GARIBALDI

Italy in 1815

GARIBALDI

Citizen of the World

Translated by Allan Cameron

Alfonso Scirocco

PRINCETON UNIVERSITY PRESS
PRINCETON AND OXFORD

Published by Princeton University Press, 41 William Street, Princeton,
New Jersey 08540

In the United Kingdom: Princeton University Press, 3 Market Place,
Woodstock, Oxfordshire OX20 1SY

Requests for permission to reproduce material from this work should be
sent to Permissions, Princeton University Press.

Library of Congress Cataloging-in-Publication Data

Scirocco, Alfonso.
[Garibaldi. English]
Garibaldi : citizen of the world / Alfonso Scirocco ; translated by Allan
Cameron.
    p. cm.
Includes bibliographical references and index.
ISBN 978-0-691-11540-5 (cloth : alk. paper)   1. Garibaldi, Giuseppe, 1807–1882.
2. Revolutionaries—Italy—Biography.   3. Statesmen—Italy—Biography.
4. Generals—Italy—Biography.   5. Italy—History—1849–1870.   1. Title.
DG552.8.G2S3513 2001
945'.083092—dc22
[B]   2007013323

British Library Cataloging-in-Publication Data is available

The translation of this work has been funded by
Segretariato Europeo per le Pubblicazioni Scientifiche (SEPS)

Via Val d'Aposa 7 - 40123 Bologna, Italy.
seps@alma.unibo.it - www.seps.it

This book has been composed in Electra

Printed on acid-free paper. ∞

press.princeton.edu

Printed in the United States of America

1   3   5   7   9   10   8   6   4   2

To my wife Angela,
after fifty years of
happy marriage

Table of Contents

Introduction

Along with Dante, Christopher Columbus, and Leonardo da Vinci, Giuseppe Garibaldi is one of the few Italians who is known and admired throughout the world, and in mod___ ___ ___ es he is the only one who is loved as well as adm__ ____ _____ ___ xtraordinary enterprises in the Americas and E_ _____ _____ ____ ure novel with its typical love of the exotic. H_ _____ ____ _____ nger adversaries earned him the aura of a her_ ____ ___ ___ as a life that inspired a sense of awe and gave ___ ____ ____ ____

Garibaldi demonstr_ _ _____ _acity, and good fortune, when for ten years ___ ___ ___ ___ reat rivers of Brazil, Uruguay, and Argentina ___ ___ ___ ___ spaces; when between 1848 and 1867 he ___ ___ ___ h fewer men and less equipment than his ___ ___ ___ enemies; and when in 1870 he fought a_ ___ ___ the Prussians. He used cunning and ing___ ___ ___ zil he transported his ships overland, ___ ___ t by three armies, and in 1860 he t_ ___ ___ withdraw while in fact he was swoopi__ ___ ___

His fame for these und__ ___ ___ d the world. He had dealings wi__ ___ ___ e Janeiro, Montevideo, Buenos ___ ___ ne, and Naples. He was the talk ___ ___ ___ yans, Italian emigrants, and Argentin__an political exiles fo_ ___ ___ nis side in South America. In Europe, he was joined in battle by Italians from all regions and all social backgrounds, democrats from France, England, America, and Germany, and exiles from Poland, Hungary, Russia and other Slav countries. Already famous in South America, his name was first splashed across European daily newspapers in 1845, and there it remained. Magazines with an international readership published his portrait and described his exploits, while newspaper illustrators and photographers followed him round the battlefields. Inexpensive lithographic portraits and illustrations of his adventures sold widely in every corner of Europe and the Americas. There was a flood of often romanticized and embellished biographies in Italian, English, French, German, and many other languages.

Garibaldi's enormous popularity amongst his contemporaries cannot be explained simply by the exceptional nature of his actions. People's imaginations were struck by his extraordinary selflessness, the firmness with which he rejected rewards and honors, the simplicity of his life which verged on poverty, the modest way he returned to the shadows once his work was finished, and his willingness to give his life in the service of the rebels of Rio Grande, the defenders of Montevideo, and the French republicans. He was untouched by the egotism of nationalistic interests. Politicians, writers, and journalists were fascinated by his personality, in which reckless indifference to danger curiously coexisted with courteous manners in daily life. Women adored him no matter what class they came from or how much wealth they did or did not enjoy.

He quickly gained a mythical status as a fighter for the freedom and independence of all peoples, which would endure for the rest of his life. The *New York Daily Tribune* greeted him as a "man of world fame" in 1850. The Russian Herzen exalted him in 1854 as "classic hero, a character from the *Aeneid*, . . . around which a legend would have been created, if he had lived in another era," and ten years later as "the only popular character of the century to have developed since 1848." The French writer Victor Hugo described him as a "man of freedom, a man of humanity" in 1860. Three years later the Argentinean president Bartolomeo Mitre called Garibaldi "the greatest man of the century," and in 1867 the Swiss politician James Fazy called him "the most courageous and selfless man of the century." In 1870, the Englishman Philip Gilbert Hamerton described Garibaldi as "the most romantic hero of our century, the most famous man on the planet, the head most sure of living in the hearts of future generations." On his death, the German newspaper *Deutsche Zeitung* appealed for a new Homer "worthy of singing the Odyssey of this life."

Garibaldi appeared to be the quintessential hero, and perhaps this was the reason why such disparate social groups as Russian peasants and Hungarian magnates believed that he would one day come to liberate them by force of arms. In 1860 news of his incredible conquest of a kingdom spread across most of Europe amongst workers and peasants through mysterious channels.

This is the image of Garibaldi that survives. Even though his greatest undertaking was achieved in Italy and for Italy, he put his energies into the liberation of all oppressed peoples and into the deliverance of the dispossessed. He followed a dream of social justice that he first conceived in youth when he was won over to the principles of humanitarianism and cosmopolitanism. Although he was a born combatant (and adopted the Spanish motto "la guerra es la verdadera vida del hombre" meaning "war is the true life for a man"), he considered war to be a painful necessity, and one that arose from injustice.

According to the organizers of the International Congress for Peace in Geneva, Garibaldi's name "means heroism, humanity, patriotism, brotherhood of peoples, peace and liberty." Indeed, he often spoke in support of peace and cooperation between peoples. In October 1860, following his famous victory on the Volturno, he appealed to the European powers to form a single state. Subsequently, he proposed a world congress to judge disputes between nations and encouraged every initiative that aspired to peace. In the spirit of human brotherhood, he expressed sympathy for incipient socialism in 1871, seeing it mainly as "a sentiment of justice and human dignity."

Garibaldi lived in an era marked by a great flowering of political systems that sought social justice: Saint-Simonianism, Mazzinianism, the anarchic socialism of Proudhon and Bakunin, and Marx's scientific version. He came close to some, particularly the first two, but never fully identified with any of them. Contemporaries and early biographers saw this as a sign of superficiality and intellectual mediocrity. In the twenty-first century, following the collapse of the ideologies that dominated the history of the twentieth century, we can show more understanding for the desire to maintain the mental independence of an idealist without ideologies.

Hostile to labels and opposed to unreasoned exclusions of other people and other ideas, Garibaldi was a free spirit and a citizen of the world. His dream provided his human adventure with a universal significance which fascinated novelists and poets such as Alexandre Dumas and Giosue Carducci, and still fascinates anyone who still believes in the power of ideals to inspire us.

GARIBALDI

1. Sailing the Mediterranean

WHEN GIUSEPPE GARIBALDI was born on 4 July 1807, Nice was a sleepy little town which had until recently been under the dominion of the dukes of Savoy for two centuries. Thus it had once been the port of Savoy and Piedmont, as they were separated from the sea by the Republic of Genoa, which extended for the full length of the Ligurian coast. It had retained this function and its related privileges when the dukes of Savoy enlarged their dominions and acquired the title of kings of Sardinia in 1722. In 1792, the armies of revolutionary France conquered Nice, and its destiny was changed. As a territory annexed by France, it found the republic's and Napoleon's grand experiments to be very disadvantageous. The empire's expansionist policy imposed high taxes to finance the war and a "blood tax" in the form of conscription, which reflected the national complexion that armies had then acquired. Its integration into the territory of France entailed an attempt to eradicate its Italian character: Joseph-Marie Garibaldi's birth certificate was written in French (but in other official documents he is called Giuseppe Maria). Competition from the large ports of Marseille and Genoa, which was also annexed by France, reduced Nice's share of trade.

Nice rejoiced at the fall of Napoleon. The return of the ancient dynasty of Victor Emanuel I raised hopes of a return to the previous monopoly over sea trade with Piedmont and Savoy, but that was not to happen. The great powers that met at a congress in Vienna had to ensure a lasting peace for a continent that had suffered twenty-five years of bloody wars, and they therefore had to strengthen all the states that bordered on France in order to contain any future aggressions. In 1814 the Republic of Genoa disappeared and Liguria became part of the Kingdom of Sardinia. Genoa thus became the principal port of the enlarged state, and Nice a seaport of secondary importance.

The Garibaldi family took little notice of these political vicissitudes, immersed as it was in the immediacy of its daily grind. The family came from Liguria. Giuseppe's grandfather, Angelo, was from Chiavari, and his father, Domenico, was born there in 1766. He later moved to Nice, where in 1794 he married Rosa Raimondo who was ten years his junior and was from Loano, also in Liguria. They had six children: two girls, who died during infancy, and four boys, Angelo, Giuseppe, Michele, and Felice. Domenico and his family lived with his brother-in-law's family, the Gustavins. They did not own the house, which was demolished at the end of the nineteenth century when the port was enlarged. Around 1814, they moved to Aboudaram House in Quai Lunel, where the children grew up. The family's financial position was fairly good. Domenico was a sea captain and owned or partly owned a tartane, a small vessel with a lateen sail that was used in the Mediterranean. The ship was called *Santa Reparata*, and he used it for coastal trade with varying degrees of success. He was not very highly educated, and had few ambitions and limited abilities (indeed his business did not always go well), but he did not let his children miss out on their schooling. In this he was influenced by his more cultured wife. A practicing Catholic, she was charitable and compassionate to the poor, who returned her kindness with affection. Giuseppe, who was known as Peppino in the family, was to hold her memory dear; in his *Memoirs* he wrote, "I can claim with pride that she is an example to other mothers." He would also worry about her: "Take care of my poor mother if you love me. . . . My mother was always such a good woman," he exhorted his wife,

Anita, who left for Nice before him in March of 1848. He also respected her beliefs, and in December of the same year he bought her a box of rosary beads in Loreto. He worried about her means of support but did not burden her with his concerns. In 1850, when he found himself in Tangiers at the start of another period of exile full of uncertainties, he rejected his cousin's advice that she had to be more frugal. He considered it improper "to sadden my aging and highly sensitive mother with reproofs that could only serve to afflict her and not to change her behavior." Instead, he asked his relation "to pawn or sell my sword—a gift from the Italian nation— should all other providential means be exhausted."

All the Garibaldi children found good positions. Angelo moved to the United States where he became a businessman and the consul for the Kingdom of Sardinia in Philadelphia. Michele (the only one to marry and remain childless) became a sea captain. Felice, a dapper womanizer, represented the shipping company Avigdor in Bari, a major center for the export of olive oil from Southern Italy. None of them reached old age, and Michele, who lived longest, only survived to fifty-six.

Although life separated them once they reached adulthood, they continued to correspond. Giuseppe was just like any other boy. "Like so many other lads, my childhood went by with a mixture of play, happiness, and misery. . . . There was nothing odd about my youth," he was to write in his *Memoirs*. However, aspects of his character were already emerging. He was a sensitive boy who cried when he unintentionally broke the leg of a cricket he had captured. He was generous and always ready to help others: as a teenager he saved a woman who was drowning in a canal; years later he rescued a sailor in Smyrna; at the beginning of his exile in Marseille, dressed for the promenade, he threw himself into the sea to aid a French fourteen-year-old; and he saved a black man in Rio.

He had a strong and independent character. He felt, as he himself was to admit, "a propensity to a life of adventure." Giving free rein to his imagination, he dreamed of daring escapades at sea and rejected his father's lazy routine. He resisted his parents' attempts to turn him into a provincial notable—a lawyer, doctor, or priest. When they sent him to study in Genoa, he found educational discipline insufferable and during the holidays, he took possession of a boat and sailed off toward Liguria with some other youths. He was soon caught and given permission to go to sea. Up to that time he had not taken much advantage of his schooling, and he acknowledged that he had been "more a friend of pleasure than of study." He regretted that his father had not made him engage in gymnastics, fencing, and other "physical exercises." Gifted with an athletic physique, he became an excellent swimmer, and used ships as his gym when they were in port. However, his early tutors did leave their mark on him. There were two clergymen one of whom taught him rudimentary English, but they were less important than a veteran of Napoleon's military campaigns, Signor Arena, who taught him Italian through readings of ancient history. Nice, positioned on a linguistic border, was not a town where Italian was particularly cultivated, but Garibaldi, at his brother Angelo's instigation, studied it in depth and developed an early interest in ancient Rome, an interest that was to remain with him throughout his life.

Giuseppe molded his unsystematic education according to his own needs and personal inclinations. He read a great deal during the hours of inactivity imposed by long sea voyages and during his moments of solitude. He studied various disciplines in such depth that when he happened on hard times, he was able to make a living by teaching them. He was a fund of scientific information, and when he farmed in Caprera, he bought treatises on agronomy. He loved literature and poetry: he memorized Foscolo's *I sepolcri* and Berchet's poetry, he often read André Chénier, and had a particular fondness for historians of Greece and Rome, and for novels full of patriotism and the desire for social justice by such writers as Victor Hugo and Francesco Domenico Guerrazzi. Once his intellectual horizons had widened and his knowledge of social doctrines and philosophical problems increased, he started to read more difficult texts: he declared himself a follower of Cesare Beccaria and considered Voltaire and Rousseau "veritable granite pillars on which universal intelligence was built." His book collection included Gaetano Filangieri's *Scienza della legislazione*, and he was well acquainted with the works of French radicals and socialists of his time. He was himself a prolific writer: he used his periods of enforced idleness to write novels, poetry, and his *Memoirs*.

However, it took time for him to open his mind to a political commitment and a comprehensive perception of the world. The first part of his life was characterized by routine professional activity, which he fulfilled with enthusiasm. He prepared for his exams to captain a ship while still in his teens. As a grown man, he found that practical knowledge of the sea was not enough for him. He took the trouble to learn the theory required for commanding a ship, unlike his father, who in his opinion did not have "the kind of knowledge that men of his class are endowed with in our generation." During his long career at sea he had no difficulty in adapting to a shift from Mediterranean routes to oceanic ones or from sailing ships to steamships. He had complete command of Italian and French; he spoke Spanish and Portuguese well, having learned them in South America; and he could express himself quite adequately in English and German. At all times, he was able to act confidently in whatever circles circumstance was to place him.

His apprenticeship started early. He was registered as a trainee in 1821, and his first officially recorded voyage took place in January 1824 on the brigantine *Costanza* when he was sixteen. The ship, which sailed under a Russian flag but was run by an Italian crew, was to remain deeply imbedded in his imagination. He always remembered its wide beam and narrow masts. Its captain, Angelo Pesante, whom he would meet again later in life, was "the best sea captain I have ever known." This initiation to maritime life—an exciting experience for an adolescent with a fertile imagination—took him as far as the Black Sea, a voyage that he was to repeat many times. When maritime routes were reopened at the end of the Napoleonic Wars, the markets were flooded with cheap wheat from the Ukraine, where it had been produced since the late eighteenth century. Odessa and even more distant Taganrog, which lies at the other end of the Sea of Azov, became regular destinations for ships supplying Mediterranean countries. In addition to wheat from the Black Sea region, Nice imported wheat from Southern Italy; less essential cereals, spices, and dried fruit from France, Sicily, and Calabria; and marble from Tuscany. Its main trading partner was France, which sent alcohol, leather, clothing, and livestock. The port also developed a very buoyant business with France, Southern Italy, and North Africa involving the import and reexport of olive oil used as the raw material in the production of soap. There was, therefore, coastal trade with Provence and the Languedoc in one direction, and with Tuscany and Southern Italy as far as Romagna in the other.

Small ships were used along the coasts of the Gulf of Lions, the Tyrrhenian Sea, and the Adriatic.

One of these was Domenico Garibaldi's tartane. Giuseppe's parents had been anxious about him during his long voyage on the *Costanza*. When he returned in July, the young man stayed with his family. In November we find him on the *Santa Reparata* for a less demanding voyage along the French coast as an unpaid apprentice in a crew of five men. The following year he made an unforgettable journey with his father. Since 1300 when Boniface VIII called the first Jubilee, the great manifestation of faith had been held at the end of each century. In 1800, it was not possible to celebrate one because of the wars that were afflicting Europe. Leo XII therefore proclaimed 1825 a Jubilee year. Captain Domenico took a cargo of wine to Rome to supply the pilgrims. The small ship this time took on a crew of eight, and Giuseppe received his first pay. Hugging the coast, it stopped off at Livorno, Porto Longone, and Civitavecchia. On 12 April it arrived in Fiumicino and was drawn up the Tiber by buffaloes to berth in the city at the port of Ripetta. A dispute over the remuneration to the contractor who provided the buffaloes extended their stay in the city for some weeks. Giuseppe was able to admire the remains of ancient Rome, about whose greatness he had read so much. He was intoxicated by the "capital of the world" and the "relics of all that was greatest in the past." Many years later, Rome was to become for him "the symbol of united Italy."

Breaking away from his family's orbit, he signed on with the crews of much bigger ships than his father's tartane. They were always sailing ships of average size, a little over two hundred tons with crews of between fifteen and twenty men. They were cargo ships but occasionally carried passengers. His frequent voyages took him to almost all of the Mediterranean, as is made clear by his *Memoirs* and the well-documented ships' log. In 1827 he passed through the Strait of Gibraltar on the *Coromandel* and reached the Canaries. That same year, he joined the crew of the *Cortese*, which set sail from Nice in September bound for the Black Sea. It was already late in the year, and there was a risk of being trapped by the ice. As it turned out, ill fortune was to dog the voyage: the ship was boarded by pirates on three occasions. As the Greeks had risen up against their Turkish rulers, the Aegean was infested with privateers fighting their enemies and pirates who plundered neutral merchant ships. Everything was taken from

the *Cortese*, including the navigational instruments and the crew's clothing. Garibaldi contemptuously recalled the captain's failure to resist, even
though the ship was armed, albeit with only twenty-four rifles. In 1832,
however, the captain of the *Clorinda*, armed with two cannon, four heavy
mounted rifles, and thirty handheld rifles, engaged in battle and the pirates fled the sustained fire. Garibaldi, who suffered a grazing wound to
his right hand, noted this skirmish down as his first military engagement.

Garibaldi became ill on the return voyage of the *Cortese*, and in August
1828 he left his ship in Constantinople. He stayed there for almost three
years, and returned to Nice only in the spring of 1831. We do not know the
reason for this long sojourn, which may have been partly caused by the outbreak of the Russo-Turkish War, but this conflict was brought to a close by
the Treaty of Edirne in 1829. We know only that he was helped by the city's
large Italian community, and in particular by Luisa Sauvaigo, who also
came from Nice—"one of those creatures who have convinced me that
women are the most perfect of all beings." He earned his living by teaching
Italian, French, and mathematics to the children of a Mrs. Timoni. Ten
years earlier he could hardly have imagined himself in the role of a tutor!

He returned to sea and the usual routes, which often took in Smyrna
and Constantinople as well as the Black Sea ports. His career in the merchant navy brought him promotion and financial advantage. In February
1832 he was issued with a second-class master's ticket. He recalled his first
command as the brigantine *Nostra Signora delle Grazie* destined for Gibraltar and Constantinople, but we cannot find any record of this. We do
know, however, that in that same February 1832 he signed on as first mate
on the *Clorinda* (which had a crew of twenty men), with a monthly pay of
fifty Piedmontese pounds, half the salary of his captain, Simone Clary. It
was a six-month trip to Constantinople and Taganrog. In 1833, it was calculated that he had completed seventy-two months of effective employment at sea. It was a hard school, and we can well imagine the kind of life
he led during his long absences from Nice. In fictional accounts, ships are
portrayed scudding across the waves and manned by colorful sailors in red
linen shirts. The reality was exhausting work on the sails, long watches,
pump duty when water seeped through the joins in the wood, the tedium
of flat calm, repetitive diet, the discomfort of restricted space, and the difficulties of personal hygiene. During the epic undertaking known as the

Expedition of the Thousand, General Garibaldi was seen crouching over the side of the ship with his trousers unbuttoned so that he could defecate directly into the sea, a practice that he had learned in his youth.

Danger was never far away. Garibaldi recalled the appalling shipwreck of a Catalan ship on the Ligurian coast, when there was no chance assisting the crew. A captain had to observe the weather constantly, and intervene in difficult moments by quickly and confidently assessing the situation, promptly making decisions, and giving orders that left no room for hesitation. This way of dealing with situations would be projected onto the methods of warfare adopted by Garibaldi the military commander. Typically he would study the terrain through a telescope, assess the enemy forces, make rapid decisions, act tenaciously in their implementation, and impose blind obedience. According to Augusto Vittorio Vecchi, his faults were also typical of a sailor: "He rarely considered the flanks and the rear, and he placed faith, too much faith, in advancing."

There were periods of quiet for the small community that made up a crew. Garibaldi probably read much of the time, and not surprisingly he formed a friendship on the *Clorinda* with the purser, Edoardo Mutru, who also came from Nice and was to join him in the first conspiracy and his military exploits during exile in South America. In port, loading and unloading imposed long periods of idleness, which were further prolonged by various circumstances and the sluggishness of officialdom. On occasion, ships were subject to quarantine, supplies of victuals and equipment could prove difficult to procure, and negotiations with local traders became grueling experiences. Taganrog and Odessa, the ports of the Levant Garibaldi visited most, were icebound for several months during winter, so they were crowded with ships from spring to autumn. The water was shallow in Taganrog and ships could not berth at the quays. Partially submerged horse-drawn carts transported the wheat, wool, copper, iron, wax, and leather to be loaded. Time passed slowly. During idle days, Garibaldi mixed with the Italian sailors from every part of Italy who busied themselves with peddling small items and contraband, or whiled away their time in taverns and brothels.

In 1833 at the age of twenty-six, the Sardinian register of seamen recorded that he was just over five feet five inches tall (166 cm), and had blond hair and light brown eyes. How did his contemporaries see him? In 1843 Bartolomeo Mitre, who met him in Montevideo, described him as "of average height, well built and well proportioned," and in spite of a degree of "heaviness" he had a "measured and lively manner." His physiognomy was "calmly serious," and his smile did not change his features. Only "his blue eyes" revealed "the intensity of his mind." In profile, his features were "authentically Greek" and "rigid and austere." His head, which recalled the busts of ancient heroes and the ideal image of Christ, was "large, well shaped, always held high, and covered with thick flowing locks, and the sun gave the glint of a lion's mane to his full red beard." In short, "he possessed the elements of good looks and physical strength, but his beauty was primarily moral, as was his power of attraction over the masses and the influence of his firmness and serenity in the midst of great dangers."

The French journalist Louise Colet had the same impression in 1860: "average height, but upright and proud," "handsome and impassioned face" held high, an extremely kind smile, an intelligent and thoughtful brow, and a blond beard, "like Christ's in the paintings of the great Italian masters," thus endowing his face with "something mystical." His first biographer, Giovan Battista Cuneo, who fought for the same beliefs in South America and shared much of his life with him, wrote a detailed description in 1850 that confirms these features of a well-balanced physique and a bright and intense expression.

He is of average height, broad in the chest and shoulders, and manages to be both burly and lithe at the same time. He gives the impression of strength and agility. At first sight, his face appears severe. This imposing effect is increased by his russet untrimmed beard, long blond hair, keen and penetrating expression, and large forehead, from which his nose continues downward in a straight and perpendicular line. But when you have looked at him a little longer, a kindly harmony of forms and features lights up as expected, and a sense of trust and sympathy suddenly fills your mind and mixes with the respect he has just commanded.

He was not handsome, then, "in the generally accepted use of the word," Giuseppe Guerzoni, another close friend, confirmed in 1882 shortly after

Garibaldi's death, while attempting in a detailed portrait to find the reasons for the great man's appeal.

> He was small. He was slightly knock-kneed, and his chest was not quite right. But above that body, which was certainly not irregular or gauche, sat a superb head that had something of Jove on Olympus, Christ, or a lion, depending on the moment in which you observed it and the emotions that animated him. . . . Nature then added strength and agility to these unique good looks. His was not really the muscular strength of an athlete but that special sinewy strength that is toughened and invigorated by exercise, and which, when accompanied by agility, makes the body capable of the most difficult trials and the most daring physical training. He knew how to swim, ride, climb, shoot a rifle, fence with a saber, and if necessary use a knife, without anyone ever having taught him how to do it. His instincts and the structure of his own limbs provided him with the technique and the mastery.

Garibaldi had great charm. Malvida von Meysenburg, a cultured and sensitive friend of Wagner's, recalled that his voice was beautiful and beguiling, and his conversation "fresh, animated, and full of delightful simplicity, as was his nature, and it was suffused with a hint of poetry. When he talked of his adventures in South America, it was like listening to one of Homer's heroes."

The merits and defects of his physique and his character were attractive to women. It is probably not the case that he had one in every port as he traveled the length and breadth of the Mediterranean, although his prolonged stay in Constantinople does increase our suspicions. In 1827, when he sailed from Nice, he promised his fiancée, Francesca Roux, that they would be married shortly. On his return in 1831, he went straight to the beautiful young woman . . . only to find her married with a son. Three years later, he wrote three passionate love letters from Marseille, where he had just started his exile, to a certain Angelina in Nice.

While at sea he was respected for his reliability and professionalism, on land he was obliged to be a fun-loving drinking partner who was not above buying sexual favors. In 1834, in an application to leave his ship during military service, he declared that he needed to be treated for venereal disease. An account written much later and unsupported by other sources claimed that one evening he was part of a group of seamen singing in the streets of Taganrog and was arrested for creating a disturbance. Having been freed, following the intercession of an influential Italian business-man, he failed to abide by his undertaking to remain on board his ship and was rearrested with the consequent risk of being deported.

He was a man of the sea like any other. He took little notice of the struggles for liberty and national independence that were beginning to make their presence felt on both land and sea, and both at home and around the Mediterranean. After the fall of Napoleon, Italy was once again politically fragmented into regional states: the Kingdom of Sardinia, made up of Savoy, Nice, Piedmont, Liguria, and Sardinia; the Kingdom of Lombardy-Venetia, which was a Hapsburg dominion; the Grand Duchy of Tuscany; the Papal States, which cut the country in two at the center, from Romagna to Lazio, with Le Marche and Umbria in the middle; the Kingdom of the Two Sicilies, which united Southern Italy and Sicily; and the small duchies of Modena, Parma, and Lucca. They were all governed by absolute sovereigns, and the middle class, which had become the governing class after the French Revolution, had been excluded from the administration of power. This resulted in the revolutions of July 1820 in Naples and Sicily, and of March 1821 in Piedmont, which failed because of the Austrian military intervention and were followed by harsh repression. The revolution of 1831 in Central Italy was also put down by the Austrians. Clearly the foreign presence in Italy was determining the political struggle. There was an increasing conviction that the ideal of achieving liberal institutions could not be achieved without gaining national independence at the same time.

Garibaldi, who was perhaps too young in 1821, has left no comments on these events. In his *Memoirs*, written in later life after he had fought against oppressors in South America and Italy, he shows that he had no understanding of another struggle for freedom, which he had witnessed while working on merchant vessels traveling to the Black Sea. In 1821 the Greeks rose up to free themselves from Turkish domination, and fought for ten years to obtain independence with the support of France, Britain, and Russia. Garibaldi was an unwilling witness under attack from pirates, but he never went beyond his contempt for the arrogance of his attackers and the cowardice of his commanders, and he never considered the reasons for the disorder that afflicted the seas of the Levant. His admiration for leaders of the Greek partisans came after the event and was never linked to memories of his youthful experiences.

This should not surprise us. Garibaldi's biographers always claim that he held patriotic ideals during his youth and take for granted that he knew about the events that troubled Italy at the time, basing their assumptions on a few lines in his *Memoirs* in which he asserts that he loved his country "from his earliest years," desired its rebirth, and sought "everywhere books and writing on Italian freedom and the individuals devoted to achieving it." They never consider that seamen are separated from society. Sailors live for many months in the company of a few people, often of various nationalities. They are engaged in strenuous work and have little knowledge of cultural life. In port, they make up for the tedium and solitude by indulging in coarse entertainments. When they get leave to return to their hometowns, often small coastal villages cut off by mountains, for a few months or even weeks, they are absorbed in the joys and miseries of the families that await them. The idea that they followed events in distant capitals or in the Italian interior ignores the difficulties of news circulation in the early nineteenth century and the presence of censorship that prevented the spread of news disagreeable to those in positions of power.

The youthful Garibaldi, working in the merchant navy, was no exception, although he was different in that he did not restrict his interests to professional matters. We know that he spent much of his time reading, and he was aware of a more complex world than the one in which he lived. He did not feel entirely satisfied with the life he was leading, even though it did give him some pleasures. He was willing to follow ideals that would direct him toward less banal aims than a seagoing career. In 1832 he heard that the Duke of Modena had condemned Ciro Menotti to death. He was deeply affected and would later call his first son Menotti. He was beginning to perceive the existence of the Italian problem.

A year later, the cause worthy of his dedication manifested itself. The occasion was a turning point in his life and involved two other events that followed in quick succession. In March of 1833, thirteen French passengers, a group of Saint-Simonians, boarded the *Clorinda* in Marseille bound for Constantinople. Count Claude-Henri de Saint-Simon, who lived in the late eighteenth and early nineteenth centuries, was one of the first socialist theoreticians. Taking the French Revolution and the Industrial Revolution as his starting points, he argued that the destruction of ancient institutions and the crisis in traditional trades and skills would lead to an era in which the *industriels*—all producers of riches, including scientists and artists—would triumph over the *oisifs*—all idlers, including nobles and members of the armed forces, who consume without producing. Saint-Simon proposed a planned society managed by bankers, as regulators of the use of capital, and industrialists, who promote profitable activities, thus raising the general standard of life. This was a society in which each would be remunerated in accordance with his or her productive capacity, as expressed through their services to the collectivity. The achievement of social justice accompanied by respect for the law was to ensure peace within societies and the happiness of the laboring classes. Collaboration between capitalists in global economic development favored by large-scale public work was to extend these benefits to the whole of humanity, leading to the unification of all peoples. To crown this new order based on science, Saint-Simon created a new religion to satisfy irrepressible spiritual needs.

Disciples developed his ideas after his death in 1825. Some were more interested in the philosophical aspects of his work, others in the organizational principles that placed the technicians of the economy in a primary role, and still others in the religious tenets that were to guide humanity toward universal peace. A movement was created under the leadership of Barthélemy Prosper Enfantin that mixed faith in the civilizing capabilities of science with a religious vision of all peoples marching toward their ultimate unification. A kind of church was formed with Enfantin at its head, and a doctrine was devised to instruct the faithful on how to lead their lives. They awaited the coming of the *Mère*, the Mother who was to unite with the Father to symbolize the unity of intellect and emotion. Saint-Simonianism spread throughout France in the 1830s, but antagonized government because it challenged the basis of bourgeois society and was accused of attacking property rights and fostering free love. A pretext was found for a trial and Enfantin was condemned to a year in prison, while his followers were expelled from the country.

The group that embarked on the *Clorinda* was part of this movement, and had decided to leave for Turkey as exiles to seek the mysterious Mother of the Orient. They came aboard the ship at night under police guard and in the presence of a crowd that enthusiastically took their leave of the departing Saint-Simonians. It was an unusual scene for the crew of a merchant ship, and they looked on admiringly. Emile Barrault, the leader of this Saint-Simonian band, was an austere and educated man (he was a professor of rhetoric), and during the voyage, he explained his convictions with great passion.

Later Garibaldi would recount those long conversations to Alexandre Dumas, the famous novelist who became his friend and biographer—conversations "during those clear eastern nights . . . , under a starry sky," according the narrative embellishment added by the great author of *The Three Musketeers*. As the Saint-Simonian ideas were explained, he caught sight of "previously unnoticed horizons." This opened up a view of humanity set on the path toward peace and well-being. He was struck by the idea "that a man who, by becoming cosmopolitan, adopts humanity as his country and, by offering his sword and his blood to every people that struggles against tyranny, becomes something more than a soldier: he becomes a hero." It was a revelation—one that made Garibaldi aware not only of "the narrow questions of nationality" in which his patriotism was trapped, but also of the possibility of fighting for the freedom of oppressed peoples in every part of the world. A single fact points to the profound emotions released by this encounter. Barrault signed a copy of Saint-Simon's *The New Christianity* and gave it to the young officer: Garibaldi would keep it with him throughout his adventurous life, and it was in his room in Caprera when he died.

The Saint-Simonians left the ship in Constantinople. They met with a hostile reception in Turkey and moved on to Egypt, where the government valued their abilities as technicians. The group returned to France after a few years, and although the sect dissolved, its main exponents continued to aim at global economic development and came to occupy important positions in the world of business. Barrault was elected to the French parliament and became involved in the development of railways, as did Enfantin.

As Garibaldi continued his journey on the *Clorinda* toward Taganrog, Barrault's words remained fixed in his brain, which was now in turmoil.

He went to one of the usual haunts for Italian sailors and ended up at a table where they were discussing politics. A young man started to talk about Mazzini, the Young Italy movement, national unification, and independence. Giuseppe Mazzini was the man of the moment. He was only two years older than Garibaldi but had led a much fuller life. He was born into a good bourgeois family in Genoa, a city that still retained a memory of republican freedom and of its role as a capital. His father, Giacomo, was a university professor and had been an active Jacobin in his youth. His mother, Maria Drago, was an educated and highly sensitive woman who was able to understand the obsessive dream that motivated him. Mazzini followed a regular university course and graduated in law. From his early youth he wrote for Genoese and Tuscan newspapers. When he was sixteen, he saw those who had taken part in the revolution of 1821 attempting to escape into exile on ships sailing from Genoa, and he began to think about the question of political activism. In 1827 he joined the secret society of the Carbonari, which revealed its program gradually to its members in accordance with a ritual full of symbols and therefore had only limited support. He was reported and arrested in 1830, and then forced into exile. He moved to Marseille, where he met the exponents of the Italian and European sectarian world, and developed a new doctrine based on his experience of political struggle in France, which was governed by a constitutional regime. Around the middle of 1831 he drew up his program, which had a philosophical and religious basis. From the existence of God, he deduced the law of progress, which was to be achieved by the actions of nations. These in turn were inspired by the development of civilization and had to be free if they were to fulfill the mission assigned to them. Independence from foreign domination, national unity, and a republic were objectives that Italy had to set itself now that it had been called upon by God to launch the peaceable coexistence of European peoples and the peoples of the world. The success of this political upheaval would then lead to the solution of social problems. Young Italy, the association founded by Mazzini, differed from previous secret societies in that its program, which was not aimed at just one of the regional states, was a set of clear ideas known to everyone and founded on a sense of duty rather than an expectation of advantage. From 1831, the group spread its views by word of mouth and in writings with the intention of inculcating its patriotic ideals in every class and every place in order to prepare a national revolution through simultaneous uprisings in various parts of the country.

It was everyone's duty to obey God's will, and not the choice of the few elect. Mazzini's propaganda was also directed at sailors, who until that time had been neglected by secret societies: their constant social mixing was very useful because they could covertly circulate incendiary writings directed at all Italians as they moved from one port to another. Indeed there were sailors from various Italian regions in the tavern that Garibaldi entered that night. Mazzini's ideas were being explained by one of them, called the "believer" because of the impassioned manner in which he spoke of his hopes of a "joyous and glorious future for the Italian fatherland." As Garibaldi listened to him, he became increasingly spellbound and then ran toward the unknown man, embraced him, and became his "bosom friend." The man was to initiate him into the doctrines of Young Italy. For Garibaldi, this turned Barrault's general humanitarian mission into the concrete ideal of the struggle for Italian independence and unification, which would be an initial stage in the deliverance of all oppressed peoples. "Columbus certainly did not feel as much satisfaction in the discovery of America as I did in finding someone who concerned himself with the liberation of the fatherland," he was to write in his *Memoirs*. The voyage of the *Clorinda* was a turning point in his life. He would no longer be satisfied with the life of a seaman sailing up and down the Mediterranean.

2. From Conspiracy to Exile

G ARIBALDI'S ADVENTURES BEGAN. The first steps toward the political activism that turned this merchant seaman into a byword for heroism—and perhaps the most popular freedom fighter in the world— have been presented by early biographers, his followers, and his admirers as a succession of sudden inspirations and encounters loaded with significance. The lack of reliable documentary evidence and the vagueness of the protagonist's memories, which were subsequently entrusted to various interviewers who partly reworked his confidential revelations, made it possible to invest an evocative chain of events, which would be worthy of his glorious future, with a quasi-religious significance.

Jessie White Mario and Giuseppe Guerzoni, both very close to Garibaldi in the 1850s and authors of two monumental biographies immediately after his death, identified the "believer" as Giovan Battista Cuneo, a companion of Garibaldi's in South America and author in 1850 of an early and partial biography that recorded the Taganrog episode. It was argued that he suppressed his own name out of modesty. They also asserted with complete confidence that the young Garibaldi, who returned to Nice at the end of *Clorinda's* voyage in July 1833, immediately rushed off to Marseille at Cuneo's behest to meet a man called Covi, and there came into contact with Mazzini, who may have personally initiated him into Young Italy, and is supposed to have given him the task of disseminating revolutionary propaganda in the Piedmontese navy in collaboration with other insurrectionary initiatives planned for 1834. This reconstruction of seamless events jumped from the revelation of his mission to his membership of Mazzini's organization, and from his meeting with his mentor to his entering the fray entrusted with a specific assignment. These biographers conjured up a picture of great patriotism, which Jessie Mario rightly considered suited to the artistry of Gerolamo Induno, the highly esteemed painter of scenes from Garibaldi's wars of liberation. From the very beginning, the herald of Italian unification and the creator of people's wars knew each other and were working together.

The little information we have and Garibaldi's own memories suggest that this fascinating representation has little credibility. The "believer" whom Garibaldi met in Taganrog could not have been Cuneo, who in 1833 was already under investigation and would have found it hard to sail for the Black Sea. In reality, he met Garibaldi in South America, where he entered into his confidence. In his *Memoirs*, Garibaldi only referred to the "believer" as "a young man from Liguria who initially provided me with some information about how our cause was progressing." He did not name him, which suggests he did not attribute great importance to the event, perhaps because his friendship was later betrayed, or perhaps simply because he forgot the surname of someone he never saw again after the sensational encounter. Equally it may be that Cuneo exaggerated the damascene nature of the event, given that the legend of Garibaldi was already being formed in 1850.

The second part of this tradition, concerning the supposed meeting in Marseille between the two future leaders of Italian democracy, is disproved by the dates: Garibaldi, who signed off from the *Clorinda* on 17 August 1833 in Villefranche-sur-mer, could not have met Mazzini in Marseille, as the latter moved on to Geneva at the end of June. Moreover, Mazzini asserted in 1860 that he had heard about Garibaldi after the failed Genoa insurrection of 1834, and in a letter of 1841 he referred to him as "a certain Garibaldi," which shows that he had not yet established any contact with him. Garibaldi himself declared that he met Mazzini for the first time in Milan in 1848.

Once we have demonstrated the inaccuracies arising from the desire of leading exponents of Italian democracy to bring forward the historic meeting and "ennoble" the hero's entrance into the political arena, we are left with the problem of ascertaining the sequence of Garibaldi's movements between August 1833 and February of the following year, and the possible motives behind them.

We should start with an established fact: subjects of the Kingdom of Sardinia were required to do military service. For merchant seamen, military service involved five years in the navy. Those who worked international routes were allowed to choose a less onerous period of service before they reached the age of forty. Garibaldi, who put in his application at the end of 1833, received orders to report for service in Genoa on 16 December, and he joined the *Euridice* on the twenty-sixth of the same month. The navy required its men to adopt a nom de guerre to avoid confusion caused by the limited stock of surnames among crews that came from the same few areas. Generally people chose a pseudonym with the same first letter as their surname, and taken from popular poems or names of flowers or gems. Garibaldi was allowed to take on the name of Cleombrotus, the twin brother of Pelopidas, who fought with Epaminondas to save Thebes from Spartan domination. Not only did this reflect his love for ancient history; it also demonstrated a clear demand for liberty.

A young officer who was close to attaining the permanent position of ship's master would have been in no hurry to exchange a brilliant career for the position of able seaman third class, unless he had a good reason for doing so. In the absence of personal or family motives, it could only have been a choice based on political commitment. The Young Italy movement had spread to Genoa, where Mazzini had many friends, and to Piedmont and Savoy (which, like Nice, belonged to the Kingdom of Sardinia). In the spring of 1833, the network of subversion was uncovered and severely repressed. Twelve of the conspirators were condemned to death, two committed suicide, twenty-eight were sent to prison, and nearly two hundred escaped abroad. Mazzini was not a man to give up. In the autumn he was again plotting against the Kingdom of Sardinia. He planned a pincer movement that implemented the tactic of multiple insurrections: a leading force of exiles was to enter Savoy from France and Switzerland, while another group of conspirators was to start an insurrection in Genoa, which opposed the monarchy because it still recalled its long period of independence and republican freedom. Putting most of his energies into organizing the invading force, Mazzini went in search of a military expert who was also a patriot. He found him in General Gerolamo Ramorino, a Genovese officer who had fought for Napoleon and was involved in the 1821 insurrection and, as an exile, in the military leadership of the Polish revolution of 1831. He undertook to create a force of a thousand men made up of Italian, Polish, and German exiles and French and Swiss republicans.

At the same time the other part of the plan was being prepared in Genoa. Garibaldi was among Mazzini's followers, but not yet a member of Young Italy, which he was to join later. This is demonstrated by his nom de guerre, used by conspirators to evade the police. He chose Borel, the name of a man who had taken part in the expedition against Savoy and was considered a martyr to the cause. Garibaldi could not therefore have joined before February 1834. It should not surprise us that this young officer did not study Mazzini's teachings or join his organization; throughout his life, Garibaldi never felt the need for thorough ideological examination of the doctrines that were to inspire his actions, and avoided joining organizations that would turn him into a subordinate and force him to follow orders with which he might not agree. He was content with principles to govern his ideas, while keeping himself free to act as he saw fit. It was an attitude that always defined him and distinguished him from the political world and from Italian and other European democrats. He had a powerful personality and, in spite of the gaps in his education, he had a core of convictions to which he remained loyal throughout his life. He used these to adapt the doctrines of Saint-Simon and Mazzini that had opened up the political world to him. As far back as 1831, Mazzini designed the political and administrative structures of the Italian republic that was the ultimate goal of his revolutionary project, but Garibaldi had no need to apply his mind to fully worked-out theories and highly detailed plans.

The supporters of Young Italy met in Marseille, Nice, or Genoa to plan the action. Mutru, who became Garibaldi's friend and knew about his mission, joined the ship at the same time, and the two set about winning followers to the cause. Garibaldi obtained leave to stay ashore one night by claiming he needed treatment for venereal disease. With money saved from his time in the Merchant Service, he stayed in an inn called the Osteria della Colomba (whose owner, Caterina Boscovich, and waitress, Teresina Cassamiglia, were to help him escape after the failure of the insurrection). He later moved to another inn, Insegna della Marina. While attempting to proselytize on board and on shore, he carelessly exposed himself to detection. He made acquaintances and offered to buy drinks for persons he barely knew in order to start debates. The court proceedings provide us with a great deal of information. We know that he openly ridiculed the king in the Caffè di Londra, a meeting place for Mazzini's followers. Some members of the armed forces to whom he recklessly revealed his intentions reported everything to their superiors (these included a gunner, a quartermaster, and an artillery officer). The court papers also show us that he was reported to the police and put under surveillance.

Following a long delay, the force that had to strike against Savoy made a move on 1 February 1834. Ramorino did not live up to the trust that Mazzini had placed in him. He stayed in Paris, where he squandered the money he had been given for the preparations. He postponed the action on several occasions, and when he finally joined the force at the place where it was being amassed, he marched it off before all the volunteers had gathered. The part of the force that had to enter Savoy from Switzerland ran into trouble with the authorities, who had been tipped off. On the French border, a group of insurrectionists attempted to take a Carabinieri barracks but was repelled. This skirmish was the only armed encounter. On 3 February, Ramorino decided to call off the attack. On the fourth *La Gazzetta di Genoa* announced its failure.

According to the plans, Genoa was to rise up on 11 February, once the victorious entrance of the volunteers into Savoy had begun to inflame public opinion. Still unwilling to give up, Mazzini hoped to start the revolution in Genoa and ordered his follower to rise up immediately. On 3 February, Garibaldi was transferred with Mutru from the *Euridice* to the frigate *Conte De Geneys*, which was the Sardinian flagship then about to depart for Brazil. Biographers have assumed that the police wished to isolate these two in order to keep a better watch over them, while waiting to arrest them along with their accomplices. It seems more probable that in view of the imminent and exacting Atlantic crossing, the naval authorities had intended to reinforce the crew with an expert mariner while being unaware of the police's suspicions.

Garibaldi hardly had time to report for duty. He went ashore as usual on the evening of the fourth. Understanding that there would be no more delay, he believed that the plan for the eleventh was about be triggered with the concentration of about three hundred men in Piazza Sarzana and then an attack on the barracks to obtain arms and take possession of key points in the city. He went to the appointed place but found no one. The other conspirators had opted for prudence, given the failure of the rebellion in Savoy and the massive deployment by the army and police who were now on alert. An incredulous Garibaldi wandered the city. He stopped at the Osteria della Colomba, where he met few of his comrades because they were either being arrested or fleeing from a police raid that occurred after his providential departure. He went to a dancehall and finally to sleep at the Insegna della Marina where Mutru also spent the night. At sunrise he left without reporting for duty, while Mutru rejoined his ship. His enrollment file was marked "absent without leave." In effect, he became a deserter. By absconding, he had admitted his guilt, and he was considered one of the leaders of the conspiracy.

As he had not properly joined Mazzini's organization, he did not know whom to turn to and found himself alone. He was helped by a few women who were friends or possibly something more. He found refuge with the greengrocer Natalina Pozzo, then at the Osteria della Colomba, and finally at the house of Caterina Boscovich, who gave him clothes to replace his naval uniform, which consisted of a black jacket with white trousers and a cylindrical waxcloth hat and had now become compromising. He cut his hair and side-whiskers to disguise his appearance further, but the net was tightening around him. On 8 February, a Captain Giribaldi was arrested, victim of his similar surname. On the thirteenth, it was Mutru's turn to be arrested, while Garibaldi's brother Felice was stopped by the authorities in Tuscany, without, however, any negative consequences. On the ninth or the eleventh (it is impossible to know with certainty), Garibaldi slipped out of Genoa to undertake the difficult journey across the mountains with long rests on the peaks. It took him ten days to reach Nice. Guessing that his home was under surveillance, he stayed with his cousins Gustavin. He received news that he was in danger and decided to seek refuge in France. After a stay of only twenty-four hours, he embraced his parents (he would never see his father again) and left for the border, which ran along the River Var, accompanied by a cousin and a friend. He would recall how he waded and swam across in winter, when the river would have been swollen and freezing cold. Perhaps smugglers ferried him across, as it is hard to believe that he came out of the river soaking and wandered around dripping wet, or that he sank his bag of clothes and provisions into the water. Less than a year after the Saint-Simonians joined the *Clorinda*, he was the one who had to go into exile.

Garibaldi did not lose hope. He reported to the frontier post of the French gendarmerie, who took him to Draguignan, while awaiting orders from above. Fearing imprisonment, the fugitive climbed out the window and took the disused paths to Marseille. He found danger at an inn where the proprietor guessed that he was outside the law and threatened to have him arrested. Garibaldi played for time and asked to be allowed to finish his meal. As he looked around for a means of escape, the inn filled up with the local youth, who started to drink and to sing. Garibaldi joined them and in his beautiful tenor voice sang a song by Pierre-Jean Béranger, the much-loved folk poet. It was a great success. They all enjoyed each other's company well into the night, and in the end the stranger was allowed to leave unmolested.

On arrival in Marseille, a busy port bristling with masts and sails, Garibaldi found trusted friends capable of helping him. And his need was very great. A military court in Genoa had passed sentence on those responsible for the failed insurrection—nine of them in all, a demonstration of its insubstantiality. If there were any others pulling the strings of this conspiracy, they managed to escape and would never be identified. Six were in detention: a lance corporal, two merchant seaman, a naval seaman (Mutru), a bookseller's employee, and a deputy clerk to the court of the prefecture. They were all acquitted, either because of lack of evidence or because there was no case to answer. Garibaldi and the other two on the run, a captain in the merchant service from Nice and another whose profession was not indicated, were accused "of being the organizers of a conspiracy . . . that aimed at an insurrection by royal troops and the overturning of His Majesty's current government," and condemned to an "ignominious death." They were declared to have incurred "public vendetta as enemies of the Fatherland and the State, and all the punishments and penalties imposed by royal laws against category-one bandits." This disproportionate sentence served to inspire fear and was decreed in the certain knowledge that it would never be implemented.

The "bandit" would not be pursued with particular vigor and was even to receive a visit from his mother while living in France. However, he had to live in the shadows. In June, a Marseille newspaper, *Il Popolo Sovrano*, carried news of the death sentence. Garibaldi would write in his *Memoirs*, "I read my name for the first time in a newspaper." It must have been a shock for someone who believed himself guilty only of desertion. For a time, he did nothing and lived a semi-clandestine existence in the house of his friend Giuseppe Pares. The money he had brought with him was about to run out, so he looked for a ship to join. This was not difficult, as Marseille was a terminus for trade around the whole of the Mediterranean, a center for important industries including tanning and soap manufacture, and it was gearing up for steam navigation. Garibaldi took on the false identity of Joseph Pane, English sailor, which he was to use on other occasions. Perhaps he bought the documents from someone he knew, but it is doubtful that he declared an Italian origin. On 25 July, he joined the French brigantine *Union* destined for the Black Sea with a crew of eight, formally qualified as a seaman (he claimed to have been born in Naples), but in reality he carried out the duties of second mate. He could not take up the position officially, because he was unable to produce the required documentation. After completing that voyage on 2 March 1835, he left in May as part of a crew charged with delivering to Tunis the frigate *Eussenie*—a ship that had been built in Marseille for the bey—and he returned on a Tunisian warship. A cholera epidemic broke out in Marseille, and with his customary generosity he volunteered to assist the sick.

After a year in Marseille, he was still facing a precarious existence. He tried to avoid places that forced him into a clandestine life, and even attempted reengage in political activity in order to pursue the ideals for which he had abandoned a lucrative career. Because of the high-profile sentence against him, he was approached by followers of Mazzini. We do not know by whom (the *Memoirs* are silent on this matter), and after Mazzini left for Switzerland, his most important followers dispersed.

We need some clues. One leads us to Luigi Canessa, an exile who remained in contact with Mazzini, although he was not considered very reliable because of his flighty character. Garibaldi wrote him his first letter from Brazil: this means that he acknowledged him as his contact in the organization he joined, which could only have been Young Italy. In April of 1834 Mazzini founded the Young Europe movement to prepare the European future that would bring together "the two fundamental ideas of the new era: *Fatherland* and *Humanity*." The organizations that he launched, Young Italy, Young Germany, Young Poland, and then Young Switzerland, all joined the new movement. He believed that they all had to aim "for a single end that embraces all humanity under the guidance of the same faith of liberty, equality, and progress," because "wherever there are inequality, oppression, or violation of human brotherhood, it is the right and duty of every man to oppose them, to work to destroy them and provide assistance to the oppressed against the oppressors." Garibaldi found in this doctrine that love for Italy and cosmopolitanism could go hand in hand, and this idea of a struggle on the part of all the oppressed peoples was what had most fascinated him when he met Barrault.

Garibaldi's introduction to this version of Mazzini's ideology by 1835 is supported by a fact that historians have chosen to ignore. In a letter to Mazzini from Rio, about which we will have more to say later, Garibaldi asked him to pass on his greetings to Ghiglione and added, "if I see him some day, I'll make him regret his silence." Antonio Ghiglione was a follower of Mazzini's who had fled Genoa during the early arrests in 1833 and sought refuge in Switzerland at his leader's house. He took part in the Savoy expedition and was one of the seven Italians who signed Young Europe's founding document on behalf of Young Italy, along with eleven Polish and German revolutionaries. Mazzini sent him to Naples in the summer of 1835. As he had to avoid the Piedmontese and Austrian police, he traveled through France and left from Marseille. Agostino Ruffini tells us that on 7 June he was "in a seaport" in France. It seems likely that he met Garibaldi on either the outward or the return trip, and initiated him into Young Europe. He may have failed to maintain contact or to keep a promise to have Mazzini write to him. In any case, his nom de guerre in memory of the Frenchman Borrel (construed as Borel) demonstrates the Young Europe connection. Borrel was killed during the Savoy expedition and perceived as a martyr—mistakenly, however, as he only joined the force for pecuniary reasons and behaved like a coward when faced with death. Although Mazzini's followers were unaware of all this, the important thing is that Garibaldi underscored his commitment to humanity as well as his nation by purposefully adopting a foreign name.

There remained the question of where to engage in this commitment. In Italy it was difficult, as the revolutionary momentum had considerably diminished for the time being. The French brigantine *Nautonnier*, which regularly worked the Atlantic routes, sailed into Marseille in August and then left for Rio de Janeiro. Garibaldi joined the crew of twelve men under the name of Giuseppe Pane, born in Livorno. As usual, he was recruited as a seaman, although he actually carried out the duties of a boatswain, as suggested by the pay of eighty-five franks (seamen earned forty-five). Canessa gave him a commission and some letters of introduction to Italians living in Brazil, whom he also notified of Garibaldi's arrival. The waiting was over, and his mind was directed toward distant lands.

3. The Rio Interlude

SOUTH AMERICA WAS occupied by Spain during the sixteenth century, and only Brazil became a Portuguese colony. During the Napoleonic Wars at the beginning of the nineteenth century, both Portugal and Spain were invaded by French armies, and this interrupted communications between colonies and their mother countries. The colonies started to demand independence.

The Spanish possessions began a process of violent separation and fought against the troops sent by Madrid following the restoration of the legitimate monarchy in 1814. The struggle culminated between 1824 and 1826 with Spain's defeat. The great viceroyships of New Spain, Peru, New Granada, and La Plata were divided into a number of independent republics in the course of several years of civil war among Spaniards born in Spain, Spaniards born in America, and mestizos, but without forming a confederation as had occurred with the United States in North America. The consolidation of the newly formed states was not an easy process, and for some time there were border conflicts and internal power struggles. The outcome, however, was inevitable. It was supported by the great

European powers, who were interested in opening up large markets and lands rich in raw materials. Spain itself started to recognize the independence of its former colonies from 1836.

Matters in Brazil were somewhat different. Following the French invasion of Portugal, the sovereign and the royal family moved from Lisbon to the colony in January of 1808. They were followed by more than fifteen thousand persons, including court officials, nobles, and employees. Rio de Janeiro became a seat of government, and was provided with the administrative and cultural institutions of a capital city. The ports were opened to trade with England and other European countries, initiating a period of economic development. In 1815 the colony was elevated to the rank of kingdom, with the same status as the mother country, but in 1821 John VI, who had remained in Rio after the fall of Napoleon, was obliged to return to Lisbon, leaving his son Pedro as regent. A few months later, Pedro took the title of emperor, and Brazil became a sovereign state in every sense; this strengthened the monarchy, whose parliamentary institutions helped establish its legitimacy. However, the centralized form of government imposed by the sovereign provoked secessionist movements, and in April 1832 increasing discontent forced the emperor to abdicate in favor of his son, Pedro II, who was still a child. A regency council governed on his behalf, and from 1835 the regent Diogo Antonio Feijó ruled the country with a firm hand, while still respecting constitutional freedoms.

When Garibaldi reached Rio at the end of 1835, there was a tense atmosphere affecting the whole of Latin America. Wars of independence and civil wars had inflicted terrible damage on agricultural production, the people's principal resource. On the other hand, there had been an increase in trade with Europe, now that it was no longer suffocated by the monopolies imposed on the colonies by the two Iberian powers. Diplomats from European states had arrived in the new capitals, along with merchants and bankers who were mainly British. The frigate *De Geneys*, on which Garibaldi had made a brief appearance, brought to Brazil Count Egesippo Palma di Borgofranco, the new representative of the Kingdom of Sardinia, which had had official relations with Brazil since 1820.

Many Italians left for this world of ferment and precarious balancing acts between the powers of newly formed classes. Most of them were attracted by the chance of employment, but some were obliged to leave Italy following the restoration of absolute sovereigns in 1815, and following the revolutions of 1820–21 and 1831. The emigrants and exiles mainly settled in the basin of the River Plate, Argentina, and Uruguay, where they numbered many thousands. Once they found work, they brought over relations and friends or formed a family locally. They did not forget their distant homeland, and they kept themselves informed about Italian affairs. Political compromises gave rise to hopes of amnesties to celebrate successions to thrones or auspicious occasions for royal families. Merchant seamen, who mostly came from Liguria, spread the most important news. In previous years, they had brought pamphlets published by Young Italy and accounts of the failure of Mazzini's first uprisings, along with those escaping repression. Diplomats representing Italian states sent their governments not only reports on the life of the countries in which they worked, but also accounts of the emigrants and their political activities, with names and factual details that often constitute our main source of information on this aspect of emigration.

We must bear in mind two things when attempting to interpret events in Brazil through letters from those involved, or endeavoring to understand how ideas and documents circulated. The first is the distance. On average a ship took sixty days to sail from the Mediterranean to Brazil, and then more time was required for a letter to be delivered to its destination. The same was true of the reply. For example, the letter Garibaldi sent Mazzini, which we will shortly examine, was sent to Canessa in Marseille, and he was charged with forwarding it to their leader in Switzerland. In general, we estimate that it took six months for an exchange of letters and three months for newspapers, leaflets, and documents to arrive. This situation applied to all countries in Latin America. We also need to take into account the difficulty of ascertaining the residence of men in hiding or who at least did not carry out any public activity. Even though Cuneo had been involved in the pursuit of Mazzini's ideals since 1835 at the latest, it was 1841 before he knew that Mazzini was living in London and was therefore able to send him a letter.

The second factor that we have to bear in mind is the inflammatory nature of the correspondence and the "subversive" press we are dealing with. This material was necessarily entrusted to intermediaries who were believed to be trustworthy. Often, however, they destroyed it to avoid trouble or handed it over to their own government's authorities. The previously quoted letter from Garibaldi fell into the hands of the Sardinian consul in Gibraltar, and the system of sending various copies by different carriers was not sufficient to get the letter to its destination. Moreover, police forces engaged in intelligence activities such as the interception and confiscation of letters written by suspect persons. The authorities could then expertly copy them and send them on. For both these reasons, we can convince ourselves in some cases that letters never reached their intended destination, and we can find them, or perhaps copies of them, in ministerial archives for use in reconstructing events.

When Garibaldi arrived in Rio de Janeiro in 1836, he found a city that was growing fast. Its status as a capital had resulted in its disorderly development. The residential area extended without any planning from the sea toward the natural defenses of its surrounding mountains. The roads were badly paved or not paved at all. The rich lived in the verdant outskirts, and the oldest part, the city's center, was by the shore and included the port and Largo do Paco, a meeting place for sailors and merchants. The population was increasing: 112,000 inhabitants in 1821, rising to 137,000 or perhaps even more in 1838. Nearly 50,000 were foreigners, many of them the British who dominated trade. The Italians did not constitute a numerous colony, as there were only a few hundred of them. Many were exiles divided by political disputes and watched over suspiciously by their respective governments.

The largest contingent was made up of Ligurians, because Sardinian ships held a leading position in trade with Latin America and were engaged in profitable coastal navigation between American ports. According to a report written in 1833 by the Neapolitan consul for his government, between 50 and 60 ships carrying 120–300 tons left Genoa every year for the Americas, and almost all were directed toward ports in South America, Cuba, Brazil, Montevideo, and Buenos Aires. Only four or five went round Cape Horn to enter the Pacific. The report claimed that the Sardinian merchant service had "achieved such a prosperous state that today it competes with England and France." The ships that crossed the Atlantic to reach South America stopped at Brazilian ports and from there sailed on to towns on the River Plate. For this reason, the government in Turin signed a trade agreement with Rio de Janeiro, and from 1835 its navy carried out a series of visits and missions: the *De Geneys* was stationed in Brazil and the River Plate for two years.

Italy exported paper, rope, woolen clothing, silk, wine, oil, wine spirit, and rosolio to Brazil, and imported from it coffee, cotton, sugar cane, leather, ipecacuanha, indigo, tobacco, and high-quality timbers. We have some, albeit incomplete, data to demonstrate the volume of trade with individual states. During the years when Garibaldi was in the region, 68 Sardinian ships sailed into Rio in 1836 and 53 in 1837, as against 11 under the Austrian flag from the Adriatic and only one from Naples. In 1838 there were 41 Sardinian ships as against 6 Tuscan ones, 3 Austrian, 1 Neapolitan, and 1 Roman. In 1832, Bahia received 11 Sardinian, 9 Austrian, 4 Tuscan, and 3 Neapolitan ships. The size and prestige of the Sardinian merchant fleet is shown by various episodes. At the end of 1833, the captain of the Sardinian ship *Temistocle* and the captain of the Austrian brigantine *Sagittario* carried out a survey of a papal ship in Rio with view to its sale, and the Genovese Giovan Battista Folco acted as intermediary in the purchase of another ship, even though he was suspected of being a member of Young Italy.

Revolutionary sentiments were widespread among the exiles. In his first report, written in June 1834, Borgofranco gave an account of the presence of rebellious fellow citizens and the intended publication of a letter from Mazzini attacking King Charles Albert. In December of the following year he reported on another patriotic initiative. A circular to the Italians arrived stating, "Our exiled brothers now dispersed around Europe have expressed their cry of solidarity with us in the idea of a memorial stone that one day the reconstituted Italian nation shall erect to remind those who come after us of these exiles." As a result the decision was made to produce a lithograph illustrating "the long and painful history of three score years of martyrdom and blood." The final design, which was offered for subscription, showed an incomplete pyramid and a cross in positions of prominence and surrounded by tombstones carrying the names of the martyrs. It is easy, then, to understand the reasons for Garibaldi's departure for such distant lands. They contained a little piece of Italy in which Mazzini's propaganda had put down roots and there was room for growth. News of political activity inspired by Mazzini reached Marseille, and prints were dispatched via sailors. The "bandit" convicted for his part in the Genoa revolt, who already had a reputation among revolutionaries because of his refusal to ask the authorities for a pardon, could have found safe refuge close to his homeland—for example, in Constantinople, where he had lived for some time. He left for South America for a specific reason. He left not as a disheartened exile but as an ardent patriot who wished to continue to work for the triumph of national ideals.

The regular presence of Ligurian seamen meant that Garibaldi's arrival in Rio could go unnoticed. He left Marseille on 8 September 1835 and arrived in November or December. He was expected. The waters close to the city contained reefs, shallows, and currents, so ships like the *Nautonnier* were obliged to remain in the middle of the bay. A boat came out to greet Garibaldi, whose fame as a patriot had preceded him, thanks to the crew of the *De Geneys* in 1834 and Canessa, who had announced his arrival. Garibaldi sent him his first letter from Rio on 25 January 1836, and this tells us something about Canessa's role in his departure for Brazil. "Your commendations have been tremendously useful to me, and thanks to your letters I have felt in my first days in this country as though I had been here for many years," he wrote happily.

However, things did not go as he had hoped. It was not easy to set up an organization, "as it is in the nature of the Italians of this country to be of an irreconcilable frame of mind," and because of the presence of "an almost infernal genius" with whom he initially attempted to make common cause. This man was Giuseppe Stefano Grondona, a Ligurian and longtime Jacobin (he had been one of Giacomo Mazzini's comrades-in-arms), who had arrived in Rio around 1815 and had been expelled in 1823 for spreading democratic ideas unacceptable to the regime of Pedro I. He then moved to Montevideo until 1834, when he was allowed to return by the more liberal regime of Pedro II. Grondona came to hear about Giuseppe Mazzini's ideas and his activities in Italy, and in 1833–34 he wrote four letters to Mazzini, which the latter never received because they were intercepted by the Piedmontese police. We know the contents of the last one, dated 30 September 1834 (found among police papers), which was sent after his return to Rio. Two points are of particular interest: he was translating into Spanish and Portuguese the *Letter* Mazzini had sent in June 1831 to Charles Albert, who had just become king, in which he asked the king to declare war on Austria and to lead the campaign for Italian unity. He was also translating a few articles from Mazzini's magazine *La*

Giovine Italia, and he asked Mazzini to send the issues he was missing. Moreover, he intended to organize a secret society called the Italian Philanthropic Society in America, which was to have branches in Montevideo and Buenos Aires, and would aim to unite and give support to Italian patriots. Then, in a postscript dated 6 October, he announced that he had already founded it.

He somehow managed to maintain contacts with Marseille and made known his desire to receive recent publications. Garibaldi brought him the *General Directions* of Young Europe and the sixth and final issue of *Giovine Italia*, whose arrival Borgofranco reported on 1 January. To gain his friendship Garibaldi made him the chairman of Young Italy, the South American branch of Young Europe founded in January 1836. In order to gain greater acceptance from the community, he became a freemason. The local lodge he joined, called Asilo de la Vertud, was not linked to the Grand Orient of London or Paris. A few weeks after his arrival he already seemed to be well on his way to achieving his mission, although the first clouds had appeared on the horizon.

He reported this to Mazzini on 27 January in a long letter that never arrived but was subsequently referred to several times. Garibaldi complained of the difficulties created by Grondona, who was a good patriot in spite of everything. He reported the formation of the association, listed the names of the office-bearers of the Confraternity (as Mazzini called the regional organizations), and explained his intention of setting up branches in Buenos Aires and Montevideo for the purpose of recruiting volunteers to return to Italy when the revolution came. In the meantime he requested "letters of marque" that would authorize him to carry out hostile acts against Austrian and Piedmontese shipping as a privateer, as though Mazzini were a diplomatically acknowledged power.

Unaware of the letter to Canessa, which was published only in 1973, even the more careful biographers could not explain how just another member of Young Italy would have the courage to write to the leader with such unfeasible proposals, and they concentrated on the plan to act as a privateer, which they considered a display of bravado by an overenthusiastic newcomer. Because the letter to Canessa, which was written at the same time, provides a reason for the decision to leave Europe, we are better able to understand the letter to Mazzini. Garibaldi received a commission from the head of Young

Italy in Marseille (or at least the person he believed to hold that position). After having reported to him, he therefore felt it was his duty to report his progress and intentions directly to Mazzini, whom he believed to have been informed of his membership of Young Europe and his mission. The central part of his project was not the plan to engage the enemy as a privateer but the establishment "of the Universal Young Europe," under the auspices of the leader. Garibaldi foresaw an operational role for this organization, which had to prepare combatants for the resumption of revolutionary activity in Italy in the not-too-distant future. He and his friends hoped that "the universal call-up will come before '36." Following the previous unsuccessful attempt to establish Young Italy, it proved possible to set up Young Europe in Rio. Garibaldi listed the office-bearers and reported the purchase of a small twenty-ton ship named the *Mazzini* in honor of their leader. "We now have a bridge to cross the ocean," he asserted confidently, "and we will undoubtedly enlarge it, as with the trumpet! The Hippogryph has reared up and will fly even before it roars," he added, giving free rein to an imagination that had fed on too many romantic works.

Young Italy was in fact an organization founded on action that, as the name implies, aimed to recruit men most suited to bear arms and therefore under the age of forty. But Grondona was not of this opinion. The aging Jacobin, who had been living in South America for many years, was well integrated in local society. His commitment to organizing the Italian exiles was mainly inspired by his humanitarian Masonic ideals, and much less by Mazzini's, which concerned the coming Italian revolution. In part this was due to his eighteenth-century upbringing, and in part it resulted from a specific political understanding of the continuing importance of Freemasonry in the spread of liberal and constitutional ideas among the Brazilian middle classes. Membership of the Masons was a means to establishing useful links with the ruling class in Rio.

The partnership between the two was soon ended, and Grondona's mischief-making and "stubborn and gossipy" character were contributing factors. Garibaldi imposed his leadership, which had resulted from Canessa's "commendations." He published an article attacking King Charles Albert in the *Paquete de Rio*, and two hundred copies of Mazzini's letter to Charles Albert were printed in Italian, along with two hundred lithographs of the previously mentioned monument to their martyrs. By circulating revolutionary writings, he made converts among the exiles and drew attention to his patriotic association in provocative ways. Its premises displayed an enormous Italian tricolor, as was reported by the Sardinian diplomat, who was both alarmed and bemused. Papal, Sardinian, and Neapolitan diplomats sent news of these revolutionary activities to their respective governments, listing the members, who were initially fifteen. At the beginning of 1838, it was reported that there were eighteen of them: thirteen Ligurians (including Folco), two Neapolitans, two from Livorno, and one Roman. There were other members, and the little group may have counted thirty members.

One of the leaders of particular note was Luigi Rossetti (nom de guerre Olgiati), a Genovese who had been in Rio since 1827 and with whom Garibaldi immediately became friends. "When we first met, it did not seem the first time, although it was in fact. We smiled at each other and were brothers for life," he would write in his *Memoirs*. The youthful Rossetti was not new to politics. In Italy he had known Canessa, and there had been some friction between them. He now sent conciliatory words in the new climate of enthusiasm. "At last good fortune has brought us Borel," he wrote to Mazzini, whose works he had not known until then. He edited the reprint of the *Letter* to Charles Albert and considered the day he joined Young Italy "the most wonderful day in this so very painful exile." Rossetti, who had studied law in Italy, now worked for local newspapers. He would translate Garibaldi's article into Portuguese and became his fellow traveler.

According to Garibaldi, Giovan Battista Cuneo (a native of Oneglia whose nom de guerre was Farinata degli Uberti) had "considerable literary talent." Cuneo, who had been involved in Mazzini's uprisings of 1833 and had not been in Rio for long, was to be Garibaldi's biographer and we will often encounter him in this book. The letter to Mazzini dated 27 January mentioned other names. Giacomo Picasso, a barber whose nom de guerre was Garelli, provided the money required for purchasing the *Mazzini*. He enclosed a note to the leader, which was transcribed by Rossetti. Domenico Terrizzano (nom de guerre Santa Rosa), a sea captain who probably left Italy for political reasons, owned a merchant ship that he renamed *Giovine Europa*. There was also Giorgio Bonelli (nom de guerre Spartaco), about whom we know very little.

Garibaldi's brotherhood was also joined by Luigi Dalecazi or Delacazi, from Verona. He was a graduate engineer and had first lived abroad in

Switzerland. It is possible that he took part in the Savoy expedition and then sought refuge in Brazil. He initially stayed in Bahia, where he married. Once he started working as a sea captain, he moved to Rio, where he met Garibaldi and struck up a friendship with him. He then returned to political activity and demonstrated his commitment by renaming his ship *Giovine Italia*. When Garibaldi visited his home, he played with Luigi's little daughters and eased his sadness at being so far from his own family.

Once the initial enthusiasm had passed, the activities of this small group faltered. In effect, Garibaldi did nothing more than complete initiatives that had previously been set in motion. Grondona had already planned to print the *Letter* to Charles Albert, the subscription for the lithograph had commenced in 1835, and Grondona—with the assistance of Rossetti and Picasso, who later shifted their allegiance to Garibaldi—had set up an association that concealed patriotic ideals behind the facade of a self-help organization. The aging conspirator found that the plan he had proposed to Mazzini was stolen, and he became hostile to the new arrival. This divided the exiles and isolated Young Italy. The isolation affected daily life, as Grondona, who was in trade, encouraged businessmen to boycott any commercial activities established by Garibaldi and his friends.

Indeed Garibaldi had been entrusted with tasks that he did not find very congenial. He lacked the cultural preparation, the experience of the Carboneria (which had been a political apprenticeship for many people, and through which Mazzini himself had passed), and the "diplomatic" ability needed to open up the old sectarian mentality and engage large sections of society as Mazzini urged. Such a profile would have required him to bring together all the aptitudes of all the people who had previously fought for freedom.

Cuneo, who was more educated than Garibaldi and more adept at dealing with groups in conflict, attempted to make their propaganda work more consistent and more incisive. He used a newspaper with a symbolic title: *La Giovine Italia*, like the magazine published by Mazzini in Marseille. Work on the first issue began in March before the initial enthusiasm started to fade. Its manifesto contained their program and claimed that it would not be long before "the era in which Italy shall rise up with terrifying threats against its tyrants" together with all the enslaved peoples of Europe. The Italian initiative was clear, as was the need to come together in an association.

With these thoughts heavy on our minds, we have decided to publish a periodical to spread our principles and to bring us Italians in America together, particularly those who reside in Brazil and the provinces of La Plata, so that Italy can receive as much assistance as possible from these countries, when it comes to the insurrection.

This was the purpose: preparation of assistance to the insurrection in Italy. The promoters of the newspaper did not hide their ambitions: they promised fortnightly issues containing no fewer than thirty-two pages in octavo, with articles, reports on the meetings of Young Italy in Rio, and foreign, particularly Italian, news "of interest to the European brotherhood." The subscription was expensive: a thousand reis every month. The first issue, of which we have no copies, came out on 1 April, but there were very few subscribers and the promised regularity could not be maintained. Only one more issue was published, and again no copy survives.

The year passed and the expected revolutionary signal from Italy never came. Relations became a little less tense, and Cuneo left for Montevideo with the intention (also borrowed from Grondona) of establishing an association there to foster Mazzini's ideals.

There were still the three ships to keep the banner of Young Italy flying. Borgofranco and the captain of the *De Geneys*, which was lying at anchor off Rio, were angered by their presence and thought about having them sunk by a friendly merchant ship (many were armed). The concerns were misplaced, for the ships were old and did not constitute any kind of threat. Besides, the *Mazzini*, in spite of the organization's bellicose intents, was used for the more prosaic purpose of providing Garibaldi with a livelihood. In January, Picasso had bought the ship "solely for employing two of us" rather than "placing it at the disposition of the association." From early 1836, Garibaldi, with his expertise as a sea captain, went to sea with Rossetti to trade in pasta, probably with the help of the Zignago brothers, important merchants whose address he considered safe enough to be given to Mazzini for their correspondence. They went north along the coast with short stops toward Cabo Frio and Campos. It was a considerable distance that required almost a day's sail, and things did not go well.

Our voyages were unlucky—Cuneo explained on 27 December—and far from profitable: the main reason arose from our trust in people whom we considered friends and who turned out to be nothing other than thieves. Our inexperience of the places we visited was not an insignificant contributing factor: *you have learn in order to know,* there can be no doubt of that.

There was a trading company at Cabo Frio that had a monopoly, and those who purchased goods there had to sell them in Rio at the same price. The two partners decided to load millet and flour at Cabo Frio and then sell it in Campos or Macaé, where they would buy sugar and spirits to be taken to Rio. Garibaldi was enthusiastic about his ship: "The caulker's daughter is beautiful, so beautiful . . . you know she's of a beauty like that often conjured up by a romantic imagination, and I have grown very fond of her," he confided to Cuneo on 17 October. He wanted to buy arms, but they did not have the money. On 27 December he again wrote to Cuneo:

I will say only this of myself: while fortune looks on heedlessly, I am far from happy and tortured by the idea of not being able to proceed with our business. I have more use for storm clouds than for tranquillity, and I am eager to go to extremes. . . . By God, I am tired of dragging out this useless existence across our earth and of being a merchant seaman. Be sure of one thing: we are destined to greater things. For the moment we are out of our element, and the time when we can put all our energies into it has been greatly delayed.

We know from the *Jornal do comercio* that at the beginning of 1837 the *Mazzini* was back and forth between Rio and Campos with goods and passengers. On 18 February (a year after his arrival in Rio), Garibaldi confided to a friend far off in Uruguay that business was much better but nothing was happening politically. He was thinking of joining him in Montevideo. But he did not, and on 22 April he made his excuses: there was a "compelling" reason that prevented him from coming, but it would have been dangerous to explain it. Another important meeting had occurred, and like the ones with the Saint-Simonians and the "believer," it was to change the direction of his life.

4. Privateer

THE OPPORTUNITY FOR Garibaldi to escape his drab life, which fell far short of the ideals for which he had left his nation, was provided by the internal conflicts of the country in which he had chosen to live. Brazil stretches over a vast territory (8,500,000 sq. km., which is comparable to the whole of Europe), and covers regions that varied greatly in terms of climate and economic development. It includes the Atlantic coast and the rain forest of the Amazon; it has both equatorial and temperate zones. The centralization of the state imposed by the monarchy did not satisfy the wide variety of local needs. There was profound discontent in some of the eighteen massive provinces, and in the 1830s during the reign of Pedro II, this discontent turned into open revolt aimed at independence.

One of the most difficult provinces to subjugate was Rio Grande do Sul (which is larger than the Italian peninsula), in the extreme south of the country, bordering with Argentina, the other large state in South America, and much smaller Uruguay. During the colonial period, the latter had been part of the Viceroyship of La Plata, and situated in the eastern part, the *Banda Oriental*, of the territory that after the fall of colonial rule became the Argentine republic. The fight for independence from Spain took a dramatic turn, when the Spanish authorities found themselves in difficulty, they called in the assistance of neighboring Brazil. The provinces of La Plata found themselves fighting both the Spanish and the Portuguese (who then became the Brazilians after the proclamation of the empire), and clashed among themselves over the form the state should take once it had unified the territories freed from Spain. The most important city, Buenos Aires, wanted centralized government, while the agrarian provinces demanded a form of autonomy that was close to independence; at the beginning of the 1830s they obtained agreement on a federal pact, which formed the basis for the Argentine Confederation. Uruguay remained outside. In 1821 it had been annexed by Brazil, which was victorious in the Cisplatine War, but in 1825 Uruguay rebelled and won independence in a bitter war that ended in 1828.

Argentina and Uruguay went through a period of great instability in the 1830s. In Argentina General Juan Lavalle, who came to power in 1828 following a revolution that aimed at greater unification, was defeated by troops raised by the provinces and sought refuge in Brazil, in Rio Grande do Sul. General Juan Manuel de Rosas took power and governed the country for a long time with an iron fist. In 1830, Uruguay elected as its president General Fructuoso Rivera, who had been a leading figure in the War of Independence. In 1835, when his mandate came to an end, he was replaced by Manuel Oribe and obtained the post of commander general of the army. However, in January of 1836 Oribe canceled his appointment, and Rivera felt that he had been deprived of all authority. The conflict between these two led to a civil war.

This series of political conflicts and personal rivalries poisoned public life in the two states on the banks of the River Plate, as it affected events in Rio Grande do Sul as well. In 1834 the province openly rebelled against the capital. The rebels were led by a rich landowner, Bento Gonçalves da Silva, who, as a colonel in the imperial army, had fought with distinction in the Cisplatine Wars. In September 1835, they took Porto Alegre, the seat of the government representative in the province, who moved to the city of Rio Grande. The authorities attempted to resolve the conflict by making concessions, but when the agitation showed no signs of abating, they resorted to armed force. In June of 1836, the imperial forces reoccupied

Porto Alegre and took control of the whole coastline with a fleet under the command of an Englishman, Admiral John Pascoe Greenfell. The Rio Grandeans, whose communication lines to the sea had been cut, embarked upon a prolonged but unsuccessful siege of the provincial capital and fought in the interior. The war took various turns. On 16 September, the revolutionaries, contemptuously called *farrapos* (down-and-outs), defeated the imperial forces at Seival and proclaimed the independence of the Rio Grandean republic. A few days later, from 2 to 4 October, it was the imperial army that prevailed. On the small island of Fanfa, they surrounded the enemy and captured the strong man of the revolt, Gonçalves, along with five hundred of his followers. The defeat did not discourage the resistance, and on 6 November an assembly in Piratinim, the republic's provisional capital, elected Gonçalves as the constitutional president, even though he was a prisoner.

An Italian, Livio Zambeccari, was captured with Gonçalves. A member of a rich Bolognese family and a little older than Mazzini (born in 1802), Zambeccari left Italy following the events of 1821. In Spain, he fought with the liberals as an aide-de-camp to Colonel Riego, a man of wide interests ranging from the natural sciences to philosophy, who had been responsible for starting the revolution of 1820. With the restoration of absolutism, he moved to England and France to devote himself to his studies. In 1826 he went to South America, and took part first in the Uruguayan struggle against Brazil and then in the Argentinean clash between centralists and federalists, fighting on the side of the former. He was forced to leave following the victory of Rosas, and after a brief stay in Uruguay he moved to Brazil, where he continued his intensive scientific and political activities in Rio Grande do Sul. Zambeccari, who joined a Masonic lodge in Porto, had been a *carbonaro* sympathetic to Mazzini's position. His ideas were humanitarian, liberal, and republican, and he argued them in the local press, which was not subject to censorship under the regime of Pedro II. He raised the morale of the revolt and he was its ideologue. He fought at the side of Bento Gonçalves, whose destiny he now shared.

The imperial government held him prisoner in the fortress of Santa Cruz on the outskirts of Rio de Janeiro, while the government of the rebel province vainly attempted to obtain his release. It was not, however, a harsh prison regime. He read, sent articles to opposition newspapers, translated philosophical works into Portuguese, and continued his scientific studies. There was much talk of politics, the rebellion in Rio Grande, the continuing struggle there, and how to help the republicans. Garibaldi's original idea of undertaking a privateering campaign along the Brazilian coast was dusted off. The rebels considered the idea of widening the conflict by taking it to the sea, dominated by the imperial fleet, and involving the great powers through the damage to trade; they decided at least to issue letters of marque to privateers of various nationalities, who were often adventurers and only interested in the right to keep one-third of the booty. In February 1837 Garibaldi spoke personally to the prisoner and declared his willingness to go to war for the liberty of a people he did not know. He did so in the name of Barrault's humanitarian ideals and the doctrines of Young Europe. The request to the republican government to set this Italian's offer on a legal footing was sent from the fortress of Santa Cruz through secret channels.

Letter of Marque Number Six, written in Portuguese, arrived in Rio on 4 May, and Garibaldi had the legal authorization he desired. It mattered little to him whether it was recognized by the Brazilians and the other states with interests in the South Atlantic. It had the appearance of an official document, headed as it was by the emblem of the new republic (two banners with green, red, and yellow diagonal bands). It was registered in the Segreteria Militar do Exercito and signed by General João Manoel de Lima e Silva. It appears to have been issued in the Candiota encampment on 14 November 1836, but in reality it must have been drawn up at the beginning of 1837 in Montevideo, where the general was being treated for serious wounds sustained in battle. In the name of the Rio Grandean government, the letter of marque authorized the cutter *Mazzini*, a vessel of twenty tons with a crew listed in the notes (fourteen men in all) "to patrol freely every and any sea or river on which naval and merchant ships of the government of Brazil and its subjects may be sailing with the right to capture and take possession of them by force of arms, as they are all suitable prize given that this letter has been issued by a legitimate and competent authority." The captain was ordered to respect the interests of other states in the hope of reciprocal recognition and assistance in the event of danger. Leaders and subjects of the Rio Grandean republic were required to give all possible assistance to the privateers.

A João Gavazzon or Gavarron was appointed captain, with Garibaldi as first lieutenant. Gavazzon must have been Giovanni Gavazzone, listed as a follower of Mazzini in the records of the papal consul in Rio. However, at the bottom of the crew list, Gavazzon was ordered to stay in Rio, and another letter of marque was made out to Gavazzon on the same date for the *Farroupilha*, a ship of 130 tons, and this document was to turn up among Garibaldi's possessions. This is a small mystery that we are unable to explain. The important thing is that Garibaldi had effective command of the *Mazzini*.

While he was waiting for authorization, Garibaldi made the necessary preparations to transform the "tiny ship" into a warship. The required funds were collected among the Italian community in Rio and totaled eight hundred lire. On 7 May the arms were loaded and hidden under the cargo. The *Jornal do comercio* recorded against the name *Mazzini*: destination Campos, captain Cipriano Alves, crew five, cargo meat, passenger the Italian Luigi Rossetti.

But the captain was Garibaldi (as in the past, he prudently adopted a pseudonym), and there were twelve men on board. Four were from Liguria: Rossetti was a passenger, Luigi Carniglia the boatswain, Pasquale Lodola the pilot, Antonio Illama and Maurizio Garibaldi (no relation) the seamen; a Sardinian, Giacomo Fiorentino, was the helmsman; Giovanni Lamberti, an Italian of unknown regional provenance, was another seaman; two Maltese, Luigi Calia and Giambattista Caruana, were second boatswain and another seaman; a Brazilian, João Baptista, was responsible for looking after the arms and issuing them when needed; a Portuguese, José María, was another seaman. There was yet another seaman, a Venetian, whose name Garibaldi did not reveal because he proved to be a coward. Some of these names differed from those in the letter of marque. This should not surprise us, because in the intervening period between the application for the document and its arrival, some must have found other work or simply had second thoughts.

"Privateer! We challenged an empire by setting out to sea with a crew of twelve on board a *garopera*, and we were the first to raise a flag of emancipation off those southern shores! The republican flag of Rio Grande."

A *garopera*, as Garibaldi explained in a note, was "a boat for fishing *garope*, a delicious fish found in Brazilian waters." It is possible to detect pride and even self-congratulation in this awareness of the almost irresponsible daring of "challenging an empire" with a fishing boat!

The captain read the text of the letter of marque. Not everyone had a clear idea of the venture for which they had been engaged. The specification of the purpose of this dangerous voyage was far from superfluous, as we shall see. The small vessel remained off Rio for a few days, possibly waiting to join up with another ship (perhaps the one commanded by Gavazzon), and this proved useful to two of Gonçalves's officers, who swam to freedom from the fortress of Vera Cruz on 10 May. Zambeccari, who couldn't swim, remained in captivity and, for the moment, left the scene. He would be pardoned by the Brazilian government in 1839, after having undertaken to return to Italy.

They finally set sail. The first prize was a cutter lying at anchor off an island not far from Rio. Given the limited value of the vessel and cargo, Garibaldi contented himself with taking a water pump, four barrels of wine, and a silver watch. As the last item was not considered war booty, it was paid for with dried meat. He also took a black slave called Antonio, whom he freed as part of the mission of liberty for which he had taken up arms. On 11 May, the privateers sighted a *sumaca*, a small coaster, and they boarded her. The terrified seamen gave up without a fight. The *Luisa*, as the *sumaca* was called, had a crew of four men, including the captain, a passenger, and four black slaves. It was transporting the passenger's property, as he had sold his farm and was moving his household goods to Rio along with 428 sacks of coffee, most of which belonged to him. Garibaldi refused the money and jewels the passenger offered him, and ordered that nobody's personal effects should be touched. Given that privateers regularly slit their prisoners' throats and confiscated their goods, some of the crew must have found such magnanimity difficult to take.

The crew and passenger of the *Luisa* were transferred to the *Mazzini*, and Carniglia, with two seamen, took command of the *Luisa*. The two ships sailed in convoy for a day, but this was not a wise policy. In the event of a naval engagement, the privateers might find themselves in difficulty, as they were divided between two ships and it was difficult to know how the prisoners would act. It was decided that they should continue their enterprise on board the *Luisa*, which was bigger (twenty-four tons) and in better condition. It had a rich cargo and was declared a prize of war. Crew, prisoners, arms, and victuals were all shifted to the *sumaca*. Garibaldi's men sank the *Mazzini* to avoid consigning it to the mercy of the waves or permitting to become an enemy prize. The *Luisa* was renamed after it, in part for ideological reasons but mainly because the letter of marque, whatever its legal validity, did not cover a ship of another name, and the new name was somehow painted on the poop. After six days when the coast was sighted, Garibaldi released the prisoners with food and water, as well as their personal effects. As he did not wish to go too close to the shore, he was even chivalrous enough to donate the only launch on the ship. The Brazilian responsible for the arms, who had not been aware of the dangers he would be exposed to, went with the released prisoners after having received his agreed pay. On the other hand, the four black slaves remained on board with Antonio, as they, too, had been declared freemen.

Even though his career as a privateer had produced pretty slim pickings, Garibaldi did not attempt other attacks on shipping. It seems improbable that along such a busy coast he did not encounter any ships during the eleven days between 17 and 28 May. Perhaps he had realized how limited his resources were. We know that other privateers had more than twenty men and were armed with cannon. He headed for Maldonado, a Uruguayan port, because he could not obtain fresh victuals in an area controlled by imperial forces, and he hoped to be well received there.

In the secret instructions he was given either verbally or in writing at the time of his departure, he had been assured of the support of the other states on the River Plate. The Uruguayan power struggle between Oribe and Rivera had culminated in July 1836 with an uprising organized by Rivera in some departments with the aid of the Argentine exiles led by Lavalle. In September, following his defeat at the Battle of Carpentería, he sought refuge in war-torn Rio Grande and joined the imperial forces. For this reason Uruguay's relations with Brazil cooled, as the latter was suspected of favoring Rivera's plots to regain power, and relations with Rio Grande improved. Argentina followed suit. But as the result of a considerable amount of highly convoluted intrigue, Rivera switched to the republican side. In March and April 1837, the alliances were reversed. Oribe,

Rosas, and the Brazilian government found themselves on the same side, and friends of the Rio Grandeans were no longer welcome in the bordering states.

When Garibaldi departed from Rio, none of this was known. Not even all Uruguayans fully understood that the situation had changed during the period that the *Mazzini* was at sea. On 28 May, when the ship arrived in Maldonado flying the Rio Grandean flag, it met with a friendly reception. Garibaldi handed over to the port authorities the ship's documents, including the second letter of marque made out to Gavazzon, and was given a receipt. In port there were a Uruguayan naval ship, which left without any hostile act, and a French fishing boat, whose captain exchanged visits with Garibaldi and lent a boat for disembarking men and goods from the new *Mazzini*, which no longer had its launch. They sold the furniture and part of the coffee, while the crew relaxed in the temperate climate of the area, the present-day resort of Punta del Este. Garibaldi sent Rossetti to Montevideo to contact Cuneo, in order to obtain supplies, news, and instructions. Given that Maldonado could not be used as a base for military operations, and intending to leave in a few days, he made an appointment to meet Rossetti halfway at Punta Jesús y María.

The situation suddenly came to a head. The Brazilian vice-consul in Maldonado notified his superior in Montevideo of the arrival of the privateer, which had already been identified owing to reports submitted by the men on the plundered cutter and the *Luisa*, when they got ashore. The Brazilian diplomatic representative in the capital demanded the confiscation of the ship and threatened a naval intervention; the government sent an order to prevent the privateer's departure. However, Garibaldi had created a great deal of goodwill, which was complemented by the mediation of an Italian immigrant, Domenico Gorlero, who dealt with the local authorities. The freeing of the five slaves had been well received throughout the country, because the port commander's report of *five* slaves was mistakenly read as a *hundred* at the Ministry of War and the Navy in Montevideo. The mayor secretly informed Garibaldi of his imminent arrest, and during the night of 5 June, the latter suddenly left port without his documents and sailed for the point where he had agreed to meet Rossetti. Dumas added a novelistic touch: the Italian "convinced" a local merchant to pay him immediately for the coffee he had purchased by pointing a pistol at his temple.

They started on a journey full of unforeseen events. June is wintertime in the Southern Hemisphere, and their departure coincided with a tempest, which also prevented the Brazilian warship *Imperial Pedro* from arriving in time to surprise the privateer in port. The *Mazzini* was in serious danger because the arms had been carelessly left close to the compass and interfered with its accuracy. At night when the ship suddenly found itself among reefs, Garibaldi climbed the foremast and shouted out the appropriate orders to enable the crew to negotiate the safe channels. He found no one at Punta Jesús y María. He later discovered that Cuneo had loaded a boat with supplies, but the Uruguayan authorities arrested him, and Rossetti was also held up.

Owing to their sudden departure, they had not taken on the usual provisions and urgently needed to find victuals. Garibaldi saw a house in the interior, about four miles from the coast. He took the ship as close to the shore as possible, but he still needed a small boat to reach it (the absence of the launch was again making itself felt). They came up with an ingenious solution: they made a raft from the dining table held steady by two well-sealed empty barrels, while clothes were suspended from a pole to form a sail. Garibaldi risked the journey along with his namesake Maurizio, whom he left on the beach while he set off for the house. He had a surprising encounter, to which we will return, but for the moment it is sufficient to know that he procured a butchered ox. It proved very difficult to load the meat on the *sumaca*. To avoid further problems of this kind, Garibaldi bought a launch from the first ship he came across. Its owner would claim that he was forced to hand it over, but as it was not a Brazilian vessel, Garibaldi would have refused to commit an act that would have made him little more than a pirate.

Eventually the *Mazzini* sighted a large cutter. Garibaldi hoped it was Rossetti, although he could not see the agreed signal of a red flag. He acted with caution. The cutter *Maria*, which had been sent from Montevideo to capture the privateer, approached with only three men visible on deck, but suddenly covered itself with armed men, and one of them gave the order to surrender in the name of the Uruguayan government. The *Mazzini* vainly attempted to make its escape, while its adversary, which with a crew of twenty-four men was the stronger, followed in hot pursuit. They exchanged rifle fire, and an attempt to board was repelled with cutlasses. Fiorentino, the helmsman, was immediately killed, and Garibaldi took his place. Shot in the neck, he lost consciousness. Carniglia took his place, and after an hour the enemy withdrew owing to lack of ammunition (according to the declaration the captain of the *Maria* made in his report). The attackers had sustained one death and two wounded. On the *Mazzini*, only the Italians had taken part in the battle, while the others, including the Venetian and the freed slaves, had hidden in the hold. Once Fiorentino was dead and Garibaldi wounded, there were only seven combatants in the naval battle on the *Mazzini*—four Ligurians, two Maltese, and Lamberti—and the enemy were not much more numerous. The armed clashes in which Garibaldi was involved in South America would often be characterized by the small number of their combatants, but their fame still spread far and wide.

Carniglia took over command and Garibaldi regained consciousness. He thought himself close to death and asked not to be buried at sea. The acting captain asked him where they should seek refuge, and showed a map of the area. Still only semiconscious, the wounded man could just make out a name written in larger letters and pointed to it. It was the distant Argentinean city of Santa Fe, on the Paraná. The *Mazzini* left the now hostile coasts of Uruguay and entered the large estuary that forms at the mouth of the River Plate, which is up to 150 kilometers wide, while the Brazilians and Uruguayans gave up the chase. The crew requested victuals and information from a Uruguayan ship. Following the direction of the wind, they reached the mouth of the River Ibicuí, where the cowardly Venetian, the seaman Lamberti, and the Portuguese decided to abandon the adventure. The *Mazzini* then sailed up the Paraná, not as a privateer, but with a Brazilian flag. When the crew signaled to the *Pintoresca*, an Argentinean schooner that ran a regular service between Buenos Aires and Gualeguay, the schooner's captain and some passengers came on board to assist the wounded. A rich merchant called Jacinto Andreus advised Garibaldi to disembark at the port of Gualeguay and offered him hospitality. It has been assumed that he did so because he was a mason, but Garibaldi had not joined a recognized lodge and we have no evidence that he knew or took part in the rituals. Andreus may simply have taken a liking to this Don Quixote whose selflessness had been the subject of many newspaper articles.

On 26 June the *Mazzini* reached land, and the following day Garibaldi sent a petition to General Pascual Echague, the governor of the province of Entre Rios in which Gualeguay was situated, who happened to be visiting the city. He explained the mission he had carried out "for the ideal of freedom and independence" in Rio Grande do Sul, notified the governor of the "mortal wound to his head," and asked for asylum and protection. Earlier, the Argentinean government had sent out notification of the possible arrival of this ship off its coast, and had ordered its confiscation and the arrest of its crew. This is what occurred: Echague notified Buenos Aires of the *Mazzini*'s arrival. On 6 July, the authorities proceeded with the inventory of the ship's assets: they found 166 sacks of coffee, partly spoilt, while another 65 had been thrown in the water because they were useless. From 10 to 17 July, a three-man commission interrogated the captain, the seven surviving crew members, and the slaves. They all gave a detailed account of the events in which they had taken part. The twenty-three witness statements were sent to the capital, and, together with the documents confiscated in Maldonado, they have provided us with most of the information we have about the voyage of the privateer.

The ship, its original name of *Luisa* restored, was in Buenos Aires on 20 October to be returned to its owner, while the instruments and equipment belonging to the original *Mazzini* were handed back to Garibaldi. The crew of the privateer remained in Gualeguay, and the governor, who had been asked by Rosas to treat the prisoners with respect, allowed them to wander the city as long as they reported to the police every day. Perhaps the subsidy of one peso per day from 8 August to 7 October, amounting to a total of sixty-one pesos to be paid by the owner of the *Luisa*, was shared among them all, or perhaps another peso per day was given to Garibaldi alone. When the subsidy ran out, the sailors left, and we hear no more of them. The five black men were returned to slavery.

Garibaldi recovered his health. Ramon de l'Arca, a young surgeon sent by the governor, healed the wound. The bullet had entered under his left ear and by some miracle crossed through the center of his throat without causing permanent damage. It came to a halt under the right ear, "half an inch from the surface." De l'Arca made an incision and removed the bullet from the foreigner who, although theoretically still a prisoner, was being feted by the local notables. He learned Spanish, and he was taught to ride a horse by some *gauchos*, "the best horsemen in the world." As soon as he could, he set about establishing contacts with Montevideo. On 26 August he confided in Cuneo and described the "deplorable situation" in which he found himself: he had no documents except the receipt from the port captain of Maldonado, and stood accused of being a pirate: "These are the real vicissitudes of adventurers." But to have the support of a people that has always been ignored was "an unparalleled happiness"! The misfortunes had not broken him, nor was he concerned about the gossip and vile lies that were being given credence in Montevideo. He intended to pursue the course of action on which he had embarked, in the company of his friend.

> Being guided by a single principle and devoted to a cause, we rejected a peaceful life and imposed silence on all our passions. We will continue on our chosen path, in spite of the shallow and thoughtless judgments of the multitude, which often considers our generous purpose to be only another form of selfishness or unbridled ambition. It is enough to have a clear conscience.

He gave an account of the life he was leading. We know that he was receiving an allowance of one peso a day, "a very comfortable condition in such a town, where you spend very little." He lived in a grand house as a guest of Andreus; indeed he had his own quarters. He spent most of his day reading books, and occasionally he would go out in the afternoon for a walk or to visit "some beauty or other," or went out in the morning with paper and pencil to write or compose poetry.

On 1 October, he devoted the day to his correspondence: he wrote letters to Nice and Rio de Janeiro, which he sent to his friend with instructions to forward them. He was still determined to continue the struggle:

> I came into this world to be a right pain in the ass for half of humanity, and I have sworn to keep being one. I have sworn it, by God! To devote my life to upsetting others, and I have already achieved something, but it is nothing compared with what I hope to do, if they let me do it or they cannot obstruct me.

He told Cuneo of his hopes of being released soon. He was thinking of going to the Rio Grande—if not to beg for rewards, at least to request compensation for his losses. He wanted to join with Cuneo and never separate again. Tired of a situation that remained unresolved, he attempted to escape at the end of the year, after having heard that he was to be taken to the provincial capital along with other prisoners. He made his escape at night during a tempest, on horseback and armed with a pistol. A guide was supposed to escort him to an Englishman's *estancia*, from where he would be able to board a ship heading for Montevideo. He may have been betrayed by his guide, and in any case he was recaptured two days later close to the Ibicuí, halfway to Uruguay. He had broken his word, and the spell on which his warm reception had been based was now broken. He was taken back to the town with his feet tied under the belly of a horse and his arms behind his back, while his skin burned under the blistering sun of the southern summer. The military commander of Gualeguay, Leonardo Millán, asked him for the names of his accomplices. When his prisoner refused, he had Garibaldi "brutally" flogged and hung by his wrists from a beam or tree. He suffered this torture for two hours, parched by thirst and exposed to the mockery of a group of young louts. When he was cut down, he was more dead than alive. His host had been arrested, and the terrified townspeople did not dare to assist him, yet a woman, "a virtuous angel of goodness," came to his assistance. The governor, informed of what was happening, had him brought to the provincial capital, Bajada. He remained in prison for another two months, and then Echague let him go without explanations. In reality, once the *Luisa* had been returned, Argentinean authorities had no charges to bring against the foreigner and preferred not to reopen a case which by then everyone had forgotten. This brings us to the end of February 1838.

"Cases of good fortune, like those of misfortune, usually come in pairs," he wrote in his *Memoirs*. In Bajada, he was given passage as far as Paraná Guazú on a brigantine, whose Genovese captain treated him with "courteous generosity," and from there he reached Montevideo on a *balandra* under the command of another Genovese. At last, he was among friends! Rossetti and Cuneo explained the background to the surprise they encountered in Maldonado and the attack at Punta Jesús y María. Garibaldi, guilty of armed resistance against a Uruguayan ship, stayed in hiding at the house of a certain Captain Giuseppe Pesente, whom biographers often confuse with the captain of the *Costanza*, Angelo Pesante. He probably knew quite a bit about the events that followed his departure from Rio, because he had always kept up his correspondence with Montevideo from Gualeguay and Bajada. He knew that, following the confiscation of the *Luisa*, Giovanni Gavazzone and Giacomo Picasso had been arrested (as they had been recorded as the captain and owner of the *Mazzini*), and Gonçalves, who was transferred to Bahia for greater security, managed to trick his jailers and escape to recover command of the rebels in Rio Grande.

Garibaldi now had to decide what he was going to do next. He did not even consider the possibility of returning to Italy or somehow eking out a living in the Italian community in Montevideo, as he had done in Marseille. Retaining the moral leadership of Mazzini's supporters that Canessa had entrusted to him, he had sent Cuneo and Rossetti to Montevideo, and they acknowledged his authority. We have ample evidence that they had also kept him up to date on events. On 6 February 1838, shortly before he left Bajada, he wrote through Cuneo "To my brothers in Young Italy" to express his pleasure in knowing of "your successful meeting in Montevideo and all the desirable plans you have conceived." He summarized recent painful experiences, and notified them of his imminent release and the penniless state in which he found himself ("I will say only that no one could be poorer"). He asked them to organize the necessary means for him to travel to Uruguay: the courtesy of the two Genovese captains could not have been fortuitous.

While he was recovering from the hardships of recent months, he had time to reflect upon his American experience. He had failed in the endeavor for which he had moved to Brazil, namely, to organize Young Italy and enroll a volunteer force to take to Italy in the event of revolution. The latter part of his plan had been the more important, but it was no longer so pressing, as the news from Italy was not hopeful. His only battle as commander of a privateer had been a disaster ending with flight and a long imprisonment marked by the memory of his torture. When he assessed his actions over the previous two years, Garibaldi realized that he was not cut out to be a political leader, and he decided to give up his organizational and propaganda role, as Cuneo and Rossetti had proved very effective in this area. Conversely, he had discovered an aptitude for command, coolness in the face of danger, and an ability to put up with privations and sacrifices. In spite of his lack of military success, he had discovered his vocation: to engage in an armed struggle to defend oppressed peoples. He ends the preface to his *Memoirs* with the assertion "War is the true life for a man" (*¡La guerra es la verdadera vida del hombre!*). He borrowed the motto from Fructuoso Rivera and made it his own. From then on it would inspire his every action.

5. In Rio Grande

G ARIBALDI TURNED TO Rio Grande do Sul for his immediate plans. The revolutionary war of independence continued. Bento Gonçalves, following his escape, arrived in the provisional capital, Piratinim, on 16 November 1837, and assumed his position as president, which injected impetus into the difficult military operations. He was in need of resources and men. He particularly needed commanders capable of fighting against his adversaries, some of whom had received their training in the Napoleonic Wars, and intellectuals capable of giving ideological support to the separatist demands. Even the document that was intended to provide a legal basis for the incipient state, the *Manifesto of the President of the Republic in the Name of the Members of His Constituent Assembly*, which was issued by Gonçalves on 29 August 1838, did not go beyond a list of the violent acts and abuses of power perpetrated by the central government and its representatives. There was no one who could provide the moral and political justifications for the revolution and defend its cause to European public opinion.

Italian exiles had an important role to play in this field. As Zambeccari's contribution was now lacking, Rossetti stepped in to take his place.

He left Montevideo and joined Gonçalves, who gave him the delicate task of running the propaganda campaign. Rosetti proposed the establishment of a newspaper as the most suitable way of explaining the government's actions and the army's exploits. The exiles had to equip a printing office with the necessary equipment sent from Montevideo. Finally on 1 September 1838 the first issue of *O Povo* appeared in Piratinim. This paper—whose full title, if translated into English, would be *The People: The Political, Literary, and Ministerial Newspaper of the Rio Grandean Republic*—was published regularly (usually every two weeks) on four crudely printed pages of small format. Nonetheless it constitutes a precious record of life in the republic and, what is of more concern to us, of Garibaldi's enterprises. The democratic and republican principles that inspired Rossetti were expressed by a statement taken from an article in the Mazzini-inspired *La Giovine Italia*: "The power that directs the rebellion must prepare citizens' minds for the values of fraternity, modesty, equality, selflessness, and ardent patriotism."

And it was the selfless and ardent Rossetti who was charged with procuring victuals, arms, and men, and who brought Garibaldi to Rio Grande. The republicans, although capable of keeping the imperial forces in check on land, were unable to challenge them at sea. They did not have possession of a single port. While they had attempted to create difficulties for their enemy by using privateers, the lack of reliable logistical support had made this a very risky strategy: Garibaldi's sudden changes of fortune in Maldonado were proof of this. They now proposed to use his professional experience as a man of the sea to hit one of the empire's nerve centers.

A significant part of the war was being waged around Porto Alegre, the province's administrative and economic center, which had been under siege by the rebels since the imperial forces had retaken it in June 1836. The city, which was cut off by land, could be easily defended because of its supply lines by the sea. It is situated not on the ocean but at the northern end of the Lagoa dos Patos (Lagoon of Ducks), an extremely calm stretch of water divided from the Atlantic by a strip of land 20–25 kilometers wide. The lagoon is 250 kilometers long, runs from the northeast to the southwest, and reaches a maximum width of 60 kilometers. It therefore has a considerable surface area: about 13,000 square kilometers, which is comparable (using examples familiar to Italians) to the whole area of

Campania or Trentino-Alto Adige, or about thirty-five times the size of Lake Garda. It is linked to the ocean by a small opening in the south at the opposite end to the one where Porto Alegre is situated. This single access was firmly in the hands of the imperial forces, who had garrisons on both shores in the cities of Rio Grande and San José do Norte.

The imperial fleet, which was completely dominant, ensured supplies to the besieged provincial capital by assembling them at Rio Grande and then transporting them by water along the lagoon, which was deep enough for navigation by ships of substantial size, but the route was surrounded by swamps and shallows that could only be used by small craft, and was therefore vulnerable to hit-and-run tactics. It seemed possible to strike at the enemy in this sea with privateers, given that ships heading for Porto Alegre were obliged to sail its entire length. Garibaldi was asked to continue the harassment to shipping he had set out to inflict in the previous year with the *Mazzini*, but this time in a more restricted theater of war.

He set off with Rossetti on the 480-kilometer journey from Montevideo to Piratinim, his "first long journey on horseback," "with enormous gratification," trying out the *escotero* system, which consisted of traveling with a group of horses and replacing the tired ones with fresh ones along the way. In Piratinim, a township with very few buildings made of brick or stone, which had been chosen as a provisional capital for the republic because of its distance from the front, Garibaldi bolstered morale by recounting the troubles of the republican government of the United States during the early part of their rebellion against the British. He was greeted "with extreme cordiality" by the minister of finance, Almeida. A few days later, he was joined in the camp by Bento Gonçalves, whom Garibaldi found to be an "extraordinary man": tall, agile, an excellent horseman, very brave, very generous, modest, and sober, he was an idol to his fellow citizens. Later Garibaldi would discover Gonçalves's limitations as a military leader and as a politician. For the moment, he was greeted "with much familiarity as though he were a childhood friend and equal," and they shared their "rustic meals" of *asado* (roast meat), the principal food of armies at war in that countryside rich with livestock.

His first impression of Rio Grande, a country for which he had fought without ever having trodden its soil, could not have been better. In June of 1838, the general situation appeared favorable to the republicans because of the very recent victory on the Rio Pardo. However, it was not easy to extend operations to the Lagoa dos Patos, where the republicans could not sail in from the Atlantic on armed ships of the same size as the *Mazzini*. The fleet to intercept imperial shipping had to be built within the lagoon. They were already working on it in a boatyard improvised on the River Camaqua, a tributary of a wooded part of the lagoon that afforded safety as well as an abundant supply of wood, because the shallows prevented enemy vessels from approaching. John Griggs, a North American of Irish origin who came to Rio Grande out of republican sympathies and a spirit of adventure, was directing the work, but it was going slowly owing to the lack of necessary equipment. Garibaldi, the new commander of the fleet, immediately instilled some urgency in the boatbuilding work: he obtained craftsmen and tools from Montevideo through Rossetti, who took advantage of an important political shift in Uruguay.

France had instructed the Argentinean government to repay a loan, and when Rosas refused, it imposed a naval blockade on Buenos Aires, which it would maintain for more than two years until it achieved its aim. In order to facilitate its operations, it had asked Oribe for the base in Montevideo. Oribe, an ally of Rosas, refused and found himself weakened by French hostility and his friend's misfortunes. This situation was exploited by Rivera, who was still an exile in Rio Grande. He gathered his forces, and on 15 June 1838 he defeated the supporters of his rival and established a government in the capital. He then declared war on Argentina, where Oribe had sought refuge. Thus Uruguay was once again an ally of the Rio Grandean republic, and became a source of men and supplies. Moreover, *O Povo* could now be distributed there, bringing news of the war and seeking support for the republican cause. From its very first issue, the newspaper had attempted to magnify Garibaldi's exploits.

Work in the boatyard on two cutters was completed: the *Rio Pardo*, of 15–18 tons, and the *Independencia*, of 12–15 tons. The crews, which overall counted about seventy men, were a "truly cosmopolitan bunch," with seven Italians, including Carniglia and Garibaldi's old comrade from Genoa, Edoardo Mutru, many South Americans, freed black and mulatto slaves, and adventurers of every nation. It was reported on 12 September (the newspaper was still only on its fourth issue!) that the ships left the yard on 26 August; they were pushed by hand through the vegetation and managed to evade a patrol of four Brazilian ships guarding the mouth of the Camaqua. On 4 September, while sailing on the lagoon, they sighted and attacked two merchant ships. One managed to escape, but the other, a *sumaca* called *Mineira*, surrendered after the first cannon shot. The crew, who escaped on a launch, were captured when they came ashore, and sent to Piratinim.

Garibaldi's report to the Ministry of the Navy, which was published in the edition of 22 September, informs us that the ship ran aground and was destroyed. The cargo was confiscated: and consisted of five hundred barrels of wheat flour, a box of documents, a box containing accessories for smokers, a demijohn of French aquavit, ten barrels of saltpeter, four crates of preserves, five crates of cloth, eight parcels of canvas, twenty-six sacks of rice, twenty sacks of beans, and forty sacks of millet. In accordance with the ship's articles as drawn up by Rossetti, the prize was to be divided into three parts, one to the shipowner (in this case the state), one to those who had captured the ship, and one to the National Treasury. However, Minister of Finance Almeida, "in consideration of the greater importance of the services rendered," ordered the prize to be divided into eight parts, four to the Treasury (half rather than an effective figure of two-thirds), one to Garibaldi "as the commander of the expedition," one to the officers, and two to the crew. This division of shares was to become the norm in the future. He also ordered that an advance should be sent to the servicemen, while the remaining sums would be paid once the booty had been sold, and he gave specific orders to the local authorities on this point.

The praise and higher remuneration were more than justified. The danger constituted by these privateers forced Admiral Greenfell to send the merchant ships in convoy escorted by warships within the lagoon. The cutters could no longer capture such rich prizes, and they had to avoid being hunted down by the Brazilians. They restricted themselves to harassing the enemy. Moving around the shallows, which were inaccessible to the larger imperial ships, they attacked the property of supporters of the enemy while rapidly moving around the interior on horses that they found at hand. In February 1839, Garibaldi's modest fleet was reinforced by a gunboat and another cutter, both of which Gonçalves had captured close to Porto Alegre, but it was still too small to take on a navy made up of thirty ships, of which two were steamships, ninety cannon, and nearly one thousand men. For this reason Almeida ordered Garibaldi to construct two more cutters, as it was not possible to build anything bigger with the available resources.

The imperial forces were closing in, and the Rio Grandeans had to transfer their capital from Piratinim, which was too exposed to military operations, to Cassapava. This involved transporting all the ministerial archives on carts. *O Povo* moved with the government and had to suspend publication between 2 February and 6 March 1839. The arrival of the Brazilian minister of war in Porto Alegre at the end of March signaled the intensification of the war against the secessionists, particularly the privateers and Garibaldi himself, considered the most dangerous of their enemies.

Garibaldi's whereabouts were not known. In fact he was back on the Camaqua, surrounded by his men, who had been joined by Rossetti following a dispute with Almeida over the running of the newspaper. He had opened a larger boatyard in a meat-salting factory that had been abandoned because of the war. Carpenters and smiths were repairing the cutters.

Major Francisco Pedro de Abreu, one of the most skilled guerrilla fighters and generally known as Moringue, was given the task of eliminating Garibaldi. In April he carefully prepared a surprise attack. On the eleventh he slipped out of Porto Alegre by night. His launches took 150 men to the Camaqua woods, and he hid them not far from the boatyard. On the morning of the day scheduled for the attack, he approached cautiously and was assisted by the southern autumn fog. The action was conducted so skillfully that Garibaldi, although warned, had no sense of the imminence of the danger, and he sent his men off to work as usual. He was alone with the cook in a *galpón*, a brick shed used for storage, when suddenly the place was swarming with armed horsemen wielding the long lances carried by mounted riflemen.

All hell broke loose. With his usual composure, Garibaldi hurried to the former factory building, where he was joined by Carniglia and ten more of his men. Now there were twelve of them, including the cook, while the workers in the yard scattered and tried to make good their escape by leaping into the river. The element of surprise was lost. The men barricaded in the factory had sixty rifles that were already loaded, a crucial factor given that there were no automatic rifles yet and reloading required a certain amount of time. They were able to produce sustained fire that held the attackers at bay, and they loudly sang the republican anthem to give the impression that they were a numerous force. The attackers made the mistake of taking up their position around the *galpón* and shooting from a distance rather than charging in. Their deadly lances were useless, and they delayed their action. As they were not equipped to breach the wall, they attempted to climb it and set fire to the straw roof, but the defenders picked them off from below. Moringue's arm had been smashed by a rifle shot. He gave the order to retreat, leaving six of their men dead in the field, while the defenders had only lost one man. They were then pursued by the boatyard workers, who had overcome their fear, so the imperial force ended up in a disorderly rout and returned in humiliation to Porto Alegre on the twentieth.

News of the Battle of the Galpón de Xarqueada spread quickly. The minister of war reported on it to the Brazilian parliament and acknowledged that he had hoped "to gain great advantage from the capture of the foreigner Garibaldi, the commander of the republican naval forces." For the first time, the privateer heard official recognition of his actions! On 24 April *O Povo* published his report. Garibaldi admitted that he had been taken by surprise and this had cost him the strongbox. He praised the courage of his men, advised that they should be adequately remunerated, and requested the deployment of a detachment of cavalry to defend the boatyard.

The Rio Grandeans were thinking of an offensive to widen the area of conflict. The republic had consolidated itself. In the new capital, the government had set up the structures of a state. In accordance with the model of Napoleonic centralization adopted in Brazil, it had formed an administration with government-nominated officials, it had organized a system of taxation to finance the war, and it was drawing up a constitutional charter. To signify the importance of the revolution, the government decreed that a new era should start from 20 September 1835, the date on which the republic was proclaimed. This provision was purely anti-imperial: the names of the months and days were not altered, and religious holidays were recognized, as the Catholic religion was always treated with the utmost respect.

Having reinforced its position in the interior, the republic rejected offers of peace from an imperial government willing to grant the rebels amnesty but not autonomy. It prepared a new strategy to isolate enemy bases by widening the rebellion's front and obtaining bases on the ocean. Discontent with the Brazilians was spreading in the adjacent province of Santa Catarina, much smaller than Rio Grande (the size of Scotland or Sicily, it had about sixty thousand inhabitants), and Lajes, a city in the interior, rebelled and asked to be annexed by its neighboring republic. The Rio Grandeans decided to take advantage of the situation and organized an expedition to assist the secession and the creation of a friendly republic, and with it the basis for a federation of rebel states to oppose the empire.

The first objective was to take the city of Laguna, a useful Atlantic port north of Porto Alegre and on the route that connected the capital to Rio Grande. The plan involved a combined attack by land and sea. Command of the operation was entrusted to Colonel David Canabarro, while "Lieutenant Captain" José Garibaldi was to lead the naval forces. First of all, part of the rebel fleet had to break out of Lagoa dos Patos into the open sea. It was not possible for them to force their way through the channel, which was the only outlet, nor was it practical to take the boats over the strip of land that divided the lagoon from the sea, as it was sandy and in full view of the Brazilians. There was no choice but to adopt an extremely audacious stratagem that bordered on the impossible: two cutters were to be taken back up the small river Capivari, which had been swollen by the autumn rains, then taken overland on large carts to the Thomás José Lagoon, assisted by the swamps created by the rains, and finally sailed down to the Atlantic on the River Tramandai.

Canabarro and Garibaldi decided to use the most recently built cutters, the eighteen-ton *Farroupilha* and the twelve-ton *Seival*. The most difficult part was moving the boats across land, which would leave them very exposed to enemy attack. They secretly concentrated two hundred oxen and the necessary workers in the chosen area. Garibaldi left command of the fleet that was to remain in the lagoon with a Rio Grandean, Zeferino Dutra, and set off at the end of June with his best men, who were all Italians. He personally took command of the *Farroupilha* and entrusted the *Seival* to Griggs. Some news of their activities must have got out, as Admiral Greenfell reached the mouth of the Capivari after the two cutters had entered it, and blocked its exit without imagining that the two ships would not reappear. Garibaldi followed his route without great difficulties. On 5 July, he arrived at the agreed rendezvous and had the boats run aground and all movable parts, from cannon to stores, removed and loaded on carts. Two enormous six-wheeled carts had been made for the hulls, with the assistance of a local engineer. The area that had to be traversed was flattened out and a kind of track laid out. The cutters were loaded by an ingenious system, given that they had no equipment for lifting heavy weights. The large carts were lowered into two enormous ditches, and the hulls were slipped onto them and tied down with ropes. The men used roping from a Rio Grandean privateer commanded by an American, Robert Bisley, which had sunk during a tempest close to the Tramandai.

Then came the difficult part. The oxen were yoked and flanked by men on foot and on horseback who goaded them with sticks and prods. It took two days of Herculean effort to pull the carts out of the ditches. Then began the march over the prepared stretch of land. The cart wheels often sank into the ground, and the men had to raise them back up again using brute force. On 11 July, the journey over land was complete, and the ships were launched into the lagoon and fitted out again. They sailed down the Tramandai, and on 14 July they took advantage of the high tide to enter the Atlantic. The plan had worked.

It was winter and there was a storm at sea, but Garibaldi still ordered them to set out into the ocean. The two ships separated and the *Seival* pulled away. The waves tossed the *Farroupilha* and crashed onto its decks. The ship was overloaded (as Garibaldi acknowledged) with thirty men on board, equipment, and provisions, not to mention a heavy revolving cannon capable of pointing in any direction. Garibaldi decided to approach land, and on arriving at the mouth of the River Araranguá, he climbed the foremast to look for a landing place. Gigantic waves smashed the rudder and capsized the ship; he was thrown into the sea far from the vessel. An excellent swimmer, he unsuccessfully attempted to rescue Carniglia and Mutru, who were in difficulty, and his two friends disappeared beneath the water. Sixteen of the thirty crew drowned, including all six Italians and the freed black slave Procopio, who had wounded Moringue in the defense of the *galpón*. The survivors, numb with cold, gathered on the beach. They refreshed themselves with a barrel of aquavit that had washed up on the shore, and they warmed themselves by running up and down. They also found hospitality and compassion at a nearby house. Then they set off overland to join the Rio Grandean army. *O Povo* proudly told the story of the ships' adventurous "escape" from the lagoon, but kept quiet about the subsequent mishap.

Meanwhile the Santa Catarinean rebels and the troops under Canabarro advanced on the city of Laguna, whose naval defense consisted of an imperial flotilla comprising the brigantine *Cometa* and four cutters. The Rio Grandeans could only count on the *Seival*, which had undergone repairs following the battering it had received from the storm. The Brazilians had no idea that it had left Lagoa dos Patos, and that their enemy could now count on support from the sea. They were greatly surprised when the *Seival* arrived, now under Garibaldi's command, while three cutters were bombarding the troops attacking Laguna.

Garibaldi found himself in an unfamiliar situation. Until then, he had fought as a privateer attacking enemy merchant shipping and fleeing warships. He was now obliged to take on the role of attacker: he had to engage in battle to end enemy dominance of the sea. The imbalance between the forces of the two sides was considerable, and Garibaldi played an audacious game based on his tactical experience in the Lagoa dos Patos. Without engaging, he withdrew to the south and lured the enemy into an ambush. Two cutters, the *Imperial Catarinense* and the *Lagunense*, entered a labyrinth of canals in hot pursuit, where they were attacked by soldiers hiding in the vegetation. They were then captured.

The Rio Grandeans exploited this success to launch an attack. The city of Laguna was situated on a lagoon; hence its name. The ships, which were immediately crewed, were used to transport hundreds of men to the northern shore by sea, flanked by boats found in the area. Two Brazilian ships, the *Santa Ana* and the *Itaparica*, took action to prevent the landing but surrendered as soon as they were threatened with being boarded, while the disoriented captain of the *Cometa* fled. It was a rout. In no time, the imperial flotilla had dissolved and the Rio Grandeans had been reinforced. For the moment it had gained control of the sea around Laguna, which was abandoned by defenders discouraged by the turn of events. Canabarro entered the city without firing a shot, and took possession of the merchant ships, arms, and provisions. In the interior of the province of Santa Catarina another military force, under the command of Colonel Joaquín Teixeira Nuñes, was advancing without encountering any resistance.

The Santa Catarinean republic was proclaimed on 25 July 1839 in Laguna, the province's second city (the provincial capital was Desterro), which was renamed Juliana, and a priest was elected as president. Rossetti, appointed secretary of state, was the driving force behind the government. The editorship of *O Povo*, which he had left some time before, was taken over by Giovan Battista Cuneo on 2 May 1840, following his move from Montevideo to Rio Grande. Canabarro, who was promoted to general, took command of the republican army now being established, and Garibaldi took command of the fleet.

The enlargement of the theater of operations achieved by the Rio Grandeans and the fall of Laguna made a great impression in Rio de Janeiro. The government reacted forcefully. Marshal Francisco José de Souza Suares de Andrea, appointed provincial governor and military commander, arrived in Desterro with many troops and a fleet of twelve ships (including the *Cometa*) and three cutters. The situation was shifting decisively in favor of the imperial forces. A foretaste came with the destruction of the Rio Grandean fleet that remained in the Lagoa dos Patos, which Greenfell surprised in its haven on the River Camaqua: three cutters were captured, the base was destroyed, and Zeferino Dutra was killed.

Garibaldi had never been in command of such a numerous fleet. He crewed it by recruiting local seamen and had others come from Montevideo. He personally took command of the *Libertadora*, renamed the *Rio Pardo*, while Griggs took over the *Imperial Catarinense*, renamed the *Cassapava*, and the *Seival* was entrusted to the Italian Lorenzo Valerigini. The other three ships had Rio Grandean captains.

The first move of the imperial forces was to blockade Laguna. Yet again Garibaldi found himself trapped on a motionless stretch of water whose outlets were all guarded by the enemy. Canabarro, however, ordered him to take three ships out on a naval raid against Brazilian merchant shipping. On 20 October he sent out a *sumaca* directed toward the north, and as he expected, the imperial ships gave chase, leaving him free to depart with his flotilla made up of the *Rio Pardo*, the *Cassapava*, and the *Seival*, each armed with only one cannon. Initially things went well, and they even boarded a merchant ship. Then Griggs broke away, and the *Rio Pardo* and the *Seival* were sighted by the sloop *Regeneração*, armed with twenty cannon in a masked battery, "a genuine warship" as Garibaldi observed in his *Memoirs*. This adversary was too powerful, and the winning tactic was the tried and tested one: approach the coast, where the larger ship would find itself at a disadvantage. During the night, the republicans managed to shake off their pursuer. They took shelter at the island of Bom Abrigo, where they took on supplies and even managed to capture three merchant ships, which they took with them after having put a few seamen on board.

The raid had produced good results. Garibaldi now had to return to base in Laguna. On the way, his ships were surprised by the brigantine *Andorinha*, which was also too powerful for the two cutters slowed down by the captured ships. The republicans took refuge in Imbituba Bay, where they found an unexpected reinforcement in the form of a detachment of two hundred Rio Grandeans. They fortified their position in the certain knowledge that the Brazilian attack would not be long in coming. The *Rio Pardo* was scuttled in the bay, and the *Seival*'s cannon was dismounted and placed on a promontory. It was 2 November. Two days later, two ships appeared and opened up an intense bombardment as they passed in turns in front of the bay, while the republicans responded from land with their inferior armaments. There were heavy losses on both sides. After four hours the imperial navy withdrew without pressing home an attack in which they were the more powerful force. Having luckily escaped better-trained enemies, Garibaldi was able to return to Laguna with the two cutters. The merchant ships were lost, but their cargoes were recovered and transported to the city overland. Yet again boldness had triumphed.

But this was the last success. The Brazilians were organizing a counteroffensive by land and sea, while the political situation in Santa Catarina was deteriorating fast. From the very beginning, Garibaldi had criticized the "the haughty attitude" of the Rio Grandeans toward the Santa Catarineans, "our friends at the beginning, and our sworn enemies at the end." The Rio Grandeans behaved like conquerors, relations between Canabarro and the local republican government were now terrible, and there was growing discontent in the country over the damage inflicted on the economy by the war. Garibaldi was forced to take action that he found repugnant: he attacked the town of Imaruí on the lagoon bearing the same name, with the *Seival* and two cutters, and he allowed it to be sacked as punishment for having massacred the republican garrison and switching to the imperial side. "I never experienced another day of such regrets and such disgust with the human family," he would write in his *Memoirs* as he recalled the "foul and evil behavior" committed by the soldiers, who were "savage beasts" and did not respond to their commanders' orders as they embarked on "threats, beatings, and killings."

The enemy prepared to attack Laguna by land and sea. It was Garibaldi's duty to organize the defense against attack from the sea, and he fortified the port entrance with three cannon and a line of riflemen. He lined up four cutters, two gunboats, and some boats loaded with marksmen. On 15 November, the city found itself in the presence of a powerful naval force consisting of 16 ships with 33 cannon, 300 seamen, and 600 marines, to which it had no adequate response. The line of riflemen was made up of 300 men instead of the 1,200 requested, and the ships were not fully crewed because seamen had been detailed to transfer soldiers in retreat. The imperial fleet attacked at two in the afternoon (it was summer), and opened up a withering fire that the defenders were simply unable to return. The defenders on board were decimated: Griggs died at his post, shredded by a cannonball with grapeshot. When he had no response from Canabarro to his request for reinforcements, Garibaldi set fire to his ships, and under cover of darkness he took the survivors to join the retreating land forces. Laguna was lost. Canabarro's decision to defend almost to the last man against superior and better-organized forces had turned out to be a useless waste of men and military hardware.

The republicans marched to the plateau in the interior. Both Rio Grande and Santa Catarina were mostly covered in forest, and distant military forces consisting of just a few hundred people were moved around with the assistance of people familiar with the terrain. Scouts were used to locate the enemy. After battles, both rebel and imperial soldiers tended to disperse and return to their families for a period. Given that there was also a lack of secure bases for holding prisoners, this situation often resulted in their having their throats cut.

At that time, the Rio Grandeans had taken about five hundred men. At Santa Vitoria, close to the river, they succeeded on 14 December 1839 in inflicting a crushing defeat on the imperial forces, who had been overconfident in their advance. On 12 January 1840, it was the turn of the imperial forces to overcome the republicans, whom they surprised with superior force.

Garibaldi, who for the first time was engaged in warfare solely on land, took part in both clashes. A report from Colonel Teixeira published by *O Povo* tells us that in the first battle "the intrepid commander José Garibaldi led his brave seamen" in an attack on the enemy's left flank, and "this officer without equal" forced the infantry to retreat. In the second, which was fought close to Forquillas, Garibaldi had command of the infantry, which amounted to five hundred men in all. Teixeira attempted to surprise the enemy by advancing rapidly with the cavalry, but was drawn into a ravine in which the horses could not maneuver and found themselves in a difficult situation. Garibaldi, who rushed to their assistance, did not know how to assess it. In difficult moments on board ship, he climbed the foremast to survey the sea and coastline. In the forest he climbed to higher ground: this was to become one of his regular precautions. On a hill he gathered the surviving cavalrymen and his infantrymen, who were catching up with him, seventy-three men in all. With Teixeira and other officers, he withdrew the group in an orderly fashion in the forest under unremitting fire. At night the survivors managed to shake off their attackers. They marched for four days in the forest without meat, their usual diet. They fed on roots as they laboriously made their way through the thickest forest. Finally they reached Vacaria, which they hoped would be friendly.

It was not to be. It was over for the short-lived republic in the province of Santa Catarina. Local soldiers were deserting and taking the horses with them. The Rio Grandeans, without allies or supplies, were suffering from the harsh climate at that time of the year. The coastal zone enjoyed a mild, almost tropical, climate, but the interior was mountainous. The cold started to become unbearable for men without the correct kit. Teixeira was obliged to take his men on the difficult march back to the plateau of the Rio Grande through hostile and almost inaccessible places. Garibaldi followed him in command of his sixty men, for the most part seamen.

The final moves were being prepared around Porto Alegre. In January 1840, the imperial commanders prepared a large-scale plan to free the city from siege and annihilate the rebels by separately attacking the two parts of the republican army, which were under the command of Gonçalves and General Antonio Netto. However, the republicans managed to foil the maneuver and bring the two forces together. At the end of April the two armies met on the river with their full forces. There were 4,300 Brazilians and 3,400 Rio Grandeans.

Garibaldi now took part in a pitched battle for the first time. This involved a large deployment of infantry and a cavalry supported on the imperial side by artillery and warships in the river. He admired the skill with which Gonçalves had been able to join Netto, by carrying out a march that would have been impossible for a European army held up by supply lines. The price for the rapidity of the maneuver was hungry troops, because for two days the pursuing enemy had prevented them from eating their *asado* or customary roast meat. Now the moment to resolve the outcome of the war had come. Gonçalves had occupied the better position, and the expert general Manuel Jorge Rodríguez ("old General George," as Garibaldi referred to him in his *Memoirs*), who led the imperial forces, had the advantage in numbers and equipment.

Garibaldi, "a follower of Beccaria who was the enemy of war," confessed to being somewhat embarrassed in having to admit that "I never encountered a more beautiful day or a more magnificent spectacle. In my position at the center of our infantry on the highest site, I could see both armies." Down on the plain views could be obstructed, but he would be able to follow every moment in the battle, which promised to be a bloody one.

His expectations were not met. Following a fierce debate between hawks and doves in the republican command, Gonçalves decided not to attack, and the battle that could have determined the outcome of the war was not fought. Perhaps it was wise not to risk squandering the already dwindling Rio Grandean troops by bringing them out into the open, or perhaps that day's decision and the skirmishes of the following day reflected

Gonçalves's "bad habit of indecisiveness," which was "the cause of the disastrous outcomes of his operations." Garibaldi did not hide his negative assessment. The experience of two years of war had convinced him of the advantage of taking the initiative, particularly when outnumbered or in an unfavorable position: his unexpected victories had been based on the tactics of attacking the enemy, putting them in a state of psychological subjection, and, once the action had commenced, never desisting, "to the point of having used one's last ounce of strength and having put one's last reserves into action." These criteria had been developed in combat that involved small numbers of men, in whom the leader could inspire enthusiasm and a spirit of sacrifice through his own example, as he was in direct contact with everyone. In the future, Garibaldi's distinction would be his ability to achieve this even when leading large forces against well-trained armies.

Time was on the side of the imperial forces, given their greater resources. The republican capital of Cassapava, which had been sacked on a previous occasion, was occupied on 23 May. The workshop where *O Povo* had been printed was destroyed, and publication of the newspaper ceased from that moment. The rebels lost the ability to disseminate information about their activities abroad and hold the attention of the international public.

The government withdrew to Alegrete to escape the enemy that was pressing down on them. There was urgent need of military action capable of restoring Rio Grandean hopes. Gonçalves decided on a move that would have been opportune from the very beginning of the revolt: the capture of San José do Norte, one of the fortified towns that dominated the entrance to Lagoa dos Patos. Its possession would have ensured victuals, arms, and munitions for the rebels, who were "in a terrible state" and would have interrupted the flow of supplies to Porto Alegre, forcing it to surrender. The preparations were carried out in secret. Gonçalves personally took command, with the assistance of Teixeira. Garibaldi prepared some vessels used for gathering the troops, and he had the task of attacking the city of Rio Grande once San José do Norte was taken. Rossetti was also involved. The force of about a thousand men and two cannon marched for eight days, advancing an average of forty kilometers a day, and attacked the unsuspecting city during the stormy night of 16 July. The walls were easily scaled, and two of the four forts were taken without difficulty. The officer in charge of the third lit the gunpowder store, blowing himself up with the attackers. The commander of the fortified town barricaded himself in the fourth, but in the morning a final assault was sufficient to assure victory.

"Finding themselves in the city, our starving and ragged soldiers thought the only thing they had to do was to eat well, drink even better, clothe themselves, and pillage. The majority therefore dispersed with the intent of looting." The imperial forces had time to take countermeasures. From nearby Rio Grande, Admiral Greenfell dispatched three ships, which opened fire while troops were deployed. The attackers were now under attack, and their situation was deteriorating dramatically. The conquerors wandered around drunk and loaded with booty. Many had damaged their rifles by using them for breaking down doors of houses and shops, or had lost their tinderboxes. The battle raged around one of the two forts taken at the outset. It was captured by the Brazilians, lost again, and then definitively wrested from the republicans. As an extreme solution, Garibaldi proposed setting fire to the city, but Gonçalves, who obviously did not want to alienate the local population, refused to do this. The only action left open to them was a disorderly retreat. The campaign had failed. Garibaldi halted in San Simón on the lagoon with the remainder of the republican navy, which now counted around forty men. Once again he was ordered to build some ships.

During that same month, sixteen-year-old Pedro II took over the throne on completion of his minority, and reopened negotiations between the central government and the rebels, many of whom considered the war to have been lost, following their failure in San José, and were favorable to negotiating an honorable peace. Rossetti, who had influence on the government, was among these. Having tired of the military's dominance, in November he wrote a letter to the president of the republic begging him to come to an agreement. But the hard-liners won because the region was not granted autonomy, and the war dragged on. The republicans, having reestablished their capital in Alegrete, set up a legislative assembly of twenty-two members, who drew up a proposed constitution. The Republic of Rio Grande was, however, being undermined by internal disputes, to

the point that the father of the country, Gonçalves, had to resign as president and supreme commander of the armed forces.

The military situation was becoming increasingly compromised: in
November 1844 the troops of Canabarro, who had become commander
in chief, were annihilated during a nighttime attack led by Moringue. In
February 1845, Marshal Luis Alves da Lima e Silva, Marquis of Caxias,
who had been put in charge of the province by the Brazilian government,
persuaded the remaining rebels to accept peace, which was solemnly proclaimed on 1 March. The twelve points of the Poncho Verde Accord
ended nine years of civil war and avoided any punitive action. Apart from
the complete amnesty, the Rio Grandeans won the right to elect their own
provincial president. Central government only retained the power of rati-
fying the appointment.

Garibaldi's involvement had ended some time earlier. The plan to
build ships in San Simón had failed, and the area had to be abandoned because of incursions by Moringue. The commander of the meager republican navy was sent again to the Capivari to build ships to transport troops
on Lagoa dos Patos, which was still at the center of the fighting owing to
the continuing siege of Porto Alegre. Rossetti was killed near Viamao during a sortie by the city's defenders on 24 September 1840. Right to the very
end, his loyalty to the republic was unswerving, and he had worked for it
with unending passion. At the end of December, Gonçalves decided to
give up on the siege and withdrew to San Gabriel, which had become the
republic's third capital. Garibaldi and his seamen had been combined
with Canabarro's force of 1,800 men, which was sent to the Sierra highlands to fight the imperial forces coming down from Lajes. The march
through the forest was very harsh and did not lead to anything conclusive,
given that the two armies did not meet. Finally Garibaldi joined Gonçalves in San Gabriel. There he met Francesco Anzani, an exile from
Lombardy who immediately became his friend. He was to have him at his
side in Uruguay.

It was March–April of 1841. For many months, Garibaldi had been pretty
much inactive. He engaged in a few tasks of little importance that point-
lessly exposed him to considerable sacrifices. He understood that there was
little room for him, and sensed the exhaustion with a war that had no prospects of victory. He had no time for the way political differences were

personalized, and was disgusted by the soldiers' insensitivity toward the suffering of local populations and the unending cycle of violence. Moreover, events in his private life had brought new personal and family responsibilities that required him to find a comfortable residence, and at the same time he had been deprived of the friendship of Carniglia, Mutru, and Rossetti. After an interview with Bento Gonçalves lasting several hours, he obtained an authorization to leave Rio Grande "temporarily" to go to Montevideo.

As payment for services rendered to the republic, Minister of Finance Almeida allowed him to take a thousand oxen with him. It was not easy to separate the animals and direct them in a herd. After working for several days in the Corral das Pedras, the herdsmen managed with great difficulty to bring together nine hundred head of oxen. Garibaldi set off in the company of hired hands, who proved either disloyal or inept, to traverse the six hundred kilometers between San Gabriel and Montevideo. The journey to Rio Grande on horseback by the *escotero* system had been a pleasant experience. On the return march the herd imposed a very slow pace, with stops for grazing and watering. It took fifty days and proved to be an extremely punishing trip. Four hundred oxen drowned crossing the Rio Negro, while others died of exhaustion. The remaining animals were used to pay the *troperos* or were put down. Garibaldi was left with three hundred skins which he sold in Montevideo, where he arrived in June of 1841. He had lived in Rio Grande for three years and was never to return.

His memories of the privations and dangers would fade with time. In an October 1859 reply to Almeida, who had congratulated Garibaldi on his part in the spring campaign of Italy's Second War of Independence (news traveled quickly with the advent of the telegraph), Garibaldi's recollection of military events was limited to "the wonderful Rio Grandean cavalry," and he expressed his desire to give orders to "a troop of your centaurs, accustomed to charging ranks of infantrymen with the same casualness with which one might treat a herd of animals."

His thoughts turned nostalgically and emotionally to the welcome accorded him "in the bosom of its [Rio Grande's] families, who treated me as a son," and to the struggles for freedom. He asserted with his usual sentimentality that he recalled this past life "as something supernatural, magical, and truly romantic." He had a vivid recollection "of so much prowess in battle, generosity in victory, of such hospitality, of such benevolence to foreigners . . . of the emotion that my inner being felt in my youth in the presence of your majestic forests, the beauty of your plains, and the manly and chivalric behavior of your courageous youth." He asked for news of Gonçalves, Netto, and Canabarro, and thought of "the many kindnesses received with nostalgia and gratitude." Of his life as a privateer and combatant he remembered only the joy of friendship and adventure.

6. Loves, Friendships, and Amusements

Even though he was obliged to live the nomadic and almost savage life of *gauchos* and *rastreadores*, even though his destiny was mixed up with that of all kinds of adventurers, outlaws, and other dregs of society, even though he reluctantly experienced the school of revolutions and perpetual wars, even though he was swept along in the midst of ferocious and bloodthirsty factions, he conserved throughout this terrible contagion the original purity of his soul. The imposition of such company did produce in him a few defects and oddities, but not a single vicious habit, not a single guilty feeling.

THAT IS HOW Guerzoni summarizes a peculiar aspect of Garibaldi's character, particularly in relation to the Rio Grandean period. What he describes, with an excessively rhetorical flourish, as "the original purity of his soul" would appear to be an exceptional willingness in a hostile environment to contemplate the beauty of nature, the attractions of poetry, the pleasures of society life and learned conversation, and feelings of love and friendship.

In his *Memoirs* there is a succession of descriptions of landscapes that he had not previously seen, and that he would never find again in Europe. After he left Maldonado on the *Mazzini*, he used a makeshift raft to go ashore in search of food, as has already been mentioned. Once he had cleared the sand dunes on the beach, he was presented for the first time with the endless plain of the pampas, "a natural phenomenon entirely new to a European and particularly an Italian, accustomed as he is to living where not an inch of ground is not covered by houses, bushes, and all kinds of evidence of man's presence." There nature was pristine. The marvelous stallion followed by a herd of mares, the bull, the ox, the gazelle, and the ostrich were all inhabitants of those lands in which man would make only a rare appearance, always on horseback, "a true centaur." Such was the emotion "felt by that privateer of twenty-five years" (in reality he was thirty), that on 20 December 1871, "huddled in front of the fire and with stiff limbs" and "deeply moved," he recalled "those scenes from the past in which everything smiled before the most stupendous spectacle I have ever seen."

No less wonderful was the memory of what awaited him in the house he had seen from the ship: "a young and very pretty woman" who greeted him in the most hospitable manner. She had been educated in Montevideo and was very cultured. She spoke to him of Dante, Petrarch, and other great Italian poets, and recited Quintana's poems in Spanish, which became conversation points. She turned out to be a poet herself and her guest was full of admiration even though his Spanish was not very good—such is the power of beauty.

Garibaldi learned to speak Spanish fluently in Argentina during his imprisonment in Gualeguay where he enjoyed such privileged treatment. We know from his letters that he passed "most of the day reading books, which the untiring goodness of the administrator (the second-in-command) provided [him]". He was well received by the local notables. From other accounts, we know that in the evening, meetings were held in his host Andreus's house, and he often went to visit the country villa of Bernardo Gallo, a wealthy man of Italian extraction. He discussed politics with the rich Spanish merchant Antonio Cuyás y Sampere, author many years later of a book recounting episodes from the imprisonment of the Rio Grandean privateer. The young Garibaldi was not afraid to proclaim his belief in the doctrines of Saint-Simon and Mazzini. The older man responded that humanitarian ideals are youthful dreams, that experience of life and the study of history had destroyed his illusions of finding happiness for the people in democratic institutions, that a nation cannot survive if it is not bound together by justice, religion, and a belief in reward and punishment, and that the poor would despair if they lost their hope in a God who will compensate them for the miseries and privations suffered in this life. He also predicted that by the time Garibaldi's hair was gray, he would have changed his opinions.

At the Camaqui base, Garibaldi was able to calm his mind through friendship and conversation. Beautiful cultivated fields and meadows with livestock stretched far beyond the shipyard, unaffected by the war: this was the vast estate of Bento Gonçalves's sisters. Dona Antonia owned a villa at the mouth of the Camaqui, and Dona Ana lived on the Arroyo Grande. Garibaldi often visited with his friends Carniglia, Mutru, Zeferino Dutra, and João Royer. In particular, the home of Dona Ana, a woman "of advanced age [and] enchanting personality," was for them "a real paradise." Garibaldi would write in his *Memoirs*:

> No circumstance in my life would come to mind with more appeal, sweetness, and pleasurable recollections than the one passed in the amiable company of those ladies and their dear families.

When he was far away, he would write to the two women "to assuage the yearning he felt in their absence." He usually asked for their assistance with the shipyard, but when he asked Ana to send some salt, he prayed that a tempest would hurl him beyond the rows of date palms, "which taught us in happier times of the home of beauty, virtue, and the most generous and pleasant hospitality I have ever encountered in my life." When he invited her to collect some barrels of flour and send a sack of tar, he asserted that his existence had been enriched by his memory of "that blessed Arroyo Grande." He described to her the storm in which his closest friends had met their deaths, and "overwhelmed with sadness," he begged her for a word of comfort.

Garibaldi's *Memoirs* are full of admiration for refined and well-educated middle-class women. Much later, while traveling in Central America in

1851, he was the guest of Doña Manuelita de Saenz, who had once been a friend of Simón Bolívar. He found her "the most charming and kind lady I ever saw," and passed a "delightful" day in her "dear company." During that journey he got to know the "picturesque" Pacific coast and saw the Andes where they are close to the sea. He confessed that he had imagined it would be much more beautiful. "As I was born on the Alpine slopes, I searched in vain for an attractive valley that could be compared with my exquisite Nice!"

We should not think that, during his time in Rio Grande, Garibaldi had with the passing years entirely abandoned his past as a seaman who frequented the bars of Black Sea ports. On Saturday evenings, he went with Carniglia and Mutru to a ranch-workers' hut to dance the *fandango*, sing, and enjoy the company of its regular customers. "The Rio Grandean women are generally very beautiful, as is the population as a whole. The colored women slaves are not bad either," he would write in his *Memoirs*. His dearest memory, however, was tinged with romanticism. He found his "ideal beauty" in an "angelic creature," Manuela Ferreira, the daughter of Bento Gonçalves's third sister. He knew she was not indifferent to him and thought of marrying her, but a privateer's proposal of marriage would not have been well received by a powerful Rio Grandean family. Garibaldi was deceived into believing that the young woman was engaged to Bento's son, and he withdrew from the courtship out of respect for his friend.

Rossetti provides evidence that Garibaldi felt the need for a worthy love affair and a stable relationship. He wrote to Cuneo from Piratinim in February 1839, "Garibaldi is in love and threatens to get married, although he will do nothing about it. He has promised me this." The woman in question does not appear to have been Manuela. Then Rossetti asks his friend to patch things up with his old friend Garibaldi. "A woman should not have upset the great intimacy and trust that existed between you." A rivalry in affairs of the heart had divided the two men—how and when we do not know. Our subject's sentimental life was more complicated than his biographers would have it.

Garibaldi felt lonely. The sense of emptiness became more overpowering in Laguna, after the shipwreck of the *Rio Pardo* and the death of all the Italians. He felt crushed by solitude and "alone in the world" now that he no longer had the friends who had almost "taken the place of his native land in those distant regions." Rossetti, the only survivor, was far away. He needed someone who loved him, "immediately, and to have that person close," and without that, life would become unbearable. Who better than a woman, "the most perfect of creatures"? And it is "infinitely easier to find a loving heart among them." This was his mood while he was looking through his telescope from the quarterdeck of the *Itaparica* as it lay at anchor in the port, when he spied a young woman between the houses along the seafront. He went ashore in search of her. By chance an acquaintance invited him home for coffee and when he entered, he found the woman he had seen from the ship.

> It was Anita! We were both silent but ecstatic. We looked at each other like two people who are not seeing each other for the first time, and we searched in each other's expressions for something that would assist our recollections.

The foreigner, who according to himself did not have complete command of the Portuguese language (but he is not to be believed, as he had lived in Brazil for years), spoke to her in Italian: "You must be mine." He was "magnetic in his impudence." She recognized the suitor as the invincible seafarer admired by everyone in Laguna, and was enchanted. They had discovered love.

We cannot assess the veracity of this account of love at first sight, which in many ways resembles the sudden conversion of the meeting with the "believer" in Taganrog or the immediate friendship with Rossetti in Rio. Perhaps the commander of the republican flotilla met her as he went from house to house to billet his sailors; perhaps there was some other occasion to meet her. The fact remains that they were immediately attracted to each other, and from that moment they would live together until her death.

Aninha Ribeiro da Silva, who would come to be known in Italy and beyond as Anita, came from a family of humble origins. They descended from Portuguese immigrants from the Azores to the province of Santa Catarina in the early eighteenth century. Her father, Bento, had worked as a livestock farmer in the interior, close to Lajes, but later moved to the coast with his wife, María Antonia de Jesús. The first three children were born in Coxillas, and Anita and two other children were born in Morrinhos. Following the deaths of her father and three brothers, her mother moved with her and her two sisters to Carniza. The names of the villages suggest a life of hardships. At the age of fourteen or fifteen, on 30 August 1835, Anita married Manuel Duarte de Aguiar, a cobbler in Laguna who was considerably older than she was. The marriage was not a happy one. At the outbreak of the insurrection, the shoemaker enlisted in the imperial forces, and when the town was taken by Canabarro, he left Laguna with the retreating troops. His wife did not follow him, as was usually the case with Brazilian women, or as she would do later for Garibaldi. She stayed behind with a family who had befriended her. She was very young: she was probably born in 1821, and if so, she would have been eighteen, some fourteen years younger than her lover. She did not hesitate to return the attentions of her passionate sea captain. From the moment of their meeting she would always be at his side.

Garibaldi spoke with remorse of a "forbidden treasure" and acknowledged a sense of guilt that while "two hearts entwined in an immense love . . . , an innocent's existence was shattered," and that this transgression was paid for with Anita's untimely death. We cannot ascertain whether this referred to his respect for the sanctity of marriage (he did not have relations with married women) or suggested obscure events we know nothing of. We do know, however, that Anita abandoned family and friends, and from then on she shared the dangers and sacrifices of Garibaldi's military vicissitudes.

She was a strong woman. According to the only description of her we have from someone who knew her in Brazil, she was tall and well-built, with large breasts, an oval and slightly freckly face, large black eyes, and loose black hair. Gustav Hoffstetter, who met her in Rome in 1849, found her to have "very dark skin and interesting features; [and to be] slim and delicate in her person. One can immediately see the Amazon in her." She was indeed an expert horsewoman, very much in the local tradition.

She joined the *Rio Pardo* on its privateering escapades. This "Brazilian Amazon" played a "glorious part" in fierce fighting in Imbituba Bay. During the ill-fated defense of the lagoon, she fired the first cannon shot against the overwhelming enemy fleet, while "shouting encouragement to the faltering crew." Garibaldi sent her to ask for reinforcements from Canabarro and implored her to send back the reply by messenger. With disregard for all danger, she crossed the lagoon standing in an exposed position on her boat and then returned with Canabarro's refusal, which convinced Garibaldi that he had to withdraw to ensure that his munitions did not fall into enemy hands.

He then set off on horseback to follow Texeira's orders with Anita at his side; "his dearest" was "no less devoted [than he was] to the peoples' sacred cause and a life of adventure." She treated "the battles as a plaything and the hardships of camp life as a pastime." Her hero was not to be outdone. The privations did not prevent him from imprinting the grandeur and beauty of the countryside in his memory. During his return to Lajes, he traveled through forests "where an incredibly vigorous and bountiful nature beneath the colossal pines of the vast forest heaps up the gigantic *taquara* (cane or bamboo), whose debris falling on other plants forms an insurmountable layer of organic material capable of swallowing up any incautious individual who attempts to stand on it." While giving an account of a military encounter in Uruguay, he stops to describe with a sensitive touch the plain that that so affected him: "A deep green grass barely protruded from the ground that undulated like the ocean in all its pacific majesty, when untroubled by storms. Not even a shrub interrupted the emptiness of that beautiful prairie."

The two lovers were happy and did not think of the dangers. During the Battle of Forquillas, Anita was left in charge of the munitions and lost contact with the retreating troops. In spite of a spirited defense, she was surrounded by imperial forces and captured. When it was rumored that Garibaldi had been killed, she obtained permission from Colonel Albuquerque, the Brazilian commander, to search the battlefield for her husband's body. She then realized that he must be alive, and during the night she took a horse and escaped. After four days of riding, she caught up with her fellow combatants. She shared the long retreat of the Rio Grandean forces through the dense forest of the Sierra, and her courage became legendary. The *Jornal do comercio* of Rio de Janeiro announced Garibaldi's arrival in Montevideo in July 1841, "accompanied by his wife, a native of Catarina, who, it is said, takes up her sword when in danger and fights at her husband's side, when he enters the fray."

Anita became pregnant, and during her pregnancy she put up with all manner of privations and hardships. She fell from her horse, and the baby had an "indentation on his head." On 16 September 1840, the firstborn, called Domenico after his grandfather, came into this world in a house in the country near San Simón. He would always be called Menotti, in memory of the martyr of 1831.

Mother and child had nothing, and the father left in the rain for Setembrina across the flooded countryside. He was to meet Rossetti for the last time, and during his absence, Anita was obliged, twelve days after giving birth, to escape an incursion by Moringue. She left on horseback with her baby on the front of the saddle, and for four days wandered aimlessly in the cold and rain. No less taxing experiences were to follow. Garibaldi was attached to a column of 1,800 men under Canabarro's command, which left the plain for the Sierra, and Anita followed him with her three-month-old baby. The rivers were in full flood and food was scarce. In the most difficult places and when crossing fast-flowing streams, Garibaldi carried his little son in a handkerchief tied around his neck, so that he could warm him with his body and his breath. The guides did not take the right *piccada* (a pathway cut into the forest), and the two found themselves almost on their own. The horses and mules could not hold out. Anita went ahead with the guide and the child, and eventually they found a clearing with republican soldiers and a fire. They were safe.

Finally the movements of the Rio Grandean army took them to San Gabriel. Life did not improve very much. The troops camped in hovels, and Garibaldi built himself a cabin to house his family. The Rio Grandean cause appeared to be lost, and he was no longer inspired by it. After six years of hardships and privations, "far from the company of my oldest friends and relations," he felt the need to get to where he could receive news of his parents. Above all, he now needed many things that previously he would never have considered necessary for himself, but which had now become essential for Anita and the baby. His responsibilities as a husband and a father convinced him that he had to move to a more secure location. He returned to Montevideo.

7. The Costa Brava Expedition

MONTEVIDEO, CAPITAL OF the Oriental Republic of Uruguay, was a cosmopolitan city. The government had a policy of welcoming foreigners capable of professional activities, unlike the other South American states, which were heavily influenced by nationalism. The result was that there were many European residents: 7,588 Basques, 2,947 Spaniards, 4,668 Portuguese, and 922 French emigrated to Uruguay between 1836 and 1841. Italians, generally defined as Sardinians, were in second place, with 5,276 immigrants. Many moved to the interior, and the Ligurians engaged in trade and coastal shipping along the large rivers. Indeed they achieved a near monopoly over river navigation. We are reminded that in 1838 Garibaldi was taken from Bajada to Montevideo by Genovese captains.

When Garibaldi returned in 1841, the Uruguayan capital had 42,000 inhabitants. The troubles caused by the siege reduced their number to 31,000 by October 1843, but they also provided posterity with exact statistics on the breakdown of the different nationalities. They were also the reason for the French and British involvement in the conflicts that divided the country. Only 11,431 of its population were Uruguayan. There were not many South Americans: 2,553 Argentineans, partly political exiles who disliked the dictatorship of Rosas, and 492 Brazilians. The foreigners were mainly Europeans: 6,324 French, 4,205 Italians, 3,406 Spaniards, 659 Portuguese, 609 British, and 183 from other states. Nationality was not indicated for 861 persons, and 1,344 were of African origin. The population was young (only 2,753 people were over fifty), with a slight majority of men over women, but this was partly explained by the fact that those who were unable to work had left the city under siege.

The presence of many Italians, particularly Ligurians, had come to Grondona's attention and had encouraged Cuneo to move to the city on the River Plate. According to an assessment made by the Sardinian consul in July 1836, there were five thousand "Genoese" in the city and, in his opinion, they were nearly all deserters from the navy and political exiles. This colorful community, although not inclined to respect its distant government, was not attracted to patriotic and republican ideals to the extent hoped for by the followers of Mazzini.

Cuneo, who left Rio de Janeiro in 1836 with the intention of setting up a branch of Young Italy in Montevideo, only found a very small group of exiles willing to engage in political activity. The brothers Stefano, Giacomo, and Paolo Antonini were of particular note (Paolo had commanded the Polish Battalion in the Savoy expedition and had been condemned to death in absentia). They were wholesalers capable of providing financial help to those who shared their ideals. For several years, Garibaldi's conspiratorial activities met with little success. One of his letters from Bajada reveals that there was a meeting of Young Italy in January 1838, and it had possibly been constituted only then, with a program full of hopes. We have no records of their activities and no membership lists showing the number and nature of their membership. In 1840, Cuneo moved to Rio Grande, where in April–August he took over the editorship of *O Povo*, which was languishing after having been abandoned by Rossetti. The destruction of the printing press after Cassapava fell into imperial hands abruptly ended this activity.

Cuneo's return from Rio Grande revitalized the association. He was one of the more cultured members of the group of Mazzini's followers in South America, and he continued his journalistic activities following his experiences with *La Giovine Italia* in the Brazilian capital and, more briefly, with *O Povo*. He managed for the first time to establish direct contact with his mentor, who was in London. When he wrote to Mazzini on 24 April, he also sent the editorial manifesto for the paper he was preparing to publish. On 22 May 1841, he brought out the first issue of *L'Italiano*, a weekly paper in Italian which took its name from a philo-Mazzini paper published in Paris in 1836. It was distributed free of charge, and because it was aimed at other Italians, it tended to gloss over Young Europe's humanitarian and cosmopolitan ideals. It set itself the task of "keeping alive and stirring up among our fellow countrymen that spirit of nationality and love of republican institutions that Italy needs if it is to set up a single, free, and independent state. Every day the number of our fellow nationals is increasing in these countries."

Garibaldi's sudden and unexpected arrival at the beginning of June posed the problem of which direction Young Italy should take. He was its leader because of the mandate he had received from Canessa in Marseille, and because his exploits in Rio Grande had turned him into the most prestigious exponent of Mazzini's ideas. It may be that he did not approve of the exclusively Italian line promoted by the newspaper, which ceased publication after its tenth issue on 10 July.

For the moment, Garibaldi remained in the shadows. He needed to sort out his family problems and the legal difficulties arising from his activities as a privateer. The Uruguayan authorities had dismissed the case against him for the clash with the cutter *Maria* in June 1837, following Rivera's rise to power. But he still had to settle matters with Brazil, the major power in South America, which maintained a naval squadron in the port of Montevideo and had often protested against the hospitality given to Rio Grandean republicans. Moreover, the squadron was under the command of two of Garibaldi's old adversaries: Federico Mariath, who had led the fleet to recapture Laguna, and Greenfell himself. As a Rio Grandean veteran, Garibaldi could not pursue his career as a sea captain engaged in coastal traffic around the waters of the River Plate, as he ran the risk of being captured in the open sea and tried as a rebel. He therefore signed an undertaking not to carry out any act of war in the future, in order to protect himself against unpleasant surprises. The journalist José Rivera Indarte acted as his intermediary and in September requested of the Brazilian diplomatic representative that Garibaldi's past misdeeds be pardoned. The imperial government granted this amnesty with a view to achieving a peaceful conclusion to the dispute with the secessionists. That was the end of the matter.

He still had to provide for his family. He earned a few hundred escudos from the sale of his leather, and he used this money to dress Anita, Menotti, and two traveling companions. For a short while he was a guest of Napoleone Castellini, one of the more active members of the association of Mazzini's supporters that had greeted him in 1838, and he then rented a small house. In his *Memoirs* he recalled the solicitude of Castellini, Cuneo, the Antonini brothers, and Giovanni Risso, but he did not intend to live on charity. Given that he "always found other people's bread to be bitter," he engaged in "two occupations which in truth were rather unproductive, but they provided enough for food." He was a middleman for merchant shipping, and he taught mathematics and languages at a college founded by a Corsican former priest called Paolo Semidei, who had left France following clashes with the ecclesiastical authorities. It was winter in the Southern Hemisphere. He was thirty-four years old, but his worries made him seem older. Pasquale Papini, an Italian emigrant, would later recall that at that time he wore a heavy, plain coat and a soft hat with a wide brim over long flowing locks. He leaned on a stick, and almost every evening he would take a book to the end of the jetty, where "he would sit for a long time and immerse himself in his reading" under the light of a streetlamp.

Once the possible causes of disputes with Brazil had been eliminated, the Uruguayan government secured the services of a man who was famous for his expert seamanship and fearlessness in battle. The war between Uruguay and Argentina was continuing, with Rivera on one side and Rosas and Oribe on the other. At the end of 1840 France lifted its blockade on Buenos Aires. Rosas immediately renewed his operations against Montevideo, and for this purpose he fitted out a squadron of ships under the command of William Brown, an Englishman who had emigrated to Argentina in 1809 and had already taken part in the Cisplatine War. He was considered the best commander in South America. The Uruguayans in turn established a small fleet under the command of an

American, Commodore John Coe, another accomplished seaman who had fought with Brown during the Wars of Independence. He left Argentina in 1840 because he did not want to serve under Rosas, and he replaced the Frenchman François Fourmantin in Uruguay.

The "Great War" (which commenced in 1838 and would end in 1851) was also a land war. Rosas was formally only the governor of the province of Buenos Aires, the most important in the Argentine federation, and in November 1841 Rivera formed an anti-Rosas alliance with the governors of the provinces of Corrientes and Santa Fe, who were themselves being challenged by Rosas's supporters. These territories were distant from the Uruguayan Republic. They could be reached along the rivers that flow into the River Plate: the Paraná (the largest river in South America after the Amazon) and the Uruguay, the first of which is entirely in Argentinean territory, and the second Argentinean on the western side and Uruguayan on the eastern. It was of the utmost importance to have control of these rivers, which were used for trade with the interior and with Paraguay, and which brought agricultural produce and livestock to the coast. The two warring nations attempted to secure that control.

At the beginning of 1842, the Argentineans prepared an expedition under Oribe's command to bring the province of Corrientes to heel. The rebels asked Montevideo to send men, arms, and munitions. Rivera's government was obliged not to abandon its allies. The success of any expedition in their aid would have had considerable political and psychological repercussions, because it would have demonstrated the coalition's cohesion and its ability to wage war inside the country. The difficulties were all of a military nature. It involved sailing a thousand kilometers up a river under the control of enemy forces on both banks. The enemy would also immediately pursue the expedition, using ships of considerable tonnage not designed for river travel. Francisco Antonino Vidal, the minister of government (prime minister), was counting on a combination of favorable conditions. He hoped that the rains would raise the river level, and, with little justification, that Admiral Brown was about to abandon Rosas, leaving the Argentinean fleet without a competent commander. Above all, he put his trust in the foreign privateer who had proved capable of seamanship and leadership.

Garibaldi, whom Vidal described in a letter to President Rivera as "well known for other risky undertakings," was summoned by the Uruguayan navy after the dispute with Brazil was resolved, although we do not know when. He was appointed colonel and entrusted with command of the expedition. Vidal kept the real purpose of the mission secret from everyone, including Garibaldi, so that the enemy would not be on its guard. He led people to believe that they would sail up the less dangerous Uruguay River, and he even went so far as to enlist pilots for this river, who had little knowledge of the Paraná, along which they would have to travel. The precise instructions to the commander were delivered in a sealed envelope to be opened after leaving Montevideo.

His orders were to enter the Paraná and to sail up it as far as Bajada, capturing or destroying all ships flying the Argentinean flag. All captured ships were to be sent to Corrientes, the capital of the province of the same name, and placed at the disposal of a "Prize Court" set up for that purpose. The proceeds from the sale of merchantmen and the fees for handing over warships to the government would be wholly divided among the members of the expedition, which thus became a privateering enterprise. It was expected that a successful outcome of the operations would strengthen the fighting force as it ventured up the river, and it was to be responsible for liaising with the troops commanded by Rivera. The government wished to carry out a strategic maneuver of considerable political and military significance.

Three ships were chosen: the 256-ton corvette *Constitución*, which had been built in France and had previously sailed under a French flag, with eighteen cannon and under Garibaldi's direct command; the 166-ton brigantine *Pereyra*, which had been built in Brazil, with eleven cannon, two of which were swivel-mounted, under the command of the Spaniard Manuel Araña Urioste; and the 71-ton schooner *Procida*, which had been built in the Kingdom of Sardinia and had previously belonged to the Antonini brothers, and was now fitted with five cannon, under the command of the Genovese Luigi De Agostini. The crews were a motley collection: adventurers, foreign sailors who had deserted their ships or were attracted by the spoils (Ligurians were preferred), and common criminals from military or civilian life whose service substituted for their punishment. They tended to be undisciplined and had to be led with firmness and flexibility.

They reached a full complement by the beginning of June, and arms, munitions, and victuals were loaded on board. Garibaldi realized that it was a dangerous venture, and he quickly legalized his relationship with Anita. He married her on 26 March at the Church of San Francesco d'Assisi in a religious ceremony, which was the only legitimate form of marriage in Uruguay. Perhaps, but we have no evidence, they had received news from Brazil of Manuel Duarte's death. Whatever the case, he legitimized the situation of a woman who had abandoned both family and country in order to follow him. In Uruguay Anita did not follow him into battle. She had other children after Menotti: in 1843 a daughter called Rosa, after the grandmother, and referred to as Rosita (who died on 23 December 1845); Teresita on 22 February 1845, named in memory of Teresa, Garibaldi's sister who died young in a fire; and Ricciotti on 28 March 1847, who was named after one of the followers of the Bandiera brothers, killed by a firing squad in Cosenza in July 1844. Her duties as a mother kept her away from her companion and his risky military operations on land and sea. Desperately unhappy after Rosa's death, she would join him in Salto. He was to worry about her condition and summoned her. She would stay for many months in the north of Uruguay but would not take part in combat.

In Montevideo, Anita suffered the discomforts of a very modest lifestyle. Various accounts refer to the poverty of the household: they didn't even have chairs, and shortage of money meant no candles and poor clothing. These conditions were the result of the siege and the firmness with which the Italian guerrilla refused assistance or monetary rewards—even ones that were due to him—which would have meant questioning the idealistic motives for his presence in Uruguay. This added to her isolation, which was also the result of the coarseness of her peasant background, her illiteracy, her Brazilian nationality, and her Portuguese mother tongue. Even though she was married to a naval commander, she did not take part in the activities run by high-placed ladies to assist soldiers and their families: we cannot find her in the Philanthropic Society of Oriental Ladies, presided over by Rivera's wife and set up to gather funds for the hospital and ensure the provision of volunteer nurses. She certainly did not go to the benefit performances at the Teatro del Commercio, where Italian operas were staged. In November 1844, *Lucia di Lammermoor, L'elisir d'amore,* and *The Barber of Seville* were performed in honor of the Italian Legion.

Contemporaries commented on her unwholesome jealousy, stemming from the fact that she was unable to be with her man as she had been in Brazil and was aware of his encounters in the higher circles within which he moved as a part of his duties. Jessie White Mario recalled having heard Garibaldi say that every so often she would show him two pistols, "one to empty into me and the other into her rival." Guerzoni was told by Gaetano Sacchi, who fought at Montevideo, that one day Garibaldi appeared before his legionnaires with his beard and hair cut short to please Anita, who feared they might attract other women. However, he appreciated her sacrifices and would remember her as "wonderful in our home life," and ready to console and assist him through those difficult years.

The small flotilla entrusted to Garibaldi left the port of Montevideo on 23 June at three o'clock in the afternoon. Two other ships remained to defend the city under Coe's command. Garibaldi sailed along the Uruguayan coast of the River Plate toward the island of Martín García, which controls the estuary of the Paraná and Uruguay, and was held by the Argentineans. Progress was slow owing to the lack of wind, and he was assisted from the land by the local civilian authorities that had been alerted by the capital. Finally they came into range of the enemy cannon. The *Constitución* immediately ran aground just out of their range. The Argentineans were able to watch the seamen struggling to lighten the ship; the cannon were dismounted and transferred to the *Procida*. It took an entire day to refloat the ship, and then Admiral Brown appeared with seven ships, having left Buenos Aires as soon as he had heard the news. Garibaldi was unable to defend himself, and only the *Pereyra* was fit for action. The Argentineans could be heard shouting for joy. But then the flagship, the *Belgrano*, which also had a large tonnage, went aground before it could get its enemy into range. At that moment, the Uruguayans got their ship afloat, and as thick fog descended on the area, the three Uruguayan ships took advantage of the low visibility to enter the Paraná Guazú. Brown thought they had entered the Uruguay and took five ships into that river. Three of them went aground, and it took days to free them. He could only recommence his journey on 13 July. Informed of his mistake, he then turned around, after having given the privateers a two-week start. This is the dramatic story that appears in Garibaldi's *Memoirs*, which provides a rather colorful version. Although the pursuers did not get very close, there was a real danger and fortune favored the bold. The flotilla sailed up the river to Bajada, following the route taken by the *Mazzini* in 1837. We will supplement Garibaldi's lively *Memoirs* with legal documents, and his and his adversaries' letters and reports.

The journey up the Paraná started at nine in the morning on 29 June. The pilots for the Uruguay River were returned to Montevideo, and they pressed sailors who knew the Paraná into service on board. Along the way, the privateers captured the shipping they encountered, engaged the seamen, and confiscated the cargoes. The small fleet benefited from the addition of two whalers which were used for sending sorties ashore to collect water and fresh food. These incursions caused the inhabitants who had prior warning to flee with their livestock and provisions. When the sailors saw farms or herds, they rushed ashore, plundered the farms, butchered the animals, and took the meat back to their ships before the cavalry appeared. As in Rio Grande, meat was the only food in those territories.

The flotilla reached Bajada on 18 July. It had covered three hundred kilometers and overcome endless difficulties. It was constantly one step ahead; Admiral Brown did not start up the river until 20 July. The Argentineans in Bajada had prepared their defenses: there were coastal batteries and three well-armed warships, as well as a merchantman. It was not in the interest of either side to commence the hostilities. After an ineffectual exchange of fire, Garibaldi continued on his journey and therefore proclaimed himself the victor. His adversary, Major Seguì, was satisfied to have kept his forces intact for Brown's arrival.

On 27 July, the squadron of "savage and filthy unionists" (as the Argentineans referred to the Uruguayans in their official reports) had reached Cerrito, a small fortified port protected by a battery. The situation reminds us of how the two cutters escaped from Lagoa dos Patos. Owing to the lack of wind and the shallow water, the ships had difficulty in moving forward. The whalers and the sailors on shore, moving "at the double to the sound of the drum," pulled the ships along against the current. For the men, this was an arduous and punishing endeavor, and fortunately the flotilla was very close to the coast and below the line of fire from the cannon, which were positioned on high ground. Indeed the raiders took possession of three merchant ships riding at anchor: a schooner, a *sumaca*, and a bilander. Another three schooners were captured in Hermandarias. In the meantime, Garibaldi sent the *Procida* to Corrientes, as he continued with the heavier *Constitución* and the *Pereyra*, and he was joined by three small vessels from Corrientes, two schooners and a bilander sent by the rebel governor, Pedro Ferré. Garibaldi's ships were in poor shape and the crews exhausted. This meeting signaled that the final destination and a safe haven were not far off: Corrientes was only thirty-five kilometers away. It would have been easy to reach, had they abandoned the *Constitución*, which was prevented by its draft from going any further. Garibaldi had no intention of doing this, as it would have compromised the propaganda value of his expedition.

The slow progression of the privateers' flagship passed the advantage to the pursuers. Brown had entered the Paraná with two schooners and three brigs, and in Bajada he enlarged his flotilla with Seguí's ships—two schooners and three smaller vessels. Along the river, which that year was rather low, he encountered the same difficulties as his enemy had done. In some places he was obliged to resort to warping (hauling ships from fixed points on the riverbank), but he could make use of military and logistical support on land. His ships were making faster progress than the Uruguayan ones, and he caught up with them in mid-August in the middle of the southern winter, close to Costa Brava. There was a massive imbalance between the forces. Brown had three brigs, four schooners, and three smaller vessels with fifty-three cannon and more than seven hundred men. Garibaldi had two warships (the *Procida* was far off), with twenty-nine cannon, many with only a short range, and no more than three hundred men.

Garibaldi found himself in a situation similar to the defense of the lagoon: he could not maneuver to make up for his inferior forces, as he had done in the open sea, and he had to remain immobile while under attack. He now faced "the most famous seaman in South America." Nonetheless he decided to engage in battle. Perhaps he trusted in his own good fortune or in his tactic of fighting to the death, which on various occasions disconcerted superior enemy forces and led them to abandon the field.

Garibaldi positioned his ships on the eastern side of the river below the bank that prevented further navigation. The *Pereyra* was in the center, the *Constitución* on the right, and a merchantman armed with four cannon on the left. They were lined up along the bank with all the cannon shifted to the side exposed to the enemy in order to increase the firepower. The merchantmen and smaller vessels were in the second row.

The Argentineans drew close on 15 August. Their ships moved forward with difficulty and relied on warping, and the Uruguayans landed sailors and marines to attack the men engaged in this task. The Argentineans landed five hundred men to repulse this attack and lined up their ships for battle. On 16 August, Brown opened fire and held his ships at a distance of five hundred meters. "Forgoing the wonderful opportunity for grapeshot and hand-to-hand fighting," Garibaldi commented in his *Memoirs*, "he kept a safe distance and exploited the greater range of his cannon." Only a few cannon on the *Constitución* and the *Pereyra* were able to return fire. Others had to use twice the normal amount of gunpowder, with the resulting imprecision in their targeting. Both sides suffered serious losses, but the privateers had the worst of it.

> Our ships were reduced to hulks. The corvette, in spite of attempts to plug the leaks, was taking water so fast that it was difficult to keep it afloat even by pumping continuously and using everyone to take a turn. . . . There were many dead and even more wounded. The remaining crew, although completely exhausted, could not rest because of the excess water in the hold. Yet there was still gunpowder and there was still shot, and so we had to fight, not to win and not to save ourselves, but to keep our honor.

This was the point: to salvage one's honor. During the night they examined possible tactical solutions. Manuel Araña Urioste attempted a land attack, but was defeated and cut down. Manuel Rodríguez used a schooner and a *sumaca* as fireships and launched them against the enemy ships, but without success. They made shot for the cannon out of chains. However, the commander of the ships from Corrientes, Alberto Villegas, did not share the decision to fight to the death, and fled with his men.

The next day, Garibaldi gave his remaining crew a stirring speech. "Those generous men repeated their battle cry in unison, and then everyone took up his station." But the situation was desperate: the ships could not move and were an easy target. They were covered with the dead and wounded, and there was no choice but to surrender or withdraw. Garibaldi would not even entertain the possibility of surrender. At two in the afternoon, the wounded and the able-bodied were embarked on a small vessel along with those supplies and confiscated goods that could be transported, and the vessel set off. A detachment stayed behind to set fire to the ships, strewing them with rum and other incendiary material. Some of them got drunk and, unable to escape, were blown up when the powder magazines on the two ships exploded. It was terrible sight, and the expedition came to its tragic denouement.

News of the victory thrilled Buenos Aires. When he returned on 9 September, Admiral Brown was hailed as the triumphal victor. In the evening the city was lit up for a holiday; large joints of beef were roasted in the streets, and then given out free. Garibaldi made the headlines, and his name became widely known in South America. His fame for being an able, daring, hardworking, and merciless warrior began to spread. The Argentinean newspapers argued that he had deliberately set fire to the ships with prisoners and wounded on board, and they accused the "pirates" of having gone too far in their plundering and having committed atrocities during the expedition, but they had to acknowledge the courage of the privateers and their leader. Fantastic versions of Garibaldi's life began to circulate. An English-language newspaper, the *British Packet and Argentine News*, which mistakenly believed him to be about the same age as Brown, claimed that he had commanded a corvette in the Neapolitan navy under Murat during the Napoleonic Wars. "This last expedition along the Paraná," it concluded, "shows that he is a hero." The Uruguayan newspapers made much of the courage with which he stood up to a superior enemy. *El Nacional* wrote, "Garibaldi leaped to the ground with the republic's flag in his hand, free from all shame. . . . The republic's honor has been saved."

The hero of this enterprise managed to save himself and the few companions who remained to destroy the ships. Luckily Brown did not pursue them, perhaps because he feared an ambush by forces from Corrientes. The two men who were incapable of going any further were strangled.

After three days of "walking in a pitiful state across islands and marshes," they reached Esquina, the first town in the province of Corrientes. They were in friendly territory. From then on, the going was much easier owing to the assistance provided by the authorities. Garibaldi moved to Goya, and then, toward the end of August, to Santa Lucia. The end of the affair was to prove distressing. The "Prize Court" set up in Corrientes sat in order to decide which of the prizes were legitimate. Under pressure from the owners of the captured ships, it carried out a detailed investigation, during which it questioned the surviving seamen and demanded documentation that could not possibly be produced. Only part of the booty was awarded to the privateers, while in the meantime a vexed Garibaldi was obliged to stay on, pending the outcome of the proceedings.

He finally received orders from Montevideo to leave Corrientes and to meet up with General Rivera by traveling through San Francisco Grande. He set off on his journey overland and along rivers with about 150 comrades. In Salto he met Anzani, who was working for an Italian businessman. On 19 November he reached Paysandú, where General Felix Edmondo Aguyar ordered him to take command of the naval squadron operating along the River Uruguay. At the end of November, he moved to the Visillac Pass with Colonel Guerra's division. Soon afterward he returned to San Francisco Grande. The Uruguayans had suffered a disastrous defeat. The situation was grave and the capital was under threat. Garibaldi was recalled to Montevideo. Before leaving, he was ordered to burn the ships in his flotilla for the third time (the first two being the Laguna and Costa Brava). "At least in the first two cases, I had been able to fight!" he commented bitterly.

8. Montevideo

THE WAR BETWEEN Uruguay and Argentina, between Rivera and Oribe supported by his ally Rosas, between unionists and federalists (as the dictator's supporters were called), and between *colorados* and *blancos* was not only fought on the rivers, but also on land in the north of Uruguay, which had been invaded by an army under the personal command of Oribe himself. On 6 December 1842 Oribe's troops came face-to-face with those of Rivera at Arroyo Grande (*arroyo* means fast-flowing stream, and therefore this topographical description is to be found in many South American place-names). The forces were almost equally balanced with 6,000–7,000 men on each side. Oribe showed greater ability in maneuvering his men, and after three hours he routed his enemy, who left the victor with all their equipment and 850 prisoners. Their captors lost no time in cutting the throats of 700 of them, and the rest were incorporated into the "federal" divisions. The situation became even more critical when Rosas reestablished control over the province of Corrientes.

If Oribe had marched on the capital immediately, he would have easily taken it. Instead he moved slowly. This delay, which has been criticized by some historians, should not surprise us. The reasons were the same as those for the battles in Rio Grande. Following a victory, soldiers celebrated and got drunk, and many returned to their families. These were not the well-trained troops found in Europe, and they were not accustomed to discipline. Oribe had to wait for his forces to reassemble and then started to march through the northern and central regions, putting them under his control as he went.

News of the defeat caused considerable dismay in Montevideo. The president's return meant that vendettas were likely to follow, and his dependency on Rosas gave rise to fears that Uruguay would lose its autonomy. It was not easy to organize the defense. The troops had dispersed, arms had been lost, and the state's finances had been completely drained by Rivera's incompetent administration. Nevertheless the will to resist was not dead. The defeated general remained in northern Uruguay to reorganize the soldiers who escaped the defeat. In Mercedes, halfway along the course of the Uruguay River, Colonel Melchor Pacheco y Obes on his own initiative called all able-bodied men in the district to arms and formed a corps of 1,100 cavalrymen and 300 infantrymen. General José María Paz took command of the army, and on 11 December a general mobilization was declared. Another decree issued on the same day abolished slavery, and able-bodied former slaves were enlisted. In January 1843, Rivera briefly returned to the capital, made a few changes to the ministries to increase the government's efficiency, and entrusted the duties of president of the republic to Joaquín Suárez. He then rejoined his troops to hold down Oribe's men, who counted more than 5,000.

The most urgent concern was defense of the capital. The city, as we know, had about 42,000 inhabitants at the time, and they lived on the *saladeros* industry: the slaughtering of cattle, the salting of meat, and the export of meat, hides, and wool. For its supplies, the city was entirely dependent on imports: dairy products, cured hams, wines, and oils from Europe; flour, tobacco, and fruit from the United States; and rice, sugar, and coffee from Brazil. Seventy percent of all shipping coming to both banks of the River Plate was French. The majority of businessmen importing luxury goods were French, while the British imported cotton and woolen textiles, hardware, and tools, and owned large ranches in the interior.

The port of Montevideo, the heart of the Uruguayan economy, was the finest in South America. The city was built above a bay, and the residential area stretched over a hill on the western side. A long wall was built to defend the city, and gun batteries were placed along it, some of which dated from the period of Spanish rule. The Cerro Fortress stood on the other side of the bay and was used as the garrison. Immediately below the fortress, Isla de las Ratas was fortified and garrisoned because of its strategic position. Domination of the sea opposite the city was essential, but the fleet had been decimated by the expedition to Costa Brava.

Garibaldi, who arrived at the end of December 1842, had the task of rebuilding it. At the time, it consisted solely of launches, and Garibaldi set about building two barges and arming some cutters. A considerable sum was raised by public subscription and used to buy a brig. Then a Spanish schooner and four other ships were purchased, and all of them were fitted out for war (even the ships used for the expedition to Costa Brava had originally been merchant ships). On 2 February 1843 and before these ships were ready, Garibaldi, with typical aggression, used four oar-propelled barges to attack an Argentinean brig that had run aground near Cerro. He sank the ship after having removed the two cannon, the munitions, and the sails.

The brig was part of Brown's squadron, which had to support the army that was now closing in. The siege was about to begin, and on 16 February, two months after the victory at Arroyo Grande, Oribe came in sight of Montevideo. He thought he would be able to enter the city without difficulties. Instead he came up against unexpected resistance, which was not restricted to military actions. As he was obliged to stay outside the city, he surrounded it with troops and organized attacks on what he considered to be the weak points, but they were systematically repulsed. He set up his headquarters on a nearby hill, the Cerrito. As he claimed to be the legitimate president of the republic, he formed a government, and the following year he set up a House of Representatives.

The siege could not be resolved by an act of force, owing to the presence of foreign subjects and their property, as these came under the protection of the European great powers. It was not possible to bombard the city from land or sea, nor could a rigid blockade be imposed to starve the inhabitants. From the very beginning the Uruguayan government had been in contact with the British representative in Buenos Aires, the most important city on the River Plate and the place of residence of European diplomats accredited for the entire region. It was in the interest of Britain and France to protect their fellow countrymen and their trade. The Argentinean dictator had closed off navigation along the large rivers to foreign ships, and many French residents had moved from Buenos Aires to Montevideo to avoid his harassment. For the moment, British and French ministers had limited themselves to requesting that Rosas suspend the hostilities, without, however, obtaining a positive result.

The foreign communities were alarmed when the siege began. The British residents turned to their own authorities, and Commodore John Brett Purvis, commander of the River Plate squadron, would not allow Brown to impose a naval blockade. Then they reached an agreement: the Argentineans were allowed to stop all ships carrying provisions from entering the port, with the exception of French and British ones, which undertook not to import arms, fresh meat, and livestock. The compromise allowed for a certain amount of trade on neutral ships and for possible action by the weak Uruguayan navy. On the other hand, the Argentinean navy was not very strong either. It had few ships, and they were old and in poor shape because of their incessant activity. In fact, the fleet consisted of the *Belgrano*, which was Brown's flagship, three ships of the same tonnage, two schooners, and some smaller vessels.

The city under siege was faced with the prospect of having all its lifelines cut off, and the situation began to deteriorate after a few weeks. On 1 April 1843, Rosas ordered Brown to tighten the blockade, and Oribe sent a circular to consular agents in Montevideo to warn them that foreigners who sided with the Uruguayans would be treated as enemies. The British again obtained the support of Purvis, who demanded that his fellow nationals be treated with respect. The French, who were much more numerous, had made known their wish to form a legion of volunteers to defend the city, and on that same day they started to enlist. More than 2,000 were recruited and assigned to many different battalions (eventually more than 3,000 would be recruited). The Spanish Basques enlisted 700 men.

The Uruguayan authorities were pleased with the foreign involvement in the war, both because of the numerical contribution to the army (in June 1843, there were only 800 Uruguayans out of a total of 6,500 troops engaged in the defense!) and because of the indirect involvement of the states they came from. Indeed they favored the organization of the larger groupings according to nationality; the British, who were too few, were integrated into the Uruguayan National Guard. Every volunteer was promised 150 square kilometers of land with 25,000 head of cattle. In the meantime, they and their families had to make do with rationed food.

The Italians also constituted a large colony, and on 1 April a commission proposed to the Ministry of War the establishment of a volunteer corps on certain conditions: service only in the city and until the end of the siege, the same benefits as those granted to the French, treatment of the wounded, and disability pensions. The offer was accepted, as long as at least one hundred men were enlisted. The division was assigned a barracks (eventually there would be three), and David Vaccarezza took charge of the recruitment. On 7 April Garibaldi visited the barracks and then took part in the organization of the Legion, in which more than five hundred fellow countrymen had already enlisted by the thirteenth. The volunteers were divided to two categories with different levels of commitment. Those who were available full-time were called *velites*, a name borrowed from the Roman army, and were lodged in the barracks at the government's expense for food and clothing. Those who continued to work and in the afternoon took part in exercises and services compatible with their part-time status were called legionnaires.

This land force, the first in South America to be made up of exiles and emigrants, had the potential to become the nucleus of a force to fight the Italian revolution, the principal purpose of Garibaldi's mission to Rio. In reality, the pro-Mazzini propaganda continued to have little effect. Mazzini, in a letter dated 8 August 1841 (which arrived a few months later), authorized Cuneo to establish a Congrega centrale dirigente i lavori della Giovine Italia nelle Americhe del Sud (Central Confraternity to Direct Young Italy's Works in South America). Cuneo actually set it up on 20 June 1842, after having received precise clarifications on the organizational structure from Mazzini and Felice Foresti, who had set up a similar organization in North America. He then started to publish *L'italiano* again during the June–September period, but with the same lack of success as in his previous attempt.

Cuneo, who was following Mazzini's directives, intended to engage in ideological discourse and to publicize a republican program, but he found little enthusiasm for these ideas. This was not Garibaldi's preferred terrain, as he believed in action based on a few humanitarian principles. Cuneo did not include Garibaldi in the governing board of the Mazzini association; for a few years they had gone their separate ways. Cuneo attempted in vain to associate the Legion closely with the inner circle of Mazzini supporters and published a newspaper, *Il Legionario Italiano*, which had four irregular issues in October, November, and December 1844, and then in May 1846.

The rush of volunteers in April 1843 did not mean that Mazzini's ideas and the ideals of Italian unification had suddenly found support. It resulted from an emotional reaction and a genuine concern that affected more or less all the emigrants. "The foreign population," according to *El Constitucional* on 4 April, came out in a procession carrying French and Italian flags, playing music, and "singing "La Marseillaise" and other songs followed by cheering for freedom, the republic, the government, France, Italy, England, and all friends of liberty." No one had an Italian flag: one evening the flag of the Kingdom of Sardinia fluttered at the head of a demonstration, which had a large Ligurian contingent. For the moment, it was significant that Italians were recognized as a nationality, and that they were training together for war under military discipline. They soon had a uniform that distinguished them: they were dressed in red woolen tunics. These had originally been made for the slaughterhouse workers in Buenos Aires and having got stuck in a Montevideo warehouse because of the blockade, they were sold off cheap to the government. The Italian community rallied round its soldiers, and the Comisión encargada de la Legión italiana, on which Cuneo (the chairman) and the Antonini brothers sat, looked after their financial and welfare interests. The Italian amateur dramatics society put on charity shows. The Hospital de la Legión Italiana was founded, and Dr. Bartolomeo Odicini, Garibaldi's family doctor, was made its director.

On 9 July, the Legion, which was organized into three divisions and a company, received its flag from the foreign minister Santiago Vasquez in a formal ceremony that it shared with the other legions. Its flag was black with an image of the volcano Vesuvius erupting. Garibaldi was absent, formally under arrest (for reasons that will be explained later). In his place, Captain Luigi Missaglia, the chief of staff, recalled that those were not the colors that would one day be adopted by the fatherland, when "it rose up again and became a free and independent nation from the Alps to the sea." While Italy suffered its misfortunes, black was the color for those who were moved to feel compassion for it. Like the lava that flowed down Vesuvius, the sacred fire of freedom would destroy the obstacles that prevented the nation from rising up to the heights that it was worthy of. Now they were fighting against tyrants in foreign lands and for "the holy cause of humanity."

These were the sentiments expressed by Garibaldi, who had become the reference point for the Italian community. British, French, and Brazilian diplomats and military men were active in the war zone, but of the small states of distant Italy only the Kingdom of Sardinia had a marginal presence, with the armed schooner *Aquila*, a consul in Buenos Aires, and a vice-consul in Montevideo, who sent reports to Turin on the attitudes of the kingdom's subjects. The cruiser *De Geneys* was a distant memory. Even in terms of their residents' influence, the Italians could not compete with the rich English and French merchants. The British, under Samuel Lafone's leadership, were able to lend money to the Uruguayan government and published an English-language newspaper, the *Britannia and Montevideo Reporter*. Louis-Philippe's government disapproved of the French Legion, because of its republican and socialist hotheads, but it was the most important because of its size and organization. Its newspaper, *Le Patriote Français*, was published throughout the years of the siege.

The Italian Legion did not have the same political and social identity, because it had no connections with any particular state on the Italian peninsula and it did not have the support of a solid mercantile group. Only Garibaldi, who was now accustomed to commanding bands of adventurers, had the prestige and the authority to hold together individuals from different regions of Italy. It was not easy to discipline several hundred men dispersed among different barracks and private residences, most of whom had no experience of combat. The Italians gave the impression of being unwilling to go to war because of the slow pace of recruitment. The French accused them of not knowing how to fight, and of being more accustomed to using a dagger for ambushes. On 2 June, the first test confirmed their distrust, as a detachment of ill-trained legionnaires withdrew in disorder at the first shots. A few days later, Garibaldi personally led two hundred men into enemy fire along with his sailors. Once they had his example to follow, they fought bravely, and the next day an admiring Pacheco, who had become the minister of war and the navy in January 1843, reviewed the Legion in Constitution Square and praised them in a speech. The friction between the Italians and the French did not cease altogether, but as time went on, the Italians earned widespread respect in the field of battle. *Le Patriote Français* was not sparing in its praise for Garibaldi and the Legion.

Garibaldi, who was in command of the fleet, left effective command of the Legion in the hands of Colonel Angelo Mancini, who was supported by Lieutenant-Colonel Anzani and Major Danuzio. Anzani, who was only slightly younger than Garibaldi (he was born in Brianza in 1809), had been won over to the ideals of liberty while studying at Pavia University and subsequently left Lombardy-Venetia, then under Austrian rule, to move to Paris. In the 1830s, he fought in Portugal and Spain on the side of the constitutionalists, and was wounded in the head and chest, which permanently impaired his health. Following a brief return to his native land, he emigrated to South America in 1839, where he set up in business. Garibaldi had met him in the Rio Grande in 1841 and renewed his acquaintance in Salto, on his return to Costa Brava. He was impressed by his loyalty to the ideals of nationhood, his sober disposition, and his sense of duty. There was also the fact that he had gained considerable military experience in the Iberian Peninsula, and he appeared to be the person most capable of training the Legion in military discipline, so in July Garibaldi summoned him from Buenos Aires (where he had since moved) in the name of his political ideals.

"He was an enormous asset for the Legion," Garibaldi would later acknowledge, "and I, who am not much of an organizer, was very lucky to have such a friend and incomparable comrade-in-arms. With him in charge of those troops, I was sure that everything would proceed well." In fact, on his arrival the Legion was structured in eight companies, and he proceeded to purge it of several officers. The harshness of the new commander provoked a certain amount of discontent.

However, the reorganized Legion acquitted itself well at the Battle of Tres Cruces on 17 November. The fighting started when a Uruguayan reconnaissance party was sent out, and this resulted in the death of the Uruguayan commander, Colonel Neiro. As occurred with Patroclus's corpse in the *Iliad*, both the attackers and the attacked made it a point of honor to take possession of the dead man's remains, which were initially defended by only thirteen black soldiers. In later phases, reinforcements arrived on both sides, until about 1,500 men were amassed on either side within a restricted space. When the reconnaissance started, Garibaldi had been on the city walls, and once the battle started, he rushed over on horseback gathering the soldiers who had taken flight and leading them back into the attack. His situation was becoming difficult when the main body of the Italian Legion appeared behind its standard. He took command of all the forces and led a bayonet attack that routed the enemy. In the evening the Uruguayans returned behind their lines and marched through the city with the body of the dead colonel carried by the thirteen black soldiers. The Legion was praised by President Suárez and Minister of War Pacheco.

Praise for the bravery of the Italians, who also took part in the fighting at Pantanoso on 28 March 1844, one of the bloodiest encounters of the siege, as well as the daily skirmishes, was offset by criticism of their lack of discipline and their violence against the local population. Garibaldi took personal command of the Legion at the end of 1843 but did not obtain the expected result; indeed his prestige was compromised by an unfortunate episode. On 28 May 1844 Colonel Angelo Mancini and Colonel Giacomo Danuzio, who had been bribed by Oribe, deserted and joined the enemy side, along with nine other officers and around twenty men. The blow was slightly attenuated when the majority of the turncoats returned, and the Legion continued to hold its place in the defense of the city.

Garibaldi, who was also a naval commander, divided his time between land and sea. His fleet defended the left flank on the defensive line between Cerro and Isla de las Ratas. Possession of the latter was essential, and both sides converged on it. For the moment it was in Uruguayan hands, and on 29 April 1843 Garibaldi reinforced his garrison and positioned two cannon there. When the Argentinean attack became imminent, he went to the island in person. On 30 April Brown appeared with three ships, and the old adversaries from Costa Brava were again facing each other. Once again, "the combat was, however, extremely unequal," he would recall in his *Memoirs*. The attackers had two brigs (one with sixteen large-caliber cannon) and two schooners, and the defenders could only rely on two cannon that had been set up incorrectly, insufficient munitions, and little support from the sea by Garibaldi's two small ships, each equipped with a small cannon. Once the munitions on the island had been exhausted and the firepower of Garibaldi's ships had proved "insignificant," the enemy started to get the upper hand. "Once again, fortune came to our rescue!" Purvis, who feared that the cannon fire might damage the merchant shipping in the port, intervened "with one of those flags that can halt tempests, that is, the British flag. He put himself between the two sides and stopped the fighting, as though he had touched the combatants with a magic wand! It was a great good fortune for me and the republic!" The island, which was renamed Liberty Island on the same day, remained in Uruguayan hands, and the Argentinean fleet took up a position at Buceo, to the north of the city in territory under Oribe's control. The siege's grip on the city was slightly slackened.

By the second half of the year, the Uruguayans had completed the armament of the merchant ships they had purchased, and could now count on a brig, three schooners, five other ships of the same tonnage, three gunboats, and three cutters. This was not enough to challenge Brown, but sufficient to harass him. Returning to the tactics of the privateer, Garibaldi carried out hit-and-run attacks on the merchant shipping supplying the enemy, while at the same time protecting the ships that attempted to run the blockade. It was principally his efforts that prevented Oribe from starving the city into submission.

These activities were full of risks. At one point, he captured an American schooner and provoked a diplomatic incident, which was, however, resolved amicably, and he became involved in several incidents involving the Brazilians, who reminded him of his undertaking to refrain from hostile acts against the Brazilian Empire. In March 1843, he captured a ship belonging to a Brazilian subject with the intent of using it for military purposes, and the ensuing controversy was resolved with payment of compensation, but a few months later another dispute arose from a raid on a Brazilian's *saladero* and degenerated into a row in the legation and an exchange of insults with Brazil's chargé d'affaires, João Francisco Regis, whom the fiery Italian challenged to a duel. The offended diplomat withdrew on board the *Imperial Pedro*, which was in port, and was accompanied by his French and Portuguese colleagues to show their support. On 25 June, the government ordered Garibaldi to be put under arrest on a warship. The delicate matter was resolved a month later, and Garibaldi wrote a declaration admitting the recklessness of his behavior and pronouncing "his enormous respect for the Brazilian government and nation." On this occasion, his impetuosity had exposed both him and his government to humiliation.

A serious crisis, again involving the Brazilians, occurred in November 1844. Greenfell, the commander of the imperial fleet, appeared with his flotilla opposite the port, and in a threatening manner demanded the handover of some deserters and the release of a seaman imprisoned by an officer in the Italian Legion. Minister of War Pacheco was outraged by this arrogance, and Garibaldi was no less determined to check Greenfell's abuse of his more powerful position. To do this, he embarked on the Uruguayan flagship, the *28 de marzo*, with the intention of an armed response, but the government preferred not to challenge the Brazilian colossus and ordered Garibaldi to hand over the individuals Greenfell demanded. There was, however, a certain dragging of feet, and Pacheco, whose prestige had been diminished, resigned as minister and commander of the army. He subsequently left Uruguay.

The effectiveness of the blockade depended on decisions taken by the British and the Brazilians, who during 1843 supported the entrance of ships into the port in order to assist trade by their fellow countrymen. Those under siege were deprived of their staple food, which was meat, and struggled to feed themselves in spite of being able to rely on a certain amount of fishing. Conversely, the troops besieging the city had an abundance of meat but few imported products. As always occurs in these cases, a black market sprang up, while life became increasingly difficult and many inhabitants left the city.

Garibaldi attempted to prevent supplies from reaching the enemy. On 21 August 1844, he carried out a surprise attack and captured an Argentinean brig bound for Buceo with a cargo of flour, sugar, and various other goods, as well as a schooner, both of which he took to Montevideo. On

27 August he captured a Spanish ship, which he had to be returned to its captain by order of his government, because it was not carrying goods subject to the blockade. On 18 September, he took advantage of the temporary departure of most of Brown's flotilla and attacked two Argentinean ships that remained close to the port with five of his own, putting them to flight. For once the Uruguayans had emerged the stronger from a clash on the high seas. The population, which had watched the daytime encounter from the land, greeted Garibaldi as a conquering hero.

The military and indeed political importance of the Italians was demonstrated in January 1845, when General Rivera made a present to the Legion "of half the lands he owned between Arroyo de las Averias and Arroyo Grande to the north of the Rio Negro, and half of the cattle and existing buildings on that land." The previous year he had made a similar offer, in addition to the compensation established at the time of enrollment, to the French Legion, which accepted it. By these offers, Rivera hoped to gain the favor of the foreign military units in the power struggle against Pacheco, the leader of the more extremist wing preferred by Garibaldi. The two men had also fought together against the Brazilians.

In reality, the actual possession of the lands was postponed until a distant future, while acceptance of the gift would have tied the Italians to Rivera's party. Garibaldi found it easy to assert the Saint-Simonian ideals that had brought him to the Americas, and to persuade the Legion's officers to refuse the offer. In his letter of 23 March, he replied that the legionnaires were "persuaded that it was the duty of every freeman to fight for liberty wherever tyranny raises its head, without distinctions between lands or peoples, because liberty is the heritage of humanity," and they had followed the voice of their consciences when they took up arms on the side of the Uruguayans. "Satisfied that they had carried out their duties as freemen," they would continue to share "bread and dangers" with their brave companions in the capital's garrison "without desiring distinctions or rewards of any kind." This noble stand, which was not made public for the moment to avoid offending the French who had accepted their gift, would put the Italians in a particularly glorious light when it finally came out.

The power struggle in the country was being played out in other theaters. Rivera wished to regain his lost prestige in the field of battle and maintained his position in the north of the country with an army of seven thousand men. On 27 March 1845 he again went into battle, this time at India Muerta against the Argentinean general Urquiza, and yet again he conducted the military operations in a thoughtless manner. He was defeated with terrible losses. There were a thousand dead and almost eight hundred men were taken prisoner, most of whom immediately had their throats cut. Rivera and some of the survivors took refuge in the adjoining Rio Grande do Sul, where the civil war had come to an end a few weeks earlier. He was arrested by the Brazilians, taken to distant Rio de Janeiro, and for the moment left the scene.

In Montevideo it was feared that the victorious general would come to Oribe's aid. This was not to happen. Urquiza acted independently of Rosas in Argentina, which was a federation of highly autonomous provinces, and he had no liking for Rosas's protégé. However, the situation in the besieged city was deteriorating. On 10 April, the government gave Garibaldi, the most popular of its defenders, the task of overseeing the security of the capital. Owing to his fear of a nighttime attack, he slept for a period in the barracks of the Italian Legion, in which he put his complete trust, and he was ready to rush to wherever danger presented itself.

9. San Antonio de Salto

Tʜᴇ ɪɴᴛᴇʀᴍɪɴᴀʙʟᴇ ᴛᴡɪsᴛs and turn of the "Great War" produced another surprise. Britain and France, whose commercial interests were being harmed by the protracted hostilities on the River Plate, decided to intervene as arbitrators and presented the two sides with a series of proposals. The war would come to an end with the withdrawal of Argentinean troops and Brown's fleet. In Uruguay, whose independence would be recognized, the dispute between Rivera and Oribe would be settled by the election of a National Assembly, which would appoint a president. In April and May of 1845, Sir William Gore Ouseley and Baron Deffaudis arrived in Montevideo as the new representatives of the two powers, and then moved on to Buenos Aires. Acting in tandem, the two diplomats opened the negotiations by putting their conditions initially to the stronger party, Rosas. At the same time, the commanders of the Anglo-French naval squadron, Admirals Herbert Inglefield and Jean Pierre Lainé, informed Oribe that he was to suspend hostilities under threat of a blockade against the ports in the territory under his control which provided him with supplies. The besieged were able to breathe a sigh of relief. Garibaldi's extraordinary powers were revoked, as they had caused some discontent among the Uruguayan armed forces. General Anacleto Medina took command of the troops that were being reorganized yet again in the north of the country.

French and British pressures did not produce the hoped-for result. Rosas rejected the proposals, and after two months of fruitless negotiations, the two diplomats moved from Buenos Aires to Montevideo on 31 July. The outcome would be decided by armed conflict. The following day the allied squadrons blockaded the port of Buceo, took possession of Brown's ships, and transferred them to Montevideo. The crews were left free to return to Buenos Aires. The British who were serving on them discharged themselves, and Brown returned to civilian life. A year later on his return to Europe, he would stop in Montevideo and visit his Italian adversary to pay his respects.

This act of force triggered a spiral of violence. Oribe retaliated by interning in concentration camps British and French subjects resident in the territories under his control. The allies strengthened the weaponry of the city's defenders. On 12 June, the troops displayed their effectiveness by marching through the main square in Montevideo. Of the 3,600 soldiers defending the city, 2,000 belonged to the Italian and French legions. However, the armies operating in the north, either established by Rivera or being reformed on Medina's orders, were made up exclusively of Uruguayans.

A resolution to the conflict did not appear close on either front, the one around the capital or the one in the interior. Oribe was incapable of inflicting the final blow, and the Uruguayans were unable to break through his entrenched positions around the city. Their supporters were unable to take decisive action: Rosas was prevented from doing so by the autonomy of the provincial governors, and the Anglo-French were unable to impose their military supremacy for political reasons. European involvement that could upset the balance of power in the River Plate region was unacceptable to nearby Brazil and the distant but vigilant United States. The latter protested and restated the Monroe Doctrine. Hence the general situations only allowed for marginal actions.

The Anglo-French alliance found a pretext for striking at Argentina. Rosas had banned navigation on the Paraná and Uruguay rivers for all ships under foreign flags. In the name of free trade, the allies organized an expedition to open up these important waterways. It was made up of ten British and French ships under the command of Admiral Inglefield and the entire Uruguayan fleet under Garibaldi's command, which had become a considerable force with the addition of the ships confiscated from Brown. The Uruguayans now had two brigs, the *Cagancha* with 74 crew and 14 cannon, and the *28 de marzo* with 36 men and 2 cannon, and five schooners and ten smaller vessels. This made a total of 323 men and 39 cannon. Garibaldi the privateer had never been in command of such a large fleet and was now for the first time fighting alongside officers in navies of world importance (their presence made the enterprise and its leading players famous in European newspapers). The ships also carried a battalion and a squadron of Uruguayan cavalry and four companies (226 men) from the Italian Legion under the command of Anzani.

The allied squadron intended to occupy the main ports of the Uruguayan coast of the River Plate held by Oribe, and then to split into two groups to go up the rivers destroying the Argentinean defenses. The expedition set off at the end of August 1845. During winter in the Southern Hemisphere, the river levels permitted navigation by large ships. The whole fleet sailed up the River Plate, and on 31 August the allies occupied and sacked Colonia, leaving behind the usual accusations of acts of violence by the Italians. On 5 September they took the Island of Martín García, which controls the entrance to both rivers. At this stage, most of the Anglo-French squadron entered the Paraná River to repeat the journey taken by Garibaldi's expedition to Costa Brava in 1842, while this time Garibaldi took his seventeen ships up the Uruguay River, with the addition of three ships from the Anglo-French squadron.

The expedition up the Paraná had the purpose of intimidating the enemy and produced a positive result. On 20 November the allied forces fought a fierce battle at Obligado Point and then reached Corrientes, in accordance with their plans. The goods confiscated along the way were sent to Montevideo. The city, which was no longer strangled by the blockade and had been supplied by Garibaldi, among others, was enjoying an upturn in its economy.

Garibaldi's mission was more complex, and its problems were not only military but also political. The western bank of the Uruguay was Argentinean and therefore enemy territory; the eastern bank was Uruguayan under Oribe's control and therefore also enemy territory, but one inhabited by Uruguayan citizens who had to be treated with some respect. Moreover, the expedition had a strategic purpose: it had to take an experienced military unit to the north of the country, where Rivera had suffered his defeats, and where it could set an example to the troops being organized by Medina.

The first phase of the military action went according to plan. Garibaldi secured the assistance of some *matreros*, who were cattle farmers, skilled horsemen, and fierce warriors. They fulfilled an important role in the forays to capture livestock and attack enemy farms. Juan de la Cruz was an "intrepid and loyal comrade throughout the campaign"—a campaign that Garibaldi considered "the most brilliant of *his* life." Another such loyal follower was José Mandell, the son of a Scottish immigrant. Along the journey, Garibaldi established a base on the Island of Biscaino, where he captured several vessels and imprisoned fugitives.

The most audacious undertaking, which was worthy of the privateer of Lagoa dos Patos, was the capture of Gualeguaychú, on a river of the same name, a tributary of the Uruguay in Argentinean territory. The town "was a rich emporium capable of clothing our ragged soldiers and providing equipment for the horses as well as every other necessity." To avoid raising suspicions, Garibaldi continued past the tributary and up the Uruguay, and then on 20 September he turned back with a few ships on which he had embarked his legionnaires and the cavalry with a few horses. The enemy was taken completely by surprise, and the military commander, Colonel Villagra, "was found asleep in bed." The local authorities and the national guards were captured, and generously not executed. Confusing this town with Gualeguay on the Paraná, where Garibaldi had been tortured, Dumas let his fantasy run wild and asserted that the pardoned governor was the brutal Millán. The occupier took possession of "many good horses, clothes to clothe all the men, equipment for the cavalry, and some money, which was shared out among our extremely poor soldiers and sailors who for some time had been suffering poverty and privations."

On 30 September, the squadron exchanged fire with the enemy at Paysandú and broke through the blockade set up by the Argentineans. At this stage one of the British ships turned back, while another British ship and the French schooner *Eclair* continued to be part of the expedition. The *Eclair*, which was under the command of Hippolite Morier who stayed with the expedition right to the end, became "very dear" to Garibaldi. On 3 October, they reached Coralito, where the shallowness of the river only allowed the passage of three small ships on which Garibaldi and his soldiers traveled on to Salto, arriving on 6 October. The first part of the expedition had come to a successful end.

The more difficult part remained: they had to set up a permanent base with a garrison capable of controlling communications throughout a strategically important area. Garibaldi had orders to occupy Salto, a town of about 10,000 inhabitants on the river between upper Uruguay and the Argentinean provinces of Entre Rios and Corrientes. In other words, it lay between the territory where Rivera's armies had been recruited and where General Medina was now active, and the provinces from which Urquiza had come and which could provide assistance from the governors who had rebelled against Rosas. At that time, Garibaldi's control of Salto favored a link-up between Medina and General Paz, who had taken command of the unionist troops in Corrientes.

The Salto garrison of seven hundred men was under the command of Colonel Manuel Lavalleja in support of Oribe. On 6 October, Garibaldi invited him to a meeting on the French schooner and suggested that he pass over to the government side. Lavalleja did not reply, or rather he replied through his actions by attacking a detachment of the Legion under Anzani's command some thirty kilometers to the south. The resistance was so fierce that a discouraged Lavalleja abandoned Salto, which Garibaldi entered on 3 November to find the town almost deserted. With his typical energy, Garibaldi took a detachment of one hundred foot soldiers and two hundred cavalrymen, and caught up with his adversary on 26 November on the River Itapebi, where he defeated him and put him to flight. The townspeople, who had dispersed on Garibaldi's arrival, returned to their homes. These included Lavalleja's family, to whom Garibaldi chivalrously granted liberty, along with the families of other enemy officers. He wrote to Anita that he had treated Lavalleja "better than you were treated by the men from Curitiba [the capital of Brazil's Paraná State, i.e., southern Brazilians of the imperial forces]," an allusion to her capture by Colonel Albuquerque.

Urquiza had remained in the north of the country, and Rosas had ordered him to attack Paz's troops in Corrientes. He therefore had to cross the River Uruguay and enter Argentinean territory at Concordia, opposite Salto, where it was easiest to cross. He decided to strike Salto to prevent his adversary from crossing the other way, and he boasted that he would use Garibaldi's ships to make the crossing. On 6 December he lay siege to Salto with three thousand men. Garibaldi had under his orders the Italians of the Legion and three hundred Uruguayan cavalrymen commanded by Colonel Baez, who had been sent by Medina. The Argentineans subjected Salto to artillery fire for eighteen days but did not attempt a general assault. Abandoning the task, Urquiza then moved most of his army away to cross the river to the north and move on Concordia, from where he started his operations in Corrientes. Seven hundred men remained to continue the siege. Garibaldi's forces retained a degree of freedom of movement and could make forays to obtain victuals. On some occasions they took the initiative, and on 9 January 1846 they surprised the enemy in a night attack and captured many horses.

Because he was counting on the Salto garrison, General Medina marched with five hundred cavalrymen to the town from an area close to the Brazilian border. On 7 February, his messengers announced that he was close. On the eighth, Garibaldi went out to meet him with 186 legionnaires and 100 Uruguayan cavalrymen under Baez. It was summer in the Southern Hemisphere, and the heat was oppressive. The detachment moved along the plain in a relaxed manner, not too far from the river. Groups of cavalrymen circled to keep a squadron of enemy horsemen at a distance. In the distance there was a rise in the ground of not more than ten meters, but sufficient to hide what was on the other side; Garibaldi showed excessive confidence and moved on with insufficient cover. The Argentineans must have had precise intelligence from their spies in the town, and when the column halted in the area of San Antonio, five miles from the town, there suddenly appeared on the crest of the high ground "a forest of lances, dense squadrons of cavalry with their flags unfurled and a detachment of infantry," which had been brought on horseback. The infantrymen dismounted and charged forward, while Garibaldi calculated that he was facing three hundred infantrymen and nine hundred cavalrymen. This time, the Argentineans had managed to gain the element of

surprise. General Servando Gómez had organized the ambush and succeeded in catching the feared privateer out in the open.

The attackers' advantage was overwhelming, and Baez wanted to retreat. Garibaldi understood that it would not be possible to cover the five-
mile return to Salto without being massacred along the way. They had
stopped by a disused meat-salting factory. As he had done at Galpón de
Xarqueada, he ordered his men to barricade themselves among the ruins
of the building, and he arranged them in the most effective manner.
Some shielded themselves behind some abandoned joists, the remains of a
wooden wall, while others took refuge behind brick walls and in a room in
the building. The legionnaires were joined by thirty cavalrymen now on
foot, while the remainder were attacked by Argentinean lancers and had
to fight their way back to Salto. The Argentineans made the mistake of not
throwing all their troops in together. Approaching with a single line, they
opened fire at a particular distance and were left with unloaded rifles. After having let them come closer, the defenders opened fire almost at point-
blank range and immediately followed this up with a bayonet charge. The
Argentineans, who had been decimated and unnerved by the initiative
taken by an enemy they thought they could easily annihilate, withdrew in
disorder and left their fallen comrades on the ground. The legionnaires
stripped the dead of their rifles and ammunition.

From that moment, Argentinean cavalrymen fighting on foot and the
remains of their infantry attacked repeatedly. Garibaldi's men continued
to fire at close to point-blank range and then charge the attackers. They
made barricades out of the corpses. To lift his men's spirits, Garibaldi began singing the republican anthem, dismounted, threw away the scabbard
of his sword, and fought alongside them. When messengers approached
with a white flag in the hope of getting his men to surrender, he repelled
with rifle fire. But the suffering was intolerable, and the worst torment was
thirst, particularly for the wounded, who drank their own urine. When
night came, around nine o'clock after eight hours of fighting, Garibaldi
ordered the retreat and organized his men into a tight column, with the
wounded in front on horseback or helped on foot by their comrades. The
able-bodied survivors formed four units. He ordered them to fire rifles
only from close range and to use bayonets in defense. The close ranks
proved capable of repelling cavalry charges, although the column was

occasionally forced to halt and face the enemy in order to drive them back. Eventually they reached a narrow wood along the riverbank, and from then on it was easy to keep the attackers at bay. The legionnaires took turns slaking their thirst, and with brief stops they made it to the town under the protection of the trees.

Anzani, who had remained in Salto because of illness, was waiting for them. He had organized the defenses and rejected the calls for surrender that came from the enemy with the false news of Garibaldi's death and the destruction of his detachment. It was midnight when the legionnaires arrived, having suffered thirty dead and fifty-three wounded (of whom thirteen were to die shortly). "No one among the garrison or the inhabitants was able to sleep at that time, and the generous townspeople came forward in great numbers to ask after the wounded, to look after them, and to take them back to their houses, where they were treated with every kindness." The wounded were treated by two French surgeons, one the doctor from the *Eclair* and the other a young man who had joined the Legion and taken part in the battle. But according to Garibaldi, the greatest assistance "to our suffering men came from the tender care of the warmhearted women of Salto."

The following day Servando Gómez left the area. In his report he would boast that he had killed 135 "savages" and captured 20 prisoners, 60 rifles, 30 carbines, 50 lances, 37 swords, "and the scabbards belonging to infantry officers, including the one belonging to the pirate Garibaldi, who threw it away when he abandoned the position he was defending in order not to be hindered by it in his flight." The reality was that he had failed to capture Salto and had failed to gain the greatest prize: the elimination of the Italian, the invincible gringo Garibaldi. The unionists remained the masters of the field. A few days later they returned to where the battle had taken place and buried their dead in a single grave on which they placed a cross with the words "Thirty-seven Italians—who died in battle—8 February 1846."

It was not a great battle, because of both the small number of men involved and the limited military consequences; indeed it was little more than the desperate defense of a handful men against overwhelming forces. Rivera and Oribe had fought with thousands of soldiers, and the outcome of their clashes decided the fate of vast territories. Yet this was the first time after a string of setbacks that the Uruguayans managed to get the upper hand during a land battle. In Montevideo the repercussions of the successful encounter were enormous. Propaganda was part of the war effort, and the government grasped the opportunity to sensationalize the event. It decreed the promotion of Garibaldi and all his officers to a higher rank; the addition to the Legion's flag of the wording in gold letters, "Act of valor carried out by the Italian Legion on 8 February under Garibaldi's orders"; the mounting of a memorial plaque on the government building showing the names of the combatants of San Antonio; the payment of a pension to the families of the fallen of twice the amount they were due; the authorization for the combatants to wear an inscription on their left arm certifying their involvement in the battle; and the concession of the Legion's privilege to march to the right of other troops during military parades until another unit achieved similar glory on the battlefield. The decree was formally issued during a grand parade of the whole garrison. Garibaldi, still in Salto, wrote a letter on 4 March to refuse the promotions on behalf of himself and his comrades, and to reaffirm that they had taken up arms "in favor of a people whom destiny had put at the mercy of a tyrant."

At that time, political changes were coming to a head in Montevideo. Uruguay was a constitutional republic, and the war had considerably undermined the working of its institutions. In January 1843, Rivera had temporarily appointed Suárez to the presidency claimed by Oribe, and Suárez had remained in office throughout the following years without any popular mandate. In early 1846 at the close of the fifth legislature, it was impossible to hold elections, as most of the country was overrun by armies and separated from the capital. The government proceeded to appoint an assembly of notables and a cabinet in which Pacheco's supporters had a majority. On 16 February, Pacheco was promoted to general, and as an admirer and student of the French Revolution, he gathered around him a group of radicals intent upon prosecuting the war until all its aims had been achieved. The moderates, who favored acceptance of the Anglo-French proposals to bring the hostilities to an end, supported Rivera.

Rivera, who was still in Rio de Janeiro, persuaded the government to appoint him as its ambassador in Paraguay, which would appear to have kept him away from the center of power, but in order to get there and take up office he had to pass through Montevideo. Pacheco vainly attempted to prevent him from disembarking. There were demonstrations in his favor, and these degenerated into street battles with the involvement of the French Legion. Rivera's supporters won the day, and Pacheco was forced to resign and go into exile. Rivera regained command of the army, placed his supporters in positions of command, and left once again for the Paraná River with the support of French warships. His major success was the conquest of Paysandú on 26 December, but in January 1847 Servando Gómez led the Argentineans in a devastating offensive in which he took Salto and reoccupied Paysandú. Rivera had been defeated once again and this time had to escape across Uruguay to take refuge in Maldonado on the Atlantic coast, which was still under Uruguayan control. Once again that control was limited to little more than Montevideo.

Garibaldi had stayed on in Salto for a few months and increased his prestige through another military action. The town was continuously harassed by two of Gómez's lieutenants, Lamas and Vergara, "eternal besiegers from a distance." On 20 May, Garibaldi marched his troops through the night and stormed Vergara's camp in a surprise attack. The Argentineans were routed and the camp sacked. During the return march, the legionnaires were followed by Lamas. When they reached a small river, Garibaldi knew that the enemy would attack as they were wading across, so he shrewdly halted and took the initiative by attacking when the Argentineans expected him to be on the defensive. His plan was completely successful.

He at last abandoned his distant posting. On 20 August, he sailed his flotilla out of Salto with the detachment of the Legion on board, and arrived in Montevideo on 5 September, where the victors of San Antonio were greeted with a parade in their honor. Garibaldi had heard something of the clash between Rivera and Pacheco. Rivera, who knew him to be close to his rival, had feared a rebellion by the Legion, and had ordered his follower General Medina to take command in Salto, but Garibaldi's position had been strengthened by his military successes, and he dispatched the general and his superior off to Montevideo on the *Eclair*. On the other hand, he did not get involved in the political dispute, in which "the squares [of the capital] had been covered with blood. In Salto there were plans for a similar farce, but they came to nothing," he would write in his *Memoirs*. However,

Rivera praised the bravery shown by the Italian Legion during the war, in a proclamation of 15 April, as he wanted to gain its favor.

In the capital, Garibaldi took command of the fleet, and for the last time he returned to the harassment of enemy shipping. At the command of the *Maipú*, which was one of the ships taken from the Argentineans, he entered the River Plate and approached the lower reaches of the Paraná, where he attacked enemy merchant shipping. It was a period full of successes, favored by the fact that Buenos Aires no longer had a navy and was subject to a blockade by the two largest European powers. He captured many ships, some of which he sank and others he took back to Montevideo. Those belonging to neutral countries were released.

Garibaldi remained undamaged by the factional struggle which the Anglo-French alliance was unable to resolve. In May 1847 Ouseley and Deffaudis, having failed in their mediation, were replaced by Lord John Hobart Howden and Count Alessandro Walewski, who reopened the negotiations. As usual, the new negotiators imposed a truce. They then proposed that the Argentineans withdraw their troops from Uruguay, whose independence they would recognize, and that in Montevideo the foreign military units be dissolved and a provisional government be formed with the task of calling an election for the National Assembly. This body would then appoint the president, which would bring the personal conflicts to an end and return the republic to its constitutional procedures. An end to the war that had lasted nine years was now in sight, and with it an end to the four-year siege that had brought Montevideo to its knees.

This time it was Rosas who gave in to pressure from the great powers, for the expedition up the Paraná and the blockade of Buenos Aires had inflicted serious damage on the Argentinean economy. In the Uruguayan capital opinions were divided. A considerable number of Argentinean liberals had sought refuge in Montevideo, and they were waging an ideological war against the tyrant Rosas, who had founded his power on political assassinations and maintained it through violence. They were in contact with Cuneo, and on 15 April 1838 they had started a newspaper, *El Iniciador*, whose debt to Mazzini's principles was clearly shown by his slogan, "Bisogna riporsi in via" (We must resume our journey), on the masthead, along with the Spanish translation, "Es necesario ponernos en camino." Using this newspaper and the *Nacional*, which was also directed by Argentinean exiles, Rosas's enemies had been opposing any compromise since the beginning of the siege. They were supported by the Uruguayan democrats, the followers of Pacheco, who wanted to pursue to the bitter end the war against Oribe, the tyrant's accomplice and enemy of their motherland. In this they could count on the backing of soldiers in various legions whose status would have been diminished by peace. They had grown used to enjoying that status, and there were no guarantees that a return to civilian life would have been easy, given that a government created through an agreement between the parties could have denied the land promised in the event of outright victory. In the opposing faction, the followers of Rivera were pushing for the acceptance the negotiators' proposals, and in this they were representing the population's desire for peace.

The dispute became increasingly bitter, and it is difficult to disentangle the defense of corporate and personal interests from the noble motivations inspired by the struggle for freedom. To support their conflicting ideas, the followers of Pacheco founded a political association, and Rivera's supporters started to publish a newspaper, *El Conciliator.* Because of his idealism, his intransigence, and his preference for resolving disputes through armed struggle rather than diplomacy, Garibaldi favored a continuation of the war. On 25 June Pacheco's men decided to make use of his prestige by appointing him as commander of the army garrisoned in the capital. On 28 June, he issued a "General Order," and General Manuel Correa, who had become minister of war and the navy, called on everyone "to support and engage in the resistance with vigor." *El Comercio del Plata* printed a song in Garibaldi's honor, which had originally been published in Lugano by Giuseppe Bertoldi, and had already been taken up by the Italian press. The first line was "Beato l'uom che al gemito—della sua patria oppressa" (Blessed the man who on hearing the cry of his oppressed motherland), and it very much reflected the crusading spirit of the democrats and legionnaires.

This was not, however, the general feeling among the remaining Uruguayan population, which, although now the minority following the exodus of many families, was still the interested party to any resolution of the conflict. The appointment of a foreigner to a position of such authority at such a delicate moment, undoubtedly for political reasons, stirred up a hornet's nest of controversies. Oribe's newspaper, *El Defensor de la*

Indipendencia Americana, spoke of the "utter shame" of subjugating the Uruguayans "to a worthless adventurer" and "Italian pirate." The officers who had been passed over and put under the command of a gringo threatened to mutiny. On 7 July, Garibaldi made a perfunctory statement in which he offered his resignation, and that resignation was promptly accepted.

This did not bring about a change of policy in Pacheco's party. On 15 July, the government in Montevideo rejected the mediator's proposals, which were, however, accepted by Oribe, who had a better understanding of the situation. The following day Howden withdrew the British troops enforcing the truce and ordered the naval squadron to leave the River Plate. France confirmed its support for the unionists and maintained its blockade on Buenos Aires. The two negotiators departed, and the shooting war recommenced.

The supporters of peace did not give up: 420 of Uruguay's leading citizens signed a petition requesting the commencement of negotiations with Oribe. The government refused to listen to these appeals, and on 16 August a new ministry, again under the control of Pacheco's supporters, decided to continue the hostilities. Rivera, who had stayed on in Maldonado during those eventful weeks of conflict, was now obliged to leave for Brazil. The core of the besieged army was made up of foreign corps, and some idea of the organizational level achieved by the Italian Legion can be obtained through an examination of its basic structure on 1 January 1848: it had 3 chiefs of staff (including Garibaldi), 36 officers (including some doctors), 42 musicians in the military band, 82 sergeants, and 552 servicemen, including corporals, standard-bearers, drummers, and, of course, ordinary soldiers.

The war took many years to end. In 1851, Brazil entered the fray as an ally of Montevideo and the part of the Argentinean army led by Urquiza, who had rebelled against Rosas. The following year the dictator, who had been defeated at Monte Caseros, abandoned power and withdrew to private life in England. Having lost Argentinean support, Oribe negotiated an honorable treaty with the government in Montevideo and left Uruguayan territory.

As in the case of the Rio Grande, Garibaldi had been absent from the conflict for some time and took no part in the final events of the saga in which he had played such an important role. From the summer of 1847 his heart was no longer in this conflict. On 8 August, he wrote to Lorenzo Valerio, who had sent him Bertoldi's poem from Turin, "Here we continue to live through this war following the failure of the peace negotiations, but today it is a sluggish and pointless war lacking in vitality and glory." He saw how it had become a matter of personalities and policies and commented on the rivalry between Rivera and Oribe, "The disagreements encouraged by the selfishness and ambition of a few competing individuals have resulted in immense catastrophes and offered up entire defenseless populations, remarkable for their generosity, to be slaughtered by the implacable victor!" In April 1851 he wrote to Cuneo from New York, "I would definitely be in Montevideo if it were not for the insufferable revulsion I feel when approaching certain people or serving alongside them."

He was disillusioned. He had tried to become part of Uruguayan society and had even joined the Freemasons. Having sworn that he had been released from all ties with the dissident Brazilian lodge called the Asilo de la Vertud, he was admitted on 18 August 1844 to Les amis de la patrie, a lodge dependent on the Grand Orient of France. Thirty-three mainly French members were present at the ceremony, and the main reason for this move was his desire to maintain good relations with the influential French colony. He took on the rank of apprentice and rarely attended, given that he was often away on military operations. When he left Montevideo, he said his goodbyes in a letter, explaining that his commitments did not allow him to take his leave personally.

The constant controversy surrounding his name for factional reasons made him feel that he was still an outsider. Much earlier, during the height of the expedition to take Salto, he had already made the bitter discovery that there was little consideration for his feelings in a country for which he risked his life every day. His daughter Rosita died in Montevideo in December 1845, and Pacheco, whom he considered a friend because of their shared ideals and struggles, informed him of this event with insensitive abruptness at the end of his military instructions. "That man was not a father . . . , because if he were a father, he would have had more appreciation of what it means to love a child," he would recall in his old age with bitterness undiminished by the passage of time.

After that, a return to Italy seemed an increasingly attractive proposition. He had the Uruguayans apply through diplomatic channels to the Piedmontese government for an authorization for him to repatriate. This was an application to *his* government, the one that had found him guilty of treason. In the meantime he considered sending Anita and their children to stay with his mother Rosa in Nice; this was the period in which Anita was very distressed about the death of her daughter. In June 1846 the reactionary Count Solaro della Margarita, Charles Albert's foreign minister, rejected the application, and even the plan to send Anita overseas was put aside, as she was recovering from the blow she had suffered and was pregnant with Ricciotti.

During the following year, news of political changes arrived from Italy, and we will examine these in detail later. At the same time that Montevideo was becoming an increasingly oppressive place for foreigners, the possibility of a less hostile government at home accepting the conspirators' return began to appear realistic. The Ligurians were overjoyed by Charles Albert's change of heart when he granted administrative reforms and freedom of the press in the autumn. The Kingdom of Sardinia's consul, Gaetano Gavazzo, wrote to Turin on 24 December:

> When news reached here of recent political events in Italy during the months of September and October, it was celebrated by these Italian residents with public demonstrations of delight. For two consecutive nights great numbers of them went up and down the main streets of the city accompanied by the military band of the Italian Legion and shouted their *Evvivas* in support of our august sovereign, Pope Pius IX, and Italian independence.

The leaders of the Legion made known their plans for transfer to Italy, and the Italian residents appointed a commission of four persons (one of whom was Stefano Antonini) to collect funds "to procure the necessary means to transport the said legionnaires, numbering perhaps two hundred." In spite of the "terrible calamities that for many years have been tormenting this unhappy country," they managed to put together a tidy sum. According to the consul, the legionnaires had helped prolong the war, and their excesses were the cause of hatred against all Italians. Their fellow countrymen were therefore quite willing to make considerable donations in the hope that the departure of the legionnaires would remove at least one obstacle to peace and mitigate the dislike of Italian immigrants in general.

In January 1848 Anita and the children left for Nice with legionnaire families. Given the uncertainty of the Italian situation, they thus avoided the dangers of landing in the company of armed men. Her José was to follow shortly afterward. The Sardinian 139-ton brig *Bifronte* was hired for this purpose and arrived in Montevideo on 1 January under the command of the captain and shipowner Gaetano Gazzolo. It seemed inappropriate for the "category-one bandit" to travel under the auspices of the House of Savoy, so the ship changed its name and flag: it became the *Speranza* under a Uruguayan flag. Garibaldi was its putative captain. On 15 April, it slipped out of port at two in the morning with sixty-three men. The departure from Montevideo had been delayed because of a wound sustained by Ensign Gaetano Sacchi in battle and Anzani's ill health. Thus a chapter in Garibaldi's life was closed forever.

The newspapers barely reported the event. Intensive preparations had been under way and in full public view: 8 February was commemorated as the anniversary of the glorious battle of San Antonio, and the victor was co-opted into the Assembly of Notables as the representative for Salto. It was in this capacity that he took his oath of loyalty to the republic. There was a reason for the ambiguity surrounding Garibaldi in the early months of 1848: the besieged had no interest in publicizing the departure from the field of battle of their most popular warrior, whose audacious raids had lessened the effects of the blockade during the most difficult years, and who had proved victorious even in distant San Antonio de Salto. Equally, it was embarrassing for their adversaries to admit that the man depicted in their propaganda as the archvillain behind the resistance to Oribe against the wishes of the Uruguayans, the perverse instigator of the government, and the true dictator of Montevideo could abandon the scene without changing the political situation or weakening the will to resist.

The Italian Legion remained in place with most of its complement. Following the initial enthusiasm, which brought to 150 the number of legionnaires willing to engage in the Italian adventure, concerns arose over an uncertain future and the break with a world in which they had ties of affection, friendship, and professional interests. The Legion, now deprived of its "illustrious leader," published a declaration to "heroic Montevideo," which was printed in *El Conservador*, restating its commitment "to the noble cause and to those united in its defense."

Garibaldi would never forget the principles that had driven him to fight for Uruguay. While the war continued, he followed the Legion's courageous deeds from afar. It was under the command of Antonio Susini, whom he complimented in March 1851 for the honor he had brought to Italy. Garibaldi also corresponded with his close friend Joaquín Suárez. At the beginning of 1860, the aged president sent him a message of congratulations for his part in the Second War of Independence. "You have brought to mind so many memories that I find enormously moving," Garibaldi replied that same month, recalling "an era of dangers and calamities never seen in other parts of the world," and a "war between giants" that had demonstrated "the resolution of patriots determined to defend the liberty and independence of my second motherland, whatever the cost. I learned from your brave fellow citizens how to fight the enemy, how to endure suffering, and above all how to resist steadfastly in the defense of the sacred rights of peoples against the liberticidal arrogance of despots." The sacred rights of peoples: in Montevideo it had become the sole purpose of his life, even more than it had been in the Rio Grande.

10. His Fame Spreads

Dᴜʀɪɴɢ ᴛʜᴇ ʏᴇᴀʀs he lived in South America, Garibaldi developed the personality of a leader: he learned to manage the organization of the men entrusted to him and to maneuver them on the field of battle with tactical wisdom. More important, during the siege of Montevideo he fought alongside the British and the French, and so his deeds were heard of far beyond the local context and achieved international resonance. In the early decades of the nineteenth century, newspapers and magazines were achieving greater circulations. Daily newspapers covered topical subjects, and in liberal states like Britain and France there were papers supporting parties, providing political news and comment, as well as reports on parliamentary sessions, while in absolutist regimes politics was the preserve of government papers. Weekly, fortnightly, and monthly magazines were often illustrated and satisfied middle-class tastes in reading. Apart from various features on literature and science, they produced articles on improved communications, descriptions of places and monuments, and accounts of journeys and explorations, particularly in distant lands. The war on the River Plate, which was fought on great rivers and across the pampas, was an opportunity for impassioned journalism accompanied by lithographs of the protagonists, landscapes, fortifications, soldiers in uniform, and dramatic events depicted in accordance with the illustrator's imagination. In Paris the May 1843 issue of the prestigious *L'Illustration* devoted a lengthy article to the situation in Montevideo, which was illustrated with portraits of Rosas and Oribe, and a view of the city. In June 1845 it reported at length on the French Legion and printed a portrait of Colonel Tiebaut and pictures of soldiers in uniform (it made only a few references to the other nationalities and did not mention the Italians). In February 1846, it gave a detailed account of the victory of the Anglo-French fleet at Obligado on the previous 20 November, and provided a map of the area and illustrations of the battle. In July 1846, it seized on the appearance of a book on Argentina as an opportunity to depict the horrors of Rosas's dictatorship, the article appeared with illustrations of scenes from daily life on the pampas.

Favorable and unfavorable articles on Garibaldi the Italian privateer appeared in newspapers in Paris, London, Lisbon, and Hamburg, this last city being the main trading center with the River Plate basin. Some reproduced the Argentinean political propaganda that depicted him as a cruel and money-grubbing adventurer. *La Gaceta Mercantil* and the *British Packet and Argentine News* in Buenos Aires and Oribe's *El Defensor* in Uruguay reported his successes through gritted teeth. They wrote such comments as "terrible crimes brought from Italy" and "he took his awful skills from Brazil to the River Plate"; they called him "the Genoese bandit," decried the "despicable thievery perpetrated by the bandit Garibaldi" in Gualeguaychú (with an abundance of invented particulars), and accused the Anglo-French of having stained the honor of their flags by allying themselves with "a pirate straight from the prisons of Genoa and Brazil." When Salto was taken, *La Gaceta Mercantil* described in melodramatic tones the sacking of the city led by Garibaldi, who "ran from one unfortunate family to another opening trunks, chests, drawers, and baskets from which he stole money and jewels with his own hands." The expedition of the *Maipú* caused particular outrage because it was an Argentinean ship (one of those taken from Brown) and was used against the Argentineans with foreign encouragement. There were complaints of European interference to protect the "Italian pirate Garibaldi" in the Chilean *Gaceta de Valparaiso* and the *Daily Union* of Washington. Garibaldi's enemies were not only to be found among his adversaries. The generosity he displayed in Gualeguaychú raised suspicions in Montevideo that this "unknown adventurer who, like so many others who have come to this land, is working for his own personal profit," had accepted a large sum from local notables.

On the other hand, those who knew him praised his courage, valued his moral qualities, and spoke highly of his humanity. He left a lasting impression on the young people he met.

"I was twenty-two at the time, and Garibaldi's personality exercised a kind of fascination on my mind and an irresistible attraction, because of the exploits associated with his name and a sort of mystery that surrounded him and arose from his moral stance," recalled Bartolomeo Mitre, a refugee from Buenos Aires who fought against Oribe. Mitre, who would become a general and president of the Argentinean republic, saw Garibaldi three times but never had a chance to speak to him. The first time he saw him was on his return from the Rio Grande, "where he had gained fame for his adventurous life of courage and moral standing," and he heard him sing the Young Italy anthem "in a soft and resonant voice." On the second occasion he saw him "standing calmly on the poop deck of a small warship, in command like the spirit of the battle." It seemed that the men and ships instinctively obeyed his will, and he understood "his power of attraction in the midst of danger." He saw him once more by chance at the barracks of the Italian Legion, where Anzani got him to leave so that he would not witness the punishment of some soldiers.

Admiration did not exclude careful observation. The young Mitre spoke of this "living enigma" in forward positions just before the battle of Tres Cruces, and produced a perceptive portrait that showed an understanding of the subject's fascination and limitations, the grandness of his ideals and the inadequacy of the means at his disposal. Writing in his *Memoirs of the Siege of Montevideo* and basing himself on his earlier *Military Diary*, Mitre recalled the profound impression Garibaldi's speech made upon him.

I was persuaded that he was a passionate republican by conviction and temperament. Behind a modest and peaceful exterior he hid a fiery spirit and a mind filled with grandiose dreams. His dream at the time was to land on the Calabrian coast with his legion of volunteers to give the signal for the rebirth of Italy and, if he failed to raise the flag of liberation over the Capitol in Rome, to die in the attempt. When he spoke of this, his language became passionate and colorful to reveal an educated man of sentiments rather than ideas. . . . His speech, although affected by moderation, was commanding and dogmatic. I had the impression of a mind and a heart that were not in tune with each other, and a spirit enflamed by a sacred fire and destined to greatness and sacrifice. I became convinced that he was a true hero in the flesh, with a sublime ideal and exaggerated and barely understood theories of freedom, and yet he had the character to achieve great things.

Decades later, Mitre recalled his manner of dress before he started to wear the red shirt: a simple blue double-breasted jacket with gilt buttons always buttoned up, and a white beaver cylindrical hat with the rim pointing upward. Another young man, the English lieutenant H. F. Winnington-Ingram, produced his portrait from life in his red tunic and in 1889 described him in his *Memoirs* as "the beau ideal of a leader of irregular troops," with a colored handkerchief around his neck tied at the front, a saber tight around his waist, two pistols in the holster of his saddle, and a black felt hat decorated with a feather in accordance with the Legion's uniform.

He met various important personalities through the positions he held in Montevideo. They all testified to his admirable qualities as a soldier and a man. Count Walewski (Napoleone III's future foreign minister) returned to Paris in August 1847 and was enthusiastic about Garibaldi, whom he judged to be "equal to the best marshals in France." Admiral Lainé congratulated him on "the splendid feat of arms" at San Antonio, asserted that "the soldiers of the Great Army that for a moment held all of Europe in check would have been proud of him," and praised his modesty, which had found favor with everyone who appreciated what he was doing for the Uruguayan cause. He also revealed that Baron Deffaudis was defending him to his government in Paris, "in order to counter the unfavorable impressions that could be produced by some articles in newspapers edited by people not in the habit of telling the truth even when the facts occur before their eyes." We should remember that some newspapers, such as the Parisian *Journal des Débats*, were spreading falsehoods about the Italian

Legion and exalting by way of contrast the activities of the French Legion. Garibaldi was mentioned when he was in the field with the French: *L'Illustration* referred to him in relation to the expedition to Paraguay and the defense of Salto.

Fearing the dishonesty of Uruguayan officials, the British minister William Gore Ouseley contacted Garibaldi because of his reputation "not only as a man of arms but also for his qualities of honor and integrity." He recalled that Garibaldi went to meet him in the evening, and that because he could not afford to buy a lamp he used daylight to do his work until sunset, and that he was always wrapped up in a poncho to hide the pitiful state of his clothes. The diplomat noted that "he is capable of taking command and acting on both sea and land, and is an excellent seaman with considerable nautical experience." He also valued the Italian's extreme modesty, reserve, and selflessness. Reporting on his integrity in 1849, Lord Howden testified to the House of Lords that Garibaldi "was the only unselfish man among a crowd of individuals who sought nothing other than their own personal aggrandizement," and he defined him as "a man gifted with great courage and supreme military skill." His selflessness was proverbial. It seems that in 1847 Rosas suggested that Oribe should offer him thirty thousand dollars to switch sides to the *blancos*, and his ally replied that it was impossible to buy him: "He is a pigheaded savage."

Mazzini started to take notice of him in 1842. On 4 October he confided to his mother, "That young man Garibaldi is a colonel in the navy and has taken an island from the enemy . . . they write to me saying that we will see him become an admiral." "Another letter from Rio de Janeiro tells me that in those countries they talk of nothing but Garibaldi," he commented in November. He complimented Giuseppe Lamberti on "the enthusiasm of those brave lads" of the Legion: "One of them, Garibaldi, is much talked of in connection with the war against Rosas. He is Genoese and was involved in the events of 1833." "We have 450 men under arms in Montevideo, commanded by one of my best men," he wrote to Nicola Fabrizi. Informed of events on the River Plate through the copies of *El Nacional* Cuneo sent him, he used news he gleaned from it to write in November 1842 about the Costa Brava expedition in *L'Apostolato Popolare*, the newspaper for Italian workers that he published in London. The

Legion and Garibaldi became part of his plans, and he looked on them as reliable pawns.

He started to correspond with the distant warrior and was overjoyed by Garibaldi's offer to bring some of his men to Italy. "I have no doubts about you," he wrote in June 1845; "I believe you to be a man who would never forget your motherland, and who would never renege on a promise. Sooner or later we must embark upon a greater destiny, one that won't involve dying in London or Montevideo." Mazzini helped consolidate Garibaldi's fame because he was so convinced that he could make use of him. For this reason, he attempted to counter the campaign of denigration in the French press in relation to the Italian Legion, which called them *condottieri* and took this to mean "mercenaries." In January 1846, Mazzini published in the *Times* Rivera's letter offering land and Garibaldi's noble refusal, while emphasizing that the French Legion had accepted a similar offer. He both exalted the military exploits and explained the ideals that motivated the military leader. European public opinion started to form a positive image of a man considered by many to be an adventurer without a country. The victory at San Antonio turned the hero (at this stage we can start to use this epithet) into a legendary figure. In July Mazzini printed a leaflet containing his letters to the *Times*, had it distributed in France, and also attempted to get it into Italy illegally. His propaganda made Garibaldi's name known to exiles of various nationalities. On 15 September 1846, the Polish magazine *Bialy Orzel* of Brussels gave an account of Garibaldi's struggle for Uruguayan independence.

During those months, unimaginable events were occurring on the Italian peninsula. In spite of his feverish organizational activity, his ability to ignite conspiracies in Italy, and the care with which he maintained contacts with other exiles, Mazzini was unable to gain the wider support for his ideas necessary for revolution. Indeed, he had alarmed public opinion with isolated insurrections that were inevitably unsuccessful, and these were attributed to his propaganda even when he had not organized them. The expedition led by the Bandiera brothers, who landed in Calabria with a handful of men in June 1844 in the vain hope of triggering a revolt against the Bourbons, caused antagonism. They were easily overcome: of the twenty-one revolutionaries who landed, two died in battle and nine were shot by firing squad, including Attilio and Emilio Bandiera. Disapproval for an ill-advised adventure was accompanied by indignation at the cruelty of the punishments.

Mazzini's political program, which foresaw the elimination of existing states, the establishment of a republic, and an end to the Catholic Church, was subversive enough to alarm the ruling classes and cause governments to react. On the other hand, there was an increasing desire that monarchs should abandon their absolutist rule, which left no space for the middle class, the class that had occupied a position of preeminence since the French Revolution. There was also support for finding a peaceful means to unify Italy so that the country could become a leading player in European politics. The need for unification arose from economic factors and the success of nationalist ideals in Europe: the Industrial Revolution, which had commenced in eighteenth-century England, spread around the continent during the 1830s. In nearby France, Belgium, and Germany, rapid changes were taking place in the use of energy resources (coal replaced charcoal); in industrial processes, with the exploitation of steam power and the widespread use of machinery; and in transport, with the construction of railways. An Italy made up of small states was unable to keep up with these enormous transformations and risked taking no part in the technological progress that was starting to distinguish advanced from backward countries. It was hoped that Italian monarchs would cooperate to provide Italy with the economies of scale required to compete in the industrial age.

The way forward was suggested by Vincenzo Gioberti, an exile from Turin living in Brussels. In 1843, his book *Del primato morale e civile degli italiani* proposed that Italy—"joined by blood, religion, and an illustrious written language but divided by governments, laws, institutions, popular speech, traditions, attachments, and customs"—establish unity through the principle of federalism. He wanted the monarchs to grant consultative assemblies to meet the middle-class demand for participation in public life, and to link up with each other through a system of states that would have the pope as their president, as he had the greatest moral authority on the Italian peninsula. This political project opened up a lively debate that was tolerated by the governments. Cesare Balbo wondered whether an Austrian possession like Lombardy-Venetia could be included in the Italian federation, and Massimo D'Azeglio criticized the local revolts and bloody insurrections, preferring peaceful demonstrations to bring moderate public opinion to bear on the various Italian rulers.

The movement for reform and nationhood was encouraged by enthusiastically patriotic literature. Following the example of Walter Scott, Francesco Domenico Guerrazzi's and Massimo Taparelli D'Azeglio's historical novels fostered sentiments of freedom and independence in the 1830s and 1840s. A moderate movement gained strength from increasing expectations of concessions from Italian rulers. Pius IX's accession to the papal throne in June 1846 was greeted with enthusiasm., and his first act was to grant an extensive amnesty to political prisoners. His attitude raised hopes of the papacy's introducing long-awaited reforms, and there was unprecedented mass participation. Thousands of people gathered in the Quirinal Square to celebrate the pope's arrival, and enormous crowds greeted Pius IX when he came out to attend religious ceremonies. Later they acknowledged his presence in silence to demonstrate their disappointment over his delays in granting the desired reforms. Popular demonstrations took place in Genoa and Turin in 1847, and in Palermo, Naples, and Milan between late 1847 and early 1848. In Milan they were marred by clashes with the forces of the law.

State organizations were modernized at a slow pace, as was liberalization of the press in order to start political debate. The Papal States introduced reforms in March 1847, Tuscany in May, and Piedmont in October. In the autumn discussions commenced on a customs union among Rome, Florence, and Turin. The rulers were unable to resist the pressure of public opinion. Their concessions were mainly of an administrative nature, but recognition of a subject's right to participate in the management of the state was accompanied by widespread impatience with Austrian interference. Austria, the guardian of the status quo, and the Bourbon Kingdom of Naples were alone in refusing to follow the pope's lead and remained faithful to absolutism.

The peaceful protests that were galvanizing Italians brought together three basic demands: reforms of a liberal nature, national unity through federation, and independence from foreign domination. The last demand, which was a precondition for consolidating the first two, was unlikely to be achieved without a war: Italians needed a charismatic leader capable of leading them to victory. Cesare Balbo claimed that he would exchange "three or four Voltas, three or four Alfieris or Manzonis, or even Dantes, or the same number of Michelangelos or Raphaels, not to mention Rossinis and Bellinis . . . for one military leader who attempted . . . to demonstrate the current actual existence of Italian courage." Garibaldi seemed the living proof of the people's warrior virtues, and someone who had to fulfill his calling on the battlefield. The moderates were won over to his legend.

In September 1846, following the election of Pius IX (a turning point that should not be forgotten), the Congress of Italian Scientists, which had met every year since 1839, was held in Genoa. The goal of national independence began to be supported openly. People commemorated the memory of Gian Battista Perassi, otherwise known as Balilla, the boy who a century earlier had thrown a stone at Austrian troops and triggered the victorious popular revolt against the occupying forces. One of the participants proposed the publication of a leaflet on Garibaldi's exploits, the proceeds of which would be donated to the victims of the earthquake in Lucca in August of that year. Written by Cesare de Laugier, the leaflet was distributed legally. *Felsineo*, which was published in Bologna, used information provided by Felice Foresti, one of Mazzini's followers then living in New York, to celebrate the Battle of San Antonio, the most famous of Garibaldi's victories.

That same month in Florence, Carlo Fenzi and Cesare della Ripa launched an appeal to raise funds for a sword of honor for Garibaldi, a gold medal for Anzani, and gold medals for each legionnaire as a reward for the "noble refusal" of Rivera's gift and the glorious day of 8 February 1846. They wanted "the whole world to know that Italy is grateful for her children's great deeds," and that "in the hour of danger the memory of the distant but watchful and solicitous motherland provides them with inspiration to carry out greater and more magnanimous exploits." The individual donations requested were set at a very low level to involve all classes in the initiative. Garibaldi's fame spread as the commemorative cards, which were banned in Lombardy, Venetia, and the duchies of Modena and Parma, circulated without problems in Tuscany, the Papal States, and the Kingdom of Naples (but not Sicily). In Piedmont, Valerio and D'Azeglio obtained permission from the king to carry out the appeal in honor of someone who was in legal terms a "category-one bandit," as long as they did so "in full public view and fully in accordance with the law," that is to say, without any implied revolutionary intentions. Among the signatories were already-famous men such as Livio Zambeccari (who had returned to Italy) and Terenzio Mamiani, and others who would become famous later, such as Goffredo Mameli, Carlo Poerio, Ruggiero Bonghi, Carlo Pisacane, and Quintino Sella. Many British residents signed in Florence and Livorno, and in Paris Cristina di Belgioioso, Giacomo Durando, and Ciro Menotti's sons also added their names. By December, the necessary funds had been collected from contributors who included thousands of nobles, priests, soldiers, workers, and members of all other social groups from every region. The sword was ready in the spring of 1847 (it was presented to Garibaldi the following year on his return to his native land). In August Garibaldi sent his letter of thanks to Valerio in Turin, and it was published in Valerio's newspaper. He expressed his hope that the time would come when he could offer to work for his motherland, and "fight and triumph for it."

Was Garibaldi therefore a turncoat? By no means. We understand from his *Memoirs* and Mitre's instructive recollections that the exiled Garibaldi thought a great deal about the Italian mission, and shared Mazzini's conviction that action taken by a group of armed men could transform popular unrest into a revolution, and that the process of national unification would only be complete with the inclusion of Rome. He therefore continued to correspond with Mazzini, who correctly continued to place his hopes in him and the group of trained soldiers he could bring from South America to bolster a revolutionary war. "Garibaldi's name needs to take on moral influence in Italy," he wrote to Filippo De Boni in October 1846. "I have never met him, but he is a man who wants to act on our behalf, and one day, I hope, he will be able to do so. Although it is right to praise him, we do so without the slightest reference to the possibility that he could ever engage in Italian affairs." He therefore attempted to counter the advantage gained by the moderates through their subscription for the sword of honor by promoting it in England, but was unable to prevent the credit for the campaign from going to the moderates.

He urged Cuneo to acquaint the Italian public with Garibaldi's exploits. Cuneo, who had made his peace with Garibaldi under pressure from Mazzini, wrote a history of the Legion, rejecting the accusation that it was a mercenary body, and sent an account of the Battle of San Antonio to the *Corriere Livornese*. An exponent of democracy since June 1847 when freedom of the press had been granted in the Grand Duchy of Tuscany, this newspaper published the long article in seven installments in July and August of the same year.

The occasions on which newspapers spoke of Garibaldi are too numerous to list. In Turin, Valerio published correspondence with the famous exile in *Letture di Famiglia* and *Concordia*. In March 1848 he published a letter from Cuneo with an account of Admiral Brown's visit to Garibaldi, and how he joked with Anita that if he had captured her husband, he would have treated him "in the same way as his brave companions deserved to be treated." The *Gazzetta di Genova* received information from Montevideo that Walewski had had "a long secret conversation" with General Garibaldi before leaving. The degree of enthusiasm surrounding his reputation and the expectations he inspired in all walks of life are demonstrated by a lengthy declaration issued by Stanislao Bentivoglio, Walewski's brother-in-law, who accompanied him on his return from Uruguay. It was published in Florence by the moderate newspaper *La Patria* in October 1847. In the new Italy rising up from the ashes of the past, the count felt duty bound to express his "friendship and admiration" for Garibaldi. He praised his bravery and selflessness, and pointed out that he fought against numerically superior enemies, put down internal disorders, punished the guilty, and inspired his soldiers with his speeches. "A thousand voices should rise up in Italy to praise his name and, by calling him back to us, restore him to his friends and his country. If the motherland ever needed to be defended, he would never fail it, and the sword that Italians sent him in order to honor him would in his hand prove to be a terrible weapon against our enemies." The legend of Garibaldi as the hero that Italy had been long awaiting was now complete.

Moderates and democrats had always claimed Garibaldi as one of their own, and were quite right to do so. He had constantly maintained a fine balance between legality and revolution. In South America he had always been preoccupied with legitimizing his position through approval from the recognized authorities. We know that he requested authorization to return from Turin in 1846. He was favorably impressed by Pius IX's reforms and the firmness with which the pope protested against the Austrians, who had garrisoned the citadel of Ferrara in 1831 and in July 1847 extended their occupation of the city. On 12 October, he and Anzani sent a letter to Monsignor Gaetano Bedini, the papal nuncio in Rio de Janeiro with responsibility for all the countries on the River Plate. The letter declared that the exiles had followed with attention and increasing interest "the advances that the pontiff was contributing to the development of the reform," and they had become convinced that the motherland had produced "the man who understood the needs of history" and was capable of advancing "the requirements of the time." During the five years of fighting in Montevideo, the Italian Legion had distinguished itself "thanks to Providence and the ancient spirit that still fires our Italian blood." Now (and it is clear that they overestimated Pius IX's intentions in relation to Austria) the Legion would devote its force "to the advantage of one who has served so well his Church and his Motherland." Because of the leisureliness of the postal services the letter reached Rio in November and Rome in January 1848. We know that the papal government decided not to take up the offer, and that the reply did not arrive in time to be received by Garibaldi in South America.

The point is that this proposal demonstrates that Garibaldi made a positive assessment of the new development in the policies of Italy's rulers and was seriously considering a return to his native land. Forty years old, he had been absent from Italy for a decade. He had a Brazilian wife and three children born in Rio Grande and Uruguay. He had lost some of his dearest friends: Carniglia, Mutru, and Rossetti. He missed his native city, his mother, and his relations. "I and all my comrades wish for nothing more than to return to our hometowns, whichever they are," he wrote in August to a friend. He was sorry to leave the unhappy country for which he was fighting, but he and his legionnaires could think only of Italy. They were open to any arrangement, as long as their dignity was respected: "therefore, my friend, find out if it is possible to serve the pope, the duke, or the devil, as long as he is Italian and gives us a living." He did not include Charles Albert, who had not lifted the sentence passed against him in 1834.

He left no stone unturned. While he was writing to Pius IX, he did not forget Mazzini, who was in London. The latter was still hoping for a republic created by a popular movement, and was counting on Garibaldi for his revolutionary plans. "Garibaldi is truly an exceptional man for us. . . . In Italy his name is beginning to be a force," he wrote to Cuneo in November

1847. However, he wanted to manipulate him for his own purposes and for many months had been pestered by the impatient exile. As far back as January 1847, he had protested because he considered Garibaldi's initiative premature; he would have preferred it to have been decided upon "by my orders, when a dozen other things had been prepared, I had found the money, and the circumstances were favorable." But he had to put a brave face on it.

Garibaldi was unwilling to wait. In the summer when peace seemed imminent in Montevideo with the demobilization of foreign combatants, he informed Mazzini that he had at his disposal one thousand "armed, disciplined, and war-hardened soldiers with complete faith in their leaders." They were the six hundred men of the Italian Legion and the men of the Basque battalion in search of fortune. As he had only a schooner capable of carrying 150, he needed to find the means to transport all the men. Mazzini attempted to procure ships and arms by using his contacts.

The planning was adversely affected by the difficulties in communication. "Do not forget," he wrote to Giacomo Medici who was in Montevideo with Garibaldi (and of whom we will hear more), "that letters take two and a half months to reach their destination, while the weakness of our governments means that things change over here every fortnight. In all conscience, I cannot take the moral responsibility for instructions that might be correct when given and disastrous when carried out."

In January 1848, events began to pick up speed. There was a great deal of excitement in Montevideo over the news arriving from Italy, and the expedition was financed by funds put together by other Italians. Of the 150 men Garibaldi had originally expected, only 63 left in April 1848. Many were dissuaded by the indecision over the destination and the renewed hostilities that meant foreign combatants were still needed.

Garibaldi, the general acclaimed by moderates and democrats, set off on his uneasy journey toward a country unprepared to receive him. He had all manner of possible backers, from the pope to Mazzini, but nothing definite. No plan had been drawn up and no safe port awaited him. With Italy undergoing a feverish period of reform and Austria firmly established in Lombardy-Venetia, it was difficult to see what role could be played by a group of armed men.

11. Italy in 1848:
The General Call to Arms

THE MODERATE MOVEMENT that developed in Italy following the election of Pius IX had a weak point. The king of the Two Sicilies, Ferdinand II of Bourbon, did not follow the example set by the pope, the grand duke of Tuscany, and King Charles Albert, who had met some of their subjects' demands by introducing a series of reforms. Neapolitans and Sicilians turned in their disappointment toward conspiracies. In September 1847, an insurrection in Calabria and Messina was put down by the army, but the Bourbon king was unable to control the separatist revolution that started in Palermo on 12 January 1848 and rapidly spread to the whole of Sicily, which could no longer tolerate its dependency on Naples. The administrative reforms that were decreed too late were rejected, and Ferdinand II with his back against the wall was obliged to grant a constitution on 29 January. The other rulers on the Italian peninsula found themselves overtaken by a concession that went far beyond their intentions because it radically changed the structure of the state, and were obliged to follow suit. The transition from absolutism to a constitutional regime that obliged the monarchs to discuss political decisions with representatives of the people, constituted a clear break with the past.

While institutions in Italy were adapting to the new order, Europe was struck by an even greater tidal wave of change. In February 1848, a revolution deprived Louis-Philippe of his throne and proclaimed a republic in France. The effects of the revolution were felt in Germany and the Austrian Empire. An insurrection in Vienna against the Hapsburg dynasty triggered further revolts in Venice and Milan, which chased out the Austrian garrisons. Charles Albert adopted the tricolor and mobilized his army. He crossed the border into the Austrian possession of Lombardy at the end of March and thus a king of Sardinia had initiated a war of national liberation.

The general enthusiasm for the early victories, which made it appear that liberation from foreign domination was imminent, induced the grand duke of Tuscany, the pope, and the king of Naples to take part grudgingly as they had nothing to gain from an Austrian withdrawal from Lombardy-Venetia, which would only have increased the size of the kingdom ruled by the House of Savoy. On 29 April Pius IX, the head of the universal church, withdrew from the war over fears of a schism with the Austrian Catholics. On 15 May, following a dispute in Naples over the recently conceded constitution, the democrats put up barricades, which were stormed by the army, and on 18 May Ferdinand II recalled his troops from Northern Italy. In June, at the time of the *Speranza's* arrival, there was already disagreement between the Italian monarchs, which weakened the coalition of Italian states. An Austrian counteroffensive looked increasingly likely, and when it came in the summer, it overturned the military situation in the Po Valley.

Garibaldi left Montevideo on 15 April. He had heard news of the Palermo insurrection of 12 January but had no idea of its further developments. His understanding of the situation was somewhat vague. As he would write in his *Memoirs*, he was ready to fight a war of liberation, "given that not only were there many signs of insurrectionary movements throughout the Italian peninsula, but, failing these, we were determined to tempt fate and trigger them ourselves by landing on the wooded coasts of Tuscany or anywhere else where our presence would be most welcome and useful." With sixty-three men, he would have risked meeting the same disastrous fate as the Bandiera brothers. When he left Montevideo, the war of the Italian states against Austria, had not yet broken out. This war overshadowed the national revolution inspired by Mazzini, which at that time had little relevance to the situation in the Italian peninsula.

He had no precise knowledge of what public opinion was expecting or of the balance of power between the various political currents. Just as he had been unable to take part in the intense activity of secret societies that preceded the formulation of Mazzini's program, because he had been working at sea in the Mediterranean, he had equally been unable to follow the cultural debate that had prepared the reforms introduced by Italy's rulers. He would probably not have approved of the economic and administrative goals that were at the forefront during the period 1846–47, and he did not assess their effects. He was struck by the patriotic fervor of the Italian unrest. He put his trust in the revolutionary plans persistently put forward by Mazzini, albeit in a vague manner that lacked any concrete and valid strategy, and constantly postponed the legionnaires' expedition until more auspicious times. He did not understand that Mazzini's reforms were unrealistic in Italy or that his theories were incompatible with the proactive policies of its rulers.

The uncertainty is reflected in the instructions Garibaldi gave to Giacomo Medici, who was sent to Italy in February 1848 with the task of preparing the groundwork. Medici, a native of Milan, was ten years younger than Garibaldi, and had followed his father into exile at the age of twelve. He then lived in Lisbon, and fought in Spain with the *Caçadores do Porto* in support of the liberal regime. He then moved to London for business reasons and there met Mazzini. Arriving in Montevideo in 1845 to join his father, he joined Garibaldi's force and then became an intermediary between Garibaldi and Mazzini.

Garibaldi did not want to make things difficult for rulers who were reformers. "Above all you will bear in mind that our purpose in leaving for the motherland is not to impede the current trend and the governments that agree to it," he pointed out to Medici, "but to join up with the good and in common cause with them go forward to do what is best for the country but, where possible, we would prefer to launch ourselves into action against the German, against whom everybody's anger must be directed relentlessly." According to the information he had received in Montevideo, the Italian rulers could not be expected to wage war against Austria. For this reason, he instructed Medici to consult with Mazzini, who in reality had neither the means nor the reputation, and was not in Italy, to seek support in Genoa, Florence, and Bologna, and lastly to make for Livorno, where the ship was supposed to be directed. In the meantime, he had to make the necessary preparations for the arrival of the *Speranza* and the men it was transporting.

The long voyage (the small sailing ship took sixty-eight days to travel from Montevideo to Nice) appears to have been "short and extremely pleasant." The enforced leisure of a sea voyage was spent in "profitable pastimes." Gymnastics kept them fit, the "unlettered" attended lessons, and in the evening everyone formed a choir and sang a patriotic song composed and put to music by one of their number. Garibaldi faced a flood of news when he stopped in Spain at Santa Pola near Alicante to take on provisions. Captain Gazzolo speedily returned on board "with news that would have excited men who were a great deal less hot-headed than we were." The popular insurrections have triumphed, and the armies of the Italian states have entered the field. It was the "general call-to-arms" that they had dreamed of in Rio back in 1836! They started to shout, "Unfurl the sails! Unfurl the sails!" The *Speranza* sailed along the coasts of Spain and France until it came within sight of Italy. There was no longer any need for a landfall in Tuscany, and they set course for Nice. On 23 June, the ship entered port, fourteen years after June 1834 when the death sentence had been passed on Garibaldi.

The usual quarantine procedures were ignored, and Anita went out to greet him on a boat. She was radiant. On her arrival in Genoa in early March after the granting of constitutions in Naples, Rome, Florence, and Turin, she was given a "singular" and enthusiastic welcome. More than three thousand persons gathered below her window, shouted their support for Garibaldi, presented her with an Italian tricolor, and expressed their hope that her husband "be the first to raise it over Lombard soil." In June, now that the war had commenced, the welcome for Garibaldi was even more enthusiastic. He barely had time to greet his mother and children.

Once General De Sonnaz, the main authority in the province with responsibility for billeting the legionnaires, had paid his respects to Garibaldi, the latter declared his position. Charles Albert was challenged by the democrats: he had only entered the war when Milan had driven out the Austrians, and was plotting to annex Lombardy in a manner typical of the House of Savoy, while conducting the war in a half-hearted way without engaging popular support. But Garibaldi did not intend to join in the dispute between parties. The important thing for him was that war was being waged against Austria, and as we know, he believed that war was the best way to resolve questions. Wars are won by uniting forces together. On 25 June, after only two days in Italy, he declared that he had never been "favorable to the monarchical cause," but this was only because the monarchies were harming Italy. In the current situation, he had become a monarchist, and had come to offer his services and those of his men to the king of Sardinia, "who has taken on the task of regenerating our peninsula." Garibaldi declared his willingness to lay down his life for the king.

On 29 June, he moved to Genoa with his legionnaires, whose number had increased to 150 following the enrolment of many young men in Nice, and was greeted by a crowd clapping and shouting their support. He repeated that he was a republican, but wanted to follow Charles Albert, who had become "Italy's champion." "Italians are concentrating their efforts on him. Heaven help us if, instead of strongly uniting ourselves around this leader, we waste our forces in varied and useless escapades or, still worse, start to sow the seeds of discord among ourselves."

The Nice and Genoa declarations say everything about the man, his pragmatism, and the way he remained outside the logic of political alignments. His convictions and his actions consistent with them tended to isolate him. Primarily he alienated the followers of Mazzini. Medici took offence, because, following the instructions he had received in Montevideo, he had awaited his leader in Livorno and enrolled three hundred volunteers. The landing in Nice and Garibaldi's offer to Charles Albert had upset the plan and yet Mazzini himself had written that the rapid change of events that typified the period meant that instructions that were valid when given could become dangerous at the time of implementation. Did not the early months of 1848, so momentous for both Italy and Europe, justify changes in plan? It was Medici's fault if he did not realize this and he vented his feelings with Anzani, who was dying—he passed away on 5 July. Anzani implored Garibaldi "not to abandon the people's cause" and asked Medici not to be too severe with his leader. "Italy's future depends on him: he has been chosen by fate," were his prophetic words to Medici.

He did not fare any better with Charles Albert. He had to borrow five hundred lira from a friend in order to reach the king at the Piedmontese military headquarters in Roverbella, close to Mantua, where he was received with coolness on 5 July. The king listened to the request to fight with his volunteers alongside regular troops, and pointed out that the volunteers should join the properly established battalions, as regulations had to be observed. He asked Garibaldi to contact the minister of war in Turin. This reply would have been wholly proper for a constitutional king, if he had not informed the minister of his "decidedly contrary" impressions: there was no means of using him at sea as a privateer, and the 1834 sentence and the republican manifesto issued in Rio barred him from appointment to the rank of general in the army. He advised the minister to provide him with "the means to go elsewhere." In Turin, the minister of war directed him to the minister of the interior so that he could find a position in a regular army unit. The minister of the interior suggested that Garibaldi go to Venice where he could be very useful as a privateer. The way to join up with the army of the Kingdom of Sardinia was politely cut off.

In March 1848, Venice and Milan had shaken off the Austrian yoke by themselves. In Venice, the Republic of St Mark's was restored at the suggestion of Daniele Manin, and in Milan the local authority constituted a provisional government. Charles Albert, who had initially hesitated, only entered the war once Milan was free. He occupied it and called for the annexation of Lombardy by the Kingdom of Sardinia, but was challenged by the democrats who accused him of sacrificing popular enthusiasm for national unity to the Piedmontese ambitions of territorial enlargement. A plebiscite was held in June and it ratified the union with Piedmont at the end of the war. In the meantime the provisional government remained in office. The Piedmontese army did not reach distant Venice, which was besieged by the Austrians. The isolated republic decided at the beginning of July to acknowledge Charles Albert as its king.

Between April and July, there was a heated debate in Milan between the king's supporters and critics of his overly cautious direction of military operations and his failure to use volunteers. Mazzini, who reached the city on 8 April, initially supported Charles Albert, deferring decisions on the organization of the state until after the war—he stilled aimed at a republic. After the plebiscite, which broke the truce on institutional matters, he launched the idea of a national constituent assembly elected by universal suffrage to establish a unified republic.

Garibaldi did not take part in the clashes between monarchists and republicans, or between unionists and federalists, which took on increasingly violent tones. During this period, he finally meets Mazzini, the man he had considered his mentor and after whom he had named a ship in Brazil. However, the meeting was distinctly chilly as their paths had divided. Mazzini had his eye firmly fixed on a unionist and republican revolution, and the ideological inflexibility that governed his actions in Milan made him appear utopian to Garibaldi. Liberation from foreign domination was the most important objective for Garibaldi, while Mazzini considered this willingness to sacrifice his republican principles to be a sign of naivety.

Goodwill was not enough. Garibaldi saw that his plans were being frustrated and was thinking of offering to fight for the Sicilian government. The island had given the signal for the revolution to start in January, and had rejected every accommodation with Naples and continued to resist the Bourbon king who denied it independence. Here was the cause of liberty.

While traveling from Roverbella to Turin, Garibaldi stopped in Milan and contacted the provisional government. When the Milanese government discovered that Garibaldi could find no role in the war in spite of having been so highly acclaimed before his return to Italy, it offered him the position of general. On 14 July, Garibaldi was in the city, and a cheering crowd gathered outside his hotel, while two bands played patriotic anthems. The newly appointed general exhorted everyone to work together. In his opinion, "a united Italy could take on not only the Austrians but the whole world."

On 21 July, his legionnaires arrived and joined up with other volunteer corps. Garibaldi formed the Anzani Battalion under the command of

Giacomo Medici. Mazzini perceived it as a manifestation of the popular will, and enrolled as an ensign. The soldiers had difficulty in obtaining arms, munitions, and uniforms—they had to use uniforms abandoned by the Austrians. On 25 July, Charles Albert was defeated at Custoza, the Piedmontese army withdrew, and Milan came under threat. Mazzini called for a popular mobilization while Garibaldi launched a proclamation, the first since his arrival in Italy, and directed it toward young men, "Italy needs you . . . . Gather around and do not hesitate."

On 29 July, he received orders to leave for Bergamo to assist in the defense of Brescia. He was joined by still more volunteers and had 3,700 men under his command. "Bergamo will be the Pontida of our generation and God will bring you to Legnano," he proclaimed with a reference to ancient glories. However, he was recalled to Milan, as the Piedmontese army was withdrawing, and the city wished to defend itself on its own. This proved impossible, because Charles Albert then signed an armistice and opened the way for the Austrians. Many volunteers lost hope and deserted, but Garibaldi was not yet beaten. From Monza he left for Como, and on the way he was joined by Medici and Mazzini, a common soldier who would be unable to bear the rigors of military life and would have to take refuge in Switzerland. Garibaldi attempted to bring other formations under his command. At San Fermo, on the morning of 7 August, he announced his intentions to continue the war and they moved into the mountain areas toward Varese. He heard about the armistice of 9 August, and greeted it with angry words, "The king of Sardinia may have a crown that he holds onto by dint of misdeeds and cowardice, but my comrades and I do not wish to hold on to our lives by shameful actions." The proclamation was met with widespread support among democratic Italians, but in the field he was left with a thousand men and the armistice had turned him into an outlaw. Charles Albert ordered that he be stopped and sent the duke of Genoa to instruct his return to Piedmontese and, if necessary, to arrest him. The Austrian general, Konstantin D'Aspre, had the task of eliminating him, and had many thousands of men at his disposal.

Garibaldi moved to Arona on Lake Maggiore. He imposed a levy on the town of 7,000 lira, 1,286 rations of bread, and 20 bags of oats and rice. In South America, armies could help themselves to the thousands of stray oxen and horses, but in Italy, a country of arable farming and dense population, it was not easy to obtain supplies. He commandeered two steamboats used for river navigation and all the barges, and took his men by boat to Luino. On 15 August, he encountered an Austrian detachment while marching toward Varese. It was his first military engagement in Italy, and as usual he was the first to attack at the head of a cavalry charge. After more than an hour, the enemy withdrew, and his ragbag army, mainly made up of young men new to warfare, had acquitted itself well in battle. The brilliant success increased the confidence of his soldiers and the population alike. However, the Austrians were put on their guard, and Marshal Radetzky sent an entire army corps against him under the command of the energetic General D'Aspre. Garibaldi feared being overwhelmed by superior forces, and split the battalion in several companies both for logistical reasons and to avoid being detected. One by one they were chased by the Austrians across the border into Switzerland.

In Varese the imposition of a levy caused considerable discontent. He was on the move again skillfully guiding his men between the Austrian detachments that were attempting to encircle him. While resting at Morazzone, he was surprised by large enemy detachments, and as at San Antonio, he stood his ground in a desperate defense. During the night he then managed to slip through the net along inaccessible paths. He had about thirty men with him and on 27 August he slipped across the border into Switzerland dressed as a peasant. He wanted to form a band to harass the Austrians with hit-and-run attacks, but was dissuaded by Medici, who had a grander plan agreed with Mazzini—the attempt at an incursion into Val d'Intelvi at the end of October ended in failure. The military adventure was over and the military leader returned from America had held at bay well-armed and equipped, numerically superior troops who had benefited from extensive training.

What is more important is that Garibaldi had shown that his skills were not restricted to his use of a saber, as the Piedmontese general, Sobrero, had claimed in Milan. During those eventful months of July and August having only just arrived in an Italy, riven by political turmoil and close to boiling point, he managed to act outside ideological prejudices and party loyalties. He met the king who had condemned him to death and the mentor who he had revered from afar, and was disappointed by both. In a brief period he was a monarchist, a republican, a general appointed by a legitimate authority, and a partisan leader on the run from friend and foe. With each military decision, he adopted a particular stance that was clearly expressed in speeches and leaflets that were distributed around Italy. The hero praised by moderates and democrats alike had proved to be quite a character.

Garibaldi traveled through France to reach Nice and the Piedmontese government allowed him to return to the territory of the Kingdom of Sardinia without reproaching him for his disobedience in Varese or his anti-monarchical proclamation. On 10 September he joined Anita and the younger children Teresita and Ricciotti, and they went to live in a house lent to him by his friend Giuseppe Deideri. The state had awarded Menotti, now eight years old, with a free place at Racconigi boarding school. Garibaldi rested for a few weeks, or rather he was in bed with malaria or the arthritic pains that would torment him throughout his life and reduce him to a wheelchair in old age.

The democrats of Liguria claimed him as one of their own. On 26 September he left for Genoa and halted at various towns and cities on the western seaboard where he was greeted with enthusiastic support. Wherever circumstance took him—Liguria, Tuscany, Romagna, Le Marche, Umbria, and Lazio—he would express opinions, exhortations, and warnings through speeches, leaflets, and open letters. In Genoa, he launched a proclamation to all Italians: Vienna was fighting for its liberty (against Hapsburg absolutism), so why were they not fighting for theirs having heard the cry from Lombardy and Venice? The Cicagna constituency, near Chiavari, elected him to the Piedmontese parliament, and he thanked his constituents for having elected a "man of the people" to defend and extend their rights, while pointing out that he only had "a sword and my conscience." It was not clear, however, where he was to use this sword. Was he to continue guerrilla warfare in Lombardy or leave for Venice, which was under siege by the Austrians? On 2 September, Ferdinand II attacked Sicily to bring it back under his control. The merciless bombardment of Messina, which opened the campaign, earned him the epithet of "King Bomba." To the consternation of Mazzini's followers, who were counting on his presence in Lombardy (this was just before the rising in Val d'Intelvi), he accepted the invitation to come to the embattled island.

On 24 October, he boarded the French steamer *Pharamond* with Anita and seventy-two volunteers. His children had been entrusted to the Deideri family. By the time he reached Livorno on his journey south, the Austrian victory had undermined the political settlement established in the spring. The grand duke's Tuscan government appeared lukewarm about the Italian cause, and Livorno, a hotbed of radical currents, had rebelled at the end of August and had resisted the troops sent to quell the revolt. This had obliged the grand duke to entrust the formation of a government to the democrats Montanelli and Guerrazzi. The *Pharamond* arrived in the midst of all this unrest and Garibaldi received a tumultuous reception. He was persuaded to stay with his men in the hope of being put in charge of the grand duchy's troops and be provided with the means to lead an expedition into Lombardy. The government equivocated and he was not content with the favorable reception to his fiery speeches and the honors heaped on him in Florence. A disillusioned Garibaldi decided to go to the assistance of Venice by crossing the Apennines into Romagna and sailing from Ravenna. The government, in its desire to get rid of him, authorized him to enroll more volunteers and undertook to provide heavy clothing, although it failed to keep this promise.

The march of the passes of the Apennines in the winder promised to be a harsh experience, and Garibaldi sent Anita back to Nice. He left with 350 volunteers. At the Filigari Pass, on the border with the Papal States, they were stopped by Swiss soldiers sent to prevent their crossing the frontier. The ground was covered with snow and the volunteers were poorly dressed and short of supplies. They refreshed themselves in a tavern at the expense of their own officers. This was not as strange as it might seem. Some 350 bands of volunteers were running around Italy in 1848, and these volunteers were mainly middle-class and capable of maintaining themselves at their own expense, at least in part, or were the recipients of generous subsidies from rich patriots. Princess Cristina di Belgioioso had hired a ship in April to take two hundred young men from Naples to the battlefields of Lombardy. Angelo Masini, who was known as Masina and was to die fighting with Garibaldi in Rome, had organized a troop of lancers at his own expense and brought these to Garibaldi's unit in Romagna.

It was in fact this unit, with its nucleus of veterans from Montevideo who had no resources of their own, that was the greatest burden to the territories it passed through. "They are a plague of locusts; we consider them worse than a plague of Egypt," Guerrazzi had said in Florence and he urged their departure. The papal authorities shared his views.

Garibaldi eventually obtained permission to take his men to Bologna. Because of his reputation, the authorities always treated him with respect, while democrats and local populations greeted him with enthusiasm, but there were concerns over the volunteers. They were hastily sent from Bologna to Ravenna, where they were to be joined by a unit of patriots from Mantua, which included the Genoese patriots Goffredo Mameli and Nino Bixio. Their stay turned out to be prolonged, much to the unease of the local authorities. The presence of a group of armed men gave further encouragement to the widespread discontent. In the Papal States, as in Tuscany, the concord between ruler and subjects had ended some time before. Pius IX's withdrawal from the war by his proclamation of 29 April had given rise to strong opposition in the capital and the provinces, which was further exacerbated by the halt to the reform process. Various governments had followed one after the other, but they had been unable to overcome the crisis. In September the pope appointed Pellegrino Rossi as the head of his government. Rossi, who came from Carrara and had taken out French citizenship, had come to Rome as an ambassador for Louis-Philippe and had then remained in the city after the latter had lost his throne. His policies, which were against any return to war and for an increasingly authoritarian state, were greeted with hostility, and on 15 November he was assassinated on his way to the reopening of parliament. On 24 November, Pius IX abandoned Rome and took refuge in Gaeta in the Kingdom of Naples under the protection of Ferdinand II. In December the parliament decreed the election of a constituent assembly and then dissolved itself.

Rome had placed itself at the center of the nationalist movement, and Garibaldi, who with the addition of Masina and the Mantuans, now commanded four hundred men in what he called the Italian Legion. He was no longer thinking of going to Venice, and by the end of November he was on the road to Rome. He stopped for a few days in Forlì, and the levies he requested for the maintenance of the volunteers caused some embarrassment. The only way to get round this pitiful situation was to put the Legion at the service of the state. He left his volunteers in Cesena and went to Rome.

On 12 December he was once again in the city that had enchanted him in his youth. "HE IS HERE!," proclaimed a poster to mark the appearance of the "great guerrilla-fighter of Montevideo." "He wished to visit the ancient ruins of the Capitol and the Colosseum. . . . The general contemplated those gigantic ruins, as did Napoleon the pyramids of the desert, and demonstrated that when divided from Italy and Europe by so great an ocean he never lost hope of kissing those August reliquaries of ancient Rome." The civil battalion mounted a guard of honor outside his hotel, and the democrats of the National Popular Association persuaded by "a greatness that emanated from a mysterious magnetism" wanted to carry him in triumph to the Capitol. He firmly rejected this proposal, but promised he would go on the day "of our liberation." The welcome he received was cause for concern among the government. He succeeded in having the Legion taken on as a salaried force, but the motley gathering of armed men continued to raise suspicions. The government would have liked to have kept them holed up in Fermo, while Garibaldi would have liked to have brought them to Lazio. Their bad reputation preceded them and prevented them from being welcomed anywhere. In the middle of a bitter winter, the Legion wandered around Umbria and Le Marche. It stayed in Foligno, and later in Macerata, but always away from the capital. At the end of January it transferred to Rieti, an important strategic position, where it remained until April. Garibaldi left only for a few days in February, when he was called to Rome for political matters.

12. The Rome Events of 1849

O N 21 JANUARY 1849 elections to the constituent assembly took place in the Papal States. In Macerata the Popular Association put up Garibaldi as one of the sixteen candidates for the constituency. He was the subject of a foreign state, but according to the electoral law passed at a time when Rome was putting itself forward as the center of the nationalist movement, anyone who was Italian could be elected. The soldiers were allowed to vote and their commander was elected; he did not perform brilliantly as he came in thirteenth place.

The people's spirits were high. On 27 January, the Teatro Argentina put on *La battaglia di Legnano*, a patriotic opera written for the occasion by Giuseppe Verdi. On 5 February the assembly met and a dignified ceremony was held. The 150 elected representatives attended mass in the Church of Ara Coeli, close to the Capitol, and then marched in procession with tricolor scarves around their waists to the Palazzo della Cancelleria. They started the operations required under the regulations with a roll call and verification of the validity of the voting procedures. Garibaldi asked to speak and proposed suspending the formal procedures and getting on with the business at hand. In his opinion, it was criminal to be wasting time on preliminaries at such a time and they should get on with proclaiming the suitable form of government for Rome, namely a republic. A brief argument followed, but the prevailing view was that it was important to show Europe that the Roman assembly was capable of dealing the problems before it with due consideration. Garibaldi was asked to be less impatient. The question of the form of state would be dealt with in a later session.

> It was 8 February 1849, and as I was in much pain owing to my rheumatism, my assistant, Bueno, carried me on his back to the premises of the Roman assembly. On 8 of February 1846, at almost the same time of day, not a few of the wounded among our valiant legionnaires were carried on my back across the battlefield at San Antonio, and settled themselves on horseback to undertake the difficult but glorious withdrawal back to Salto. Now I was witnessing the rebirth of a giant among republics, the Roman Republic! On the stage of the greatest events in the world! In the Eternal City! What hopes for the future! So that mass of ideas and foresights that had crowded my mind since childhood and my eighteen-year-old imagination were not made of mere dreams.

Garibaldi remembered the glorious day at San Antonio. He was still the member of parliament for Salto in Uruguay and for Cicagna in the Kingdom of Sardinia. He had only made a brief appearance in Montevideo and in Turin he had not attended a single session. In Rome, however, he did not intend to be absent. The proclamation of the republic had a profound significance for him, because of its association with the country's unification. He listened with ill-concealed impatience to complex legal arguments and political assessments of whether it was sensible to have an outright rift with Pius IX. He spoke to recall attention to the facts. Given the unquestionable rebirth of Italian nationality, the assembly should declare that "Sicily's cause and Venice's cause *represented* Italy's cause."

The decision to give the state a new expression was not a purely formal matter, as was asserted by the warrior Garibaldi who was impatient to come to the defense of Venice and Palermo. The debate extended into the following day. At one o'clock on 9 February, the *Fundamental Decree* was approved. It declared that the papacy had ceased to exist "in fact and in law" as a temporal government, adopted "pure democracy" as its form of government with the "glorious name of the Roman Republic," and declared that the republic would maintain with the rest of Italy "the relations required by common nationality." There was no undertaking to support their imperiled brothers, as proposed by Garibaldi.

He returned to Rieti and his legion on 19 February, when his painful attack of rheumatism subsided. Rheumatism would torment him throughout the rest of his life and occasionally completely debilitate him. For the moment he had a fixed address, and in mid-March Anita joined him. In late April following an untroubled few weeks together (a fifth child was conceived in this period), she returned to Nice. Garibaldi devoted his time to organizing his men, and had received permission to increase their number to one thousand. He launched an appeal, and recruits flocked from all parts of Italy. They were middle-class youths, students, and even teenagers. His legion increased its number to 1,264, and the quality and appearance of its members was improved. He also received coats, shirts, and arms, but in insufficient quantities. Given the lack of rifles, Garibaldi had local craftsmen make lances, which were naturally of great use to the cavalry.

While the assembly proceeded with drawing up the Constitution, executive power in Rome was assumed by a triumvirate. On 6 March Mazzini arrived after Mameli had summoned him with three dramatic words: "Rome. Republic. Come." In February the grand duke fled in the same manner as Pius IX, and Tuscany was under a democratic government. It appeared that Central Italy would provide the rising for national unification and replace the initiative taken earlier by rulers with a popular movement.

In reality, the dreams of 1848 were coming to an end. Events came to a head within a few weeks. On 12 March 1849 Charles Albert repudiated the armistice signed with the Austrians in August of the previous year, on the twentieth hostilities recommenced, and on the twenty-third the Piedmontese army was defeated at Novara. The king abdicated and his successor, Victor Emanuel II, reopened peace negotiations. During the same period, Ferdinand II suspended the Constitution in Naples and launched the final offensive to subjugate Sicily (Palermo capitulated on 15 May). In

April, the grand duke was placed back on his throne by Austrian soldiers—he then repealed the Constitution. Meanwhile Venice was under siege, yet managed to resist until August.

The Roman Republic found itself alone in an Italy that had been returned to the status quo that had existed before 1848 and in which Austria was once again the dominant power. In mid-March, at Mazzini's suggestion—he had been elected to the assembly in a by-election—a war commission was set up to study the structure of the army and the defense of the state. It was headed by the Neapolitan and former officer in the Bourbon army, Carlo Pisacane, who had fought as a volunteer on the Alps near Brescia and had been wounded by the Austrians. He was an expert in military problems. The commission presented its report in early April, and included a plan for the use of the available forces. In the meantime, the situation in both Italy and Europe as a whole had become less favorable. The pope had appealed to Catholic countries and requested assistance in restoring its temporal power. Austria, France, Spain, and Naples had offered to help. There was an urgent need to make military preparations and engage on the diplomatic front, as far as that was possible, in order to weaken the alliance that was ready to support the pope.

On 21 March, the assembly decided to send ten thousand men to support Charles Albert. On 29 March, following the disaster at Novara, it conferred "unlimited powers for the war of independence and salvation of the republic" on a new triumvirate. Mazzini was appointed one of the triumvirs along with Aurelio Saffi and Carlo Armellini. Danger was imminent. In France the republic had taken an authoritarian turn in 1848. In December Prince Louis Napoleon, the nephew of the great emperor, had been elected president and was considering a coup to take on the imperial title (he actually carried this out in 1852). He needed to gain favor among French Catholics and France therefore took on the task of restoring the sovereignty of the pope in Rome, while Austria was left with that of reestablishing order in Tuscany and the Papal states outside Rome. The Neapolitan army and a small Spanish contingent were of secondary importance.

On 25 April, the French expedition of seven thousand men under the command of General Oudinot landed at Civitavecchia and occupied the city in order to make their base for the imminent operations. In Paris it was believed that a single division would be enough as the Romans would not want to fight. In Rome there was anger at the foreign arrogance that wished to deny them the right to choose their own form of government and the sovereign power. On the evening of the twenty-fifth, the assembly decreed that it would meet force with force.

At the time, Rome had little more than 170,000 inhabitants and was not a fortified city in the proper sense of the term. It was surrounded by a city wall, part of which went back to the third century A.D. (the Aurelian Walls) and part of which had been built by the popes (particularly Urban VIII in the seventeenth century), but it lacked more modern defensive devices. People entered the city through eight gates straight into built-up areas divided up by extensive areas without buildings. The city was bordered on one side by the River Tiber, which was crossed by very few bridges, and on the other side by the Quirinal Palace and the Capitol. St. Peter's Church and Square were far from the center, beyond the Tiber in an area dominated by the hills of Vatican and Janiculum, one of the critical points of the defense, because if taken they would dominate Rome and make it possible to threaten it with artillery. For the French who landed in Civitavecchia, that was the part of the wall that was easiest to approach as they marched along the Via Aurelia. The defenders therefore set up their headquarters at St. Peter's, and they cut down trees and placed these and other obstacles across the roads along which the enemy would travel.

On 30 April, Oudinot launched his attack against the Janiculum as had been expected, and it was Garibaldi who defended it. He had heard news of the developments while in Rieti and had written to Mazzini calling him a brother and reminding him that in Rieti he had "unswerving friends of shared beliefs," but he did not receive a reply. One of his officers, Francesco Daverio, had urged the dispatch of rifles without success. Pisacane, who believed the Legion could not be combined with the regular units of the army, had decided to leave it close to the Neapolitan border at Anagni. On 23 April, as the French approached, the new minister of war, the Piedmontese Giuseppe Avezzana, appointed Garibaldi brigadier general and recalled him to Rome.

Pisacane's contempt for a body more picturesque than martial was not without foundation. The British sculptor Gibson described the bizarre spectacle of the Legion entering Rome. "The men were tanned by the sun, had long and disheveled hair, and wore conical hats decorated with fluttering black feathers; their faces were white with dust and framed by unkempt beards, and their legs were bare; they crowded around their leader who, seated on his white horse, was perfectly statuesque in his virile handsomeness."

The disorder among Garibaldi's legion that made an impression on an artist also appeared to be the dominant characteristic for a volunteer who fought alongside it. Count Emilio Dandolo from Milan was in a unit of Lombard light-infantrymen made up of aristocrats and members of the middle class who followed the Legion in the Roman campaign. He was described by his commander Luciano Manara as "disciplined, proud, taciturn, and chivalrous." Garibaldi's men were quite the opposite, and he defined them as "a pack of brigands." Confusion, indiscipline, and brawling were the rule in the Legion. Dandolo was surprised to observe:

> Garibaldi and his staff officers wore scarlet "blouses" and caps of all shapes and sizes without any badges and without bothering with any military decorations. They mounted on American-style saddles and were keen to show their contempt for everything that regular armies care about and impose with great severity. Followed by their orderlies, who all came over from America, they disperse, gather together, and rush here and there in a disorderly manner, and are active, reckless, and untiring. When the troop halted to rest and make camp while the soldiers collected the weapons, it was wonderful to watch them leaping down from their horses and personally attending to them, even in the case of the general.

Dandolo did not approve of the excessive number of officers chosen from the most courageous and promoted "to the higher ranks bypassing others and with complete disregard for length of service or protocol," but he admitted that the majority "justify their grand appointments through the most courageous actions." He also marveled at other acts of indiscipline: if they did not receive provisions through the proper channels, they rustled sheep and oxen, which they then slaughtered and roasted.

> Meanwhile, if the danger is distant, Garibaldi is lying in his tent, but if the enemy is close, he is always on horseback giving orders and

visiting forward positions. Often he takes part in dangerous recon-naissance expeditions dressed as a peasant. More often, he spends hours seated in some high position with a telescope examining the landscape . . . . With his patriarchal and possibly slightly affected simplicity, Garibaldi resembles an Indian chief rather than a general, but when danger is at hand and closing in, then he is truly admirable for his courage and shrewdness. What he lacks to become a good general he partly makes up for with his incredible energy.

It should be pointed out that the government asked Garibaldi to dress the Legion in a uniform determined by a regulation, and following the Battle of Palestrina in mid-May, Garibaldi ordered everyone to wear a tu-nic of red wool. Before that, there were two features that struck the foreign sculptor and Italian aristocrat alike: the mish-mash of clothing and the di-verse behavior (unusual in an era in which restricted communications made ethnic and cultural exchanges a rarity) and the personality of their leader, whom the artist considered "statuesque in his virile handsome-ness," and the soldier "admirable for his courage and shrewdness." The general's exotic clothing, his bizarre military force, and the simplicity with which he had himself carried to the assembly by Ignazio Bueno, who had come with him from Uruguay, as had his inseparable and athletic black attendant Andrea Aguyar, and had heroic exploits in America and, more recently, in Lombardy were all part of a mix that fascinated the crowds.

In May the English magazine, *Illustrated London News*, published a wonderful portrait of the "Roman general" and in July it published one of the general "and his negro servant," both on horseback (Garibaldi, on a white horse, was talking with an officer), one of a group of grim-faced le-gionnaires dressed in a variety of clothing, and one of Garibaldi's lancers with a pike and feathered hat bringing a dispatch and riding a horse at great speed. The magazine often extolled Garibaldi's valor. His soldiers were encouraged to fight by the calm way he confronted danger and the courage with which he put himself in the front line facing the enemy.

He was greeted by the people in triumph when he entered the city by Porta Maggiore on 27 April. His presence galvanized the defenders, who considered him their true leader. The republic could count on seventeen to eighteen thousand men spread around the extensive territory of the

Papal States, including regular soldiers of the former papal army, units of the National Guard, which had fought in Venetia in 1848, and volunteers. Four thousand were in Romagna, a thousand in Le Marche, and eleven to twelve thousand along the lengthy border with the Kingdom of Naples from the Adriatic to the Tyrrhenian Sea. As the French approached many units were recalled to the city and a force of between seven and nine thousand men was built up, including the six hundred Lombard light-infantrymen under the command of Luciano Manara, who had landed at Civitavecchia at the same time as the French and were initially cut off by Oudinot.

Garibaldi, who was responsible for the defense of the most critical sector around the Janiculum, had 2,500 men under his command and 1,800 in reserve at the orders of Colonel Bartolomeo Galletti. As usual he explored the terrain, and noted some country houses outside the walls that were higher up than the city gate, Porta San Pancrazio. These houses, Villa Corsini (also called Casino dei Quattro Venti) and Villa Pamphili, would have made defense of the walls impossible if they were to fall into enemy hands, so he had them occupied.

The French attacked on the morning of the thirtieth with a force of five thousand men. They advanced confidently and did not expect any serious resistance. They aimed for the Vatican Hill and the Janiculum. They headed for the city gate called Porta Pertusa only to discover that it had been walled up for years, although this was not shown on the maps they had used for their plans. The officers were not discouraged: the French army was one of the foremost in the world for preparation and experience in battle. The column divided in two to find entrances at the nearest city gates. One part was directed toward Porta Cavalleggeri and had to march for a kilometer out in the open exposed to enemy fire, and the other went toward Porta Angelica, and the soldiers marched without protection at the foot of the wall. They attempted to climb the walls with grappling-irons, but were repulsed. The maneuver was a failure.

Garibaldi saw the opportunity to attack the unit, amassed under Porta Cavalleggeri, from behind. He stormed them from the country houses on the Janiculum. Many of his men had never been under fire before, and when they entered the narrow Via Aurelia Antica they came across a battalion positioned to defend the flank against attack. There followed an engagement that recalled the Battle of Tres Cruces in that fresh units were successively brought into play. Initially the French had the upper hand and Garibaldi therefore brought in Galletti's reserve and, on horseback at the center of his troops who now numbered over two thousand, he led a bayonet charge. The two country houses, which had been lost, were retaken, and the French withdrew toward Castel di Guido, where they had set up camp. They left behind them five hundred dead and wounded on the ground and 365 prisoners. The defenders suffered two hundred dead and wounded. Garibaldi had also been hit by a rifle shot, and the wound in his side, although not serious, would give him problems for a couple of months. He showed it to no one and had it tended to during the night.

That evening the city was lit up and the population was in festive mood. Morale was sky-high. The citizens and many outsiders visiting the city to see its monuments took part in its defense. Barricades were put up in the streets, and a committee of ladies—including the Lombard Princess of Belgioioso and Pisacane's Neapolitan wife, Enrichetta Di Lorenzo—organized medical assistance. Garibaldi, following his often expressed convictions, wanted to exploit the favorable moment by pursuing the demoralized enemy. "We could have driven them into the sea by exploiting the weakness and their fear, and then we could have done the reckoning," he would comment in his *Memoirs*, but Mazzini stopped him. France was not an adversary that could be disposed of with one lucky battle. The problem was political. The democratic opposition, which was a powerful force in the parliament in Paris, was against the expedition. Napoleon had said that he was sending the troops to avoid an Austrian attack and France would favor the maintenance of the constitutional regime established in Rome by the pope in 1848. Mazzini hoped that the attack was over, and therefore the defeated enemy had to be treated with courtesy. The prisoners were released, and in exchange Oudinot released the Roman prisoners and allowed four hundred volunteers held up in Civitavecchia to leave for Rome. In reality he was playing for time while awaiting reinforcements.

In the meantime, the republic had to deal with other belligerents. Austria, which already had an army in the Po Valley, took Bologna. The Bourbon king of Naples, who was the pope's host and had destroyed all opposition within his kingdom, entered Lazio from the south. At the time, the border between the two states was at Terracina, and the invading army of twelve thousand men soon reached Castelli Romani, where it was able to threaten the city from Frascati and Albano. Garibaldi, who was sent wherever danger appeared, left Piazza del Popolo on 5 May with the Legion, Manara, Masini, and other units that had not fought on 30 April. As in Lombardy, he moved between built-up areas and countryside creating the kind of fast-changing warfare he preferred and attempting to deceive the enemy as to his real intentions. He spread the word that he was moving against the French and turned toward Tivoli, almost as though he were going to Abruzzo, and finally he moved toward the towns of Castelli Romani to threaten the right flank of the Neapolitan army. On the ninth he occupied a favorable position. The Bourbon army could have driven a wedge between him and Rome, and cut off his chance of withdrawal, but even in victory this would have given him the opportunity to cross over the border with his men. They decided to unleash a frontal attack and drive him from whence he came. They attacked with two columns, one repulsed by Manara and the larger one by Garibaldi after three hours of combat. The Bourbon army withdrew leaving about fifty dead. Ferdinand II's advance on Rome had come to a halt.

Events speeded up, and some suspicious maneuvers by Oudinot alarmed those responsible for the defense of Rome, and Garibaldi was urgently recalled to Rome on 11 May with a march through the night. Then came a dramatic twist: on 15 May Napoleon instructed Ferdinand de Lesseps, the future builder of the Suez Canal, to negotiate. This was what Mazzini had been hoping for, but in reality the French president was waiting for the end of the parliamentary session in order to avoid criticisms from the democrats while providing Oudinot with adequate means to finish the job. When this became clear, it was too late. For the moment, Lesseps acted in good faith and signed a truce on 17 May to last until 4 June.

Ferdinand II was resigned to letting the French have the honor of bringing the pope back to Rome, and decided to withdraw the entire army back to the Kingdom of Naples before the Roman forces made a concerted attack on him. The republican government, while the danger represented by Oudinot was temporarily removed, decided that it would be opportune to force the king into battle and demonstrate the new state's military capabilities. The command of the forces deployed along the southern front was given to General Pietro Roselli, who had a force of eight thousand men. Like Oribe's supporters in Montevideo, the propaganda from the pope's supporters attacked the presence of so many Piedmontese, Lombards, and Ligurians among the defenders of the republic, and claimed that the Romans wanted the pope's return and were victims of "foreign" fanaticism. Roselli was not a military expert, but he had the advantage of being Roman. He had been an officer in the papal Corps of Engineers and had taken part in the Venetia campaign during the weeks in which Pius IX had joined the war of national liberation. He earned promotion to major, but without actually taking part in any combat. In the republic, he was rapidly promoted to colonel, then general, and later commander-in-chief, with the Neapolitan Pisacane as his chief of staff.

Roselli left Rome on 16 May. He moved his troops in accordance with military expertise and advanced slowly with the intention of bringing his army before the enemy at full strength. He gave order not to engage the enemy until all the units were gathered in order to avoid numerical inferiority. However the circumstance demanded an acceleration of deployment to take the Neapolitans by surprise. Garibaldi was in the advance guard near Velletri, and realized that the Bourbon army was withdrawing. He decided to ignore express orders and attacked, while sending notification to Roselli with a request to speed up the advance of the main army.

Masina's forty lancers sent on reconnaissance found themselves up against a powerful cavalry detachment. They withdrew in disorder and Garibaldi on horseback committed the imprudence of barring their way to stop them. He was swept along by horsemen unable to halt their horses and fell in "a pile of men and overturned horses." The enemy was on top of them slashing with their sabers. Fortunately the Legion charged and the fray was joined by a group of very young volunteers who saved their commander and drove off the enemy cavalry, thirty of whose number were taken prisoner. Once again Garibaldi had escaped death by a whisker. "Having been trampled by horsemen and horses, I was suffering from contusions that prevented me from moving. When I finally managed to stand up, I touched my limbs to feel if any were broken." The account of an unhappy incident was extremely terse.

The advance guard reassembled and drove off the enemy who took up position in Velletri on a hill. The republicans were obliged to halt.

Garibaldi had his men fed with animals hastily rounded up and seized, while Roselli waited for provisions to arrive. He was angry at Garibaldi's disobedience, and refused to deploy the reinforcement requested by the advance guard. When he arrived in the afternoon at the time agreed in the original plans, he did not attack the town immediately and made no attempt to cut off the Neapolitan escape route. According to Garibaldi, the opportunity to engage the enemy in a pitched battle from a favorable position had been lost, and according to Roselli and Pisacane, his untimely attack due to impatience had prevented the deployment of an encirclement of the Bourbon army.

The southern front was not the government's greatest worry. The Austrians, who were advancing through the former Papal States, were more dangerous. The army was recalled to the capital, and Garibaldi was given permission to carry out an incursion into the Kingdom of Naples toward Cassino and Capua, using the Legion, Manara's light infantry, and Colonel Luigi Masi's regiment. But when he had only reached Terra di Lavoro, he was recalled as Rome was faced with more immediate dangers. At the end of May he entered the capital again covered in glory. However, he regretted having lost the "perfect and decisive" opportunity to penetrate the heart of Southern Italy where he had support among the population. This was his conviction, as demonstrated by his proclamation to the Neapolitans in Frosinone on 28 May, which exhorted them to "break the ignominious chains" of tyranny. But 1848 had shown that peasants cannot be moved by ideals of nationalism they do not understand. Garibaldi had personally experienced this in Lombardy, but refused to accept it. With his volunteers willing to fight like lions, the Bourbon army demoralized, and Sicily "not yet brought to heal," he felt there would be "every chance of success in pushing forward audaciously." He blamed Mazzini for having stopped him, as he had done a year earlier in Switzerland. His reverence for his mentor, which is clearly stated in his letters from America and reflected his belief that Mazzini's doctrine was a call to action, was now giving way to an inability to understand an attitude that appeared to be governed by indecision and jealousy over his own initiatives.

Garibaldi thought like a soldier and Mazzini like a politician. The latter therefore had his eye firmly fixed on France. But Napoleon now revealed his real intentions. He had sent over an army of thirty thousand men armed with six artillery batteries, siege equipment, and substantial engineering units. On 1 June, Oudinot notified the republic that the truce was over and that he would attack on the fourth, in order to give French civilians time to leave the city. The government was now facing a fundamental strategic decision. Pisacane advised concentrating the army outside Rome in central position close to Terni in order to meet the French, Austrians, and Bourbons separately with the assistance of bands of volunteers. Clearly they could not keep such superior forces at bay for very long. Garibaldi was substantially in agreement and offered to hurry the enemy in the provinces to the north of Rome. Mazzini knew that from a military point of view the game was over. The defense would only have a symbolic value. By concentrating the forces in Rome, it would provide an example of heroism and sacrifice, and would consecrate the Eternal City as the future capital of the Italian nation. There was no choice but to fight stubbornly with no hope of immediate success.

The final act in the defense of Rome started with a sudden attack by the French. Oudinot had announced that on 4 June he would attack the *piazza*, which was understood as the fortress. He would later say that by piazza he meant the city within the walls. During the night between 2 and 3 June he took Villa Pamphili while the defenders were resting. The previous evening Roselli, on visiting the forward positions, had asserted that there was no need for vigilance as the French had given an undertaking to reengage in hostilities on the 4 June. Part of the troops was quartered in the city, and the officers were sleeping in private homes. Garibaldi was also resting in the city, and was suffering from the wound he had sustained on 30 April and the endless exertions of that period. He had suggested that Villa Corsini be fortified, though throughout May nothing was done about it. On 26 May Mazzini asked him for his honest opinion of the military operations. He replied in a letter, "Given that you have asked me what I would want, I will tell you: here I can only do good for the republic in one of two capacities—either dictator with unlimited powers or soldier in the ranks. You choose." There was no answer to this. The government could not turn an eccentric guerrilla-fighter into the symbol of its defense, but neither could it take authority away from its most popular combatant. Garibaldi kept responsibility for the Janiculum and the right bank of the Tiber, where the attack was expected to come.

The surprise attack on the 3 June was a success. The French reached the outer wall of the country house in silence, destroyed it with explosive charges, and broke into the gardens through the breach. The four hundred defenders were either captured while they slept or withdrew to Villa Corsini and the San Pancrazio Convent. Galletti's troops arrived as reinforcements, but the French threw in significant forces according to a carefully worked-out maneuver with artillery support. The villa and the convent, which were the key to the defense of Rome, fell into enemy hands.

June third was taken up with a continuous counter-attack. It was not possible to organize it immediately because officers and troops were dispersed throughout the city. Garibaldi, who was informed of events at three in the morning, gathered his men in Piazza San Pietro who came rushing at his command. He considered the possibility of leaving by Porta Cavalleggeri to attack the occupiers of Villa Pamphili and Villa Corsini at their flank and their rear, but decided against it because they would have to get past a high wall. Instead he decided to attack from Porta San Pancrazio. It was dawn and he was on horseback outside that city gate. He launched his units into the attack. They could not advance en masse, as the road to the country house was initially narrow and under fire from the defenders, and then with slight upward gradient it reached steps where the attackers had to use bayonets. It was a murderous stretch of road, and yet the villa was taken after two hours, only to be immediately lost again. More fighting broke out around Villa del Vascello. For the entire day, there was a succession of attacks on the country houses by volunteers and deployments of French reinforcements with artillery support using well-organized regiments that could count on superior numbers and equipment. Garibaldi lacked the weapon that had given him so many victories in South America: the refusal to give up fighting even in desperate situations, which in Rio Grande and Uruguay had on many occasions broken the enemy's spirit. The French were no less tenacious in defending and attacking, and just as willing to die on the battlefield. But they were also well equipped and well trained. By evening they were in control of Villa Corsini and Villa Valentini. The defenders still held Villa del Vascello and Villa Giacometti.

There were a thousand dead, and more than sixty officers and six thousand men had been engaged in the successive military operations. Daverio, Enrico Dandolo, and Masini had been killed, and Nino Bixio and

Goffredo Mameli had been wounded (Mameli would die a month later from gangrene). Garibaldi would be accused of deploying units in successive groups rather than a mass attack, and sending them into extremely dangerous frontal attacks without supporting them with reinforcements so positions taken at great cost could be defended. In his defense, it should be noted that the country houses were located in a small area with only a few hundred meters of circumference and with obligatory approaches where it was not possible to maneuver or surprise the enemy. The French had deployed sixteen thousand men against the six thousand available to Garibaldi, and his men arrived at irregular intervals as they gathered together. Manara brought his men to the Janiculum three hours after Garibaldi, who had to wait another three hours for Medici's men.

On the other hand, as Gustav Hoffstetter, a Swiss volunteer who fought on the side of the Roman Republic, would write in his diary, Garibaldi impassively directed operations on horseback where the gunfire was thickest. He did not remove himself from danger, but considered it the duty of anyone who believed in the ideals of liberty and the motherland to be willing to sacrifice his life. The volunteers who consciously risked their lives shared his sentiments; hence the great authority he held over the combatants after the terrible slaughter. The heroism with which young men from every corner of the Italian peninsula demonstrated faith in Italy's destiny to the astonishment of Europe and turned 3 June into the first of several events that made it increasingly difficult to reverse the momentum toward national unification.

On 4 June the siege started in earnest. The French occupied various positions around the city. They made it difficult to keep supplies reaching the besieged, damaged some aqueducts, and fired shells into build-up areas. One of these hit the facade of the Church of St. Andrea della Valle, where Giacomo Puccini would set the first act of his *Tosca*, and others caused civilian casualties. They were loath to launch an attack into the streets: citizens had created serious difficulties for regular troops with their barricades across the streets of Paris, Milan, Vienna, and Naples. The area in which resistance was concentrated was again the Janiculum, from Porta San Pancrazio to Porta Portese, and Garibaldi was coordinating the defense. Outside the city walls the defenders were holding positions around Villa del Vascello, with three hundred volunteers under Medici's

command, and the Giacometti country house, both of which were connected to the city gates by trenches.

Pisacane proposed breaking the French line with a mass attack from
Porta Cavalleggeri. Garibaldi considered such an audacious action imprac-
tical now so many of the best officers were dead and given the volunteers'
lack of training. A night attack attempted on 10 June ended in confusion.
There was no choice but to let the enemy increase the pressure, and any
remaining hopes vanished. In Paris the opposition was defeated in parliament and the authorities dispersed a demonstration organized by the
democrats who used the attack on the Roman Republic to denounce Napoleon's increasing authoritarianism. Rome was on its own.

On the night of 21 June a French spearhead broke through the lines.
Garibaldi and Manara organized the defense along a line of rear positions
that included strongholds like Villa del Vascello and Porta San Pancrazio
to Villa Spada. Mazzini insisted that Garibaldi launch a counter-attack to
retake the lost positions. He sent Roselli and Pisacane to urge him to follow this order. In the hope of the attack being made in the afternoon of 22
June, he had the bells ring the tocsin and called out the population to give
him support. Garibaldi held firm to his conviction that such an action
would end in disaster. Tempers became frayed. Garibaldi suggested a di-
versionary tactic: he would lead out a thousand men to threaten the enemy lines from the rear, and draw some of the French forces away from
the siege. The plan was approved and then revoked, because it did not
meet with Roselli's agreement. An angry Garibaldi withdrew his legion
from the front line and headed back to the barracks. Manara, who had become the chief of staff following Daverio's death, persuaded him to return
to the front. It was now simply a matter of saving one's honor. On the
morning of 28 June the legionnaires put on the legendary red shirts they
had worn at Montevideo, as these were finally ready.

When Garibaldi was on the Janiculum he took up a position at Villa
Spada. On the twenty-ninth, the cannons fell silent out of respect for St.
Peter's feast-day. The dome of the basilica was lit up for the festivity, but a
downpour extinguished the torches. Two French detachments attacked at
two o'clock in the morning, and the defenders fell back. Garibaldi retook
the lost positions leading a bayonet attack. The strongholds used by the
resistance were now reduced to a pile of rubble. He ordered Medici to

abandon the Villa del Vascello and withdraw to Porta San Pancrazio. The French took Villa Spada with an assault using fresh troops. Emilio Morosini and Luciano Manara were fatally wounded and Andrea Aguyar also fell in battle, while Garibaldi fought like a tiger. "He was ancient Leonidas at Thermopylae. He was Ferrucci at Gavinana Castle. I trembled at the idea of him falling at any moment," recalled Candido Augusto Vecchi. The French were gaining the upper hand and at midday a truce was agreed so that the dead and wounded could be removed from the battlefield.

During the morning Mazzini had convened the military leaders. They were faced with three choices: they could capitulate; they could put up barricades as the French entered the city; or they could leave with the army, the government, and the assembly to continue the war in Umbria, Le Marche, and Emilia-Romagna. Garibaldi, who remained at the front, let it be known that he preferred the third solution. The decision was referred to the assembly, which was discussing the republic's Constitution, and it was decided that Garibaldi's opinion was required. He appeared covered with dust and sweat during the truce: the Janiculum front was close to collapse and barricades would induce the enemy to bombard the residential areas, while in his opinion it would be possible to continue the resistance on the Apennines. He was opposed by Roselli, who was convinced that the army would not comply. There was no choice but to succumb to the greater force without dignifying Napoleon's arrogance with a negotiated surrender. "The Roman constituent assembly remains in sitting and ceases because defense is no longer possible" was the formula adopted. In effect, the assembly continued to examine the articles of the Constitution, which was formally approved on 2 July as the French were about to enter the city.

13. The Bold Defiance of 1849

O FFICIALLY THE REPUBLIC had renounced its right to defend itself. The assembly conferred full military powers on Roselli and Garibaldi, jointly and severally. Garibaldi thus received the authority to continue the war in the provinces from a government that had declared itself legitimate. He was determined to do this and rejected the offer of safety on an American sloop from the ambassador of the United States. He arranged to see those who intended to continue the struggle with him in St. Peter's Square on 2 July.

In his *Memoirs* he recalled that he had already told Mazzini that it would be best "to leave Rome and march with all the available forces, materials, and means of transport, which were not inconsiderable, toward strong positions in the Apennines. . . . The people's representatives, who, for the most part, were young and energetic patriots much respected in their own constituencies, should be sent back to them where they could foment the population's patriotism, and find out what fortune would bring." He was forgetting that very few defenders had come from the countryside and during its march from Le Marche to Lazio the Legion had often encountered hostility. He also neglected the volunteers' exhaustion, as they were now worn out by weeks of constant fighting and demoralized by the useless sacrifice of so many brave young men. Very few of Manara's light infantry followed him, which demonstrates their misgivings over continuing a struggle that was clearly over.

Given his fame, Garibaldi's initiative caused a sensation and made people think again when they were on the point of giving up. The Dutch painter Jan Philip Koelman, who lived in Rome between 1846 and 1851 to follow his artistic career and vividly depicted many scenes of popular life in his memoirs, described the square crowded with volunteers, Roman soldiers, their families, and onlookers. Koelman had first learned of Garibaldi in May 1848 through a short biography containing his portrait, which circulated widely in Rome, and in his diary he expressed his skepticism over Garibaldi's splendid exploits in America and his supposed selflessness. Later he became convinced of the leader's exceptional nature. He had seen him in the convent where his men where billeted and he described him, like many had done before him, as "of medium stature and well built with wide shoulders and powerful chest clearly shown through his uniform jacket, which all gave the impression of a strong figure." He was greatly impressed by "the blue eyes tending toward purple" (we know they were actually brown), which "had an extraordinary quality both because of their color and because the candor of their expression." His eyes and his hair, which was "very light brown and flowed freely down to his shoulders," contrasted with the black eyes and hair of the men who surrounded him. "His thick, pointed and light-blond moustache gave a warrior-like touch to his open and oval face covered with freckles and bright red from the sun." In his opinion (an observation we have not found anywhere else) "the most distinctive feature . . . was the nose with its exceptionally wide bridge, which earned him the comparison with a lion, and he certainly did make you think of a lion. According to his soldiers, this resemblance was even more marked in battle, when his eyes caught fire and his blond hair bobbed around his head like a mane."

The painter took part in the defense of the republic and wrote in some detail about the epic battles against the French in his diary. He experienced the conclusion when the general called on them to continue the struggle, and produced a very effective account.

We could see Garibaldi's black plume in the midst of the undulating pressing crowd that was pouring out of Via del Borgo into St. Peter's Square. He was surrounded not by his own staff officers, because they were trapped in the crowd and were struggling vainly to reassemble, but by members of the middle class and women who crushed against him. He very slowly and with great effort managed to get to the Egyptian obelisk in the center of the square. There he stopped and turned his horse, and when his staff officers had gathered around him, he gestured with his hand that the cheering should cease. After this had continued with even greater force, complete silence fell upon the whole square. It was an awe-inspiring moment, and the behavior of that immense crowd before us was perfectly in harmony with the historical memories of the square in which it stood.

As usual, Garibaldi exhorted everyone to continue the fight, but his words were partly lost in the vastness of the square.

"Fortune, which today has betrayed us, will tomorrow smile on us,"— this was the substance of his speech. "I am leaving Rome. Those of you who wish to continue the war against the foreigner should come with me. I cannot offer you pay, quarter, or provisions; I can only offer you hunger, thirst, forced marches, battles, and death. Those of you, who have Italy's name not only on your lips but in your hearts as well, must follow me." He warned them grimly, "Once you have passed through the gate of Rome, one step backward will mean death."

This passionate tirade was greeted with acclamations, thunderous applause, the sound of swords being unsheathed and shouts of "We are all coming! You are Italy! Long Live Garibaldi!" He told them to gather in Lateran Square that evening, and at eight o'clock that evening a considerable force of about 4,700 men left Rome through Porta San Giovanni to the cheers, good wishes and blessing of the crowd.

Garibaldi was setting off on a very bold undertaking. Politically he was completely on his own. No government representative had joined the expedition. Mazzini did not perceive the initiative as grandiose as the government's and the assembly's continued prosecution of the war. He remained in Rome to demonstrate that he was not the hated tyrant depicted by the enemy propaganda. In mid-July he left for England, stopping at Marseille on the way. A demoralized Medici also sought refuge in England. Militarily Garibaldi was surrounded by overwhelming forces: 40,000 Frenchmen, 20,000 Neapolitans, 15,000 Austrians, 9,000 Spaniards and 2,000 Tuscans, in all 86,000 men. His men were mainly volunteers: the remains of his legion, a hundred odd Lombard light-infantrymen, the survivors of Masina's lancers, and a few hundred cavalrymen, mainly papal dragoons who had joined the republican forces. He no longer had his best officers, such as Daverio and Bixio, who were dead or wounded, or Medici, who had so bravely defended the Villa del Vascello. His was a bold act of defiance with little chance of success, and in this sense similar to the suicidal expedition to Costa Brava.

As always he prudently did not reveal his plans. In all probability, he was hoping to trigger a popular insurrection in Umbria and Tuscany, where there was widespread discontent with the Austrian occupation. On leaving Rome he headed for the Alban Hills, almost as though he wanted to march toward Capua against the Bourbon throne. Then he turned toward Tivoli, and there stopped to organize his forces. He created two legions, the first under his command and the second under that of Gaetano Sacchi, as well as a cavalry regiment at the orders of Colonel Ignazio Bueno, a brave legionnaire who had fought with him in Uruguay, and his Polish second-in-command Emil Müller. When the column was on the move, it was about five kilometers long. Garibaldi was usually at its head on his white horse along with some thirty horsemen. Then came the infantry, the baggage train, the ambulance, and an artillery piece pulled by two pairs of horses. The cavalry guarded the rear.

A French division of between seven and eight thousand men was on their tail, and in front of them laid a Spanish division and a Neapolitan division, each of the same size as the French one. These two divisions also had effective artillery support. Garibaldi used all his abilities in guerrilla warfare to keep them in check. His cavalry was particularly useful, as he could deploy small units and send them in different directions. This had three benefits: it kept him informed of enemy maneuvers, led the enemy to be believe he had more forces than was actually the case, and misled the enemy as to his intentions. Fortunately for him, his enemies were not coordinating their operations. Thus while the French, Spanish, and

Neapolitans were searching for him around the Castelli Romani and Terra di Lavoro, he pretended to move against the Abruzzi, but instead veered off to the north and escaped his pursuers. He abandoned his baggage train in Poggio Mirteto, and on 8 July reached Terni. The hope of a popular insurrection proved illusory, indeed many volunteers were deserting. In Terni he found a battalion recruited by the English colonel Hugh Forbes, which brought the numbers back over 4,000, and he was able to obtain supplies. The Austrians were approaching and the possible directions in which to march were being blocked off one by one.

He displayed his usual cunning by putting out the word that he intended to march to the Tuscan coast to embark for America. He then halted at Todi, where the cavalry intercepted a supply convoy on its way to the French army. He reached Orvieto on the morning of 15 July and left in the afternoon with the French on his heels. But the French decided to abandon the pursuit because they were far from their base camps, and this left the Austrians in pursuit. Garibaldi now faced twenty thousand Austrian and Tuscan soldiers, and decided to anticipate their moves. They were commanded by General D'Aspre, who he had come up against the previous summer in the area between Lake Maggiore and Varese. He crossed over into Tuscany and on the 17 July was warmly received in Cetona. His men and horses rested in the open and his officers were lodged in private houses. On the twentieth he entered Montepulciano, where he was again well received, but by that evening he was on the move again. In Torrita he notified his men that he had decided to go to Venice, which was still fighting. Continuous marches (usually eight hours by night and three hours in the afternoon), thirst, and the summer heat were exhausting his men. Many were deserting, and their numbers were halved. Major Müller had gone over to the enemy and his extremely loyal Colonel Bueno left during the night of 28 July taking his case and returning to America!

The populace was becoming hostile. They feared violence and theft, and not without good reason. On 5 July Garibaldi had threatened the death sentence against anyone guilty of theft "of objects of any value or nature," and personally executed a soldier caught stealing. The column had difficulty in obtaining provisions in Arezzo on 23 July. The daily supply of rations for nearly five thousand men was a terrible burden for these communities. Garibaldi had left with insufficient money, and what's more, it was in republican banknotes that Oudinot had recognized as valid only up until 10 July. As a legally appointed general, he used the powers with which he had been invested to demand the exchange of banknotes for coins, to requisition and to impose compulsory loans. In Tuscany his authority and money were running out.

The encirclement was closing in as he moved from the high reaches of the Tiber across the Apennines with the intention of reaching the Adriatic and sailing for Venice. The volunteers were at the end of their tether. The column had been reduced to 1,500 men with 300 horses. On the evening of 30 July, several hundred deserted under the rain on Mount Copiolo, at a thousand meters above sea level. Garibaldi finally gave up hope. He took the survivors on the extremely difficult march over the mountain ridges to the small republic of San Marino. On 31 July he declared to the captain regent that he was laying down his arms and had come "as a refugee." The captain regent promised hospitality and assistance, as well as humanitarian mediation with the Austrians concerning the safety of the survivors. The general gave orders that released his soldiers from the obligation to follow him, and he acknowledged that "the Roman war for Italian independence" was over.

The odyssey of Garibaldi and Anita, who accompanied him on his grueling march, was not finished. She had joined him at Villa Spada on 26 June at the height of the French bombardment. She had traveled by sea to Livorno, and then on to Rome by coach. With the fall of the republic, she had again not wanted to leave her husband. She dressed as a man, cut her hair and left with the volunteers in the uniform of an officer of the Legion. She rode in the advance guard at her husband's side. She was pregnant, and suffered more than the others from the endless hardships. At Cetona, she was billeted in the home of the *gonfaloniere* or chief magistrate, and was finally able to change her clothes and wear feminine ones that had been made for her. She did not discard her customary boldness. Even at the gates of San Marino, the "American Amazon" shouted her contempt for the cowards in the rear-guard who fled before an attack by Austrian patrols.

"A most dear and extremely painful hindrance was my Anita, who was far advanced in her pregnancy and unwell," Garibaldi would write. The hindrance arose from the fact that he had decided to avoid capture and continue the fight. *La guerra es la verdadera vida del hombre.* He could not see any future that did not involve fighting. A few days earlier he had reached forty-two years of age. His athletic physique had already recovered from the tremendous exertions he had gone through. After so much suffering, he and his wife were billeted in two rooms as guests of Lorenzo Simoncini, the owner of a café. Just when Anita could finally rest, she was struck down by a high fever. It would have been prudent of her to stay in bed, but this would have meant parting from her husband who was thinking of leaving San Marino. The Austrians were imposing harsh conditions: surrender of arms, return of officers and men under an armed escort to places of birth, and Garibaldi's departure for America. He rejected them in agreement with his officers. He was thinking of reaching Venice, the last symbol of liberty in Italy. The city would finally capitulate on 22 August. He quietly put the word around that he intended to leave, but without any publicity that could have put the Austrians on their guard. He left San Marino during the night with about 200 men, a hundred of whom were on horseback. Those who remained, who numbered more than a thousand, had to wait for months before being able to leave the small republic.

His group included Anita. He had begged her to stay "in that land of refuge," but in vain. "That generous and stout-hearted woman became indignant at each of my warnings concerning this matter, and forced me into silence with the words, 'You want to leave me.'" Her obstinacy was understandable. She was alone in a foreign land, whose language she could barely speak and without her friends from Uruguay, who were either dead or on the march with Garibaldi as they, too, had nowhere else to go.

The fugitives marched along little-used pathways, and some of them got lost. Gustav Hoffstetter fell behind and abandoned the enterprise to return to Zurich. After twenty-three hours and into the following night, the remains of the detachment reached Cesenatico on the Adriatic. A worker called Nicola Zani had acted as their guide from San Marino, and a young man from Forlì took over when they approached the coast. Anita suffered from a high fever and was racked by thirst. She was given a melon, a fruit in season. One of the brief stops involved resting with her husband in priest's parish house in Musano, and the church authorities would later reconsecrate the church they considered to have been contaminated by an enemy of the papacy.

In the fishing port of Cesenatico, Garibaldi intended to find a boat to reach Venice. A small garrison of papal gendarmes and Austrian soldiers was surprised while they slept. The fishermen were also asleep and the intruders had to wake them to open the stores for provisions. Garibaldi's men then requisitioned thirteen fishing boats, the distinctive local *bragozzi*. These were sufficient to take everyone, the provisions, and the fishermen who were forced to come on board. Fortune abandoned the bold expedition. A storm blew up and prevented them from leaving the port. They needed several exhausting attempts and complex maneuvers before they finally succeeded and these required all of Garibaldi's supreme knowledge of seamanship, "with sleepy and unwilling men who had to be hit with the flat of a sword before they would move or provide the necessary." By leaving the mainland, Garibaldi was obliged to abandon his horse. He left strict instructions that it should not fall into Austrian hands.

The day was well advanced by the time the boats were out to sea. It was 2 August and the weather was now excellent. They had sufficient provisions, but lacked water. Anita in particular was suffering from thirst. They sailed along the coast throughout the day, and the night unfortunately was splendidly calm and clear. Not far from Goro Point (only about eighty kilometers from Venice, the moonlight revealed their little fleet to an Austrian brig, the *Oreste*, which was supported by some smaller vessels. The squadron maneuvered into a position closer to the *bragozzi*, and intimidated the fishermen with cannon fire, given that they were in no mood for risking their lives. Garibaldi gave orders to approach land where there were sandbanks that would bar the way to the ships. The owners of the boats, however, refused to cooperate, and eight *bragozzi* fell into enemy hands. One hundred and sixty-two legionnaires were captured and taken as prisoners to Pula. Three boats offloaded their unwanted passengers and returned to sea to give themselves up. Two, with Garibaldi, and thirty odd volunteers ran aground in the shallows. He took Anita in his arms, lowered himself into the water up to his chest, and then waded for four hundred meters to the beach. All hope of bringing a group of combatants to assist Venice was now definitively lost. Even Garibaldi realized this, and finally faced the facts. He took leave of his comrades, who included the Barnabite chaplain for Garibaldi's men, Ugo Bassi, and Captain Giovanni Livraghi, who had returned from Montevideo on the *Speranza*.

These two were shot by firing squad in Bologna, where the archbishop, monsignor Bedini, who two years earlier had been the papal nuncio in Rio, allowed the Austrians to apply rules of warfare. Angelo Brunetti, who was also called Ciceruacchio and the most famous of the popular leaders in Rome, and his sons, Luigi and thirteen-year-old Lorenzo, were caught on the road to Venice by the Austrians and executed by firing squad.

> I stayed close to the sea in a maize field with my Anita, and my inseparable comrade, Lieutenant Leggero, ... The three of us remained in that maize field for some time, uncertain what to do next. Finally I told Leggero to advance a little toward the interior in search of a house in the vicinity.

Garibaldi had landed not very far from Magnavacca, not on the mainland but on one of the islands in the Comacchio Lagoon, and this complicated their escape. Leggero, a recruit from Montevideo whose real name was Giovan Battista Coliolo, was wounded and his resulting limp was a further complication. When he returned, however, he brought a friendly face, that of Colonel Nino Bonnet, who had met Garibaldi the previous year in Ravenna. He belonged to a patriotic family. His two brothers had fought in Rome: Gaetano had died in battle and Raimondo had followed his general as far as San Marino. Nino had heard the cannon fire and rushed toward the beech. He called on the assistance of Battista Barillari, also known as Baramoro, a poor man in search of driftwood and other items washed up on the shore. The three fugitives headed for a nearby farmhouse, and Garibaldi and Baramoro carried Anita, who was finally able to quench her thirst. The two men removed their red shirts and put on the ragged clothes of a peasant.

Bonnet returned to the boats with the intention of recovering something, but the place was crawling with Austrians. He changed his mind and went back to the farmhouse with the news that they had to leave urgently. It was eight o'clock, and the sun was still low. The group had a distressful two-hour journey on foot and covered a distance of about two kilometers (the tradition asserts that Anita rode on a donkey). They halted at Cavallina. Garibaldi was still thinking of reaching Venice. Bonnet persuaded him that it was impossible, and offered to take him to safety in Tuscany. He insisted that he had to leave Anita behind, as she would not have been able to put up with the hardships of their flight. She seemed resigned to her fate, and they started off on their journey again. Anita was placed on a cart pulled by oxen. At the Zanetto farm at the edge of the Comacchio Lagoon, which had to be crossed by boat, she was assisted by the lady of the house, Teresa De Carli Patrignani. She rested on a bed and Garibaldi dressed in some of Bonnet's clothes. In the evening the boat procured by Bonnet arrived to take Garibaldi across the lagoon. Anita clung to her husband and he gave in. "You cannot imagine what and how many things this woman has done for me . . . and what affection she holds me in! I have for her an immense debt of gratitude and love . . . . Let her follow me!" he said to Bonnet.

Then everything became more difficult. As the boatmen became suspicious and were frightened of Austrian reprisals, they dumped their passengers halfway along their journey near a shack at Tabarra d'Agosta. However, they did not report their passengers to the authorities. Bonnet, who got word of this, was able to obtain assistance from more courageous boatmen. They set off again at eight in the morning on 4 August. After five hours they reached Chiavica di Mezzo, on the northern bank of the Po di Primaro. Anita was in agony and Garibaldi asked the weir keepers' children to get her some soup. They killed a hen, but Anita who was now suffering from convulsions was unable to take the soup made from it. They needed to cross the Po and travel three kilometers. It was impossible transport Anita over such a distance. Battista Manelli, a carter and Italian nationalist known to Garibaldi, was called upon to provide his services. Anita was settled on a mattress and cushions on the cart. She was dying.

The carter led his cart along slowly under the afternoon sun. An inconsolable Garibaldi walked alongside and used a handkerchief to wipe away the white frothy liquid that dribbled from Anita's lips. A doctor was waiting for them in the evening at the farm of the Ravaglia family in Mandriole. Four people took a corner of the mattress and carried the dying woman into the Ravaglia's bedroom. "As I placed my woman on the bed, I felt I could see the physiognomy of death on her face. I felt her pulse . . . it was no longer beating! My children's mother, who I love so much, was a corpse before me!"

It was a miserable death that ended a miserable life. She died on a cart or on someone else's bed, wearing clothes given to her out of charity and far from her homeland and family. She left everyone behind, included her children that she loved, and she had their father promise to do his best for them during one of her last moments of lucidity. She had wanted to stay close to her husband right up to the end, as he was the great passion of her life. The only comfort was that he was next to her during her last moments.

Her tragic end was described in tones of Christian piety by a member of the clergy who was charged with sending a report to the archbishop of Ravenna, Cardinal Falconieri: in the Papal States the religious authorities also had civil and political roles. "At this unexpected blow," wrote the priest who interrogated the witnesses, "the loving husband became motionless from his terrible suffering and then he broke into the most bitter wailing, which could not be stopped by the vain attempts of bystanders to comfort him. . . . He would have liked her to have had an honorable Christian burial. He begged that she be taken to Ravenna to receive a proper funeral, yet with what means, if he, so wretched and miserable, did not a have a single coin with which to pay for the cart on which he had place his devoted wife?"

In fact Manelli would not accept payment. Everyone around him was crying and entreating him to flee. He went down the stairs, but then came rushing back to the corpse. "It was difficult for him to leave, because that was the most bitter moment of his life so far, the one that divided him forever from his beloved companion. . . . He climbed the stairs, entered the room, saw the cold corpse and threw himself upon it with all his soul that dissolved through his eyes into bitter tears." He took off her coat, sandals, handkerchief and ring, which he offered to the farmer. The latter rejected them and felt that Garibaldi should keep them as a memento. He went back down the stairs, and asked reassurance of everyone there that she would have a proper burial. "On the point of complete exhaustion, he asked if they would be so good as to give him a piece of bread."

The misfortunes of that intense early August were not over. They were not even over for Anita. A regular burial of a woman who was not local would have attracted attention. That same evening as the sun went down, the Ravaglia brothers wrapped the dead body in a sheet, loaded it on a cart, hurriedly dug a shallow grave on uncultivated ground less than a kilometer from the farm, placed the body inside, and covered it with a little earth. Six days later, a girl who was playing nearby saw a hand and a forearm, which had been gnawed by animals, protruding from the sand. She ran in horror to her father who notified the gendarmes. The body was disinterred, examined and dissected by the medical examiner. She was recognized as the women who accompanied Garibaldi and quickly buried because of the advanced state of decomposition. The parish priest for Mandriole was authorized by the bishop to accept her body for burial in the local cemetery.

The doctor who carried out the autopsy thought that he found signs of strangulation. The Ravaglias were arrested for "complicity in the alleged murder of the unknown woman of the well-known Garibaldi" and for harboring a wanted man. Fortunately the magistrate acquitted them. After a few weeks they were released, but their adversities continued. The rumor went around that the fugitive had abandoned treasure. The most terrifying brigand in Romagna, Stefano Pelloni also known as *Il Passatore*, rushed to the farm, turned the house upside down, and threatened, and beat Stefano Ravaglia, the head of the household who had been absent on the 4 August, to make him reveal the hiding place of the nonexistent treasure.

Nino Bonnet's position proved to be more serious. He was arrested by the Austrians on 5 August and taken to the civil rather than the military prison in Ravenna. This probably saved his life because it delayed his transfer to Bologna "to face a firing squad," as announced by the *Monitore di Bologna* on 9 August. General Gorzkowski, who had issued menacing proclamations and insisted on the execution of Ugo Bassi, was replaced by General Strassoldo. Now the alarm was over, the Austrians were interested in reestablishing better relations with the local population and producing some signs of normalization. Even though he had saved Garibaldi, Bonnet was a free man again in September.

The main fugitive evaded capture, and on the evening of 4 August Garibaldi and Leggero left Mandriole on a cart. They changed their hiding place three times during the night. Austrians and papal gendarmes, who had received a tip-off, searched houses in the area. A young man, Ercole Saldini, led the hunted men across fields, had them ferried across the Po di Primaro, and rested them in the extensive pine wood near Ravenna. On 6 August they were moved to Capanno del Pontaccio. The irrepressible Garibaldi asked yet again to be taken to Venice, and yet again the patriots who took care of him explained that with Austrian troops crawling over the entire territory this would amount to suicide. The least dangerous route led to Tuscany. In Capanno, Garibaldi and Leggero were joined by republicans from Ravenna. Partly on foot and partly by boat, the two men reached a farm on the outskirts of Ravenna. For greater safety they changed their lodgings several times. On the night of 15 August, they were taken to Forlì, and then in a gig to Terra del Sole.

At this point, the parish priest of Modigliana, Don Giovanni Verità, enters the scene. "A true Christian priest," Garibaldi would write later, ". . . from the moment a man persecuted by priests for his love of Italy approached that district, he made it his job to protect him, feed him, and take him or have him taken to safety from those persecutions." Verità personally took care of Garibaldi. Along the road to Modigliana he waded through a stream swollen by the rain with Leggero on his shoulders. Garibaldi refused assistance with the words, "Water has long been my acquaintance." His guide replied, "Seawater, not the water of our dangerous gullies." The seaman gave in and was carried across. They were sheltered in the priest's home for a couple of days, dressed in hunters' clothes. To cross the Apennines, Don Verità chose inaccessible paths that were not guarded. They engaged a mule driver, nicknamed Pius IX, who in turn called one of the mules Garibaldi. When the general heard his name shouted, he gave his identity away but fortunately was not betrayed. They reached the ridge of the Apennines, not far from the Filigare Pass where in November 1848 Garibaldi and his legion had asked permission to pass through the Papal States.

Due to a mishap they then lost their guide. Don Verità went to look for an acquaintance of his and left them in a secluded place. He was late in returning and the two feared that he was unable to show up. As they were now in the Grand Duchy of Tuscany and close to the busy road between Bologna and Florence, they hired a gig to take them to a tavern in Santa Lucia allo Stale. Austrian soldiers entered but did not recognize them. Other units were arriving and the two men took refuge in a hut where they slept on straw. Having lost Don Giovanni Verità, they did not know how to contact the patriots that were to take them to safety. They took a lift on another cart and then were accompanied by a peasant toward Prato. In a country hotel they met a civil engineer specialized in road-building called Enrico Sequi, who was hunting in the area. Garibaldi revealed his identity and luckily the young man turned out to be a liberal. He put them back in contact with the organization that helped political refugees to leave the country.

It was not prudent to attempt entering the Kingdom of Sardinia over the mountains close to La Spezia, as the Austrians were policing them very carefully. Sequi, who would be arrested and imprisoned for over two months, advised them to go by sea. He took them to Prato, and entrusted them to others. Garibaldi gave him Anita's wedding ring as a memento. From Prato, they left in a closed carriage for Poggibonsi, and from there to Colle Val d'Elsa, to a seaside resort at Bagno al Morbo and finally to San Dalmazio in Maremma, where they stayed for four days in the opulent home of Doctor Camillo Signorini. Garibaldi passed the time reading Vittorio Alfieri's autobiography.

On the evening of 1 September, the escape plan was put into action. The fugitives were taken near to the coast. At sunrise on the following day a group of men pretending to be hunters went to Cala Martina, close to Follonica. Paolo Azzarini's boat, *Madonna dell'Arena*, was waiting for them with a crew of six. Garibaldi displayed an almost childlike joy on seeing the sea, and took his shoes off to paddle in the water. In a very emotional state, he thanked the men who had saved him and wished to compensate them in some way. They asked him for a piece of his handkerchief to remember him by. The boat stopped at Elba, and its owner had two men go ashore to keep the number of the crew unchanged and the passengers to count now as crew. He had a travel license issued illegally.

The small vessel did not go into the open sea but sailed up the coast, although they went wide of Livorno. On the morning of 5 September the boat arrived at Porto Venere in the Gulf of La Spezia, which was friendly territory, and Garibaldi was safe. On 7 September he wrote from Genoa to Don Giovanni Verità, "the bales of silk arrived safely." "It was truly a miracle that he managed to save himself this time," La Marmora would comment.

14. The Gray Years

IN SEPTEMBER 1849 the Kingdom of Sardinia was the only possible refuge in Italy for a freedom-fighter. During the early months of the year, the constitutional regimes had ended their short lives in Naples, Rome, and Florence, and Lombardy-Venetia were once again under Austrian domination. Only the House of Savoy kept faith with the concessions that had been made in the Kingdom of Sardinia. Victor Emanuel II, who succeeded to the throne of his father, Charles Albert, promised in a proclamation to "consolidate our constitutional institutions," which meant maintaining the parliament, political parties, and freedom of the press. There was no shortage of tensions at home and abroad. When the armistice was announced on 27 March, Genoa rose up and demanded a continuation of the war, and following a brief siege the rebellion was quelled militarily by General Alfonso La Marmora's troops on 10 April. One of the rebel leaders was General Avezzana, the commander of the National Guard in the city, who left for Rome on an American ship after the capitulation. There was an urgent need to lessen the residual resentment in the country, and at the same time conclude a peace with Austria without angering it by untimely manifestations of patriotism. Massimo D'Azeglio, who was appointed prime minister in May, started the process of normalization and settling the outstanding matters resulting from the war.

Among the possible causes of the disturbance to public order was the return of volunteers who compromised themselves in the defense of Rome, which also risked damaging relations with France. On 6 July, the minister of the interior, Pier Dionigi Pinelli, instructed the authorities not to allow them to enter the country, particularly "Mazzini, Garibaldi, Mameli, [and] Bixio." Garibaldi had not been able to follow developments in the political situation in Piedmont—as we shall call the Kingdom of Sardinia for reasons of brevity—either when he was in Rome or, still less, during July and August given that he was entirely absorbed with the expedition that ended in San Marino, the attempt to reach Venice from Cesenatico, and his lucky escape through Tuscany. However, his memory of the treatment he had received in 1848 at the hands of Charles Albert and his Piedmontese generals was hardly of comfort to him.

I had no doubt of the unfavorable reception I would encounter from the government in the Sardinian States, and it occurred to me on the way past Livorno harbor to ask asylum on board a British ship that was riding at anchor. However, the desire to see my children before leaving Italy, where I knew I would not be able to stay, prevailed and in September we went ashore to safety in Porto Venere.

On the evening of the fifth he arrived in Chiavari, where he had been elected a member of parliament (for the constituency of Cicagna). But he no longer held that position because the chamber had been dissolved by D'Azeglio, and new elections had been held in July. He found lodgings in an inn and later with relatives, and was greeted by the inhabitants with the same warmth as he had been the year before. The quartermaster for Chiavari found him at supper in the presence of about twenty people and had him recount his adventures, "while the audience listened to his story not without a few surprises; it was a curious episode in the extremely curious history of these times." News of his arrival spread around Liguria. The Genoese democrats prepared a great welcome.

The events of 1849 had increased his fame in both Italy and the rest of Europe. The democrats, who had won the elections in the Kingdom of

Sardinia, were keeping the patriotic ferment alive. The press, which had remained free, had provided considerable coverage of the defense of Rome
and the deeds of its most famous defender. While the Royal Army had collapsed before the Austrian troops, which following the armistice had set up
a garrison in Alessandria, Garibaldi, by his heroism, had restored Italy's
military honor. The newspapers had enthusiastically followed his incredible incursion among well-armed enemy armies and anxiously reported the
little news they had on his fate during August. It was not so much news as a
series of speculations. On 16 August *La Concordia* of Turin even reported
that Garibaldi had arrived in Venice with Anita, and provided details of
how he was received by the population, Daniele Manin (the moving spirit
behind the resistance), and his wife. Was this a colossal mistake or an attempt to put the Austrians off the scent? On 21 August, *Il Fischietto* published a cartoon deriding the Austrians who had let their prey slip through
their hands, although at the time their failure was only probable. Artfully
distorted news of his sojourns in towns, the imposition of levies, and threats
against the clergy were reported in the press in the countries that had returned to absolutism, such as Tuscany, which had been directly affected by
the incursion. The Austrians themselves had contributed to the increased
fame of the elusive guerrilla by publishing wanted notices against him,
which appeared in the official press in Milan and other capitals on the Italian peninsula, and were then reproduced in foreign papers along with criticisms of the Austrian repression.

As had occurred in the case of Uruguay, the direct intervention of the
great powers had raised international profile of the Italian events. The
misadventures of the head of the Catholic Church had religious repercussions and mobilized public opinion, parliaments, and the press, particularly in France where the armed intervention demanded by Napoleon was
violently challenged by the democratic opposition and supported by Catholics. *L'Illustration* in March produced a lithograph depicting the proclamation of the republic in Rome. In April–May it illustrated the departure
of the French expedition, the landing in Civitavecchia, and the entrance
of the advance guard into Rome, and believing the march would not encounter any obstacles, the illustrator allowed himself to be led by his imagination. On 26 May the first page showed a portrait of "Garibaldi, général
romain." It followed Italian affairs carefully throughout the summer and

in August reported news of Garibaldi's flight from Rome, while speculating on an engagement between him and the Austrian fleet. It then reported his arrival in Venice where he was received "with acclamations," and when the Venetian Republic fell he was supposed to have fled to Dalmatia.

Britain was opposed to the papacy because of its own Anglican confession and was hostile to an excessive Austrian dominance of the Italian peninsula. It was also worried about the presence of socialists in the republican leadership, and the events in Rome in particular had attracted a great deal of interest. The *Times* sent a special envoy who took an unfavorable view of the republican government, but did not hide his admiration for Garibaldi and his ability to hold the line against superior forces. A current of opinion sympathetic to the Roman Republic formed in the United States.

Apart from political considerations, the conflict caught the public's imagination, as military operations on this scale in the heart of Europe had not occurred since the end of the Napoleonic Wars. Detailed accounts of military events, in which Garibaldi played a considerable part, appeared in the foreign press, and not just the French and British press, while foreigners in the city sent private letters with comments on and impressions of the defenders' behavior. For these reasons it would not have been easy to push a popular leader in the defense of Rome to the margins, given that his movements continued to be an object of great interest to the foreign presses even after he had returned home safe and sound. Once he arrived in Liguria by unknown means, the problem became one of rendering him politically inoffensive. Garibaldi was depressed and dispirited, and had already decided to leave his native land. He intended only to stay a few days in Liguria and go to Nice to visit his family. He put up no resistance to the precautionary measures taken against him by the authorities.

General La Marmora, who was still in Genoa with the powers of extraordinary commissioner, feared "some kind of rowdy demonstration." La Marmora had Garibaldi arrested during the night with his inseparable Leggero, and had him moved to Genoa in a closed carriage. According to the authorities, Garibaldi adopted a "prudent conduct" and used "his surprising influence" to calm the crowds that formed at each stop to cheer for him and curse the king, the government, and the *carabinieri* who accompanied him.

At four in the morning on 7 September, he was locked up in a room in the Ducal Palace, and an official informed him that the government wished him to leave the country. Garibaldi assured them that he was quite willing to emigrate very soon but first desired to visit his family in Nice as a free man. La Marmora understood that it was impossible to stop him from seeing his family "so that the opposition would not *exploit* this circumstance to start decrying a state of tyranny and making Garibaldi the victim." This fear was well founded, as at the same time, the Chiavari town council was sending a petition to parliament in support of Garibaldi. It was treated as urgent and debated on 10 September. Many leading members of parliament took part in the debate, including the future prime ministers Giovanni Lanza, Urbano Rattazzi, and Agostino Depretis. Angelo Brofferio obtained a massive majority for a motion censuring the government, because the general's arrest and threatened expulsion were "violations of the rights enshrined in the Statute and the sentiments of nationality and Italian glory." In order to ensure parliamentary immunity, his supporters presented Garibaldi as candidate at the by-election for Recco.

Garibaldi did not exploit this support. He cooperated with the authorities to avoid demonstrations in his favor, and this led to some subterfuges. To get to Nice he boarded a naval ship, the *San Michele*, which was lying at anchor in the port, and then he transferred to the *San Giorgio*, which provided a regular service between Genoa and Nice. They made him wait for several hours in Nice for bureaucratic formalities. In spite of all the precautions, he was greeted by a vast and adoring crowd. The meeting with his seventy-three-year-old mother was an emotional affair. It seemed very likely that they would never see each other again. He stayed with his children for as long as possible, and did not have the courage to tell them what had happened to Anita. It was painful to leave: the boys were with his cousin Augusto Garibaldi, the little girl with the Deideri family, and Menotti would continue his education in boarding school.

In Genoa he remained on board the frigate *San Michele*, commanded by Carlo Persano, whom he would meet again later in Naples in 1860. He had accepted a government pension for his family and had brought two thousand lira for his mother. Initially he had also refused one for himself, as was his typical of his character. During his difficult times in August, he had politely rejected the donations offered him by wealthy patriots. But now the uncertainty over his future was becoming a burden. He felt drained. "I believe we are in submissive times, because they are disastrous times," he wrote to Lorenzo Valerio on leaving Genoa. He ended up accepting a pension of 300 lira a month during his sojourn in Tunis where the Piedmontese government hoped he would stay. He was also paid an advance of 1,200 lira. Ultimately he decided it was right that the state should provide for someone who had sacrificed everything for the nationalist ideal.

La Marmora went to visit him on the *San Michele*. Like many others before him, he was greatly impressed by a man who had become famous as a revolutionary. He wrote to General Dabormida:

> Garibaldi is no ordinary man. His physiognomy, although coarse, is very expressive. He does not talk much but he speaks well. He is very discerning. I am increasingly persuaded that he threw himself into the republican cause in order to fight and because his services had been rejected. Nor do I believe him to be a republican in principle. It was a terrible mistake not to make use of him. If another war were needed, he would be a useful man to have on our side.

For the moment war seemed far off. Garibaldi left for Tunis on 16 September on the naval steamship *Tripoli* in the company of Leggero and Luigi Cucelli, the Italian Legion's musician who had come with him from Montevideo. In Tunis the government would not allow him to come ashore, because they did not want to harm their relations with France. The possibility of taking him to Malta came to nothing. The steamship set off for Cagliari, but the governor did not want him to stay in his city (on the eighteenth, during a brief stop, dozens of boats approached the ship and the Garibaldi spoke to them from the deck), and on 25 September the governor had him taken to the Isle of Maddalena to the northeast of Sardinia where Leggero had been born and Francesco Susini lived. Francesco was the father of Antonio Susini who had taken over command of the Legion in Montevideo. There he could do no harm, although there was fear that he would make a sudden return to the political scene. Garibaldi and his comrades remained on the small island for a month, where they were watched over from a distance and treated well by the local authorities. This was the first respite from his troubles, and on leaving he wrote to Susini, "I have rediscovered peace in my soul anguished by the vicissitudes of a tempestuous life.

It was not easy for Garibaldi to settle, nor did he have any clear idea of where he wanted to go, although he had thoughts about London or the United States. The Piedmontese government still had fears about his popularity, and there had been another collection in the kingdom for another sword to honor him, which would be presented to his cousin Augusto. The government obtained permission from Britain, which was open to exiles from all nations, to land in Gibraltar, while waiting to choose his destination, and paid him another thousand lira to cover the predictable problems involved. On 24 October, the little group left on the naval brig *Colombo*, and arrived on 9 November. A surly governor ignored his government's instructions and only allowed him a brief stay. It was the beginning of winter, and Garibaldi, who was demoralized, suffering from ill health and had lived in hot climates for many years, did not find the cold climate to his liking. On 14 November he accepted the chance to travel to Tangiers on the Spanish ship *Nerea*.

As a guest of the Sardinian consul, Giovan Battista Carpanetti, he "experienced a peaceful and happy life, as far as an Italian exile can be peaceful and happy far from his dear ones and his native land. At least twice a week we went hunting and bagged an abundance of game. Then a friend put a *guzzetto* [small boat] at my disposal, and we also went on fishing trips along that coast where fishing was very good." "While awaiting some useful employment, I lived as a hunter," he wrote to his cousin in January 1850. "On my last hunting trip, I killed a wild boar. I am also the scourge of the rabbits." Such a leisurely life could not have satisfied him indefinitely. He wrote in April 1850 to his friend Francesco Carpaneto:

In the last few days, I have wanted to go for a trip around the Bay of Gibraltar without any other purpose than that of being on the move and fishing, perhaps just to prove that I am still a good seaman. But it was impressed upon me that diplomacy, the Governor of Gibraltar, and whatever else . . . . For the moment, I am allowed Africa, which would be a great deal if the people who have been given the official task of giving me a pain in the ass understood that we are a long way from the times of the knights errant when people only had to think about righting wrongs and never about where the next meal was coming from. Even if I were to take work as a seaman, I would encounter difficulties arising from these diplomatic scruples. But as I have gone through much worse, I will not let this drive me crazy, and they will have their work cut out if they want to starve Garibaldi to death.

After many years of fighting wars, Garibaldi was presented with the problem of finding a professional activity that reflected his skills and conformed to his agreed permanent residence outside Italy. While awaiting the possibility of work, however uncertain, he set about writing an autobiography. Memoirs of the events of 1848 and writings that defended them or reflected upon them were publishing successes, as the whole of Europe was interested in them. He thought that a publisher might be willing to pay him for an account of his fantastic adventures. He started work on this project while still in Maddalena, and he returned to it in Tangiers, partly to pass the time.

In early 1850 Cuneo published the *Biography of Giuseppe Garibaldi* in Turin. It was a pamphlet of 94 pages, a concise but effective political account of his character and the principal events of his life from childhood to his second exile. It was a response to the campaign of the moderates against the democrats, who were beaten in Piedmont in the elections of December 1849. Using a lively journalistic style, Cuneo summarized his support for Mazzini's ideas (but not his Saint-Simonianism), the expedition of the *Mazzini*, his involvement in the cause of Rio Grande, the war in Uruguay, his campaigns in Italy during 1848–49, and his exile in Tangiers. He emphasized the high esteem in which he was held by many foreigners, such as Admiral Lainé, Lord Howden, and, more recently, Pacheco. Cuneo concluded with a long panegyric on Garibaldi's commitment to civilized values not only in relation to Italy, although Italy was his preference. "Motherland and humanity" had always been "the goal for which he struggled." He had therefore defended the American cause "with the same ardor with which he took arms in Lombardy and Rome." He wanted Italy to gain its freedom through its own efforts, because he believed that Italy needed "to rehabilitate itself in world opinion by strong and magnanimous acts."

"As a man who believes in humanity, he hopes for a brotherhood of peoples in the future, but he wishes to sit at the banquet of nations as an equal or not at all." For this purpose he was ready to return "as the thunderbolt of war to give new glories to his country, new reasons to be hated by the evil and, let God confirm this wishful prophecy, the final blow to the Austrian in flight across the Alps!"

Garibaldi had no intention of stirring up controversy. He thanked Cuneo for sending him the pamphlet and continued to write on the more adventurous aspects of his life, which he believed would be of more interest to those who were not interested in politics. Alongside the autobiography, he wrote biographical sketches of "the most important fellow combatants in America and Italy from 1833 to 1849," who had fallen in battle. In April–May he sent the first samples to his cousin and Carpaneto in the hope that they would find a publisher, but their replies were disappointing. Carpaneto advised him to touch on recent events, something that Garibaldi did not intend to do, partly because the obligation to write the truth might have tarnished the fame of men who one day might be of use to Italy and partly because the events were not entirely clear and he therefore risked providing imprecise information. "If I were obliged to write for history," he declared, "I would really want to be as scrupulous as possible and try to resist the craze for writing that is sadly all too common among us." Hence the attempt to earn money by writing in Tangiers turned out to be fruitless.

In late 1849 and early 1850 he was presented with the possibility of returning to Montevideo. The war between Argentina and Uruguay was still continuing. Pacheco was sent to Paris to consolidate support for Uruguay in France. Rosas's supporters, of whom there were many in the French capital, attacked him and brought up atrocities committed by the unionists. The dispute ended up with a libel action in the courts. Garibaldi's name came up, and he was attacked as a cruel adventurer and murderer of the French in Rome, while Pacheco defended him as a brave and chivalrous soldier. Alexandre Dumas made himself the champion of the Uruguayan cause in his book, *Montevideo, ou une nouvelle Troie*, in which he paid homage to Garibaldi, while regretting the fact that in 1849 he became an enemy of the French. Garibaldi therefore continued to be the subject of much discussion, and his name was associated with the war in Uruguay. The return to Montevideo appeared a reasonable solution to his precarious situation. In a letter to Valerio published by *La Concordia* on 21 September, Pacheco reminded everyone that Garibaldi was still "a general of the [Uruguayan] republic to whose fate he was linked by his glorious service." He also wrote to Garibaldi personally. The Piedmontese government was also thinking about establishing a colony in Uruguay for its own population and entrusting it to Garibaldi. However, this plan risked stirring up opposition in France, which had many interests of its own in the country, and Garibaldi did not encourage the dialogue with Pacheco. He had been very disappointed with the behavior of the Uruguayan political class, and there was no question of him returning as an ordinary citizen. He did not take up the offer.

Instead he wanted to move to North America and there return to his career in the merchant navy. In Genoa, Carpaneto "devised a plan to collect sufficient funds from persons known to him and to myself to build a ship which would be under my command and would provide me with a living." Ideally the ship, a four or five-ton sailing ship, would be built in the United States and sail under an American flag, if the Piedmontese authorities refused to issue him with the captain's ticket they had withdrawn at the time of the Genoa incident in 1836. Garibaldi intended to oversee the construction of the ship and personally conduct the negotiations for it purchase. In June of 1850 he left Tangiers without Leggero and Cucelli, but took Major Paolo Campeggi Bovi, who was "unable to work because he didn't have a right hand" and had lost it in the defense of Rome. On the thirteenth he stopped in Gibraltar and on the twenty-second he reached Liverpool, where on the twenty-seventh he sailed for New York on the sailing ship *Waterloo*, which brought him to his destination in thirty-three days.

During the crossing Garibaldi suffered from rheumatic pains. On the morning of 30 July, he could no longer move and was lowered "like a trunk . . . from a hoist" onto Staten Island, where travelers from abroad had to undergo a short quarantine. Over the previous few decades, New York had become a city of 700,000 inhabitants, the country's financial center and a great port connected by channels to the river systems of the interior and equipped with quays and shipyards of considerable importance. It had mainly relied on immigration from Europe, and there were many exiles and no shortage of democrats of every nationality. There was also a large Italian colony. General Avezzana had been honored with great pomp and put up in the Astor Hotel. A committee was set up for Garibaldi, "a man of worldwide fame, the hero of Montevideo and the defender of Rome" (*New York Daily Tribune*, 30 July 1850), and an occasion of similar importance was planned. To honor him they came up with the idea of a tricolor cockade decorated with Mazzini's words "God and the People," a Phrygian cap and the wording "Honor to the champion of liberty in both the hemispheres." This title was a precursor to the one that became so much a part of the Garibaldi legend: "the hero of two worlds."

On Staten Island, Garibaldi was carried on people's arms to a divan, where he was received by a crowd of visitors. With his usual modesty, he rejected any kind of welcoming ceremony and found accommodation at Hastings, about fifteen miles from the city. In the *New York Daily Tribune* of 7 August, he reaffirmed his rejection of any kind of ceremony however great the gratification would have been for him, "exiled from my native land, separated from my children, and lamenting the overturning of my country's liberty by means of foreign intervention." He hoped to become a "citizen of this great Republic of Free Men, sail under its flag, follow a career that will allow me to earn my living and await a more favorable occasion to free my country from its domestic and foreign oppressors."

"Earning my living" turned out to be anything but easy, while awaiting the funds that Carpaneto hoped to collect. After a fortnight he went to live with Felice Foresti, in the house of an Italian, Michele Pastacaldi.

The proposed ceremonies to honor him created something of a sensation, and his name was already known because of the encounters with American shipping during his days as a privateer on the River Plate. His exploits had turned him into a romantic figure. Harro Harring's novel, *Dolores*, which had been published only a few years earlier, was mainly devoted to the subject of Garibaldi. Sensing a story, the journalist and publisher Theodore Dwight went to visit him and asked him for a few pages on his adventures. Garibaldi handed over the manuscript of the memoirs written in Tangiers, which concerned his early exploits up to the expedition to Costa Brava. However, he did not authorize their publication and would not do so until 1859. Instead he published the biographical sketches of his fallen comrades. Here he did not keep to his commitment not to discuss recent history. In his biography of Anita, he recalled her courage during the withdrawal from Rome, and described her as an "American Amazon, a martyr for Italian freedom." In his biography of Ugo Bassi, he railed against the Catholic Church. During the defense of the Roman Republic, he had become fiercely anticlerical, because he had been able to observe the clergy's aversion to the national cause. Most of the clergy were loyal to the pope and therefore allies of the Austrians who, with the French, had put him back on his throne. In his words, the priests had guided the Austrian bullets and sold Bassi's life to protect their own interests, just as they had betrayed Italy. Italy's true religion was the one Bassi had believed in, whereas theirs was "the religion of hell. . . . The Pope is Lucifer. . . . On the day of vengeance, the cry that will go up will be *Bassi!*"

The harshness of his anticlerical tirade, which pleased the majority of the American ruling class due to its Anglican confession, revealed the strength of his convictions, an inner certainty that manifested itself in his self-possession and was commented upon by those he spoke to. One of them, Henry Theodore Tuckerman, marveled at how much he differed from the Italian stereotype:

Without the superficial vivacity and the exaggerated manner so common to the Italian temperament, there yet was revealed a latent force and feeling all the more impressive from the contrast it afforded to the voluble and dramatic utterance of his countrymen. His calm manner, comparatively slow movement, and almost Saxon hair and beard, might have seemed characteristic of a northern rather than a southern European; yet his eye, voice and air were essentially Italian. [*North American Review*, XCII, pp. 34–36]

Dwight was struck by "the courtesy of his movements . . . the freedom of his utterance and the propriety and beauty of his language," and described his physical appearance:

He has a broad and round forehead; a straight and almost perpendicular nose, not too small, but of delicate form; heavy brown moustaches and beard, which conceal the lower part of his face; a full, round chest; free and athletic movements, notwithstanding ill health, and a rheumatism which disables his right arm . . . an easy, natural, frank and unassuming carriage, with a courteous nod and a ready grasp of the hand. [G. Garibaldi, *The Life of General Garibaldi written by himself. With sketches of his Companions in Arms. Translated by his friend and admirer Theodore Dwight* (London and New York, 1859), p. 5]

The good opinion and respect he induced in others opened the way for work he found congenial. In October he went to live on Staten Island with Antonio Meucci, a successful businessman who many consider the inventor of the telephone, in a house belonging to a man called Fasi. In the late autumn, he traveled to the Caribbean on the *Georgia*. He left New York on 11 November, almost certainly as a passenger, passed through Havana in Cuba, then still a Spanish possession, and reached the Isthmus of Panama in Central America, from where he returned to Havana and then back to New York on 7 December.

There was very little to do on Staten Island. The ban on hunting rabbits, quails, and other animals restricted even that pastime. He fished, played bowls, and occasionally went to New York, where he met friends and Italian exiles. He was a member of the committee set up to use the remaining funds from the collection in 1848 to assist revolutions in Italy. All these activities were insufficient for a man of Garibaldi's energies. Fortunately Meucci set up a factory producing candles: "I therefore spend my time making wicks and handling tallow with unbelievable skill," he wrote on 10 February 1851 to Eliodoro Specchi. "Next to the boiler the temperature is almost that of Cuba." It was not what he was looking for, and he felt he was a burden. One day he went to the port, approached some of the ships and asked to be signed on as a seaman. Sailors had to carry out heavy duties and were subject to harsh discipline. They would not even give an answer to such an elderly man, however robust he might have appeared. He offered to work as a longshoreman for free, just to warm himself up, as there was now snow on the ground. He was not accepted.

In April, Carpaneto found him "in the clothes of a simple seaman, mending the sail of a small boat, which during the hours of enforced idleness he took out to sea for fishing or into the river estuaries to hunt wild ducks." He deplored that they were leaving "to rot a man who has given such service and brought such honor to the name of Italy, both at home and abroad. If he were a jester, a buffoon, a singer, or a theatrical hero, he would be rich by now, and revered by the whole world. But the man who has put into practice the virtue extolled in theaters is ignored and left to perish in penury. Shame on us!"

Carpaneto had come to New York for business reasons. He had been investing in trade with Central America. He had sent one of his own ships, the *San Giorgio*, from Genoa to England to complete its load and from there to Peru. He left New York on 28 April on the steamship *Prometheus* to meet up with the *San Giorgio* in Peru and took Garibaldi with him. Garibaldi took the name of Captain Anzani and devoted his time to astronomical observations. Later he took the name of Giuseppe Pane, which he had already used in Marseille. He sailed as a passenger to recover his confidence as a seaman. Being the scrupulous person he was, he had already bought "the books necessary to win back my original trade" in Liverpool in June of 1850. In reality he wanted to learn about the seas that were unfamiliar to him.

They changed ship at Chagres in Panama, and traveled across Nicaragua partly by land and partly by sea, encountering many adventures along the way (Garibaldi suffered from tropical fever). They crossed the isthmus and boarded a British steamboat to reach Callao on the Pacific coast of Peru on 5 October, where Carpaneto met up with the *San Giorgio*. He then proposed to travel on board to California along with Garibaldi. The discovery of gold in the region, which had only just become part of the United States, had triggered the Gold Rush. Often ships that visited there were abandoned by the seamen attracted by the mirage of sudden fortunes, and then put up for sale at very low prices. This could have been the opportunity to buy a ship for Garibaldi.

In Lima, Garibaldi had a "splendid reception from that rich and generous Italian colony." Since 1840, Europeans had been attracted to the Pacific coast of South America by the increasing importance of the trade in guano, a fertilizer formed from the droppings of thousands of birds which were deposited in enormous quantities in some parts of Peru. This natural fertilizer was very effective and very much in demand, and it generated considerable maritime trade. There was a large Italian community in Callao and Lima, the capital of Peru, which is about ten kilometers inland (in that year of 1851 the first railway in Latin America linked to the two cities). In 1844 the community consisted of about one thousand people, of whom five to six hundred were subjects of the Kingdom of Sardinia. Some of them were well placed in the local economy. The events of 1848 had brought in republican and liberal exiles of some stature. The doctor Emanuele Solari, a follower of Mazzini, held the chair of clinical medicine at the university and was the founder of scientific medicine in Peru.

In Lima Garibaldi obtained the much-desired command of a ship. Recently acquired documents have shown that the brig *Carmen* was purchased in California with capital provided by Pietro Denegri, a businessman from Liguria who had become rich in Peru, Carpaneto, Gabriele and Giovan Battista Camozzi (both from Bergamo), and Luigi Piazzoni (an exile from Genoa). To obtain his master's ticket Garibaldi sat the exams required by the maritime authorities of Callao (it was, in fact, obtained in very short time, perhaps with the assistance of some connections). The general returned to his career as a sea captain in every sense. He started to earn a salary, which allowed him to look after himself better than he had with just the pension from the government of the Kingdom of Sardinia.

The purpose for which he was signed on was the transport of a cargo of guano to China. While preparing the cargo, his fiery temperament led him into an incident similar to the encounter with the Brazilian chargé-d'affaires in Montevideo. On 30 November during a wedding reception, a Frenchman called Charles Ledos made some disparaging comments about the Italians who defended Rome, to which Garibaldi answered in kind. Four days later, the *Correo de Lima* published a letter signed "a Gaul" and entitled "Paltry Heroes," which ridiculed Garibaldi as a military figure. The latter read the letter while in Callao, preparing for the voyage. On Saturday afternoon, he went to look for Ledos at his home in Lima, which was a large *magazeno*. He gave him an abrupt talking-to accompanied by "four blows of a light cane" that he was in the habit of carrying about. One of Ledos' French friends ran over armed with a rapier, but Garibaldi disarmed him. In the meantime Ledos came up behind his attacker and hit him a glancing blow with a large piece of wood. Garibaldi held both of them at bay and withdrew bleeding to the home of an Italian across the road. Many other Italians quickly arrived to give assistance, and the police, who had attempted to arrest him after he had been reported by Ledos, were obliged to retreat. The Italians and the French were on the brink of attacking each other, and the authorities had the city patrolled by cavalry units.

The consul for the Kingdom of Sardinia, Giuseppe Canevaro, who was also a rich businessman and Denegri's brother-in-law, had been in favor of the decision to help Garibaldi find an appropriate position, but he had a dislike of republicans and hated the way they exaggerated "General Garibaldi's deeds, who in their eyes was the only great man in all of Italy, and a thousand other boasts." Now Garibaldi was dragging him into a troubling dispute. However, national honor was at stake, and so he defended Garibaldi's behavior and rejected a humiliating settlement of the dispute whereby Garibaldi would pay a penalty of 200 pesos dressed up as a contribution to charity, and persuaded Ledos to give up any attempt at obtaining compensation. Garibaldi's prestige played its part in obtaining a favorable solution. As Canevaro had reported, he was greatly admired by the Peruvian military, "for his brilliant exploits both in the war against Rosas and in the defense of Rome against the invasion of endless phalanxes of French soldiery." The legend of the indomitable warrior accompanied him everywhere.

On 10 January 1852, the *Carmen* left for China flying a Peruvian flag with a crew of fifteen men and loaded with guano. They passed by Hawaii and reached Canton after three months on 10 April. Overall it had been a peaceful trip, apart from a typhoon on 19 March. While it raged around the ship Garibaldi dreamed that he was at his mother's funeral, and later he discovered that his mother had died that very day. We should again remember the lengthy periods it took for news and letters to travel from one continent to another, while Garibaldi's voyage around the Pacific continued. One example demonstrates the point: on returning to Lima in January 1853 after his year-long sea journey to China, he received a letter from Lorenzo Valerio posted in Turin on 18 July 1851 and another from Avezzana posted in New York on 5 March 1852. We do not know when they received his replies.

In Canton he could not find buyers for the guano, so the agent sent him to Amoy, where he found some. He returned to Canton, and then sailed to Manila in the Philippines with a mixed cargo. Back in Canton, he replaced the masts on the *Carmen*, and also the copper that lined the ship's bottom. In the various Chinese ports he visited, he frequented the local bars frequented by seamen and made friends with other captains. He left with a cargo of silk and chinoiserie. There have been theories that he was taking on cargoes of coolies who were carried off as slaves to various localities in Central America and Peru, but it recently became possible to demonstrate that this rumor was entirely groundless. To exploit favorable winds he took the long route south, which took him along the coasts of Australia and New Zealand. The round trip took 142 days (according to some recent very reliable calculations), and he was back in Callao on 24 January 1853.

The Sardinian consul informed Turin that the republicans in Lima had organized a banquet in his honor, and he had been offered the opportunity of returning to Europe, either to Spain or Genoa. There was no truth in this, as Garibaldi left as captain of the *Carmen* for Valparaiso in Chile, where he took on a cargo of copper and then sailed back toward Peru. In Islay, he completed the load with bales of wool. He returned south, rounded Cape Horn, sailed up the Atlantic coast of Argentina, Uruguay, and Brazil, crossed the Caribbean and offloaded his cargo in Boston on 6 September 1853. He would never return to South America again.

From Boston he went to New York. Having ended his voyage, he calculated the expenses and earning, and presented Denegri's agent, Theodore Riley, with his fee. Because of some debts that had not yet been collected, a dispute arose over these accounts and it took years of negotiations to sort it out. The proud sea captain left the command of the *Carmen*. He did not blame Denegri for the disagreement, and wrote in his *Memoirs* of the great kindness Denegri had always shown him. He blamed instead a "parasite," who had made the ship-owner suspicious of him.

"I know nothing of Italy, and I believe there is nothing of importance except its servitude and the passivity of its sons," he wrote to Avezzana from Lima on 28 January 1853. "Many think they see rebellions from one day to the next, but I see nothing and continue to work at sea. As you know, I cannot settle down in one spot and wait to see what happens. If it were possible, I would circle around the nest and stay nearby." He was missing Italy, then, even though he had no hope of another war with Austria, because of Italian submissiveness.

The opportunity to return to his native land was provided by Captain Antonio Figari, who came to America charged with buying a sailing ship.

He bought the *Commonwealth* in Baltimore, and sailed on 16 January 1854 loaded with flour and wheat. The ship was flying an American flag, and Garibaldi was not allowed to have regular command, which was taken by a man of straw. He arrived in London on 11 February, and there met Mazzini and other leading figures of European democracy. He left for Newcastle, where he loaded coal, and on 6 May 1854 he was in Genoa. Four and a half years had passed since that 16 September 1849 on which he had left that port.

In Genoa various citizens came on board to greet him. There was not the warmth of the previous occasion and memory of his exploits had started to fade. Even the authorities made no difficulties over his return. In America, Garibaldi had notified the Sardinian consul of his intensions, and in London the ambassador, Emanuele D'Azeglio had notified Turin of his arrival and departure. Cavour, the prime minister from 1852, had replied, "If he is only coming to see his family and children, we will not interfere with him at all, but if he has any intention of coming here on Mazzini's behalf, then we will not tolerate his presence for a single moment." In fact he had no intention of political activism, and still less did he share Mazzini's plans. However, it did not prove possible to stay out of politics.

He was suffering from rheumatism when he arrived, and he stayed with a friend for a couple of weeks. As soon as he his health improved, he went to Nice. His mother had died on 20 March 1852 at the age of seventy-seven. He set up home in his native city, something he had long dreamed of. He took seven-year-old Ricciotti with him, and left Menotti (now fourteen-and-a-half) in boarding school and ten-year-old Teresita with the Deideri family. He led a simple life: he rose at sunrise, lunched at midday, slept in the afternoon, and went to bed at nine in the evening. He played bowls and checkers, went fishing, and hunted on the mountains behind Nice. He was often tormented by pains in 1854 and 1855, particularly in his arms. In July 1854 he went to take the spa waters in Acqui.

In the autumn, he was visited by Emma Roberts, a middle-aged widow, one of those educated and fascinating women about which Garibaldi had often written with admiration. He made no mention of her in his *Memoirs*, because in London the friendship had turned into a love affair with plans for marriage. This wealthy woman came to Italy on a long journey in the company of one of her daughters and a young journalist, Jessie Meriton White. Garibaldi accompanied the three English women to Sardinia. As he went hunting and watched folkloristic events staged in honor of the foreigners, he started to think of moving to the island. Nice was no longer the city of his youth. New neighborhoods had been built, gas lighting had been introduced, and the city had become an attraction to holidaymakers and foreigners. In 1851 the government had removed its privileges as a free port, and it started to feel closer to France than to the Kingdom of Sardinia. Garibaldi no longer felt at home. Now close to fifty years of age, suffering from arthritis and disillusioned with politics, he wanted to live in a peaceful place away from the center of things. Initially he considered Capo Testa on the Bocche di Bonifacio opposite Corsica, but then the Susini brothers encouraged him to buy a piece of land on Caprera, a small almost deserted island close to the island of La Maddalena. The purchase was signed on 29 December 1855. Garibaldi invested his saving from his seagoing and an inheritance of 35,000 lira left to him by his brother Felice, who had died in November. For the moment he did not go to live there, and would only occasionally visit with a few friends with whom he would live in a tent. He started to build a house with materials brought over from Genoa.

The group of English travelers left Sardinia for Naples, Rome, and Florence, all in states with absolutist governments, where Garibaldi was not free to go. In the spring of 1855 they returned to Nice. Ricciotti was suffering from pains in his legs, and his father feared that he would become lame. His women friends took the boy back with them to England where he underwent successful treatment. Because of his parents' difficult lives, his education had also been neglected, so Emma, with his father's agreement, put him in a good boarding school in Liverpool.

Garibaldi was alone, and returned to his seagoing life. In August 1855 he was issued with a first-class master's ticket, and took command of the screw-driven steamship *Salvatore*, the first of this kind under a Sardinian flag. Built a few months earlier as a tug, it was fitted out for coastal trade. Until 5 October, Garibaldi traveled between Genoa, Nice, and Marseille. In March 1856, he went to England (he traveled through France on a French passport in the name of Joseph Pane) to see his son and implement a plan to free some Neapolitan political prisoners facing life sentences on the Island of Santo Stefano. He met Emma Roberts, and the plans for a marriage between two people of such different social classes were dropped. "A servant every step you take," he confided to White, "three hours for lunch and never time to go to bed! A month of this life would kill me!" He remained on very good terms with the English lady. He bought the forty-two-ton English cutter *Anglo French* with some of his own money, some given to him by his friend Felice Orrigoni, and a substantial gift from Mrs. Roberts, and he renamed the sailing ship *Emma*.

On 13 March, Garibaldi, who was already back in Nice, had the cutter brought over by an English captain. He had it fitted out for carrying cargo. The main destination was Caprera: he took building materials out and returned with agricultural products and firewood. On 7 January 1857, the sailing ship loaded with lime mortar was hit by a storm off La Maddalena. The ship started to take water and the lime started to froth up. There was no choice but to run it aground, which at least saved the cutter. The cutter was insured, and Garibaldi was paid compensation, but his career at sea was over. Perhaps because his arthritis was worsening in the marine climate, he became a farmer.

Caprera, a predominantly rocky island of about sixteen square kilometers some two kilometers from the Sardinian coast and a few hundred meters from La Maddalena, was inhabited by a few shepherds and an English couple, Mr. and Mrs. Collins, who owned half the land. Garibaldi, with help from his friends and his son Menotti, surrounded his land with a wall to protect it from the neighbors' animals. He built a single-story house out of stone and with a terraced roof in the style of South American houses, and over the years he enlarged it with rooms as needs required. Professor Galante, an agricultural expert, wrote on Garibaldi's death:

Garibaldi was a true agronomist and transformed his Caprera into a real farm with a farmhouse, stables, cowsheds, ordinary manure pits, a barn for fodder and straw, a store for foodstuffs, an excellent dovecote and henhouse, a lean-to for tools, agricultural instruments, a stationary steam engine, a windmill (because the wind there is a powerful source of energy), a well equipped with a pump, an oven, a vegetable garden, a garden, boundary walls and convenient roads.

He introduced fruit trees, cereals, vegetables, and silage, and kept horses, cattle, sheep, and bees. It took time to do all these things, and in 1865 his admirers purchased the land owned by the Collinses and donated it to him. He became the sole proprietor of Caprera. He lived the simple life he dreamed of with his family and a few people he trusted, took care of his land and animals, produced his own clothing (he worked hard at cutting and sewing his own trousers), and reading books in his library. It was a patriarchal life from which he was drawn by his other great dream, that of Italian national unity.

15. In the King's Service

DURING THE GRAY years of his second exile, Garibaldi had not been able to keep himself out of politics as much as he wished. The return of a papal government to Rome did not extinguish all comment upon the defense of 1849. The Pole, Adam Mickiewicz, who had fought in Italy with the volunteers, published several articles in the Parisian *Tribune des Peuples* describing Garibaldi's courage and energy, and insisting on his popularity. Another Pole, Count Edward Lubienski, who was a Catholic conservative, published *Guerres et révolutions d'Italie en 1848 et 1849* in Paris in 1852, and devoted ample space to the "famous military leader, Garibaldi." He was described as "an energetic, courageous, but not very capable general who could have defended Rome much longer, and whose esprit de corps had made him a hero." Even an adversary had to acknowledge his importance, albeit through gritted teeth. His name was known even in countries that had no national or social demands: on Christmas Eve of 1857 in Stockholm a Finnish exile, Adolf Erik Nordenskiold, found a plaster bust of Garibaldi, and put it on his desk to make the longing for his native land less painful.

Governments and public opinion could not believe that the warrior had returned to the normality of civilian life. They gave credit to completely groundless rumors such as the one that in January 1851 he left New York for Italy with three ships carrying volunteers, or another that he had taken command of the Peruvian army in October of the same year. He found it difficult to avoid events held in his honor. Accounts of his deeds followed him everywhere. "Illustrious defender of liberty, we salute you," wrote the *Correo de Lima* on his arrival in Peru, and in 1854, while he was loading coal in Newcastle, a local newspaper published a rather romanticized version of his biography in installments, and a democratic society presented "the glorious defender of the Roman republic" with a sword, a telescope, and a scroll of honor, all paid for by money collected from 1,047 workers.

In Italy those who took part in the events of 1848 reflected upon the reasons for the rapid triumph of the revolutions and the subsequent defeat of liberal and national ideals. Democrats in particular agonized over their inability to involve the masses and fuse the demands of the peasantry with those of the movement for national independence and unification. They needed to identify a political strategy capable of creating a consensus in the same way that neo-Guelphism had made possible the enormous conquests of 1848.

Unlike others, Mazzini held onto his convictions. In his opinion, the success of the urban insurrections and the glorious defense of Rome and Venice proved that it was possible to defeat reactionary monarchs through popular movements. It was now necessary to coordinate the European revolutions that had been defeated separately in 1848–49, and use an Italian uprising to give the signal for a new wave of radical demands. He therefore reestablished a clandestine organization throughout the Italian states that had returned to absolutism, and resumed his previous tactics.

Mazzini was counting on Garibaldi. He rightly believed him to be the right man to lead a daring exploit and to inspire young men to take action. Putting aside the past the resentments caused by the disagreements in Rome, Mazzini's newspaper *L'Italia del Popolo*, which was published in Lausanne (another newspaper with the same title would be published in Genoa in 1857–58), acknowledged in 1850 that an "aura of glory" had formed around Garibaldi's name and "nothing could remove it." In November 1851 Mazzini wrote to Garibaldi in America to inform him that before May an uprising would occur in Italy in coordination with a European revolution. But these plans proved unsuccessful. A group of conspirators was discovered in Lombardy-Venetia and nine of them were hanged at Fort Belfiore in 1852. In Milan on 6 February 1853 his plan for a group of working-class insurrectionists to take the Austrian garrison by surprise turned out to be a miserable failure. Following this attack there were many executions and the resulting bitter arguments included the accusation of attempting to organize a social revolution. These failures were attributed to his irresponsible trust in badly organized insurrections.

Mazzini was not discouraged by either failures or criticism. When he met Garibaldi in London in 1854 for the first time since the defense of Rome in 1849, he believed that Garibaldi was "ready for action." "His name is all-powerful among Neapolitans following the Velletri affair," he wrote to C. A. Taylor; "I want to send him to Sicily, where they are ripe for insurrection, and invoke him as their military leader." He was deceiving himself over the number of his followers in the Kingdom of the Two Sicilies and over Garibaldi's willingness to implement his plans.

Yet again Garibaldi was absent from Italy at a time of ideological debate, but it is unlikely that he would have gotten involved in the theoretical discussions and contributed his own considerations on the suitable means for creating a popular revolution. In his usual manner of simplifying problems, he believed that the priority was to fight for the country's independence from foreign domination. Writing from Boston in September 1853, he confirmed to Candido Augusto Vecchi that he still hoped for "the emancipation of our land" and was horrified by "the probability that he would never again take up sword or rifle to fight for Italy." He had no intention, however, of setting off on adventures that were compromised from the very start and, as in the past, he wanted his actions to be sanctioned by recognized authorities. We should remember that in 1837 he would not sail until he had been issued a letter of marque, that in Rio Grande and Uruguay the governments of those countries assigned him a position in their armed forces, that in Italy he was appointed general of the Milanese provisional government and later the Roman Republic, and he only set off on his highly dangerous march that ended in San Marino once the assembly had granted him full military powers. It is unlikely that his enemies, especially Austria in August 1849, would have recognized the legitimacy of this position, had he fallen into their hands, but this does not alter the fact that he had sought out legitimacy for his actions.

When, following the events of 1848–49, the prospects of further military actions revived, he demanded the same guarantees, and above all he wanted to know exactly what they wanted of him. He was not "a passive instrument that works unthinkingly for us," as Costantino Nigra wrote to Cavour in July 1860. He would not work "unthinkingly" for either Mazzini or Cavour, but consciously for the ideal of Italian independence.

Encouraging news was arriving from Italy about the attitude as King Victor Emanuel II of Sardinia, who had retained the Constitution. In practice this meant that an elected chamber of deputies debated the government's directives, political parties could be formed, and there was freedom of the press even for opponents of the monarchy, although there were a few restrictions. Hence newspapers that supported Mazzini and his republican ideals could be published. Some twenty to thirty thousand refugees from persecution by the absolute monarchies had found asylum in liberal Piedmont, and they were fully integrated into the life of the country. Some obtained citizenship, were elected deputies, and became government ministers, while others obtained university posts or rose to high ranks in the army. This presence of men from the whole of Italy in positions of high office turned the Kingdom of Sardinia into a foretaste of the united Italy patriots dreamed of.

From 1852 Count Cavour was head of government in Turin, and was put there by the centrist majority in parliament. He undertook domestic reforms and reforms to assist the defense of the small state's autonomy against unwanted interference by the regional power Austria. Following the Milanese revolt in February 1853, Marshall Radetzky, the governor of Lombardy-Venetia, confiscated the property of those who had fled the country, and even considered a war against the Kingdom of Sardinia to force it to repeal its Constitution. The Sardinian government set up a fund to assist the refugees, who then became its citizens. Republicans approved of the firmness with which Cavour countered the arrogance of the Hapsburg Empire.

Garibaldi's rapprochement with the House of Savoy commenced when King Charles Albert went to war with Austria. "Anyone who knows me is aware that I have never been favorable to the monarchist cause. But this

was solely because monarchs were harming Italy. Now, however, I am a realist and come to present myself to the king of Sardinia, who has made
himself the champion of Italian renewal, and I am ready to spill my blood
for him. I am convinced that all other Italians are of my opinion." This
was his first unequivocal declaration and he made it on his arrival in Italy
at a banquet organized in his honor in Nice on 25 June 1848.

"I was republican, but when I heard that Charles Albert had become the
champion of Italy, I swore to obey him and follow his colors," he repeated
in Genoa on 3 July. His indignation at King Charles Albert's armistice of 9
August had been offset by the king's recommencement of hostilities against
Austria and then his abdication. In September 1849, Garibaldi told La
Marmora, "experience has taught us to acknowledge the need to rally everyone around the Piedmontese army and put up with any government in
order to be able to reengage in the war of independence when the time
comes." He expressed these opinions quite publicly. In a letter of 11 September from Genoa to *Concordia*, "the valiant general" argued for unity
and harmony "so that Piedmont can grow stronger, go up in everyone's
opinion, and become the bastion of Italy's liberty and independence."

Always the realist, Garibaldi assessed the experience of 1848, starting
with the balance of power. He compared the modest results obtained by
the heroic actions of his volunteers with the political and military weight
of the great powers involved in the Italian conflict. He came to the conclusion that when it came to fighting an organized and well-trained army,
such as the French and Austrian ones, it was indispensable to have an
equally well-organized army on one's own side. In 1854 he made this point
very clearly to the Russian revolutionary Aleksandr Herzen, who was in
exile in London.

I have been a republican all my life, but now it is not a question of
having a republic. I know the Italian masses better than Mazzini. I
have lived among them and shared their lives. Mazzini knows educated Italy and dominates their thinking, but you cannot create an
army out of them to defeat the Austrians and the pope. For the
masses, for the Italian people, there is only one flag to which they
will rally: that of unification and the expulsion of the foreigner! And
how can you achieve this, if you antagonize the only strong Italian

monarchy, which for whatever reasons is willing to fight for Italy but is fearful? Instead of seeking to ingratiate themselves with it, they are rejecting and offending it. The day in which that youth [Victor Emanuel] believes that he is closer to the archdukes than he is to us will be the day in which Italy's destiny will be put off for one or two generations.

Once he returned to Italy permanently, Garibaldi was obliged to make public his disagreement with Mazzini, which he had already made known privately at the meeting in London. On his arrival in Genoa, Mazzini's newspaper, *Italia e Popolo*, wanted to show that "Rome's heroic defender" was in agreement with Mazzini and organized an event in his honor. A journalistic war was being waged around Garibaldi. *Il Parlamento* of Turin, which was the mouthpiece of the moderates, published a report from Genoa attacking *Italia e Popolo* and asserting that everyone knew that Garibaldi was in "radical disagreement" with that newspaper's faction. *Italia e Popolo* pursued the matter, and when Garibaldi visited Turin in June, it referred to "some wiseacres or dreamers" who wanted to use him as "a lever to create popular support for Piedmontese constitutionalists." The question of his support for one party or the other was not purely academic at the time. Mazzini had attempted a second uprising in Lunigiana, and was preparing another in Valtellina. The word was being put around that Garibaldi would take part in these.

On 4 August Garibaldi stamped on the rumors and distanced himself from Mazzini by sending a letter to the newspapers, but mainly directed at *Italia e Popolo*.

Since my arrival in Italy, I have twice heard my name in connection with proposed insurrections of which I do not approve, and consequently I believe it is my duty to make this known and make sure that our youth, who are always ready to confront dangers to free our fatherland, are not led astray by the false arguments of deceivers or the deceived who are ruining or, at the very least, discrediting our cause by their untimely actions.

This harsh declaration created a sensation, and in the moderate camp, *Il Corriere Mercantile* considered it:

an excellent avowal of common sense and pure and independent Italianness against a system that perceives actions solely in terms of impulses that are condemned to failure from the very start—against a system that considers it the duty of Italians to organize perpetual defeat and the decimation of our boldest and most candid young men who die by the *fives* and the *tens* on each occasion.

There followed a lively debate among the democrats themselves, many of whom, such as Medici, Agostino Bertani, and Enrico Cosenz, were against Mazzini's methods. Francesco Bartolomeo Savi, the editor of *L'Italia e Popolo*, published a clarification and his own antagonistic comment. He also produced a declaration from "some officers of the Roman Republic" who were against Garibaldi, and inserted a resentful letter from Pietro Roselli on the Battle of Velletri in May 1849 with severe criticisms of Garibaldi's indiscipline, which was responsible for the failure of the maneuver against the Neapolitan army. An indignant Garibaldi challenged Savi and Roselli to a duel. On similar occasions in South America, justice had been achieved by physical aggression, but this dispute was entrusted to a court of honor made up of Medici and Cosenz to act for Garibaldi, and Bixio and Oreste Regnoli to act for Roselli. Its chairman was Admiral Giorgio Mameli, Goffredo's father. The court found that Garibaldi's honor had not been impugned, and Garibaldi had to let the matter drop. It should be remembered that during this period Bixio was critical of his former commander. In 1851, following the publication of Pisacane's book, *La guerra combattuta in Italia nel 1848–49*, which contained carefully argued criticisms of the way Garibaldi conducted military operations, he had associated himself with the accusations and refused "to contribute to the magnification of some reputations that history will only know from evils that flowed from them."

Garibaldi and Mazzini went their separate ways. The Crimean War provided the occasion for exacerbating the disagreement. In 1853, Russia, which had not been affected by the 1848 revolutions and had indeed intervened on Austria's behalf to subjugate Hungary, believed that the time had come to force the Ottoman Empire into opening up the Bosphorus and the Dardanelles to its warships. France and Britain did not want the Russian fleet in the Mediterranean and encouraged Turkey to stand up to this aggression. In 1854 they entered the war on its side. Russia was counting on Austria returning the favor and coming to its assistance, but Austria declared its neutrality as it feared any enlargement of its powerful neighbor. Turkey's allies were separated from its aggressor, and an Anglo-French expeditionary force had to go to the Crimea to attack the enemy. It laid siege to Sebastopol, Russia's main naval base in the Black Sea. The war promised to be long and difficult, and France and Britain put pressure on Austria to enter the conflict on their side. Austria played for time and argued that it feared a Piedmontese attack from the west while engaged in the east. The two powers then put pressure on the Kingdom of Sardinia to send their own expeditionary force against Russia so that it would be unable to attack Lombardy-Venetia.

In Turin, most public opinion was against an undertaking that would be a heavy financial commitment and promised few benefits. Cavour, on the other hand, saw that an alliance with the great powers would be an opportunity for little Piedmont to enter the stage of international diplomacy. With the king's support, he convinced the government to take part in the war and sent a contingent of fifteen thousand soldiers to the Crimea. Mazzini believed it an error to send battle-ready men away from Italy, and publicly adopted a position against what he considered a deportation. Garibaldi did not adopt a position in public, but in private he argued that it was useful to the Italian cause for the Piedmontese army to give a good account of itself on the European stage. "Our neighbors should be reminded every day that we know how to fight and how we will soon fight for our own interests," he wrote in November 1855. He was becoming more hopeful. "I hope to do my little bit to build Italy," he wrote to Valerio in November 1854, and in February 1855 he sent him a plan to be presented to the king involving a secret organization of ten thousand armed men on top of the fifteen thousand soldiers being sent to the Crimea, and these would be sent to Sicily to trigger the struggle for unification and independence.

At the end of the war in 1856, a peace conference met in Paris to decide the conditions. France, Britain, Russia, and Austria took part, and the Kingdom of Sardinia was admitted as well. On 8 April, they debated the anomalous conditions in Italy, where the Austrians had garrisons in Ferrara and Piacenza, French troops stayed on in Rome since 1849, and the

Bourbon rulers of Kingdom of the Two Sicilies continued to impose brutal repression. Cavour argued that the conduct of the reactionary monarchies discredited the properly constituted governments, increased the strength of revolutionary forces and constituted a threat to peace in Italy and Europe.

Even though he made no territorial gains, Cavour achieved a diplomatic success, and established liberal Piedmont as the alternative to Austria and the absolutist states of Italy. Longtime republicans, like the Lombard aristocrat Giorgio Pallavicino Trivulzio, who had been imprisoned by the Austrians for many years in Spielberg Fortress before emigrating to Piedmont, and Daniele Manin, an exile in Paris, started to look favorably on the House of Savoy. They argued that there was an urgent need for monarchists and republicans to unite together in a "national party" bent on independence and unification with the assistance of the Kingdom of Sardinia. On 25 May 1856 following the Paris peace conference, Manin publicly announced his break with revolutionary methods in a letter to the *Times*, in which he accused Mazzini of being the exponent of the "dagger theory."

The national party's program coincided with the ideas Garibaldi had developed some time before. "Italy is marching toward national unification," he wrote to Cuneo, who had returned to South America in April 1856; "this is beyond question. Most people are in agreement with Piedmont's leading role." "Unless I am deceived, we are on the threshold of great events for our cause," he added in June. In July he told Pallavicino that he was with him and Manin, and he informed Cuneo that Italy was "in a happy position, and we must be proud of this," and that, "although my body had aged, I *still have* a young man's soul."

He was ready for action. In 1855 he accepted the proposal to carry out a raid worthy of an ageing privateer. The purpose was to free some thirty political prisoners in the Kingdom of the Two Sicilies. These prisoners, who included Silvio Spaventa and Luigi Settembrini serving life sentences, were held on the Island of Santo Stefano in the Tyrrhenian Sea. A group of exiles and politicians in England collected money to buy a ship which, under Garibaldi's orders, was supposed to launch a raid to release the prisoners. The ship, the *Isle of Thanet*, sailed from Hull but was wrecked on the English coast. Funds were collected for a second ship, but in mid-1856 the project was abandoned as it was believed that the Bourbon government was about to grant an amnesty to the political prisoners.

Garibaldi believed that the plan was feasible, because it involved a lightning attack and an immediate escape: more an act of mockery than an act of war. He did not believe that it was possible to trigger a revolution with a few hundred men without the population being already in revolt. With Jessie White, a fervent supporter of Mazzini but also his friend, he was quite frank about his disapproval of movements that had no chance of success. It was more sensible to put one's trust in the Kingdom of Sardinia. He wrote in February 1857:

> In Piedmont [the Kingdom of Sardinia] there is an army of forty thousand men and an ambitious king. Those are the factors capable of taking the initiative and obtaining success, and most Italians now believe in them. Let your friend [Mazzini] match that and show a little more good sense than he has in the past, and we will bless him and fervently follow him. On the other hand, if Piedmont vacillates and does not live up to the mission to which we believe it has been called, then we will turn our backs on it. Let others prepare for the holy war, with boldness perhaps but not with laughable insurrections, and you will find your brother on the battlefield. Fight! I am with you, sister! But I will not tell Italians "Rise up!" to make the rabble laugh.

He was therefore against Mazzini's plan to make Southern Italy rise up with a handful of volunteers in 1857. On 26 June Carlo Pisacane, on this occasion in agreement with Mazzini (he was a socialist and did not share Mazzini's philosophical and religious theories), boarded the steamer *Cagliari* with twenty-two comrades, and took control of it once it had left port. They landed on the Isle of Ponza, where they took the Bourbon garrison by surprise and freed the prisoners, mainly criminals and soldiers undergoing punishment who joined him. They then went to the agreed meeting place with the southern democrats, Sapri in the Gulf of Salerno, where they should have met hundreds of armed peasants ready to start the revolution. There was no one there: the rising had not been properly organized and there was a lack of forces prepared to take part. On 2 July the small band was wiped out in Sanza. Pisacane was wounded and committed suicide. Mazzini had combined this expedition with an insurrection in Livorno on 29 June, to start the rebellion in Tuscany, and another in Genoa, to stop the Sardinian monarchy from taking charge of the insurrection: both were easily put down.

The tragic outcome of the Sapri expedition provoked widespread condemnation of Mazzini's methods, which sent groups of patriots on hazardous exploits in the mistaken belief that the country was ready to rise up. No less was the abhorrence at the Genoa uprising, which was directed against the only constitutional state in Italy. The liberal and national movements had been increasingly looking to the Sardinian monarchy for leadership, and now democrats and republicans were also increasingly sharing the opinions Garibaldi expounded to Jessie White. She, however, was arrested in Genoa for her part in the uprising of 29 June, and after she was released she married the Venetian exile Alberto Mario, thus strengthening her commitment to the democratic camp.

Garibaldi was taking decisive steps toward working more closely with the monarchy. On 13 August 1856 he met Cavour for the first time. According to Felice Foresti who went with him, Cavour greeted him "in a manner that was both courteous and familiar, gave him much to hope for and authorized him to pass on those hopes to others." Garibaldi then authorized Benedetto Cairoli and Giacomo Griziotti, both from Pavia, to collect money "for the Italian cause." He was beginning to gain a reputation in politics. In the elections of November 1857, which registered gains by conservatives and Catholics, he stood as a candidate for the liberal opposition in the Genoa V constituency, and was beaten in the second ballot by the lawyer Cesare Leopoldo Bixio, the candidate for the right opposition.

Since 1856, Cavour had been giving Italians the impression that the Kingdom of Sardinia was preparing to play a decisive role in the national cause. He was gambling for high stakes. He led people to believe that the sympathies expressed by France and Britain at the Paris conference could be transformed into outright support. His provocative policy toward Austria called people's attention to the Italian question. Austria fell into the trap. It responded to the provocation with an attitude of intolerance and this led to breaking off diplomatic relations between the two countries.

The Paris Conference had increased Napoleone III's prestige, and he was interested in reviewing the European settlement decided upon in the Congress of Vienna in 1815, which was fundamentally anti-French. The unresolved conflicts in Italy made him think of embarking upon a policy of territorial expansion. In July 1858, he met in secret with Cavour at Plombières, a spa town. A plan was drawn up that provided for a French alliance with Piedmont in the event of it coming under attack from Austria. After victory, the Kingdom of Sardinia would annex Lombardy, Venetia, the Duchy of Modena, the Duchy of Parma, and the Papal Legations (the Legations correspond to modern Emilia), and in exchange, the Kingdom of Sardinia would cede Savoy and Nice to France. They also considered the wider reorganization of the Italian peninsula and a possible solution was to form a Kingdom of Central Italy under a French prince and place Gioacchino Murat's son on the throne of the Two Sicilies, while the pope who would remain the sovereign of Rome and the surrounding region of Lazio, could preside over a confederation of these states. All these plans involved a great deal of uncertainty, and if they were implemented, it was clear that Austrian supremacy was going to be replaced by French supremacy, but Piedmont had little choice. The project also depended on Austrian aggression, without which France had no justification for going to war. In January 1859 Napoleon III snubbed the Austrian ambassador, and Victor Emanuel opened parliament with a king's speech in which he declared that he was not deaf "to the cries of pain that so many parts of Italy are directing toward us."

Garibaldi met Cavour on 20 December 1858. They were thinking of provoking an insurrection in the duchies in order to force Austria to declare war. Garibaldi was the right man to lead it. He was vice president of the Società Nazionale, and there were no doubts about his loyalty to the crown. Cavour was thinking of putting him in command of a volunteer force made up not of irregular troops, who had been expressly ruled out by Napoleon, but organized formations like the *bersaglieri* who belonged to the Guardia Nazionale. Garibaldi was full of enthusiasm. He notified Giuseppe Deideri in Nice, Eliodoro Specchi in Millesimo, and Giacomo Medici in Genoa in order to organize the recruitment. "I believe we have an infallible movement in Italy, and one that has a grandeur that we have not seen for twenty centuries," he wrote to Cuneo. On 19 December, he met some democrats in the Genoese villa of Gabriele Camozzi. He asked Luigi Mercantini, a poet and the author of *Spigolatrice di Sapri*, an anthem commemorating Pisacane ("They were three hundred men, young and strong, and yet they are dead!), to compose another for the volunteers. The result was *L'inno di Garibaldi* ("The graves are opening and the dead are rising"), and it was put to music by Alessio Olivieri, a regimental bandleader. The song accompanied the combatants with the chorus, "Leave Italy! The time to leave has come; leave Italy! Leave, foreigner!"

The principal feature of the War of 1859 was the enthusiasm that accompanied the preparations, which were carried out quite openly. The monarchy's commitment, which was public and official, ended all opposition to the Kingdom of Sardinia's leadership of the nationalist movement. On 21 December 1858, Garibaldi, while passing through Genoa on his return from Caprera, informed his friends of the details of his conversation with Cavour, and the promise of war in the spring with the involvement of volunteers. Democrats in disagreement with Mazzini, who had been inactive since Sapri, now aligned themselves with Garibaldi, who was becoming a leader around which a considerable part of the democratic and republican movement could rally. Only Mazzini held firmly to his ideas of a popular revolution leading to a republic, and opposed support for Victor Emanuel.

Thousands of volunteers, perhaps twenty thousand, left Lombardy and other regions and made their way to the Kingdom of Sardinia. Their recruitment into the Piedmontese army was enough to provoke Austrian resentment. On 2 March Garibaldi went back to Cavour, who presented him to the king. It was his first meeting with Victor Emanuel. Garibaldi would say nothing about their conversation or the impression the king made on him. Like Garibaldi, the king was a simple man who loved women and hunting. He knew how to be affable without detracting from his authority. He established a rapport with Garibaldi, which was to survive the passing years in spite of the setbacks and disputes. Garibaldi explained in his *Memoirs*:

Although born a revolutionary, I have never failed, if so required, to subject myself to the necessary discipline which is indispensable to the success of any undertaking, and from the moment that I was convinced that Italy had to march with Victor Emanuel to free itself from foreign domination, I have believed it my duty to follow his orders at any cost, even if it meant quieting my republican conscience.

The plan for the volunteers came to fruition. On 17 March, a royal decree established the corps, *Cacciatori delle Alpi*, under Garibaldi's command, and he was appointed a major general in the Sardinian army, though not everything was agreeable. The newly appointed general found that he had to "appear and not appear"; he had to attract the volunteers, but also hide himself so as not to compromise diplomacy. Most importantly command of the different volunteer corps was given to Enrico Cialdini, an exile from Modena since the uprisings of 1831 and a combatant in Portugal and Spain who returned to Italy in 1848 and was recruited into the Sardinian army: he brought together the qualities of an exile and of a serving officer in the Royal Army. Then "the strongest and most suitable young men," between the ages of 18 and 26, were assigned to army units, and the *Cacciatori* were getting the youngest and the oldest, as well as those who failed their physical examination. The officers, however, were those chosen by Garibaldi, combatants from 1849 in Rome and Venice.

The *Cacciatori* were about 3,200 men, with around fifty scouts (horsemen trained in reconnaissance), who included nineteen-year-old Menotti. They had their own horses, no artillery and no sappers. Their rifles were second-rate, but they had an effective field hospital under the command of Agostino Bertani, a Milanese doctor exiled in Genoa, who would play an important role in the Expedition of the Thousand. They wore the uniform of the Sardinian Army, and even Garibaldi put it on in place of his red shirt, although he occasionally wore a poncho. For training purposes, they were assembled at the depots in Cuneo, Savigliano, and Rivoli, near Susa. Garibaldi, who had left Caprera, created three regiments, and put the best two under the command of Enrico Cosenz and Medici.

The likelihood of war appeared to fade. Britain wanted to avoid a clash between the great powers in the heart of Europe, and proposed a conference on the Italian question. It also suggested the simultaneous disarmament of Austria and Piedmont. This would have meant an end to Cavour's dream, after he had put all the small state's resources into his military preparations. Fortunately for him, Austria rejected mediation, and gave

Turin an ultimatum to dissolve the corps of volunteers. The much sought-after war had come. Cavour rejected the ultimatum, and on 27 April, Austrian troops crossed the Ticino River. Napoleon could now enter the war. He had promised to send 120,000 men to Italy, and there were another 60,000 men in the Piedmontese army. The enemy had 170,000 men.

Austrian interests would have been best served by a rapid offensive attack to overpower Piedmont and push its army as far as Turin before Piedmont's allied forces could arrive. Marshal Gyulai, who had replaced Radetzky, failed to do this. He advanced slowly and provided time for the French troops to reach the front. On 14 May Napoleon took supreme command at Alessandria, on 4 June he defeated the Austrians at Magenta and on 8 June he entered Milan with Victor Emanuel. Emperor Franz Joseph in turn took personal command of the Austrian forces. On 24 June, after a savage battle on the heights of Solferino and San Martino, close to Lake Garda, the French won the day, but on 5 July Napoleon proposed a truce. On 11 July, he signed an armistice at Villafranca and agreed with Franz Joseph that only Lombardy would be ceded to the Kingdom of Sardinia. He had been affected by the savagery of the war, he faced considerable domestic hostility to his Italian campaign, and he feared a Prussian attack on the Rhine. For Italians this was an anticlimax.

Garibaldi had acquitted himself with distinction. Neglected by the Piedmontese command, he moved from the depots at the request of Victor Emanuel. The king received him at military headquarters on 8 May. His orders were to take part in the defense of Turin, and he was therefore to carry out operations in the area around Lake Maggiore, "harrying the Austrian right flank in the manner you think best." He authorized him to gather all the volunteers and recruit others, and the ordered the civil and military authorities and local government administrations to provide him with all assistance.

Once the capital was free from danger after 16 May, Garibaldi was effectively free to move around an area he was already acquainted from the campaign he fought there in 1848. At that time he had been an irregular who continued to fight after Charles Albert had signed the armistice, but now he was a general in the Piedmontese army. On 25 April he made a brief proclamation to his men, "We have come to the moment we have all desired, to the purpose of our hopes. You will be fighting the nation's oppressors." He demanded "the most severe discipline and complete obedience." He needed to be followed blindly if he was to carry out his intended maneuvers to disorient the enemy. He was counting on his expert and courageous officers, Medici and Nino Bixio, who had defended Rome, and Enrico Cosenz, who distinguished himself in Venice.

He marched toward Arona on Lake Maggiore, and notified the authorities that they should prepare rations and billets, as though he intended to skirt the lake. Instead he took his units to the River Ticino during the night, after giving instructions not to talk, smoke or light a match, and on 23 May he crossed the river on boats and surprised the Austrian garrison at Sesto Calende. He had entered Lombardy with one of his typical surprise attacks without even informing his own officers. On the main front, the armies were still studying each other, so his action created a sensation among the population.

The following night he reached Varese under pouring rain and greeted by a delirious crowd of its citizens. At the same time an Austrian division of three thousand well-equipped men with cavalry and artillery was bearing down on him under the command of General Urban. Garibaldi could not abandon the city to the enemy without a fight. He ordered his men not to open fire until the enemy were fifty paces away (an expedient that he had successfully adopted in America). The men obeyed, even though they were under fire from the artillery. The Austrians were hit by a deadly hail of bullets and then subjected to a bayonet attack. The attack by the *Cacciatori* forced them to retreat. The tactic imposed by Garibaldi meant the sacrifice of many lives: that day, Ernesto Cairoli fell; he was the youngest of five brothers, four of whom would die fighting for Italy.

Garibaldi could not allow himself to become a target for an enemy that was receiving reinforcements. His war had to be one of movement. He left for Como, and pretended that he would take the Camerlata road, when he actually went by San Fermo. There he came across fierce resistance, which he overcame in a bloody encounter. During the night he entered Como, where the inhabitants led the way with torches and lit up their windows.

Garibaldi drove the Austrians from the part of Lombardy around Lake Maggiore, and the government acknowledged his bravery by awarding him the gold medal and bonuses for his men. However his small detachment was far from its bases and needed supplies. "Continuous marches;

never still for more than six hours; no regular meals, only bread, cheese, salami and occasionally a little roasted meat: that is all the soldiers get. Our misfortune was the continuous lack of shoes," wrote Bixio. Garibaldi returned toward Lake Maggiore. He was heading for Laveno, where there was a fort in which he could find arms, munitions, clothing, and three Austrian steamboats for lake navigation. On 31 May, the raid under the rain and again during the night ended in failure due to an inability to coordinate the movements of the different units. On the same day, General Urban entered Varese and imposed a heavy fine on the city for having abandoned the Hapsburg government. He soon moved on to join up with the main body of the Austrian army, which, after Magenta, withdrew from Lombardy.

Garibaldi returned to Como. In the new situation, he saw his task on Lake Maggiore as complete. He embarked the *Cacciatori* on boats to cross the lake to Lecco, and from they moved to Bergamo, which they entered on 8 June. The following day he was received by Victor Emanuel in Milan. On 11 June, he awarded the decorations received to the officers and soldiers in Bergamo, and read a declaration in the name of the king that exalted the exploits of the small corps. That same evening he marched on Brescia. He chose tortuous mountain road to avoid meeting General Urban, who was still covering the right flank on the Austrian lines with seven thousand men. Along the way he stopped for a few minutes to listen carefully. Everyone went silent and wondered about the reason for halting, only to discover that he had been enchanted by the song of a nightingale. It was one of the many anecdotes that demonstrated Garibaldi's serenity during military operations. Witnesses described his behavior while he ate his rations with soldiers, drinking water from a spring, or sleeping on his poncho under the shade of an oak tree while awaiting the battle.

He entered Brescia in the morning to the waving of tricolors. Here his freedom of action ended. On 15 June he received orders directly from the king to go immediately to Lonato, where Franz Joseph's headquarters were located. The brigade of *Cacciatori* was supposed to take part in a complex operation that was then cancelled without informing Garibaldi. Cosenz and Colonel Stefano Türr, a Hungarian officer who had left the Austrian army, found themselves in difficulty. Garibaldi arrived, reorganized the demoralized men, and sent Menotti to inform the king. The arrival of army units redressed the imbalance between the sides. The Austrians boasted that they won a victory at Tre Ponti, but Garibaldi simply complained that he had been sent into a situation in which defeat appeared inevitable.

On 18 June the brigade returned to Salò on Lake Garda. In little more than a month, the *Cacciatori* had grown into a corps of twelve thousand men, due to the volunteers full of enthusiasm who were rushing to join them, but Garibaldi was put under the command Cialdini. Due to fears that a strong Austrian detachment could come down from Tyrol, Garibaldi's men were sent to the Stelvio Pass. At Edolo, Tirano, Tresenda, and Bormio, "they gave further demonstrations of their valor and determination in a new kind of war among the gorges and crags of the perennially snow-covered Alps, where the enemy was more acclimatized and familiar with the terrain as they were nearly all Tyrolese." These were the final adversities they had to suffer. On 7 July the supreme command entrusted Garibaldi with defense of the Alpine valleys, but the following day Napoleon signed the armistice with Franz Joseph at Villafranca. After little more than two months, the war Italians define as the Second War of Independence had come to an end.

16. Political Frustrations and Disappointments in Love

THE VILLAFRANCA ARMISTICE poured cold water on the plans of liberals fighting for unification. Even though it had ceded Lombardy, Austria retained its role as major power in Italy and it used that power to restore the *status quo ante* following the successes of the nationalist movement in the spring of 1859. On 27 April, when the hostilities began, the grand duke of Tuscany had to flee, and following the Franco-Piedmontese victory at Magenta the dukes of Parma and Modena left their states. The Papal Legations, no longer garrisoned by Austrian troops, rose up against papal rule. Provisional governments were set up in Florence, Parma, Modena, and Bologna, under Victor Emanuel's military and diplomatic protection. There was a real possibility of a large kingdom covering central and Northern Italy under the House of Savoy. But when the two emperors met in Villafranca, they decided that Austria should hold onto Venetia, and that the former sovereigns should be restored to the lost dominions without, however, the assistance of the Austrian army. As usual, hopes were expressed that the absolute monarchs would grant reforms and that an Italian confederation would be formed and presided over by the pope.

The Piedmontese government was informed of the decision only after it had been taken. Victor Emanuel had to adjust to the new situation and ratified the part of the agreement that concerned him, but not the decisions on the overall political structure of the Italian peninsula. Cavour, who was devastated by the collapse of the plans for which he had worked so hard, handed in his resignation. His place was taken by General La Marmora, while the government's political mind became Urbano Rattazzi.

The unexpected manner in which the war came to an end left Italy in state of considerable uncertainty. French troops, who still garrisoned Rome, were to remain in Lombardy until the peace treaty was signed, but Napoleon was not to be ceded Savoy and Nice, because he had not liberated all of Lombardy-Venetia. There was a power vacuum in Central Italy. The provisional governments, which were made up of moderates who, since 1856, had been guided toward support for liberal Piedmont by the National Society, prevented a return to the previous political systems. In Florence, Modena, Parma, and Bologna, the assemblies met and declared their annexation by Piedmont. A diplomatic crisis resulted from this "Revolution of the Moderates," the name that came to be used for the ruling class's refusal to accept a peaceful return of the former monarchs. While Victor Emanuel limited himself to taking note of the decisions of the assemblies presented to him by delegations, the four provisional governments set about establishing a united front particularly when it came to organizing their defense, and on 10 August they reached an agreement to form a military alliance called the League. They called on Garibaldi to lead their armed forces, and he took command on 16 August.

The campaign by the *Cacciatori delle Alpi* had again brought him to the attention of the public, both in Italy and abroad. Naturally the events of the war were followed in the Kingdom of Sardinia and the countries freed from absolutism with trepidation in the early weeks and with glee as one Franco-Piedmontese victory followed another. Newspaper articles discussed the generals, units in the two armies, their uniforms, and their weapons. Surprisingly a great deal of information was circulating in Naples, too, and this demonstrates the importance attributed to what was happening further north. Although public opinion was concerned about Ferdinand II's deteriorating health after a long illness (he died on 22 May), the Bourbon government allowed the newspapers and magazines to provide plenty of news on the war and its protagonists.

The clash between the two great powers was also attracting international attention. Observers and journalists were coming to Italy from all parts of the world, including Britain and Russia, which was now hostile to Austria following its disloyalty during the Crimean War. The spotlight was also on Garibaldi, even though he was confined to a military sideshow. The reporting was sympathetic to him, as the situation was different from the one ten years earlier when, as the general of the Roman Republic, he was looked on as the enemy of established order. *Le Siècle* and the *Times* followed his exploits in a war that had the support of liberal Europe. Karl Marx and Friedrich Engels often mentioned him in their articles on the war for the *New York Daily Tribune*.

L'Illustration produced illustrations from sketches, drawings from life, and photographs sent by their correspondents (photography was becoming more widely used), and the subject matter mainly concerned the emperor, the French units involved, their departure, their life in Italy (in the barracks and cafés), fraternization with Piedmontese units, the battle lines, acts of valor by the Zouaves, and the torment of the wounded. The Sardinian troops, including the *Cacciatori delle Alpi*, also obtained some coverage. The magazine's May issue showed four uniforms of the *Légion Garibaldi*, and the June issue published a portrait of Garibaldi *commandant les Chasseurs des Alpes*, a view of Como as it was Garibaldi's headquarters (taken from a photograph), Austrians taken prisoner by Garibaldi's troops landing at Arona, the warship *Radetzky* on the lake bombarding a convoy of supplies being sent to the *Cacciatori*, and the night attacks on Fort Laveno and Fort San Fermo.

In June *Le Monde Illustré* published not only Garibaldi's portrait, but also his entrance into Como on horseback with the cathedral in the background, and some members of his contingent. The illustrations were based on photographs sent by Léonce Dupont. In June, the *Illustrated London News* produced a full-page portrait of him on his white horse, wearing his poncho and his dark feathered hat, and brandishing his sword. This was followed by a detailed biography that covered all periods of his life and bestowed much praise upon him.

Another novelty was the explosion of popular biographies based on Cuneo's but filled out with unbridled fantasies. Dwight's *Memoirs*, whose publication Garibaldi finally authorized, were not used, and in any case they were not published until after the war. The French novelist Louise Goethe speedily put together a biography which was published at the beginning of June and then translated into Italian and Dutch. It was imitated and partially plagiarized by the German Ludwig von Alvensleben and the Frenchman Claude Pitz. The books invented incredible embellishments: Garibaldi was born in a rowing boat during a tempest, at the age of nine he killed a Moroccan pirate chief while boarding the enemy ship, and after the Mazzini plot he escaped and became a brigand in the Italian highlands. Then a count engaged him as a tutor for his daughter, he fell in love with the girl and when the noble dismissed him, he set the castle afire and had a hermit marry them in the woods. When the girl died, he went on to other amorous adventures in Tunisia and later in South America, where he married a Creole woman with whom Rosas was infatuated.

Garibaldi was depicted as a barbaric warrior in these biographies, as he was in the less fantastic, but still invented, ones published in England. Journalists and foreign tourists went to meet him out of curiosity were surprised to find him so normal. *Le Pays* correspondent, Léonce Dupont went to interview him in Como and admitted that he expected to see "a felt hat, a savage physiognomy framed by a mass of uncombed hair, a smock and wide belt adorned with a dozen cavalry pistols, and unsheathed saber in his hand." The more serious papers did not present this picture: the portrait in *Illustration*, made from a photo taken in Turin before his departure (as specified in the paper) showed a man who looked after his appearance and correctly dressed in the uniform of a Piedmontese general: a blue tunic with silver braid on the collar and cuffs. This photo was reproduced on leaflets and widely distributed in Italy and abroad. Dupont had to admit that Garibaldi's hair was short, his beard was similar to those worn in Paris, and the frightening warrior used spectacles. We know that they were a type of pince-nez held with a cord that went round the back of his neck.

This same bourgeois appearance was described in a letter to the *Times* by some English tourists who went to Como from Switzerland. Garibaldi spoke to them and entertained them not with talk of war but with his memories of China and his travels in the Pacific. The visitors had expected a sallow man with a black beard and the romantic appearance of a Spanish bandit. They were surprised to find that he had "a healthy English complexion" and spoke "without the gesticulations of southerners, but with the calm manners and appearance of a British officer and gentleman."

A legend had in fact been formed around Garibaldi, and it reflected naive popular beliefs. Austrian soldiers feared him and called him "the red devil," because of his unpredictable maneuvers and his ability to escape numerically superior forces. People in the countries he passed through applauded him and attempted to kiss his hands or his garments. They kept portraits of him in their houses and lit candles to him, as though he were a saint.

Once the hostilities were over, the Sardinian government, which no longer needed to attract volunteers and keep them under control, found Garibaldi something of an encumbrance. When, at the end of July, he was invited to Florence by Bettino Ricasoli, who had become head of the provisional government in Tuscany, the Piedmontese army gladly accepted his resignation. Garibaldi, who was keen to engage in new exploits, was in Livorno by 13 August. In the meantime, the military alliance between the provisional governments had been agreed, and on 16 August he found himself head of the forces gathered in Central Italy.

From both a military and a political point of view, it was not the most suitable task for Garibaldi. The forces that he had to unify were made up of the Tuscan army, which had been reorganized by the Neapolitan exile Gerolamo Ulloa and consisted of two brigades of infantry and some cavalry and artillery units, with the addition of volunteers from Romagna, the small parts of the armies of Modena and Parma that did not transfer over to the Austrians with their masters the dukes, and some units of the papal army which had mainly withdrawn to those provinces that had remained loyal to the pope. After Villafranca, there was an urgent need to consolidate and enlarge these disparate forces and enable them to repel attacks from their deposed monarchs. They needed an organizer and not an inciter of men like Garibaldi. The *Cacciatori delle Alpi* had been a disciplined corps because it had been trained in accordance with the Piedmontese army practice before the war in training camps. Now the situation was different and required a commitment that Garibaldi did not find agreeable.

"For me organizing troops is a very tedious occupation," he would write in his *Memoirs* as he recalled those months.

Turin sent General Manfredo Fanti, who originated from Carpi, had been in exile since 1831, and was a veteran of wars in Portugal and Spain. He had returned to Italy in 1848 and joined the Piedmontese army in which he had fought in the Crimea. He was the man for the job, as he had been born in the Duchy of Modena and had trained in both irregular militias and the regular army. He was put in command of all the forces at the end of August. Garibaldi stepped back and became second-in-command. Moreover he was the commander of the Third Division recruited in Emilia (the name given to the union of the Papal Legations and the two duchies) while the First Division was commanded by Pietro Roselli and the Second Division by the Neapolitan Luigi Mezzacapo.

Garibaldi found himself in a subordinate position. He had to witness the rejection of his officers and the *Cacciatori* on any pretext, who "came as a barefoot crowd dressed canvass jackets, all tired and broken by the long journey" only to be refused even food and the means to return to their homes. More serious is the disappointment at being unable to act in accordance with Mazzini's political proposals. After Villafranca, Mazzini attacked the limitations imposed by the moderate policies of the Sardinian government, which were dependent on diplomacy. In his opinion, the nationalists needed to develop the insurrectionist policies that had succeeded in Central Italy. The situation in Italy was such that it was now possible to recruit volunteers in the Papal Legations, invade Le Marche and Umbria, remove them from papal rule and then invade Abruzzo to trigger an uprising in the south and Sicily. In a few weeks the papal dominion would have been reduced to Lazio and the Bourbon kingdom would have been eliminated: Italy would have been unified, with the exception of Rome which was garrisoned by the French, and Venetia, which was in Austrian hands. To implement this plan in the summer of 1859, Mazzini left England to return to Italy and lived in hiding in Florence during August and September. He then withdrew to Lugano, as he wanted to stay close, and there he wrote *Letter to Victor Emanuel*, in which he called on him to lead a people's struggle for national unification.

This was not an initiative that you could ask of the king. The territorial changes in Italy, which had been recognized by the great powers and guaranteed by Napoleon, were conditional on the maintenance of order and stability in Europe, and the blows inflicted on the church's temporal dominion were upsetting Catholics. Even many democrats, who had previously broken with Mazzini, feared that an imprudent move would provide Austria with the pretext for restoring the deposed monarchs to their thrones. Garibaldi's inclination was always to carry out an aggressive maneuver likely to confound the enemy's plans. Mazzini was counting on him and thought of stimulating Garibaldi's ambition by making him supreme commander or dictator. In the state of uncertainty that persisted in Central Italy—the peace treaty signed in Zurich 10 November was to confirm the Villafranca accords—it seemed possible to justify an armed intervention if there were an insurrection in Le Marche. Fanti made provisions for this eventuality in an operational order of 19 October, which spoke of the case of an uprising in "a whole province in Le Marche or a city like Pesaro." On 29 November Garibaldi asked to be joined by Medici and other loyal officers. "I am considering an attack that could put us in a favorable position and immensely advance our cause. General Fanti is a good and true Italian, but he is a little indecisive. I will take full responsibility for this undertaking."

Garibaldi was put in command of the troops on the border with Le Marche on 26 October, an imprudent decision if League did not want to attack, given that Garibaldi's ideas were well known, and in that position he issued proclamations inciting papal subjects to rebel. Within the governments of the League there was dissent over the appropriateness of an attack. Victor Emanuel became involved and called Garibaldi to Turin on 28 October. He requested him to desist, but did not obtain any undertaking. The king then wrote to Fanti telling him to resign and to advise Garibaldi to do the same. Fanti resigned but he did not involve Garibaldi; indeed, he handed him the command. It appeared difficult to remove a man of Garibaldi's prestige from Romagna. He was adored, and everywhere he went he was greeted by large demonstrations of support. "This man enjoys an immense, universal, and almost unlimited popularity," wrote an Englishwoman to Ricasoli on 26 October. On the thirty-first of the same month, Farini asserted, "We all know the prestige carried by the name of General Garibaldi, whose presence calms the suspicious, reassures the impatient, and constitutes a considerable element in the concord we are seeking."

In Turin, Fanti became aware of the need not to create difficulties for the government, which had been asked by Napoleon to prevent any further actions by volunteers. He therefore returned to Modena to take back command of the armed forces. Garibaldi, who came under pressure from the moderates and General Solaroli who had been sent by the king, decided not to go ahead with his plan. But on 13 November, on hearing the mistaken report that an uprising was taking place in Le Marche, ordered his troops to cross the border. Fanti bypassed him and peremptorily ordered Roselli and Mezzacapo to ignore Garibaldi's command. Garibaldi's position was unsustainable. Following a violent argument with Fanti and Farini, whom he held responsible for having prevented an initiative that would have led to success and therefore considered his personal enemies, Garibaldi left for Turin and on 15 November was persuaded by the king to resign.

The succession of contradictory decisions was a result of the uncertain situation in which assessments kept changing. The only thing that remained unchanged was Garibaldi's obedience to the king as he had broken with Mazzini in 1849, and it now adhered to Mazzini's plans. He did it only in as much as they coincided with his own desire to break the diplomatic deadlock through a popular initiative. He trusted Victor Emanuel to develop the political strategy, but he had little faith in the men who surrounded him. On 19 November, he declared in a proclamation to all Italians that he was withdrawing from military service for the moment, because his freedom of action was restricted by the devious arts of others, and he asked them to give full support to the king, a brave and loyal soldier for independence. Once again, we should bear in mind that Garibaldi always wanted to be invested with power by some legitimate authority, and always worked with a politician who held an official position. In Rio Grande he had followed Bento Gonçalves in spite of his reservations about his character, in Uruguay he had remained loyal to Pacheco y Obes in spite of being hurt by his indifference to Rosita's death, and in Italy Victor Emanuel was his point of reference.

During the final months of 1859 Garibaldi did attempt to carry out some independent political activity in the belief that it was agreeable to the king. In September he launched a popular campaign to raise five thousand francs to buy a million rifles with hopes of arming the people, and he put

Enrico Besana from Milan and Giuseppe Finzi from Mantua in charge of this enterprise. Following his resignation, he went to Nice and then Genoa, with the intention of leaving for Caprera. But he was persuaded to remain on the continent in the hope of new developments, and therefore stayed on in Sestri. On 28 December he went to Turin and was received by the king, who had demonstrated his friendship by sending the gift of a hunting rifle and appointing him as his aide-de-camp. The king now wanted to engage him to organize a rapid-response unit called a *guardia mobile* in Lombardy. Garibaldi accepted and hoped "to be able to recruit all our poor roving comrades," something that was a great worry to him, as he confided to Giacomo Medici.

In the capital, there were attempts to return Cavour to power, and some democrats who supported Rattazzi tried to exploit the general's prestige to shore up the Left against him. Garibaldi resigned from the presidency of the National Society, which he had only taken on in October, in order to become the president of a new association, the Armed Nation. This maladroit move soon proved a failure and the king then got involved. "He summoned me and told to desist from all plans." The *guardia mobile* was cancelled and the Armed Nation had to be dissolved. Garibaldi's prestige had suffered a blow. "The giant has been cut down to size in recent times," noted Pallavicino; "Garibaldi is not an *eagle* but a *lion*. A lion is distinguished by its *strength* and not its *intelligence*. Here I am discussing Garibaldi as a politician; I will not judge him as a soldier."

During his stay in Romagna, Garibaldi paid due homage to the memory of Anita. On 7 August just before leaving for Tuscany, he informed Teresita of his intention of taking the opportunity to go to Comacchio and have his wife's "sacred remains" moved to Nice close to those of his mother. This was carried out in September. On 20 September he arrived in Ravenna, accompanied by Teresita, who had come from Nice with Colonel Deideri and his wife, Menotti and a female friend, and Esperance von Schwartz who would leave us details of the journey. They were greeted with particular warmth in memory of the events of 1849. He took a cart to the Guiccioli farm, where a jubilant crowd awaited. Stefano Ravaglia had expected him and prepared a banquet with eight guests. The house was crowded with visitors and his rescuers, in particular Nino Bonnet, wanted to see him. When

it came to the toast, Garibaldi gave a short political speech in which he recalled the comrades who fell in 1849. He had thought that they had found
safety abroad.

This, of course, was not the purpose of the journey. Some fifty carriages
went to the little church where Anita was buried. Her remains were placed
in a coffin covered with flowers close to the altar. After the benediction,
Garibaldi went on his knees and remained with his head on the coffin absorbed in his own thoughts. Then he offered money to the parish priest,
who wanted to refuse it, but they forced him to accept it with the words, "For
the poor of the parish." The coffin was entrusted to Colonel Deideri, who
transported it overland to Nice. The Brazilian wife was buried next to
Signora Rosa, where she remained even after the city passed into French
hands. On 4 June 1932, Anita's remains were again disturbed and moved to
Rome and their final resting place on the Janiculum, at the foot of a monument erected in her memory in the place where her José demonstrated his
valor in 1849. Another monument stands in his memory. Her love for Garibaldi made her a heroine in a country in which she lived for little more than
a year, while shifting between Nice and the places in which her husband
was living: she understood Italy very little and only felt part of it through her
relationship with her husband.

The melancholy ceremony concluded the long process of mourning
Anita. For some time and since he had set up home in Caprera, he had
been feeling the need to have a wife and companion who loved and understood him. He had forgotten Emma Roberts, and discovered his ideal
woman in Baroness Maria Esperance von Schwartz. She had had a cosmopolitan education (she could speak English, French, German, and Italian fluently, and she knew Greek, Spanish, and Arabic) and an adventurous
life (she had traveled in the East, Africa, and Europe), and she was also
beautiful, elegant, cultured, witty, and audacious. Moreover she was a passionate and observant traveler (she described the views and customs of the
places she visited, followed the tracks of events and personalities, and went
to the prison in Civita Castellana to meet the brigand Gasparoni). The
baroness was born in England in 1821 to rich German parents, and studied in Geneva and Rome. She married a cousin who committed suicide,
and then a Hamburg banker, whom she divorced in 1854, after having
had a son. She then moved to Rome, where she started a busy literary and

journalistic career under the pseudonym Elpis Melena, which was her name translated into Greek.

Esperance saw Garibaldi in Rome in 1849 and was thrilled by him. In Germany and Austria she had heard the incredible stories associated with his name. Wishing to know more about his life, she got hold of the manuscript of his *Memoirs*, which stopped, however, in 1848. In the autumn of 1857 she went to Caprera to persuade Garibaldi to finish his autobiography with the Roman events. He invited her to sleep on the island, but she preferred to return to Maddalena. The following day she (thirty-seven-years-old) visited him (fifty-one-years-old) again, and was captivated by him. He in turn was captivated by her.

When she left the ship in Livorno, she sent clothes to Teresita and presents for other members of the family. Garibaldi wrote to her on 28 November.

> If there has ever been a circumstance in which I have wanted to be something and possess qualities that I could lay at a woman's feet, then this is certainly it. It was natural that I should love you before knowing you! You were interested in my personality and became something dear in my imagination. But reality has been good to me, and I felt truly happy and honored that so dear, kind, and generous a lady should take interest in me even for a moment.

This was the beginning of an intense exchange of letters. On 24 January 1858, she expressed "the boundless affection" she felt for him and would always feel for him. She regretted that she lacked "all the qualities that *he would want* from a woman" and wanted him to know "that I am with you in spirit and with all my heart no matter where you are and I have no thought that is not directed to you." She asked him not to forget "her deeply felt and profound love, which cannot end even when life ends in the soul of a woman who is with all her heart yours, yours, yours."

In the summer of 1858 she returned to Caprera. This time she accepted the frugal hospitality. During a romantic walk, Garibaldi asked her "to unite her destiny with his, take the place of Anita, and become the mother of his children," who had in fact accepted her with great goodwill. Esperance was surprised (is it possible that such a worldly-wise woman was unaware of the sentiments she had provoked?), and said she needed time to reflect upon his proposal. Perhaps she feared impoverishing her personality in his island hermitage surrounded by sheep and the sea. Perhaps she did not want to get mixed up in a rather undignified situation.

When he set up home on the Isle of Caprera, Garibaldi brought over from Nice a domestic help, a young illiterate girl of peasant family called Battistina Raveo. She was the only woman among the few inhabitants on the island in whom he could have a sexual interest. On 5 May 1859, as military operations commenced, he received news that he had become a father for the fifth time: he had a daughter who was christened Anna Maria Imeni, but would be called Anita. To acknowledge her by marrying her mother, he needed the death certificate for his Brazilian wife. The trip to Comacchio also had this prosaic purpose. But the Caprera entourage did not want the illustrious general to marry an obscure woman of humble origins. Signora Deideri accused her of infidelity and sent her back to Nice.

The girl was to have an unhappy life. Her father, who was taken away by his political commitments, spent little time with her and only on an irregular basis: a few months after the failed marriage in August of 1860 during a quick trip to Maddalena at the time the Expedition of the Thousand. When he returned to live on the island in November of the same year, the little girl was already in Nice with her mother. Garibaldi provided them with means of support but could not oversee his daughter's upbringing. After a while, Esperance took action and obtained custody. She sent her to a school for young girls in Switzerland (Ricciotti, too, had been entrusted to female friends and brought up far away from his father in England. The intention was to give Anita the best of educations, but in practice the girl, who was then nine, was torn from the environment in which she had always lived. As she was not given sufficient emotional support, she opposed the move as hard as she could, and her father was not content with the education that she received, which in his opinion was too upperclass. He responded coldly to her letters or not at all. Later Esperance took her to her villa in Crete and handed her over to the care of hired staff.

In the spring of 1875, the girl, now sixteen, managed to inform her father that she was being mistreated. Garibaldi, who at the time was in Frascati, sent Menotti to bring her to him. He was appalled and wrote to his friend, "My beloved Esperance, Menotti arrived today with Anita, who is in good health and has become a woman, but infested with more fleas than I have ever seen on any human being!" The young girl could now start an untroubled existence in Caprera, but fate was not going to allow it. One day in August, Anita died after a meal of seafood, struck down by a sudden attack of meningitis. "My poor daughter, I couldn't even send you some words of love," the father acknowledged with a belated sense of guilt. His faith in Esperance began to fade.

In 1859 the noblewoman remained close to him, in spite of rejecting a further marriage proposal. Garibaldi asked her to join him in Modena. She rushed from a spa town in the Pyrenees, and accompanied him on the trip to Mandriole and Anita's grave. But his plans for marriage were now taking him in different directions. In Bologna he had fallen in love with thirty-year-old Paolina Pepoli, the widow of Count Zucchini. It was a brief love affair. Then his heart was lost to the seventeen-year-old Giuseppina Raimondi of Fino near Como, a marquis' daughter. He met her in a manner worthy of an adventure novel: while he was fighting near Varese, she came alone on a gig to bring him a message and had to pass through an area patrolled by the Austrian. He was immediately struck by her. He wrote her a passionate letter from Bologna on 3 September, but revealed that he belonged to another woman. He met her in Como and declared his love to her on bended knee.

On 30 November, he explained to the marquis' daughter the conflict between love and duty that was tormenting him. Duty called him to the side of a plebeian woman with whom he had had a child: but "I can no longer love her and I must never marry her!" On the other hand, if he married a noblewoman, "I would repudiate my characteristic self-abnegation which provided me with some of the popularity I greatly prize and could be of value to me in assisting our nation. When Italian affairs call me once again to lead soldiers into battle, it will be said of Garibaldi: he has schemed to get his fortune! He has separated himself from the people for whom he has so often boasted his willingness to lay down his life." He emphasized the age difference and his faltering health, but he did not want to lose her and demanded an immediate reply, because he loved her and could wait no longer. He went to her villa in Fino in December 1859. During the night of the 3 December, she put aside her doubts and entered his bedroom. The deed was done! A contusion of the knee caused him to postpone the marriage, which took place 24 January 1860 in the chapel at the villa, with Teresita as bridesmaid.

According to a well-established tradition, a letter was handed over to the bridegroom immediately after the ceremony, and it revealed that the bride had had a love affair with an officer, along with other embarrassing details about her behavior. Garibaldi showed Giuseppina the letter, and she confirmed its content. Harsh words were exchanged: "Whore!" "Beastly soldier!" In his outrage, he brandished a chair. They were not to see each other again.

By placing the revelation immediately after the fateful marriage vows, Garibaldi's biographers achieved two things: they lessened the humiliation for the intrepid general, who otherwise would not have realized that he had conquered a fortress already taken by others, and they supposed his application to annul the marriage on the grounds of nonconsummation. However, a dispassionate examination of the facts reveals that the ardent suitor had already tasted the fruits of his passion without discovering the deceit, and it has been shown that the marriage lasted a few days before the letter arrived and revealed the truth. It was probably written by the bride's cousin and former lover.

The letter must have arrived on the evening of the twenty-seventh or the morning of the twenty-eighth, because that is the date on which Garibaldi wrote to his friend Lorenzo Valerio, the governor (prefect) of Como, of his "well-founded suspicions concerning Giuseppina's honesty" and his desire for "separation from her that is as complete as possible." Giuseppina Raimondi had had a busy romantic past, and had just had a relationship with a young and brilliant cavalry officer called Luigi Caroli. Knowing that she was pregnant and without hope of marrying the father, she accepted the offer from the ageing and lovesick suitor. She then precipitated things so that she could write to him on 1 January that she was expecting his baby.

The scandal was hushed up, but the consequences of the affair would weigh upon the three protagonists. Caroli, as though to redeem himself, left with Francesco Nullo to fight for Polish independence in 1863, and was taken prisoner by the Russians only to die in Siberia in 1865. Giuseppina Raimondi's child was stillborn in the summer of 1859. She spoke very little of the affair, and would attempt to justify herself by pointing out how difficult it was for an eighteen-year-old girl to resist pressures from her parents. Following her divorce, she married again and her long life ended in 1918. The divorce was a torment for Garibaldi, and he was smarting from the affront. On 29 January 1860, shortly after moving to Milan, he asked Valerio "to warn Giuseppina not to sign herself *Garibaldi*, because if I come to hear of it, I will certainly prevent her by any means." He wrote to Deideri from Caprera requesting information and documents, and informed him that he wanted "an annulment, not merely a separation." His version was clear. He wrote to Valerio:

The marriage has not been consummated. Before the marriage, between 8 December and around 20 January, I had sexual intercourse with her, but on the 20th she became ill with what was believed to be smallpox and there were no more carnal relations. Given therefore that marriage occurred on 24th and having never again had sexual intercourse, I believe that we can consider the marriage *unconsummated*.

Unfortunately for the spouses, whatever happens in the privacy of a bedroom has no witnesses, and the assertions of an interested party have little value. Garibaldi attempted to obtain an annulment at all costs, and asked for the assistance of influential friends, even the king. This desire became even more pressing when he had more children by a new cohabitant who insisted upon the union being regularized. Finally in 1879, the ingenious lawyer Pasquale Stanislao Mancini came up with a legal nicety to resolve the problem. He made use of the fact that in January 1860 the Austrian Civil Code was still in force in Lombardy, as this permitted the annulment of a legally sanctioned but unconsummated marriage. This opened the way to the dissolution of his marriage to Giuseppina Raimondi, which was delivered by the Court of Appeal of Rome on 14 January 1880. Thus the most bitter experience in Garibaldi's private life came to an end more after more than twenty years.

17. The Epic Campaign
of the Thousand

THE SITUATION OF uncertainty in Central Italy was a danger to peace in Europe. Neither the little Kingdom of Sardinia nor the weak provisional governments could decide with their forces the destinies of the territories removed by revolution from their legitimate sovereigns. A new political physiognomy of the Italian peninsula depended on the great powers. Cavour, who returned to power in January 1860, concluded an agreement with Napoleon. France came out of the war without making the territorial gains agreed in Plombières. The enlargement of the kingdom ruled by the House of Savoy would have made it possible to return to negotiations on ceding Savoy and Nice to France. An agreement between the French emperor and Cavour removed the impasse.

In March 1860 the populations of Tuscany, the duchies, and the Papal Legations voted in plebiscites to become a part of Victor Emanuel's constitutional monarchy. On 25 March, a general election was held in the whole state, both the previous possessions of the House of Savoy and the newly acquired provinces. But when the parliament met on 2 April, it was made known that Victor Emanuel had signed a treaty that permitted the return of Nice and Savoy to France. Two plebiscites were held, in Nice on 15 April and in Savoy on 22 April, and they both ratified the decision with a large majority.

The territorial concessions, the final result of the mechanisms set in motion by Plombières, had to be approved by parliament. Garibaldi was elected deputy for Nice, and was indignant that his native city was being transferred to France. He wrote to Cremona, Pavia, Brescia, Bologna, and Faenza requesting that councils and associations send pleas to parliament against the transfer of territory. He thought of carrying out a putsch to prevent the plebiscite, but this route proved infeasible. On 12 April he spoke to the chamber in defense of Nice as an Italian city. The opposition requested the postponement of the voting on the annexation, which had been arranged for 15 April in order to give parliament time to discuss the question. Cavour's majority rejected this proposal. The debate was actually held at the end of May and the beginning of June when the whole thing was a *fait accompli* and Victor Emanuel had carried out his triumphal journey around Central Italy to confirm the House of Savoy's commitment to Italy following its renunciation of its transalpine dominions.

Garibaldi was far away. During the early months of 1860 he continued to busy himself with assisting wounded volunteers and officers in financial need. He was still working on collecting the funds for a million rifles: modern Enfield rifles had been bought and Colonel Colt had sent a hundred of his famous revolvers from New York as a gift. What was the purpose of these weapons? As things stood, another war against Austria to take Venetia or an invasion of the Papal States was unthinkable.

In the summer and autumn of 1859, there had been a plan to trigger a rebellion in Sicily in unison with Mazzini's plan to widen the Italian revolution to the south by marching through Le Marche and Umbria. Sicilians were hostile to Naples which, they believed, treated them as a colony. Up until the beginning of the nineteenth century, the island had been an independent kingdom linked to the Kingdom of Naples simply through a union of the crowns. Up until that time it had retained its own parliament and its own institutions that had a long history. Between 1806 and 1815 Ferdinand IV of Bourbon, who had been driven from Naples by the French army, took refuge in Palermo under the protection of the British fleet, and there he clashed with Sicilian feudal interests, which had been strengthened by the prerogatives granted by the Constitution. In 1815, when he recovered Southern Italy, he united the two states in the single Kingdom of the Two Sicilies with its capital in Naples, and declared himself Ferdinand I. He abolished the Sicilian Constitution, and extended the southern administrative orders to Sicily. These orders were based on the Napoleonic model of centralization. Sicilians never accepted this loss of their own state, and rebelled in 1820 and 1837. In 1848, they managed to expel the royal troops, declared the Bourbon dynasty to be forfeit, and placed a son of Charles Albert, King of Sardinia, on the throne. Ferdinand II had to crush the rebellion militarily and it took more than a year to take Palermo.

The island had remained in a state of ferment resulting from the strength of separatist sentiment and the weakness of central government. It should be remembered that Sicilians refused to submit to military conscription, which had become essential for national armies since the end of the eighteenth century, and the Bourbon troops, which were made up of Neapolitans and foreign corps, found themselves in the situation of an occupying army in Sicily, much as the Austrians occupied Lombardy-Venetia.

Ferdinand II died in May 1859. His successor, the young Francis II, refused the Kingdom of Sardinia's invitation to take part in the war against Austria by granting a Constitution. Austria's defeat deprived the kingdom of its principal ally, but the king kept faith with absolutism and made no attempt to get emigrants on his side, as they were willing to return if he started to introduce reforms. Opponents of the regime in the south were mainly moderates under strict police surveillance, and they looked toward the House of Savoy, but they were not willing to take the initiative and were awaiting external intervention. In Sicily, opposition to the government, which was fueled by hatred of Naples and widespread poverty, was much stronger and raised hopes of widespread popular participation in any insurrection. Francesco Crispi, who secretly went to the island on Mazzini's behalf in July–August of 1859 following Villafranca, reported that a revolution would be supported by everyone. To start it, Crispi decided in December to use the volunteers left behind by Garibaldi in Romagna, and to send them off from the Isle of Elba under Garibaldi's command. The plan could not be implemented for the moment.

Unrest in Sicily was on the increase in early 1860, and this was serious enough to cause concern among European governments, who feared that the insurrection was imminent. In January–February, Victor Emanuel sent Enrico Bensa, in whom he placed great trust, to Palermo to establish contact with moderate aristocrats. The ideal of national unity started to gather strength alongside the separatist movement and there was an increasing willingness to accept Victor Emmanuel's leadership. In March, news of the annexations in Central Italy increased expectation of an anti-Bourbon initiative and exiles increased their efforts to bring one about.

Many hopes were placed on Garibaldi. Rosolino Pilo, a follower of Mazzini who was about to leave for the island, asked him for financial assistance from the fund for a million rifles, and invited him to take command of the country "militarily" by bringing together "all the active elements." On 15 March, Garibaldi clarified some points on which there was to be no argument. Above all, his program was *Italy and Victor Emanuel*. Although willing to take on any enterprise "however risky it might be, when it came to fighting enemies of our country," he did not believe that at that time "a revolutionary movement in any part of Italy" was opportune "unless it has a reasonable probability of success." In short, he was not willing to embark on some adventure aimed at triggering an insurrection that had not started, as had been the case with the Bandiera brothers and with Pisacane. He had put down these views on paper many times: he was ready to lead an expedition with the support of Victor Emanuel's state to strengthen a revolution that was already being fought. He therefore required that the revolution break out and acquire a certain magnitude. Besides, Bensa, who was in the king's service, had come to the same conclusion.

A revolt broke out in Palermo on 4 April from the Monastery of Gancia da Pasquale Riso, and involved seventeen insurrectionists. It was immediately suppressed, but a series of local uprisings was triggered and forced the Bourbon army to control the island with mobile detachments. A concentration of rebels was annihilated at Carini on 18 April. The contrasting news on the magnitude of the insurrection caused indecision in Piedmont. After the Gancia uprising, Cavour was interested in taking the initiative away from the democrats, and summoned General Ignazio Ribotti to Turin. A native of Nice, he had been an exile in Portugal and Spain after 1831, and in 1848 he fought in the Sicilian army. Cavour asked him to lead an expedition, but let the matter drop after the success of the Bourbon repression. In mid-April he was again considering the possibility of armed intervention and this time he thought of the Sicilian Giuseppe La Masa. At the same time, he had the king write a letter to his "dear cousin" Francis II (son of Maria Cristina of Savoy) exhorting him to adopt the liberal and national principles of the House of Savoy: this was a means to demonstrate to Europe that the government in Turin was willing to negotiate with the Bourbons.

Officially peace reigned in Italy, and was guaranteed by France. It was up to the democrats to shift the balance of power between the two major Italian states. Pilo, who reached the island in April, did all he could to keep the revolutionary ferment alive by encouraging the resistance and promising Garibaldi's imminent arrival. A committee was set up in Genoa to give support to the uprising, and included Bertani, Bixio, and Crispi, who renewed his request to Garibaldi, but the latter was still uncertain. He feared ending up like Pisacane, but started to sound people out while he was in Turin to debate the Nice question in parliament. Many things had to be put in place. He convened Finzi to ascertain the availability of rifles bought from collected funds, talked to friends about the possibility of procuring a steamship to transport the volunteers, and he went to the king to ask for command of the army brigade for use in a Sicilian expedition. The leading officer of the brigade he wanted was Gaetano Sacchi who had been his officer in Montevideo. After some hesitation, the king rejected his proposal on 10 April: it was not possible to use the army against a sovereign with whom he was not at war.

Garibaldi, who was bitter about the Nice affair, decided on 13 April to go ahead with the Sicilian project. He took up residence in Genoa at Villa Spinola with Candido Augusto Vecchi, a veteran of the 1849 Rome campaign. The organizing committee was set up in Bertani's home. The propaganda to enroll volunteers was made publicly throughout the Kingdom of Sardinia. Cavour, who was passing through Genoa on 22 April on his return from Tuscany, received Giuseppe Sirtori, who came on Garibaldi's behalf, given that the latter did not want to meet the man who had made him a foreigner in his own country. Sirtori explained the plan, which was not without its difficulties. There was to be a twin attack on Bourbon territory: in Sicily and across the border from Le Marche, which more or less copied the planned invasion of Abruzzo through the Papal States. Cavour vetoed the involvement of the Papal States, but he promised to do what he could for the expedition to Sicily.

The government was between a rock and a hard place. It could not disown Garibaldi at a time when public opinion was unhappy about the price it had had to pay France for its assistance, and it had to demonstrate very clearly to European diplomacy that it was completely extraneous to any plans to subvert international order. The main diplomatic fears were that a reckless move could upset Franco-Austrian relations again. Foreign observers noted that the authorities made no attempt to prevent the build-up of volunteers in Genoa. Former officers in the *Cacciatori delle Alpi* came running in response to their general's request. Young men and not so young men flocked in and were keen to liberate their oppressed brothers from the tyrant. Recruitment centers were opened, particularly in Bergamo, Brescia, Milan, Pavia, and Como, all cities in Lombardy. Venetian, Tridentines, Southern Italians, and Sicilians were also joining up. The committee in Genoa proceeded with the selection, allocation of billets, collection of funds, and procurement of arms and supplies. Weapons were the main problem for the organizers: Massimo D'Azeglio, the governor of Milan, would not let the twelve thousand excellent Enfield carbines, bought with the collected funds, leave the depots in the city because he would not condone assisting a revolution against a sovereign with whom there were diplomatic relations. The carbines were used by the later expeditions. Little more than a thousand rifles were eventually obtained by using the ones Giuseppe La Farina, the secretary of the National Society, had prepared for La Masa. They were in poor condition, but were accepted in the absence of anything better.

While they were busy with the preparations and enthusiasm was continuously rising, a mixture of reassuring and disappointing news was arriving from Sicily. The organizational difficulties and impossibility of having reliable information on events on the island caused the departure to be postponed. The delay favored the arrival of more volunteers and increased the available men and equipment. On 12 April Garibaldi was ready to sail with two hundred men, on the twenty-eighth he could count on five hundred, but in the end he decided to take a thousand volunteers, and this proved to be a wise decision because it gave substance to the landing force, which initially did not encounter the promised assistance on the island.

Garibaldi was counting on massive support from the insurrectionists and wanted to be certain that the revolution was spreading throughout the island. On 27 April Nicola Fabrizi sent a coded telegram from Malta. Crispi, who had the code, read, "Complete failure in the province and city Palermo. Many refugees on British ships that have come into Malta. Stay where you are." The preparations were pretty much in place. Garibaldi had set about collecting money and equipment from every possible source. The departure date had been set for 28 April. Giambattista Fauché, agent for the company Rubattino of Genoa, had identified two steamships in the port that could be used for transport. It seemed impossible to turn back. Garibaldi convened the main participants. Crispi, La Masa, and Bixio insisted that they should go ahead, whereas Medici and Sirtori were against leaving without being sure of having the ground prepared. Garibaldi, decided to cancel the enterprise, which had begun to look reckless, and this was consistent with his often expressed views. On 29 April, he asked Fauché for a steamer to return to Caprera and announced his imminent arrival to his daughter Teresita. He notified Anna Pallavicino in the afternoon of the thirtieth of his departure for Caprera the following day. "We were ready, but news of a setback on the island has held us back," he wrote to Giovanni Verità.

There was immense disappointment. Some volunteers returned home, and many others expressed their desire to go with another leader, if Garibaldi was frightened. Bixio and La Masa said they were willing. Crispi persuaded them to wait, while anger, recriminations, and exhortations abounded. He was the one who found a solution to the impasse. On the twenty-ninth he informed Bertani and Garibaldi that he had incorrectly decoded Fabrizi's telegram, which should have read, "Insurrection defeated in the city of Palermo, holding up in the provinces," and then produced further communications that confirmed gains by the insurrectionists. Crispi probably falsified the content of the messages, as only he had the code to interpret them. In the existing atmosphere, it took only one pretext for enthusiasm to triumph. The following day, 30 April, while Villa Spinola celebrated the anniversary of the 1849 victory over the French in Rome, Garibaldi was persuaded and announced the expedition's departure. This was, after all, exactly what he wanted. He wrote on the 4 May to a friend:

The Sicilian insurrection carries the destinies of our nation. In the end I will find myself in my element: action in the service of a noble idea. Nothing else was needed to reawaken my courage in the midst of disappointments of every kind, which have left me embittered.

The die was cast. The doubters went silent. The preparations went on, and were completed within a few days.

On the evening of 5 May in the port of Genoa, around forty men gathered a few at a time on a small vessel with a lateen sail. They were not under surveillance, but all the same it was best not to attract attention. On 2 May Cavour rushed by train to Bologna to meet the king, who came up from Florence by carriage. It has never been known what they said to each other, but the fact is that Garibaldi was left in peace to carry out his preparations. The armed group under Bixio's orders, came alongside anchored steamships, the *Piemonte* and the *Lombardo*, both property of Rubattino Company. Fauché had ensured that they were unladen and ready for sea. The new arrivals board the ships. Some of the seamen refused to cooperate and are allowed to leave, while other stayed on to run the ships. Departure was not immediate as they needed to force a few doors, whose keys could not be found, light the boilers, build up steam, and start the engines. The *Lombardo*'s engines refused to start, and so the *Piemonte*, more quickly under steam, towed her out of port.

At half past eight, Garibaldi left Villa Spinola. He was wearing his red shirt, which from now on he would always wear: it was not the smock he wore in Montevideo, but a real shirt tucked into his trousers. Over it he wore an American poncho with a colored scarf around his neck. He was fully armed with saber, dagger, and pistol. He was aware that time was passing and started to worry that some problem had arisen. He took a dinghy and went out to the ships, boarded the *Piemonte,* and took command of his flotilla. The moonlight was splendidly clear. The ships steamed until they were just off Quarto, where the volunteers had been amassed for hours on the shore. They were crowded onto boats and barges, and then boarded onto the ships. The rifles were taken on board, while food and munitions were to be obtained at sea. Bertani handed over ninety thousand lira to Garibaldi. With other small sums of varied provenance, the expedition

started with a capital of barely ninety-four thousand lira. The general justified his undertaking in a message to the king.

> Sicily's cries of pain have reached my ears and moved my heart and
> the hearts of a few hundred of my comrades in arms. I have not en-
> couraged an insurrection by my brothers in Sicily, but given that they
> have risen up in the name of Italian unification of which Your Maj-
> esty is the personification, and against the most infamous tyranny of
> our age, I did not hesitate to accept the leadership of this expedition.

"Unity and Victor Emanuel" was then his battle-cry. In the event of victory he would add "this new and most brilliant jewel" to his crown. The
same program appeared in his proclamation to all Italians, who he invited
to assist the Sicilians "with their words, their gold, their weapons, and
above all their labor," and to rise up in Papal States and in the south.

He left Bertani the task of gathering together all the equipment and supplies that he could in order to assist the enterprise, and reminded him that
"the Sicilian insurrection does not only have to be assisted in Sicily, but
also in Umbria, Le Marche, Sabina, the Neapolitan region, etc.—wherever
there are enemies to be fought." On the operational side, he entrusted
Medici, who remained in Genoa, with the task of sending "reinforcements
of men and weapons" to Sicily and everywhere the revolution breaks out.
He could now see the image of Italy ready to take up arms against the Bourbons, the pope, and Austria.

As dawn broke on 6 May, the *Lombardo*, under Bixio's command, was
carrying eight hundred volunteers, and the *Piemonte* three hundred under
the command of its Sicilian captain, Salvatore Castiglia (he had been able
to provide Garibaldi with information on the speed and weaponry of Neapolitan warships). Not everyone who turned up could find a place on
board. There were already enough volunteers for the next expeditions.

Exactly how many men were squeezed into the two merchant ships?
1,162 departed from Genoa. In Talamone, as we shall see, the *Thousand of
Marsala* had become 1,089, or at least that was the number when they were
registered on the official list in 1878. They were professionals, students, ar-
tisans, and workers; they included about 250 lawyers, 100 doctors, 20 phar-
macists, 50 engineers, 50 sea captains, 100 shopkeepers, and around 10
artists, painters, and sculptors. There were a few priests, and one woman,

Rosalia Montmasson, who was Crispi's wife dressed in men's clothing. They were nearly all Italians, and the great majority northerners: the best represented provinces were Bergamo (163) and Liguria (154), whereas there were less than a hundred subjects of the Bourbon king. There were veterans, raw recruits, patriots who had escaped the noose and prison, idealists who followed dreams of glory, literary types in search of excitement, depressives who sought an early death, and the destitute who hoped to gain a place in society. The oldest, Tommaso Parodi from Genoa, was almost seventy-years-old, and the youngest, Giuseppe Marchetti of Chioggia, was an eleven-year-old who came with his father.

Only 150 wore the red shirt. Most were dressed in very different clothes. Garibaldi defined them as "multidressed," an effective neologism. Giuseppe Bandi, one of the volunteers on the expedition who would write his memoirs, was very attentive to anecdote and colorful aspects:

> [S]tarting with Sirtori's great black fur-lined coat and top hat and going down the range of clothing to the Ernani type of clothing [artistic dress, after one of Victor Hugo's characters]; all styles of dress, old and new, were represented. Crispi, with a long and very closefitting frock coat that was showing the string; Carini, with his English flatcap and a very short threadbare coat; Calona, an old Sicilian with white hair, wore a bright red suit and a large black hat *à la* Rubens with a long fluttering ostrich feather. Then there was Canon Bianchi who was partially dressed as a priest, several elegant young men from Lombardy dressed in the latest fashion, uniforms of the merchant service, the navy and the *Cacciatori delle Alpi*, and a great crowd of red shirts, whose lively mass constituted the background to the picture.

Uniforms were worn by the fifty-nine Genoese *carabinieri*, a group from the National Shooting Society who brought their own carbines which would deliver deadly fire at critical moments in the campaign—as many as ten would die at Calatafimi. Bixio wore the uniform of a Piedmontese colonel, and Türr dressed as a Hungarian.

Garibaldi scanned the horizons. The ships were supposed to meet up with two barges at sea to collect munitions, percussion caps, all the carbines and revolvers, 230 rifles, and small arms. They failed to make the appointment, as some smugglers who had been engaged to act as guides had disappeared to deal with their normal business. After waiting in vain, Garibaldi decided to continue on his route. At Recco he took on oil and tallow for the machines and he set sail for Tuscany. On board, the volunteers found it difficult to make themselves comfortable: many had to stand up because of lack of space and quite a few suffered from seasickness. There was a shortage of food and water.

On the morning of 7 May, the two ships docked at Talamone, where they hoped to find arms and munitions. Garibaldi visited the commander of the fort in the uniform of a general in the Royal Army. There was very little there, although there was a well-stocked depot at Orbetello, twenty kilometers away. He sent Türr off in an officer's uniform, and he came back with gunpowder, lead, percussion caps, cartridges, a hundred or so Enfield carbines, two cannons without gun carriage, one with, and a culverin. They stocked up with victuals, bread, meat, rice, and tallow. On the ninth they bunkered with coal for the engines in Porto Santo Stefano. They thus sorted out the deficiencies of an improvised departure, which had to have the appearance of secrecy even though it occurred under the eyes of the authorities.

The two-day stay in Talamone served to reorganize the volunteers along military lines, given that they had begun the journey just as they came. When they came off the ships, they gave their names, and were divided into eight companies, each under the command of a captain appointed by Garibaldi, and these in turn chose their officers and petty officers partly on the basis of previous military experience. The companies were then formed into two battalions under the command of Bixio and the Sicilian Giacinto Carini. Sirtori was appointed chief of staff, Giovanni Acerbi head of the commissariat, and Türr first aide-de-camp with the assistance of another four, one of whom was Bandi. Life on board was now disciplined. During sea voyage, weapons were distributed (the best to the more expert), and they worked on putting them in prime condition. They improvised a workshop to make cartridges and each man was issued with twenty.

In Talamone some strict supporters of Mazzini abandoned the expedition because they would not accept the monarchist flag, as did the sixty-four men under the command of Callimaco Zambianchi of Forlì, who had fought for the defense of Rome in 1849 and was well known for his fierce anticlericalism. Together with other volunteers from Livorno, they were to cross over from Tuscany into Umbria to trigger a revolt among subjects of the pope. From the very beginning, Garibaldi had been thinking of provoking an uprising in Le Marche, Umbria, and perhaps even Lazio in unison with the Sicilian expedition, in the hope of finding a following. The group did in fact move toward Orvieto, but was repelled by the papal gendarmerie, and it then withdrew and abandoned the enterprise. The diversion in the Papal States, which Cavour had advised against, failed because of fears of bringing Napoleon into the war on the papal side, and they discovered once again that the population was not ready to rise up. However, fear of invasions did keep papal and Bourbon troops on the border.

Then Garibaldi encountered more serious difficulties. To reach Sicily the ships had to cross the Tyrrhenian Sea, off the coasts of the Southern Italy and the continental part of the Bourbon kingdom, which was the largest and most populous of the states established in Italy in 1815. It had an army which on paper seemed quite formidable, with a force of sixty to eighty thousand men. It had been very well looked after by Ferdinand II after 1848, and reached its maximum size in 1859, when an invasion was feared across its northern border. Its navy was made up of twenty-two steamships and ten sailing ships, which were patrolling the Sicilian coasts. Twenty-five thousand men were garrisoned on the island, with cavalry, artillery, and well-equipped fortresses. There were twenty thousand men in Palermo alone.

He had to decide the point on the island where he would direct a surprise attack on an enemy who was already on alert due to the publicity surrounding Garibaldi's departure, and he had to choose the appropriate route to avoid the Bourbon ships. Garibaldi did not want to sail close to Sardinia in order to avoid compromising the king, whose noninvolvement in the enterprise he emphasized in his message of 5 May. If he had done this, he would have put the whole expedition at risk. Garibaldi had no idea about the doubts that were troubling Cavour, who could not prevent the embarkation in Genoa, because in April and May parliament was debating the transfer of Nice and Savoy to France. Were the government to make any further insult against the most famous combatant for Italian independence, there might have been adverse effects on public opinion. On the other hand, it had to show the great powers that it was not involved in the enterprise. Therefore on 7 May, the government ordered Admiral Persano and all other authorities to seize the two ships if they took refuge in any port in Kingdom of Sardinia, but not to seek them out outside its territorial waters. In reality the volunteers were taking on provisions in Talamone, and after that they would not stop in any other port considered friendly.

Garibaldi knew the Tyrrhenian Sea very well. He had sailed it in his youth, when he was in the merchant service. He chose a route that fooled the Bourbon navy. He sailed so far west that some people on board thought he wanted to land in Tunisia or Malta. Then he changed course toward the Aegadean Islands. There was much to worry about during this period, but the prevailing mood among the volunteers was one of light-heartedness. The heterogeneous mix of people of different ages and social conditions amassed in a restricted space engendered a sense of brotherhood based on their shared ideals; they debated various questions, played games, and sung songs. Garibaldi invented some patriotic lines which he wanted put to the chorus in *Norma*, but everyone preferred to sing *La bella Gigogin*. One volunteer attempted suicide by throwing himself into the sea, but they managed to save him. The most significant event, which could have had serious consequences, occurred toward the end of the journey. The *Piemonte*, which was the faster vessel, accelerated as it approached Marettimo in the Aegadean Islands, and the two ships whose lights were off lost sight of each other. Bixio discerned a shape in the darkness and, fearing that it was an enemy ship, was about to ram it when a cry from Garibaldi in unison with the volunteers on the *Piedmont* managed to overcome the noise of the engines and reveal his error. Garibaldi then swore at him in Genoese.

On 11 May, Sicily came into view of the two ships. Garibaldi had been planning to make landfall at Sciacca, but the morning was well advanced and he opted for Marsala, which was closer. He stopped a fishing boat at sea, and the skipper gave him information and acted as his pilot. The Bourbon government had predicted that he might head for this little port, and had sent a few army detachments there, but they were withdrawn on the tenth. Six warships—two sailing ships and four steamships—were patrolling the coast. None of them were in port and the town was undefended. The *Piemonte* anchored close to the jetty, but the *Lombardo*, which was larger, ran aground on the shallows. While the volunteers started to disembark, the arrival of two suspicious steamships with no flags was reported by telegraph to Trapani, the provincial capital. *Stromboli*, a steam-corvette with paddlewheels and six cannon, approached Marsala. The captain, Guglielmo Acton, saw the two merchantmen and the men in red shirts on the jetty, and understood that Garibaldi had arrived. His enemy was in range while they were unloading. He could have started a murderous bombardment, but he hesitated. On the jetty he saw the factory buildings of Woodhouse and Ingham, which belonged to British subjects and were used for the production of the valuable Marsala wine. There were merchant ships of various flags in the port (one was leaving as Garibaldi's ships were entering and Bixio had shouted to it that they should take news of the landing to Genoa). That morning two British warships, the *Intrepid* commanded by Marryat and the *Argus* commanded by Winnington-Ingram, had arrived for the purpose of protecting property belonging to British nationals. Moreover Winnington-Ingram had been in Montevideo and had drawn the uniforms of the Italian Legion in his album. The Bourbon captain, who feared hurting the British, parleyed with colleagues on the two ships, who asked him to wait for some seamen to come back on board. He only opened fire once the volunteers were on shore—a few ineffectual shots which were imitated by the sixty-gun sailing frigate *Partenope*, which in the meantime had also arrived. "The noble flag of Albion yet again contributed to the prevention of bloodletting," Garibaldi was to comment, "and I, the blue-eyed boy of these Lords of the Oceans, was protected by them for the hundredth time."

There were no marines on the Bourbon ships, which remained at sea. Garibaldi's men spread out through the town, but they were not greeted with enthusiasm. The population did not want to compromise itself with these badly armed and strangely dressed conquerors, who did not look capable of competing with the well-ordered Bourbon army. General Garibaldi issued two proclamations exhorting the Sicilians to take up arms and inviting Bourbon soldiers, whom he addressed as "Italians," to fraternize with them. There was talk of dictatorship, and Garibaldi immediately accepted, because he believed it to be "the safety plank in urgent cases and crucial situations in which peoples can find themselves." Crispi, a Sicilian and the political mind behind the expedition, had the matter debated by the Municipal Council. The council met for the first time in the afternoon and a second time in the late evening. Garibaldi took part in both sessions. We know how important it was to him to act within a legal framework. The council in this Sicilian town was made up of thirty decurions, and Garibaldi was able to obtain a proclamation from the ten who were present, declaring Bourbon rule in Sicily to be forfeit and offering him the dictatorship of the island "in the name of Victor Emanuel, king of Italy."

Garibaldi's men passed the night in the town. They refreshed themselves as best they could and slept in private houses or makeshift shelters. Garibaldi slept in a luxurious home, where he ate a frugal meal of bread, cheese, and beans, of which he was passionately fond. There was white wine on the table, but being teetotal he did not drink any. He requested blankets from the convents for future use, and he instructed the Sardinian vice-consul in Marsala to reclaim the two steamships, but when the Bourbon forces returned to the town, they towed the *Piemonte* to Naples and the *Lombardo* remained aground on the shallows.

The following day, the invaders marched inland. Garibaldi rode a white mare called Marsala, which he would take to Caprera. The officers and scouts were on horseback, and were thus able to carry out vanguard and reconnaissance tasks. Two carriages brought along the old and indisposed, and baggage was carried on wagons and carts. The volunteers received their first pay from municipal funds requisitioned by Crispi. It came to eighty-five centimes a head, and they each received a round loaf. As always, Garibaldi gave strict orders to respect the persons and properties of the inhabitants. The expeditionary force set off for Salemi, over thirty-five kilometers away along lonely and badly maintained country roads. After four hours on the road, they made a brief stop and were joined by the first group of insurrectionists, about sixty of them. This was enough to reassure them that anti-Bourbon unrest existed.

In the evening, the force, which no one had pursued or confronted, halted at a farm in Rampingallo. Paolo Bovi, who was responsible for provisioning, bought fourteen sheep from a shepherd and the farmer gave what he could. It was not easy to feed 1,200 men. He gave plenty of straw to the volunteers and this served as both mattress and blanket. Garibaldi slept with them in a tent on a saddle: an American saddle made up of various layers of leather, which in some ways was comparable to a sleeping bag. The officers slept in the open. La Masa left for Salemi to request that the municipal authority prepare 4,000 rations of bread, an equal number of pasta or riso, and 2,000 of meat, and then wine, oil, coffee, sugar, salt, and candles. They would also obtain horses, carts, ropes for the artillery, equipment for a workshop, and money.

On Sunday 13 May, they received an enthusiastic welcome in Salemi. The volunteers, broken by tiredness and the heat, found themselves among flags and band music; they took refreshments and slept indoors. They were joined by other groups of insurrectionists, groups of *picciotti*, armed and on horseback. Together they came close to another thousand. Unaccustomed to military discipline, they were of little use on the battlefield, but their presence alongside the volunteers had political significance because it demonstrated that the people were taking part in the liberation of their island. Garibaldi and Sirtori imposed an initial organization on them and called them the *Cacciatori di Etna*. One of their squads was led by a Franciscan monk called Fra Giovanni Pantaleo from Castelvetrano: in Sicily much of the clergy sympathized with the revolution. Garibaldi issued an appeal "to good priests," in which he invited them to join his cause. On 14 May, following a decision taken by the municipal council and brought to him by the mayor, he spoke to the crowd and exhorted them to fight for the unification of Italy: "given that in times of war it is necessary for the civil and military powers to be concentrated in the same hands," he formally took on the dictatorship of Sicily in the name of Victor Emanuel II, "King of Italy." He appeared on the balcony to continuous applause. Copies of the decree were put up in the streets, while the town criers read them out in loud voices. During the two-day halt, they worked on the weaponry: they made cartridges, lances, and pikes, and the cannons were provided with gun carriages and horses to draw them.

On hearing of the landing, Prince Castelcicala, King Francis II's representative in Sicily, requested reinforcements from Naples, and more troops arrived in Palermo. A committee of generals decided to recall the mobile units to concentrate on defense around Conca d'Oro. In the meantime General Francesco Landi, who was already in the western provinces with 2,800 men, 4 cannon, and cavalry units, marched on the invaders. From 7 to 12 May, he stayed in Partinico and Alcamo to disarm the population. He did not have precise information: he believed that he was facing a "Piedmontese battalion." On 13 May he took up his position at Calatafimi, a hilltop town with a castle that dominated the road. He sent out three reconnaissance units, and one of these, under the command of Major Michele Sforza, was sent toward Salemi and encountered the enemy.

Garibaldi studied the map of Sicily, and as was his custom, he went on horseback to explore the area in which he thought he would encounter Bourbon forces. When he slept, his favorite orderly officer Bandi slept nearby, and on the morning of 15 May he called him at three o'clock. He appeared to be in good humor. While he was drinking his coffee, he was singing part of *Gemma di Vergy* to himself, and it seemed appropriate: "I believe I can see the shining day that is coming." Garibaldi's love of coffee is worthy of a digression. Bandi recalled:

> Wherever Garibaldi stayed, he could easily go without bread, wine, meat, and even salt, but he never went without coffee. For that man, who was quite used to living on three or four pairs of dried figs with a sharp apple or a few wheat grains, it would have been like going through hell if he had ever gone without his cup of coffee.

For this reason, enough coffee had been loaded on board in Genoa "to ensure that every morning and even every evening Garibaldi had his dose of excellent coffee made there and then, perhaps in a wood or on a deserted plain."

At the moment that Garibaldi was having his ritual morning coffee in Salemi, he heard reveille being played on the bugle, and he sent for the bugler. He was Giuseppe Tironi, a soldier from Bergamo who had played reveille in Como for the *Cacciatori delle Alpi*. He gave him a *scudo*. The volunteers were on the march at half past five, and in the mid morning they stopped for their frugal rations of bread and beans. Then, four days after their landing in Sicily, they saw the Bourbons.

The area was undulating with hills of around four hundred meters. Major Sforza had eight hundred men with artillery pieces and forty horsemen. He was on a rise called Pianto dei Romani, from *Chiantu* meaning vineyard. Garibaldi drew up his force on another piece of high ground, Monte Pietralunga, and there was a valley between the two lines.

Sforza examined his adversaries in the distance, and could see that they were not in uniform. Their red shirts looked like the jackets prisoners wore, and he decided they were a bunch of adventurers whom he could easily disperse. Around midday he took the initiative, left his favorable position, descended into the valley and climbed toward the position held by Garibaldi's men. The fire from the Genoese *carabinieri* took the Bourbon soldiers by surprise, and when this was followed by a bayonet attack from the volunteers, Sforza's men withdrew to their previous position.

The hill of Pianto dei Romani was cultivated in terraces. Garibaldi's men pursued their enemy, and on each terrace the fight was resumed. Landi brought in reinforcements, and in the middle of the battle the expeditionary force of a thousand with a few hundred Sicilians was facing an enemy of 1,800 bourbon soldiers. Garibaldi was fighting with his saber at the head of his soldiers and encouraging them to fight on. One volunteer, Daniele Piccinini, covered Garibaldi's red shirt with his own cape because it was drawing fire, while another volunteer, Augusto Elia, protected Garibaldi with his body when he saw a Bourbon soldier aiming at his leader, and was seriously wounded. The Bourbons fought like "lions"—better than the Austrians in Lombardy, Garibaldi would acknowledge—and made use of their better weapons and favorable position. At one stage, Bixio whispered to Garibaldi that it would be advisable to withdraw, but the solemn reply that passed into the folklore of the *Risorgimento* was simply, "Here we either create Italy or we die." It may be that Garibaldi said more prosaically, "Withdraw, but where?" given that a defeat would have lost Sicilian support and led to failure of the expedition.

In the end, around a hundred volunteers waiting in the rearguard joined the attack, and the impetus of the new arrivals was enough to win the day. Yet again, Garibaldi had triumphed with the tactic of keeping his enemy under continuous pressure. With his usual disregard for the dangers both he and his men were exposed to, he had lost some of his best men. Of the thirty-two dead (not many if we think of the statistics for twentieth-century wars, but a great deal at a time when rifles fired one shot at a time), Garibaldi would recall Simone Schiaffino, one of the *Cacciatori delle Alpi* and of great assistance to Bixio in Quarto, who fell in a vain attempt to defend the colors, the Bourbon's only trophy (it was the flag donated by the women of Valparaíso for the war of 1859). The 180 wounded included Menotti, who had been hit in his hand, and Bandi, who with five wounds was almost given up for dead and would stay behind for treatment. He returned to his post later in Palermo. Among the *picciotti* there were about ten dead and forty wounded.

The Bourbons (who had suffered little more than thirty dead and one hundred and fifty wounded) withdrew to Calatafimi, and Landi decided to abandon the position. He received orders from Palermo to return to the capital and was unnerved by popular support for the rebellion. In reality, the scale of the battle was very limited, but numerous bands were springing up around the battlefield. "Send help, send help quickly," he wrote to Palermo, "the rebels . . . are popping up all over the place. . . . The Sicilian masses united with the Italian troop are of an immense number." Flour depots were looted, munitions for the artillery were nearly finished, and those for the infantry were much reduced. The letter, which did not arrive because it was intercepted, demonstrates General Landi's concerns over the general hostility. The decision was challenged by his officers, and Major Sforza, who was convinced of Garibaldi's death (he had confused him with Schiaffino, who was also blond), and wanted to maintain a base in the town and continue military operations. But the Bourbon troops left for Palermo during the night, and along the way they were attacked by the population in revolt. In Valguarnera they had to use their weapons to open the way, and in Partinico it took four hours of fighting with the use of artillery fire and burning of several houses. The bodies of the Bourbon dead were torn to pieces by the rebels. Garibaldi would later comment:

> The victory at Calatafimi was of little importance in terms of what we actually took, which amounted to no more than a cannon, a few rifles, and a few prisoners, but it had an immense effect in terms of morale, because it encouraged the populace and demoralized the enemy army. The victory at Calatafimi was unquestionably decisive for the brilliant campaign of 1860.

It was in fact a turning point. The Bourbons, Sicily's rulers, were on the defensive. The legend of Garibaldi's invulnerability was spreading among their troops, and dejection prevailed among the high command. The "freebooters" (*filibustieri*), as they had been called by *Il Giornale del Regno delle Due Sicilie*, now struck fear into their enemies' hearts.

Francis II could not count on any reliable officials and advisors. His father, out of a mistaken desire to cut costs, allowed those in high office in all branches of his administration to remain in office well into old age. In the army, he did not send ageing officers into retirement: Landi was sixty-seven, and General Ferdinando Lanza, a Sicilian who on 16 May replaced Castelcicala as the king's representative and took supreme command of the armed forces in Sicily, was seventy-three. Moreover the army had no experience of war. The men who formed the core of the Expedition of the Thousand had fought the French in 1849 and the Austrians in 1848 and 1859, two of the strongest armies in the world. The Neapolitan troops had only had the brief and inglorious campaign of 1849 against the Roman Republic. The monarchy had used them against Calabrian rebels in 1848 and Sicilians in 1849, and for policing work against brigands. They were to encounter difficulties fighting against a determined adversary who used aggression as its most powerful weapon.

Garibaldi had to take the initiative, given that his enemy was putting no pressure on him. He could either fortify himself in the interior and gather bands of insurrectionists around his forces, or he could advance on the island's capital and challenge the Bourbons where they were strongest. He opted for the second solution. From Marsala he had got in touch with Rosolino Pilo, whose bands were not far from Palermo. After Calatafimi he sent La Masa to gather other bands. On 17 May he left Calatafimi and reached Alcamo, on the eighteenth he was in Partinico, where pay of 85 centimes was distributed for a second time, and on the nineteenth he could see Palermo and the sea from the Renda Pass, just fifteen kilometers away.

The city was garrisoned by twenty-one thousand men. Garibaldi had the Thousand (now nine hundred), who were now almost as organized as the regular troops, and then a few thousand rebels. He was relying on the people of Palermo, and assuming they were ready to rise up. The odds were heavily against him. He was also counting on Pilo, now a few kilometers away, but on 21 May a Bourbon detachment under the command of a Swiss colonel, Luca Von Mechel, attacked the build-up of insurrectionists, destroyed them, and killed Pilo. The monarchy had had four regiments of Swiss mercenaries in its service between 1826 and 1859, and it still employed Austrian and Bavarian mercenaries in support of its national army.

Garibaldi had wanted to join up with Pilo for an attack on Monreale. In this changed situation, he could no longer attempt a frontal approach on Palermo. Using one of his now familiar maneuvers, he took his men along the Road of the Greeks and difficult mountain pathways in infernal weather. They walked through mud and along precipices for an entire night, and had to ford a river in full flood due to the rain. They used ingenious systems to transport the guns and gun carriages. On 22 May they consolidated their position on a mountain peak, Cozzo di Crasto, while in the village of Parco nearby the volunteers, "ragged, wet, and covered with mud," washed and dried their clothes, and were provided with others by the inhabitants. Garibaldi hoped the enemy would attack frontally, but the Bourbons actually employed a circling maneuver at some distance so that he was forced to withdraw onto a plateau called Piana dei Greci, after having contained their operation with difficulty. It was a delicate moment. It looked as though the volunteers might have to retreat into the interior of the island. Fortunately the Bourbons did not exploit the favorable moment and delayed their final assault, while the rebel forces were receiving reinforcements, money, and victuals.

Garibaldi, always a very skilful guerrilla fighter, implemented his plan on 24 May. At dusk, he sent off a detachment toward Corleone with about forty wagons with baggage, the wounded, five cannon with around fifty gunners, and 150 *picciotti*, under the orders of Colonel Vincenzo Orsini, the Sicilian commander of the expedition's artillery. Everyone, including the Bourbon informers, believed he was withdrawing to the interior. During the night he took off the rest of his force in the same direction, but at the first crossroads he moved onto another road and then used secondary roads to go down to the coast in order to approach Palermo along a wide circle. The stars were bright that night, and he took this to be a good omen. Once again his men were willing to suffer an exhausting march. On the evening of the twenty-fifth they were at Misilmeri, which again was about fifteen kilometers from Palermo. They were well received, and after being given refreshments, they slept in the open.

At the same time, Von Mechel was occupying Piana dei Greci. He moved with the slowness of regular armies, the slowness about which Roselli and his impatient subordinate had argued at Velletri in 1849. He was proceeding more slowly than usual because he was aware of the hostility of the population and did not want to risk detaching small groups of scouts and isolated patrols. He was led to believe that Garibaldi was marching on Corleone and set off on the same road certain that he was close on the rebels' heels. On 26 May Lanza telegraphed Naples to inform them that "Garibaldi's band has been routed and is withdrawing in disorder toward the district of Corleone," and had posters put up to notify the populace of this fact. On the twenty-seventh Von Mechel occupied Corleone, caught up with Orsini and defeated him, but Orsini was able to withdraw and draw Von Mechel further into the interior. On the twenty-eighth while in Giuliana, a messenger brought him the news that Garibaldi had entered Palermo. Only then did he realize that he had been tricked into removing three thousand of the best soldiers from the capital.

At dawn on 26 May, Garibaldi held a council of war in Misilmeri. The odds against them were overwhelming. The Thousand had now been reduced to 750, and a few hundred *picciotti* had joined up a few days before. They were also joined by the squad recruited by La Masa, amounting to about 2,000 men. In the hills not far from Palermo, Giovanni Corrao had gathered together the remains of Pilo's bands. It might have appeared wiser to withdraw along the coast where there were less Bourbon troops, but the majority opinion was to move forward.

The true position of the attackers was known only to the rebels and foreign observers, but not to the Bourbons who believed them to be on the way to Corleone (the rebels recruited by La Masa could be seen from Palermo but not the volunteers). Palermo harbor was crowded with nine Neapolitan warships and some hundred merchant ships. There were also two Sardinian (Victor Emanuel's new kingdom had not yet changed its name to reflect its new territorial spread), three British, three French, two Austrian, one American, and one Spanish warships, which were there to protect the interests of their own subjects, as had occurred fifteen years earlier on the River Plate. The British, in particular, were fascinated by Garibaldi. In Britain this adventurous and romantic leader was looked on sympathetically by all classes. Even before his entrance into Palermo, committees were being formed and funds collected to support him.

A group of naval officers went out in several carriages to meet Garibaldi. There were three British officers and two Americans, as well as Ferdinando

Eber, the Hungarian correspondent for the *Times*, who had been notified by his fellow-countryman, Türr. This authoritative newspaper was devoting several columns to the war on a daily basis. It was not easy to get reliable information, as the Neapolitan government, like the Argentinean one many years before, was accusing the expeditionary force of marching across the island "threatening peaceful citizens, and inflicting robbery, arson, and destruction of all kinds on the towns through which they go." Using these defamatory statements, correspondents in Rome and Naples wrote of incredible atrocities for foreign reactionary newspapers. On 9 June *Le Journal de Bruxelles* reported that a Bourbon sentry who had been captured "was found still breathing and nailed to a wall with his arms and legs apart," and once Palermo was taken, they would denounce assassination on a large scale and cases of cannibalism. The use of misinformation to defame the enemy led to some clamorous mistakes. After Calatafimi, the foreign minister released information to foreign capitals on the complete defeat of the volunteers who left on the battlefield "their flag and a great number of dead and wounded, including one of their leaders."

Although the Bourbons toned down their triumphalism later, the diffidence over the reliability of their information was justified. Foreign correspondents wanted to find direct news. A description of the meeting with Garibaldi in his camp was published on 24 June by the *New York Herald*, and Eber sent London an article on the encampment at Misilmeri. He did not fail to pick up on the colorfulness that had always struck observers of Garibaldi's encampments. He described the picturesque disorder in which men huddled "around a steaming pot of large pieces of beef, a sack of onions, a basket stuffed with fresh bread and a cask of Marsala." He commented at length on the shabby appearance of the volunteers, who had marched, countermarched, fought in the rain, and slept in makeshift bivouacs. He emphasized Garibaldi's calm and his certainty of victory.

The sympathies of the foreigners, who went out to meet Garibaldi, lay with those involved in this incredible enterprise. They provided precious information: the Bourbon military command were expecting the attack along the road from Monreale, and had positioned most of their troops to the north and west of the city, while the southeast was undefended and that was exactly the direction from which Garibaldi's troops were to approach. The southeast was also the working-class district of Fieravecchia, a network of narrow streets. Garibaldi could take them by surprise. The city was surrounded by twelve bastions, each of which contained a gate. He decided to break through Porta Termini, after approaching along not the main road next to the sea but an internal road through the Gibilrossa Pass. The *picciotti* wanted to lead the attack, but their arms were improvised and they had more enthusiasm than experience. Nevertheless Garibaldi could not refuse them without offending them, so he backed them up with thirty of his best volunteers.

The force moved off on the evening of 26 May, in accordance with Garibaldi's well-established tactic of attacking the enemy at night. Fires were lit on the nearby mountains to give the impression of soldiers bivouacking. They moved forward in complete silence along an almost impassible path. The surprise element was not complete. On the outskirts of Palermo, the inexperience of the *picciotti*, who shouted and fired in the air to show their joy, set off the alarm in the small Bourbon garrison, where they took action. The advance guard came to a halt at the Admiral's Bridge. The main body of the attack arrived with Garibaldi in the lead and brandishing his sword. The attackers carried out a bayonet charge and reached Porta Termini. Here the defense became fierce, and the bourbons were supported by two cannon and the cannon of a warship. The Hungarian Luigi Tüköry fell, Benedetto Cairoli and Giacinto Carini were seriously wounded, and Bixio slightly wounded. A barricade barred their way. Garibaldi rode up and encouraged his men to break through it. The attackers advanced under fire, with serious losses and the poorly armed *picciotti* occasionally wavered. Eventually the defenders fell back. At six in the morning of 27 May (Whit Sunday), Garibaldi's troops reached the main square of Fieravecchia, and from there moved out into the other districts of the city.

Palermo had 160,000 inhabitants. The population, which the police had disarmed in the previous months, initially remained closed up in their homes. Then little by little, as the bells were rung, they came out into the streets armed as best they could. The crowd grew thicker and barricades were erected. The Bourbon soldiers were targeted from windows and balconies with improvised projectiles. Lanza was obliged to turn around his troops which he had positioned on the outskirts to counter an attack from another direction. By now the rebels were in the city, and Garibaldi was attempting coordinate their actions, which were fragmenting into hundreds of small episodes in its streets, squares, and buildings. He set up headquarters in Piazza Bologni (where he slept peacefully for two hours on the floor), and later in the city council building in Piazza Pretoria.

The fighting continued for three days. Both attackers and defenders were unable to develop a proper plan. The Bourbons attempted to keep control of the barracks, public buildings, and Castellammare Fort, while their warships bombarded the city, which caused widespread damage, terrible fires, and many victims among the civilians. Garibaldi's men and the insurgents fought street by street and put up barricades at strategic points. They gradually took control of the residential areas, encouraged by the incessant bell-ringing. They had the shops reopen and received food from the monastery kitchens. There were episodes of savagery: soldiers looted buildings and carried out acts of violence on defenseless fugitives while rebels went off to search out and kill policemen in the service of the oppressor. On 28 May 2,000 prisoners escaped from the Vicaria Prison; some of them were political prisoners who rushed to the barricades, but the majority were dangerous criminals. Garibaldi decreed the death penalty for anyone guilty of theft, looting, or violence. Both sides received reinforcements: Corrao's bands came to the insurgents' assistance, and two battalions of foreign mercenaries from Naples joined the Bourbons.

Lanza gathered his troops around the Royal Palace. In the surrounding area there were attacks and counterattacks with alternating fortunes. In the afternoon of 29 May the Bourbons mounted a dangerous attack, and Garibaldi personally intervened. Up until then he had been directing operations in Piazza Pretoria, but now he rushed over on horseback and threw himself into the thick of the fight. He appeared invulnerable, and drew his men on to take back the positions they had lost.

Both sides had little strength left. The Bourbons were short of food, and were unable to bury their dead or treat their wounded because their hospital had fallen into enemy hands. The insurgents were running out of ammunition. Lanza was the first to break. On the morning of 30 May he wrote to Garibaldi, and invited him to meet on the British warship *Hannibal*, commanded by Admiral George Mundy. "The leader of the Thousand, who had been treated as a freebooter up to that moment, had suddenly become His Excellency," Garibaldi would later observe. Lanza's offer was timely, as it was a critical moment for the attackers. Garibaldi lost no time in demonstrating his willingness. An immediate ceasefire was agreed and was to come into force at midday, followed by a meeting between the parties. By an irony of fate, Von Mechel arrived just after midday with his four battalions, entered the city by Porta Termini overcoming weak resistance from the *picciotti*, and pushed on into Fieravecchia. He clashed with men gathered together by Sirtori and Carini, who were wounded, but then two Neapolitan officers informed him of the armistice and Lanza's orders to stop hostilities. To obtain partial satisfaction, he stayed put in the heart of the residential district to await the outcome of the negotiations, but was soon surrounded and trapped by barricades.

General Giuseppe Letizia, representing Lanza, and Garibaldi in the uniform of a Piedmontese general met on the launch that would take them to the ship. The negotiations took place in the presence of French, American, and Piedmontese commanders. Mundy did not invite the Austrians, because they had previously refused to sign the request to avoid bombarding the city. The conversation was animated. The Bourbon general wanted to avoid negotiations and impose his conditions with Mundy's backing. The latter refused to accept this role. Letizia buckled. Garibaldi was willing to allow safe passage for victuals and medical aid for the enemy wounded, but he would not allow the people of Palermo to be asked to send a petition of submission to the Bourbon king. The armistice was prolonged for eighteen hours of the following day. In the evening Garibaldi spoke to the people from the balcony of Palazzo Pretorio, and delivered a stirring speech that won their commitment to the struggle. Balconies and windows were lit up. New barricades were erected and existing ones strengthened. The people worked on the production of powder and cartridges. The determination of the insurgents impressed the Bourbon generals.

On 31 May General Letizia returned to negotiations with Garibaldi in his headquarters with its improvised furnishings. Bandi, who was present in his role of aide-de-camp, described the scene. Garibaldi, as calm as ever, was seated in an armchair with a chair in front of it that acted as a table. He listened while pealing an orange with a small dagger. He offered a segment of the orange on the point of his dagger to the general and Colonel Buonopane who had accompanied him. While the three ate the orange they discussed terms. Bandi stayed close throughout because the informers (the secret services of the time) had let it be known that the Bourbons were planning to assassinate the dictator. For this purpose they had brought to Palermo a corporal in the marines and the Calabrian brigand Giosafatte Talarico, who had been pardoned in 1845 by Ferdinand II, but they gave up on the plan when they too fell for Garibaldi's charm.

The armistice was prolonged for three more days. The agreement was signed by Crispi, "secretary of state of the provisional government of Sicily": for the insurgents this was an important recognition. Garibaldi obtained control of the mint, which provided an enormous sum, and he managed to stock up with gunpowder. In the afternoon he toured the city to a rapturous crowd. Bread and flour arrived from the nearby towns. The position of the attackers was improving. Lanza consulted with Naples but received no precise directives. The terrible bombardment had not produced the desired effects, and it was not possible to resume it without incurring the indignation of European public opinion. Colonel Buonopane noted the determination of the people of Palermo as they escorted the wounded. The city was a network of barricades, and the rebels were driven by a hatred of the Neapolitans, who had been forced to abandon the city by popular rebellions in 1820 and 1848. A discouraged Lanza capitulated on 6 June. The following day the first contingents boarded ships to leave. By the nineteenth the whole garrison had left Palermo.

18. Dictator of Sicily

If there ever was a favor granted by Providence for which a man had to humble himself before her with immense gratitude, then that is what has happened to me during the fortuitous events of these recent days in Sicily, in which I have had the good luck to take part.

I T WAS 21 June, and Garibaldi was firmly established in the island's capital. These words addressed to Ruggero Settimo, president of the Sicilian government of 1848, reflect the extraordinary sequence of events that favored the daring enterprise. It seemed impossible that a handful of badly armed men with no government assistance could bring a centuries-old government to its knees, and humiliate its army with its mighty fortresses, artillery, and well-trained navy. There was an unfounded suspicion of British complicity: at Marsala the expedition benefited from the absence of the defenders, and the presence of British ships had little influence on the delay in the Bourbon response (this was officially acknowledged by the Neapolitan government). In Palermo the foreign commanders, although sympathetic toward Garibaldi, maintained a position of strict neutrality, and even Alessandro D'Aste, who was in command of the Piedmontese warships *Authion* and *Governolo*, refused to provide assistance under the counter. The success of the expedition was due to Garibaldi's abilities, the heroism of the volunteers, and Sicilian impatience with Bourbon rule.

The astounding news from Sicily was immediately disseminated around the world by telegraph. In Britain, they recalled the Uruguayan battles and the defense of Rome in 1849. This rekindled the antipathy in which they held the Bourbons, who were accused in lively press campaigns of having established a tyrannical regime. The *Times* of 10 May did not mince its words when Garibaldi left Quarto.

> Such an enterprise is beyond criticism or praise. It would make no sense to judge this act on the basis of the rules applied to political compromises. The man, the cause and the events are so exceptional that they have to be assessed by their own rules. Success will give Garibaldi the importance of a general or statesman of the highest standing; defeat, ruin and death will classify him as an adventurer, a Don Quixote of great courage but mediocre intelligence, who would have lost his life in a desperate freebooting attack. . . . The only thing that cannot be doubted is the heroic daring of the leader of this expedition.

Success quietened the doubters. Public opinion was mobilized: funds were collected and the takings from shows were offered. The famous (the Duke of Wellington's son, Florence Nightingale, and Charles Dickens) and the not so famous made donations. The quick succession of victories in Sicily and Southern Italy would only increase the enthusiasm. The arms manufacturer that created the Enfield rifle offered an artillery gun to be sent duty free. The workers at the Glasgow arms factory and the Liverpool longshoremen worked free overtime to prepare and dispatch munitions and medication kits. "Sketches from life" of events and personalities filled the pages of the *Illustrated London News*, which on 19 May produced a front-page news story entitled "Sicilian affairs: Portents." On 2 June it portrayed Garibaldi at Quarto while boarding a boat and waving goodbye to women and children, and sent various "special artists," one of whom, Frank Vizetelly, would gain Garibaldi's friendship. Historical truth was not always respected: on 23 June an illustration depicted the armistice negotiations and showed the dictator, Major Bosco as the Bourbon envoy, and various witnesses including a priest with a wide-rimmed hat. A wonderful portrait of Garibaldi was produced on 14 July from a photograph by Orsani, and on 18 August there was a crowded illustration depicting Garibaldi at Milazzo as he killed a Bourbon officer who was about to strike him.

The French public had never ceased to be interested in the general who had fought with Napoleon's soldiers in 1859. The republican journalist, Charles Paya, who had studied in Italy (in 1858 he published a book in Paris, *Naples 1130–1857*, which was unfavorable to the Bourbons), wrote a biography of Garibaldi which was published in January 1860, and fifty thousand copies were printed. In spite of concerns that a shift in the balance of power in the Mediterranean could damage France, the liberal press gave prominence to the Expedition of the Thousand. In July, the authoritative *Revue des Deux Mondes* emphasized Garibaldi's support in Europe, partly because he "did not have the regular military resources that have turned wars of civilization into something almost scientific and have destroyed its poetry; he is fighting the war of ancient times, in which personal bravery shined through and inspired adventure novels." On 1 September it continued in a similar vein,

> The thing that most interests us, though not the only thing that interests us, is following this singular and prestigious military leader on his heroic and stunning peregrinations. . . . Every day we are all asking the same question: what has Garibaldi done and what is he about to do? . . . His portrait is being sold in our villages. . . . If by any chance the whole of Europe were in this moment to carry out a collective act of universal suffrage around a single name, the name that would triumph from the ballots of that European universal suffrage would be Giuseppe Garibaldi. Who could possibly doubt that?

His popularity was enormous. "In these last seven days have you heard anyone utter a name other than that of Garibaldi? In all Europe we have discussed nothing but the famous partisan," asserted *L'Illustration* on 19 May, accompanying its reports with views of Sicilian cities and sketches of moments in the war by various artists. In July, it sent a special correspondent to Sicily, the painter Jules Duvaux. "The French are impatient," it observed on

2 June, "they would like the insurrections to follow the regular progression of theatrical productions with exposition, adventure, and conclusion." *Le Monde Illustré* used several correspondents, especially the painter Durand-Brager, who was a specialist in naval engagements and was assisted by Dumas' young secretary Edouard Lockroy, Colonel Bordone (a Frenchman who would draw extremely well), and Captain Paugham. However, they too often let their imaginations run away with themselves: their portrayals of the armistice negotiations took place in the open on the jetty with Garibaldi and the Bourbon generals standing. On the other hand, the photographer Legray was responsible for the excellent half-length portrait of the dictator, published on 21 July, showing him in his red shirt, his head uncovered, and the hilt of his saber at his side. The dailies, *Le Siècle* and *L'Opinion National*, followed the expedition day by day, and praised the activities of the volunteers. On 15 May *Le Siècle* launched an appeal to collect funds and enroll volunteers. The newspaper also published Garibaldi's *Memoirs* in installments reworked by Dumas, and reports from the novelist himself (he rushed to Palermo on his yacht in early June), who compared the conflicting versions of the battles in Sicily on adjacent columns, and drew attention to the Bourbon misinformation.

Dumas was not the only French writer to heap praise on Garibaldi. The famous writer George Sand wrote that he "is not like anyone else and there is in him a kind of mystery that calls for reflection!" The physical and moral portrait that Sand painted reproduced considerations already made by others, but worthy of note is that she saw the enterprise as "a poem," called Garibaldi "the man of portents . . . banner of the new age," and asserted that "all Europe looks to him obsessively and wakes in the morning to ask where he is and what he did on the previous day."

On 14 June, Victor Hugo, who was in exile in England, wrote an impassioned denunciation of the tyrannies of the Bourbon monarchy and asserted that Garibaldi's enterprise was necessary. Who was this man? "He is a man, nothing more. But a man in all the sublime meaning of the term. A man of liberty; a man of humanity. *Vir*, his fellow-countryman Virgil would have said. . . . What is his strength? What makes him win? What does he bring along? The soul of the peoples. . . . He has brought the Revolution; and now and then in the chaos of battle, among the smoke and flashes, the goddess can be discerned behind him, as though he were one of Homer's heroes." Hugo imagined what it would be like if, following Palermo, the march of freedom continued on to Naples, Rome, and Venice. Italy exists: "where once there was a geographical expression, now there is a nation." The whole of Europe was electrified by Garibaldi's deeds, and Italy was once again the land of liberty and the rule of law.

The enthusiasm was unbounded. In Spain, the Italian military leaders were compared with the national heroes of 1808. Garibaldi's enterprise was discussed in Serbian and Bulgarian newspapers. However, the reporting was not always sympathetic to him. In France, as in Poland, the Catholics expressed their fears that changes to the Italian political system could compromise the Papal States. In Belgium, as we have seen, they gave credence to the worst propaganda against Garibaldi, although *L'Echo du Parlement* did publish the *Memoirs* fictionalized by Dumas.

In the United States, there was controversy over the value and purpose of the expedition that recalled the activities of freebooters, a controversy that became caught up in the debate on the abolition of slavery. The prevailing arguments were favorable. In the *New York Daily Tribune* of 17 May, Karl Marx, its London correspondent, emphasized the backwardness in which the Bourbons had left Sicily. On 22 June, Friedrich Engels commented in the same newspaper on the "spectacular march" from Marsala to Palermo. He considered the conquest of the city "one of the most stupefying military undertakings of our century," and asserted that "here Garibaldi has masterfully demonstrated that he is a general capable not only of partisan warfare but also of much more important operations." The operations Garibaldi carried out in Palermo "immediately mark him out as a general of great stature . . . we see him acting on a good strategic terrain; and he has passed the test as a consummate master of his art." Engels concluded by writing that Garibaldi's operations were ones "that carry the imprint of more military genius than any other event in the Italian war of 1859". The *New York Times* of 27 June compared the Italian military leader to Washington, and he was often defined as "Italy's Washington." In September the *New York Herald* considered the conquest of the Kingdom of Naples to be "an undertaking that has no equal in modern times." "No similar fact has been encountered in history," the newspaper asserted, "not even in the deeds of mythological heroes."

Long and short biographies with varying degrees of fictionalization were reprinted and translated. Funds were collected in Europe and America—in Sweden just as they were in Uruguay and Chile. Working-class rallies to express sympathy and support were held in many U.S. cities. A concert was held in New York on 11 July to collect funds: they staged *Lucia di Lammermoor* and parts of *Lucrezia Borgia* and *Vespri Siciliani.* Garibaldi received a flood of messages from well-wishers, poetry and musical compositions, and infallible military plans. The fascination of the adventure attracted more volunteers. Applications came raining in from all European countries, Algeria, Turkey, India, Canada, and the United States. Thirty-three Englishmen rushed to Genoa and left with the expeditions of Medici and Cosenz. The French socialist Paul de la Flotte went to Sicily. The ageing general Avezzana hurried back from New York in time to fight at Volturno. He brought with him a group of American volunteers, and Colonel Charles Carrol Hicks, who had distinguished himself in the war against Mexico, was his chief of staff.

The sympathy was not so much for the Italian cause as for Garibaldi, who one English admirer defined as "the man of action of the moment." He provoked enthusiasm at the reactionary Russian court and among British statesmen and across the class divide. The examples are endless. The Garibaldi myth caught the popular imagination from the very beginning and engendered support even in countries where there were no problems of liberty and independence: on 4 July 1860 the inhabitants of Helsingborg in Sweden decided to send him a sword of honor. "This is an heroic enterprise that recalls ancient times," wrote the Russian democrat Nikolai Alexandrovich Sernosolovyevich on 16 May. Where there were existing political and social demands, admiration was accompanied by expectations: Bakunin, who at the time was in exile in Siberia, noted that Garibaldi's march was followed with passionate interest in Irkutsk. In St. Petersburg, they spoke of Garibaldi with gratitude in the taverns because he was fighting for the freedom of all Europe and insisted on the need to free the peasantry from serfdom.

Even in Russian-controlled Poland, it was felt that Garibaldi was fighting for the freedom of all peoples: by the end of 1860 his name had become familiar, and his portrait was venerated in homes and meeting places next to that of the national hero, Tadeusz Koshciuszko. That autumn in Warsaw, a greengrocer who asked for her son, a political prisoner, to be released, shouted at the chief of police that in a week's time Garibaldi would come and free her son. A rebellion by shoemakers against their treatment by the police was carried out to shouts of Garibaldi's name.

In Hungary, the entire press devoted considerable coverage to the Expedition of the Thousand. There too the peasantry expected Garibaldi to come and liberate them, and one youth believed that his name was being used as a cover for Kossuth, the leader of the struggle for national independence. In July and August, a long series of anti-Austrian demonstrations shouted the names of both Garibaldi and Kossuth. The latter, who was in exile, had met the former, admired his audacity and honesty, and carefully followed his exploits.

Reactionary governments favorable to the pope and the Bourbon king found Garibaldi unstoppable. Austria, Russia, Prussia, and Spain muted their protests. Napoleon III, to whom the Bourbon king turned for assistance, limited himself to giving advice. The protests were naturally directed toward the government in Turin, the beneficiary of the recent upheavals in Italy's political structure, and presumably the beneficiary of the successful revolution in Sicily. In the kingdom ruled by the House of Savoy, now stretching from Piedmont to Central Italy, the enthusiasm for the expedition was now mobilizing public opinion as a whole. Newspapers of all political persuasions published lengthy reports and detailed up-to-the-minute news. In Turin, *Il Mondo Illustrato* revealed the places, personalities, and events of the expedition. Democrats and moderates were competing in the dispatch of men and supplies. Considerable sums were collected, particularly in Lombardy. Some twenty thousand volunteers were enrolled and dispatched. A network of associations was set up under the auspices of the National Society, and then specially organized Action Committees (*Comitati di provvedimento*). With the funds raised, steamships were bought to carry later expeditions, arms, munitions, shoes, pullovers, trousers and coats.

Bertani, following instructions left him by Garibaldi on 5 May, wanted to take the revolution to the Papal States with the encouragement of Mazzini, who had secretly arrived in Genoa on 7 May (the death sentence passed on him while Charles Albert was on the throne had not been cancelled). Mazzini, with the optimism that had already landed him in so many disasters, took it for granted that Garibaldi would succeed in Sicily, and was pressing for another expedition against Umbria and Le Marche to strike the Bourbon king in Abruzzo. The government, which was willing to accept the enthusiasm for Sicily (and it could do little to prevent it), took control of the situation and ensured that funds were directed solely toward Sicily. It used the fleet to protect the subsequent expeditionary forces that followed shortly after the Thousand. A ship under the command of the Sicilian Carmelo Agnetta arrived in Marsala with 89 men and a massive cargo of arms munitions on 1 June. These were the first reinforcements and were immediately sent to Palermo.

Following his victory Garibaldi was left dangerously short of troops and arms. Lanza took all his equipment with him. The majority of the *picciotti* (as occurred in South America) returned to their homes, and those who remained were not very disciplined, so on 13 June their bands were demobilized. The Expedition of the Thousand was now reduced to a few hundred able-bodied men with little equipment: barely 390 rifles and little ammunition. Fortunately, on 7 June Salvatore Castiglia arrived in Palermo from Malta with 1,500 rifles and munitions. On 18 June, a large force led by Medici landed at Castellammare del Golfo, about fifty kilometers from Palermo. It was made up of three American steamships with 3,500 volunteers, 8,000 excellent rifles and 400,000 cartridges. Another sizeable contingent of two thousand men, under the command of Enrico Cosenz, landed directly in Palermo on 6 July, immediately followed by one of nearly a thousand men under the command of Clemente Corte, which left before Cosenz but was captured at sea by the Bourbons off the Isle of Elba and taken to Gaeta. They were later freed because they were on American ships and formally on their way to Cagliari. They returned to Genoa, only to set off once again for Sicily.

Garibaldi had initially counted on Sicilian support. On 14 May in Salemi, he decreed mass conscription of men between seventeen and fifty years of age, divided into three categories. On 27 May, as soon as he entered Palermo, he issued a proclamation. "He calls to arms all the municipalities of the island in order that they should make their way immediately to the capital and complete the victory." On 4 June he decided to call his troops the "Southern Army," and he formed a division with 940 men, which he called the Fifteenth, as though it were part of the Piedmontese army. This division was supposed to grow with the conscripts that presented themselves for duty by 20 June. On 8 July, he reviewed the division. It had its own flag, donated by the women of Palermo and similar to the Montevideo one—a volcano on a black background with a red border. Garibaldi was thinking of a large army to liberate Italy; on 5 May he wrote to Bertani that Italy had to arm half a million men. He wanted to create the nucleus right away, but the reinforcements of Sicilian soldiers did not arrive. Conscription was not accepted on the island, given that the Bourbons had exempted them from military service. Young men refused to report to the army, partly because of the imminent harvest, and Garibaldi had to accept the unpleasant reality and water down the orders he had given. He was obliged to replenish his troops with volunteers.

For the first time in his long military career, he had command of an entire army and responsibility for its deployment. In Rio Grande, Uruguay, and Italy, he had always fought under someone else's orders. Either a minister of war or a general had provided him with specific tasks and a specific sector, and he followed his orders even when he disagreed with them. This time he was answerable to no one. On 20 June he visited the commanders of the warships anchored in the port: the Piedmontese *Maria Adelaide,* which had just arrived with Admiral Persano, greeted him as a general of high command with a nineteen-gun salute; Admiral Mundy brought out the guard of honor and military band; the French admiral Jehenne greeted him as a simple "guest of note" but the following day he returned the visit. Garibaldi was the dictator, and had to exercise full powers particularly on the military front. He had to develop strategy and conduct operations, while taking into account a general overview of the available forces and the immediate and future aims.

The war still had to be fought. The departure of the Palermo garrison did not mean the withdrawal of the Bourbon army. In eastern Sicily at the beginning of June, the Bourbons still had five thousand men. Whatever the future plans for Southern Italy and the Papal States, Garibaldi had first to complete and secure the conquest of the island. The first phase of the Expedition of the Thousand, in which a few poorly armed men challenged a powerful monarch, was over. More volunteers, arms, munitions, clothing, and money were arriving all the time. On 20 June having just received reinforcements, the dictator sent the division of the Southern Army into the interior toward Enna and Caltanissetta to make the presence of the victors felt, gather conscripts and, if necessary, re-establish public order. Türr was put in command, but as he was ill, he was replaced by Eber, who had now enrolled in Garibaldi's army. On 25 June, he sent of a detachment of 1,200 men (700 northern volunteers who came with Medici and 500 Sicilians) under the command of Bixio, who also moved toward the interior around Corleone, and from there to Agrigento and Licata where he boarded his troops for Terranova. In mid-July he arrived in Catania, and joined up with Eber.

The two small detachments had the task of carrying out an armed reconnaissance, gathering support and favoring the implementation of conscription. This latter part of their duties met with little success. They did not encounter the enemy army. The Bourbons remained in the eastern part of the island, and abandoned Catania: in spite of having suppressed a revolt on 31 May, General Tommaso Clary preferred to withdraw to Messina. Francis II entrusted him with the counterattack. The Bourbon king received him in Naples on 19 June and approved his plan for retaking Palermo. Francis II also gave Clary command of all the forces in Sicily, which at the time stood at 22,000, of which 18,000 were in Messina, 2,500 in Siracusa and Augusta, and 1,000 in Milazzo on the coastal road that led to Palermo. On 29 June, Garibaldi sent a third detachment against them. This was made up of Lombard and Tuscan volunteers who had just arrived, and was under the command of Medici, his most trusted commander. Medici was one of the few people (all known during his youth in America) whom he addressed with the informal *tu*. The Medici detachment advanced along the northern coast of the island as far as Barcellona (now Barcellona Pozzo di Gotto), close to the enemy.

Clary still had not implemented the offensive maneuver agreed in Naples, and was using various pretexts for postponement of operations. On 14 July he sent three battalions of light infantrymen (three thousand crack troops) with the order to liaise with the Milazzo garrison. These battalions were under the command of Colonel Ferdinando Beneventano del Bosco, an energetic officer who had been Von Mechel's second-in-command. Like Von Mechel, he had fallen for the ploy that sent them chasing after Orsini and had been boxed up in Palermo by the armistice. He had left with the surrendered garrison and later returned to the island to exact retribution. The two opposing detachments came into contact. Medici was concerned about defending Barcellona, which had greeted him with jubilation, while Bosco was using Milazzo as his base. The town is on a small peninsula, and Medici blocked access, and thus threatened to bottle up his enemy and cut them off from Messina. In the morning of 17 July, Bosco sent Major Maringh to attack and open up the road. The major succeeded in forcing Medici's troops to retreat and occupied Archi, a village of strategic importance. Then, feeling satisfied, he withdrew and abandoned the position! Bosco had him arrested, and in the afternoon sent Lieutenant Colonel Marra to lead another attack: Medici sent in reinforcements, and at the end of a day of fierce fighting, Archi was once again in Bourbon hands, but Bosco abandoned it in the evening and shut himself up in Milazzo. In the meantime, he was desperately demanding reinforcements by semaphore, as he feared the imminent arrival of another five thousand "Piedmontese" of whom he had been informed by a prisoner. The reinforcements were not to arrive. In Naples, the Minister of War, Giuseppe Salvatore Pianell, had decided to concentrate his forces on the defense of Southern Italy and did not approve the offensive strike, while Clary asserted that he did not have available means of transport by sea or land.

Medici had his own fears of being overwhelmed by superior enemy forces, and requested reinforcements. A month and a half after the fall of Palermo, Garibaldi's troop and Bourbon troops were again facing each other. Garibaldi understood that his prestige was at stake. The following day he sent six hundred men under the command of Colonel Dunne, an Englishman. They were mainly youths recruited from the streets by Jessie White's husband, Alberto Mario, and following military training they were to acquit themselves very well. Mario himself had left on the *City of Aberdeen* with a group of crack Genoese *carabinieri*, and the ship had also brought nine hundred volunteers led by Vincenzo Strambio. In Palermo, this ship took on board another thousand men under Clemente Corte who arrived in port at the same time. This large contingent then landed at Patti, close to Milazzo. Another contingent of Cosenz's volunteers arrived overland under the command of Major Specchi. Garibaldi's only warship also joined the scene. It was the ten-gun steam corvette *Veloce*, which had defected from the Bourbon fleet and been renamed *Tüköry*.

On 19 July, Garibaldi concentrated all his available forces at Milazzo and with Medici and Cosenz, he examined the terrain. Guerzoni would recall,

Milazzo sits on a narrows isthmus joined to the mainland by three main roads. . . . The city is surrounded by its ancient walls built on the slope and above them at the northern extremity there is a castle with two levels of fortification, capable of garrisoning a few thousand men and several gun batteries. The surrounding terrain, drier to the east and more fertile to the west, is mainly low lying, covered, lacking views of the horizon, broken up by houses and windmills, and ob-structed, one might say, in the cultivated part by a network of lanes with continuous garden and vineyard walls and in the uncultivated part by thick reed beds that reach down to the exposed and sandy beech dominated by the castle's embrasures. It was excellent terrain for anyone who had to defend it from a stationary position and equally inhospitable to anyone who wanted to cross it inch by inch and con-quer it by force.

On 20 July Garibaldi attacked. He had nearly five thousand men, mostly newly arrived and with little training, as well as two old guns. Bosco had nearly 4,700 soldiers, a cavalry unit, and eight guns. The en-emy line was a three-kilometer semicircle, with the right flank supported by the navy and protected by the fortress, and the left flank positioned so as to enfilade the attackers with the artillery. Garibaldi's initial plan was to attack before dawn en masse to break through the center of enemy lines and isolate the left flank which could be then defeated separately. This did not prove possible, because the concentration of dispersed units took time, and the fighting started after daylight and under the blazing heat. He di-rected operations from the roof of a farmhouse. His troops advanced and found themselves under the deadly fire of the well-positioned Bourbons and their artillery support. They were forced to retreat. Supported by rein-forcements, they recommenced their advance and captured one of the guns. The battle was extremely fierce and by midday, Garibaldi's troops were burnt by the sun, tired, thirsty, and hungry, but they held firm. His enemy was no less determined. Bosco rushed to the firing line, and Garib-aldi moved into the thick of the battle. Under his leadership, his men got the upper hand and captured another gun. Bosco sent in a cavalry unit, which charged and momentarily dispersed the attackers. Garibaldi was in the open and a cavalry captain rushed at him. Yet again, his boldness was about to lose him his life, but Missori shot the horse while the officer was bringing his sword down, and Garibaldi parried the blow and killed his adversary. The cavalry, which had no infantry cover, withdrew.

The battle continued. The combatants on both sides fought bravely and hard in exhausting conditions, but neither seemed capable of placing the decisive blow. Garibaldi then understood what he had to do. Perhaps he remembered the conquest of Laguna. He ran to the beach and took a boat to reach the *Tüköry*, from which he bombarded Bosco's troops. It was four in the afternoon. The battle had been raging for eight hours. The Bourbon troops were taken by surprise, their morale collapsed, and they took refuge in the fortress abandoning the residential part of Milazzo, which was occupied by volunteers and looted by peasants. Garibaldi entered on his horse Marsala and set up his headquarters in the garden of a church, where he ate whatever came to hand—a piece of bread sprayed with water. He then laid out his saddle on the ground and fell asleep. Dumas, who was sailing in the Mediterranean, had come to Sicily and was in the waters off Milazzo on the day of the battle. His imagination conjured up the figure of Cincinnatus.

There were too many soldiers crowded into the castle. There was insufficient space, provisions, and water. Bosco was demoralized, and asked for help from Messina. Clary was again lost in his doubts over the appropriateness of moving the majority of his troops out of the city, and in the end he decided to take no action. In Naples, they decided to abandon the fortified town. On 23 July the Bourbon naval squadron appeared off Milazzo. Garibaldi was prepared to fight off an attack, but the commander had orders to negotiate the surrender of the castle and the removal of its troops. On 24 July the Neapolitans boarded their ships with the honors of war. The victor kept the guns, munitions, horses, and half the mules, while in Palermo Lanza had left "with equipment, stores, artillery, horses, and baggage." One of the horses taken in Milazzo belonged to Bosco. Garibaldi had wanted it for a facetious vendetta. The Bourbon colonel had asserted that he would enter Palermo on Medici's horse, and now Medici would enter Messina on Bosco's horse. Garibaldi relaxed. In the castle courtyard he amused himself by lassoing the horses in the South American manner.

The Battle of Milazzo had been particularly bloody. Garibaldi's troops had suffered eight hundred dead and wounded, and the Bourbons barely one hundred and fifty, but on 20 July they lost Sicily. Clary, who still had fifteen thousand men, gave up the fight. On the twenty-eighth, he signed an agreement with Medici, who had moved toward the Strait of Messina. He abandoned the island with his men, leaving only a small garrison in the Messina citadel. On 1 August, Siracusa and Augusta also capitulated. Sicily was free. Garibaldi entered Messina on 27 July to a delirious and cheering crowd who removed the horses from his carriage and carried it in triumph. They repeatedly insisted that he appear at the balcony.

By accepting the dictatorship, Garibaldi had concentrated all powers in his hands, not only military ones. In every field they awaited his decisions, which had the force of law. For the first time in his life, he did not have a politician to whom he was responsible. In Rio Grande it had been Gonçalves, in Uruguay Pacheco, in Rome in 1849 the republican government, and in Lombardy in 1848 and 1859 the House of Savoy. In a sense he was still responsible to someone, King Victor Emanuel, but he was far away and had to pretend that he did not favor the revolutionary enterprise. It was up to Garibaldi, who was surrounded by democrats (i.e. longstanding republicans and followers of Mazzini), to take the decisions and maintain the line based on "Italy and Victor Emanuel." The political aspects of managing Sicilian affairs were quite significant. In the first place, he had to govern the territory as it was gradually removed from Bourbon rule, guarantee public order, and make local government work, while removing supporters of the fallen regime and initiating the transition to liberal forms of government.

Francesco Crispi, who had been appointed secretary of state, was the inspiration behind the first measures. Crispi, a Sicilian, was a lawyer, a student of the Bourbon state and an expert on the island's problems. In Alcamo, immediately after the Battle of Calatafimi, he appointed a governor to each of the island's twenty-four districts with powers to reorganize council administrations and install new police officials, and he made these changes as though Garibaldi's forces were already in control of the country and capable of enforcing them. A politically important move was his insistence on issuing all decrees "in the name of Victor Emanuel King of Italy," because this made clear the revolution's aims and was a promise of stability for the middle class. In Palermo on 28 May while the city was not yet in his possession, Garibaldi laid down the basis for the financial administration and entrusted the functions of treasury minister to the army quartermaster. He installed a new city council. On 2 June, following the armistice (but when Lanza had not yet capitulated), he formed a regular government with six ministries (Crispi had the Interior and the Treasury). On the seventh, the ministries were increased to eight (the Treasury became autonomous).

At the same time, Garibaldi introduced a series of measures aimed at satisfying popular expectations. On 19 May while still in Alcamo, he abolished the grist tax, which was the principal form of taxation under Bourbon rule on the island. It was universally hated because of the oppressive way in which it was collected. He also abolished duty on the importation of cereals and pulses, which kept the prices high. In Partinico on twenty-eighth, he ordered councils to bring forward the payments of compensation for damage inflicted by Bourbon troops (who during their movements imposed requisitions and imposed fines) and to give assistance to the families of volunteers. He did not intend to disappoint the peasants, who he hoped would become soldiers in the war of liberation. On 2 June, as soon as he had set up a government, he ruled that combatants would have a given percentage when it came to sharing out crown property in the hands of municipalities. The question of crown property was one of the main causes of discontent in the Sicilian and Southern Italian countryside. At the beginning of the nineteenth century at the time of the suppression of feudalism, the former feudal lands were allocated to the municipalities with instructions to distribute them among the peasants—to all of them if there was a sufficient number of plots or by drawing lots if there was not. The distribution never took place and the middle class appropriated the lands by illegal confiscation or token rents. The Bourbon government had in vain attempted to carry through the division and distribution of the land. Any upheaval that weakened the forces of repression caused the peasants to rebel. In June, Garibaldi's promise was understood as a commitment to distribute municipal lands as soon as possible, and this caused ferment in the countryside.

This was not what was being proposed by the dictator, whose government activities were guided by a spirit of reconciliation and attempted to win support from all sections of society for the new regime. He gave instructions for paying out assistance to the poor families of Palermo, the state adoption of orphans of the war dead, and compensation for damage from bombardments. He visited the almshouses, and put abandoned boys into a military institute (entrusted to Alberto Mario). He also decreed the abolition of the appellative *Eccellenza* and the kissing of hands between men, and attempted to gain the support of the nobles, the middle classes, and the clergy: in other words, the dominant groups.

He did not lack consensus. Nearly all the bishops paid tribute to him. The bishops of Monreale and Palermo took part symbolically in the demolition of the fortress at Castellammare, which had come to represent tyranny. Garibaldi returned the courtesies by visiting convents and showing his respect for the forms of popular devotion. At Calatafimi, he kissed the crucifix brought to him by Father Pantaleo, and in Alcamo he accepted a benediction in church. In Palermo on 15 July, the festival of Santa Rosalia, the city's patron saint, he went to the cathedral for the Pontifical Mass dressed in his red shirt. He sat on the throne reserved for the sovereign, and thus assumed the office of Apostolic Legate which belonged to kings of Sicily. When it came to reading the gospel, he held his sword unsheathed to symbolize his status as defender of the church. An immense crowd filled the streets, and the civil and religious authorities, dressed in their most sumptuous clothes for the occasion, paid homage to him.

The core political feature of dictatorship in the classical sense was its duration as an exceptional and transitional regime. The need to emphasize the difference between the new government and the former Bourbon one led to a development of the state structures. It was not just a matter of providing financial stability by resuming tax collection and placing trustworthy persons in positions of responsibility: Garibaldi needed to give the state a new physiognomy which would suggest the form it was going to take on in the near future. There were two models that needed to be borne in mind: the institutions of the independent Sicily of 1848 and those of liberal Piedmont, the nucleus of Italy as it was being unified around the House of Savoy. The latter were imitated more than the former. By a decree dated 13 June Garibaldi ruled that Sicily's coat of arms would be the same as that of the state rule by the Savoys. He confirmed that public deeds should be made out in the name of Victor Emanuel, and enacted the Piedmontese electoral law, given that the Sicilian people would not tardy "to be called to pronounce its vote on the island's annexation to the emancipated provinces of Italy, either by direct suffrage or by means of an assembly."

In the meantime, Sicily claimed its own identity, and confirmed its separation from Naples by appointing its own diplomatic representatives in Turin, Paris, and London. Garibaldi announced the imminent annexation to Victor Emanuel by specifying that Count Michele Amari, who was sent to Turin, did not claim "to exercise the representation of a special and distinct state," but was the interpreter "of the thoughts and sentiments of two and a half million Italian men." He informed Queen Victoria that Sicily desired nothing more than "to take part in national life and liberty under the scepter of a magnanimous prince, to whom Italy had entrusted itself."

Garibaldi and Cavour disagreed on the timing of the annexation—a disagreement between revolution and diplomacy. Garibaldi wanted to keep hold of Sicily for as long as possible to use it as a base for popular campaigns to liberate Southern Italy and Rome. Cavour was pressing for the immediate transfer of the island to the sovereignty of Victor Emanuel. The statesman feared that the dictator might be influenced by Mazzini's followers, or that that the great powers would decide against Italian unification. The future of Sicily was a matter of diplomatic concern. In mid-June, the *Times*, although favorable to the liberation, posed the question of the future of the island, too small to become an independent kingdom and too distant from the Kingdom of Sardinia to become part of it.

The Bourbon king appeared to have given up any attempt to take Sicily back, but he was still dangerous. By a sovereign act of 25 June, he restored the Constitution granted by his father in 1848, which had never been formally abolished, adopted the tricolor as the national flag, and promised specific institutions for Sicily. In his new role as a liberal sovereign, he commenced negotiations for an agreement with the Kingdom of Sardinia, which was now virtually the master of Sicily and the accomplice of the invaders who were now being reinforced with men and equipment. The House of Savoy was not interested in compromising possible further territorial gains by giving a hasty undertaking. Giovanni Manna, who took over the Treasury in the new liberal ministry, was sent to Turin where he found the Piedmontese implementing a delaying tactic. The Bourbons did obtain more concrete results from their diplomatic envoys to Paris and London, and on 4 September when Garibaldi was at the gates of the capital, the Duke of Cajaniello vainly pleaded with Napoleon for military assistance to save the Bourbon monarchy.

Indeed the transition from absolutism to constitutional regime only served to aggravate the crisis in the Bourbon kingdom. The political system created after 1848 by Ferdinand II collapsed, and there was no time to make the new structures of the liberal state work. The change in personnel threw the administration into disorder, the weakened forces of repression favored unrest and resumption of the uprising over the question of former feudal lands in the countryside, and uncertainty over the future interfered with trade. The exiles, who put little trust in Francis II's sudden conversion to liberalism, either did not return to their homeland or returned with the specific intention of fighting to overthrow his dynasty.

After Garibaldi's early successes at the beginning of June, the depth of the crisis in the Bourbon monarchy was not immediately clear, nor did people understand that it would prove to be irreversible. The Bourbons had been driven from Naples in 1799 and 1815, but had later returned. In 1820, 1837, and 1848, it had managed to suppress Sicilian rebellions. The army had remained loyal in the fighting against the Expedition of the Thousand, and it was believed that in Southern Italy the dynasty was popular and its rule well established. Cavour immediately took action to make Sicily's secession from Naples definitive, and was encouraged in this by the Sicilian ruling class which was aware of the impossibility of creating an independent Sicily and wanted the protection of the House of Savoy in the face of increasing unrest among the working class and the peasantry. He made a mistake in his timing and in the man he chose for the task. He sent Giuseppe La Farina, who arrived in Palermo on 6 June just after the capitulation, on the *Maria Adelaide*, which was under the command of Admiral Persano.

La Farina overestimated his influence in Palermo, made contact with exponents of the pro-Savoy party, promoted a campaign in the press to promote annexation which depicted a dire state of affairs in the island (obviously unsettled by the war), attacked Crispi who was his personal enemy, and put pressure on Garibaldi. He was the inspiration behind a deputation from Palermo municipal council on 22 June to the dictator to offer him citizenship and express its "vote to join the Kingdom of Italy under King Victor Emanuel." On the twenty-seventh he organized a demonstration in the streets that shouted, "Long live Garibaldi! Down with Crispi!" as Crispi was supposed to be an ardent republican. But the dictator pointed out that he had come to fight "for Italy and not Sicily alone; and if all of Italy is not freed then the cause of no part of it will be won." For this reason, he intended to maintain his freedom of action. On 7 July in the face of persistent unwanted demonstrations, he ordered the arrest and expulsion of La Farina, who was removed with two spies. It was an offensive response to Cavour's interference.

This did not mean that Garibaldi did not want to commence the union with Piedmont. He simply wanted to keep power in his hands. For the management of the civil service, he actually requested Turin to send a man *super partes*, who was agreeable to both him and the Piedmontese government. He suggested Agostino Depretis, an exponent of the Piedmontese left who had followed Mazzini in his youth but later became much closer to the monarchy. Cavour would have preferred Lorenzo Valerio, but had to bow to the specific request from the dictator. Depretis arrived in Palermo on the day of the Battle of Milazzo. On leaving the capital, Garibaldi had appointed Sirtori as his pro-dictator. On 22 July in Milazzo, he appointed Depretis to this position, while strongly advising him to make use of Crispi's experience.

The pro-dictator undertook in a sense to provide continuity with previous policies, but he did immediately accentuate links with Piedmont. On 3 August he promulgated King Albert's Statute, which was in force in the territories under the House of Savoy, as the "fundamental law of Sicily," and removed the specter of a republican order. On the same day, he imposed an oath of loyalty to Victor Emanuel and observance of the statute on public officials and state employees. Depretis introduced various Piedmontese laws in Sicily: the laws on shipping and of particular note, the law on provincial and municipal structures with a view to the election of local-government representatives. Union with the Victor Emanuel's other territories was pretty much a foregone conclusion. Garibaldi was in agreement. However the fact that he was postponing annexation and announcing that he wanted the people to decide in a plebiscite appeared to be a contradiction. On the other hand, the imposition of Piedmontese legislation from above prejudged the future structure of the unitary state and alarmed the autonomist movement, which had a large following. There was therefore a heated debate on the methods and timing of the annexation, which was further exacerbated by the concerns of property owners over the disorder in the country.

In every province, local disputes and peasant rebellions were resulting in bloodshed. The revolution for unification, as Garibaldi understood it, had become a class struggle. A young friar told Giuseppe Cesare Abba, before Garibaldi's forces entered Palermo, that he had observed that liberty was not enough for those who had no bread, and what was needed was "something more" than the fall of the Bourbons, and this was a war "of the oppressed against oppressors big and small, who *were* not only at the court but also in every city and town." Anger at the levels of poverty and the eternal question of the former feudal lands had provoked a series of uprisings, a tumultuous and spontaneous movement of peasant masses, which was particularly widespread in June, August, and September. Landowners lost no time in putting pressure on Crispi and even Garibaldi. The government took harsh action using units of the National Guard, and summary justice was dispensed by Councils of War and Special Commissions.

Large private landowners of longstanding were not alone in the chorus of protests. The Spanish consul reported the occupation of lands belonging to the Duke of Ferrandina, and the British consul contacted Garibaldi, because he believed that the property owned by descendents of Admiral Nelson in Bronte was under threat. From Messina, the dictator wrote personally to the governor of Catania to order the immediate dispatch of "a military force capable of suppressing the disorders in Bronte which were threatening British property." It was the least he could do for the protection he had received from "these Lords of the Ocean."

In Bronte, as elsewhere, the peasant masses had risen up to obtain the allocation of the former feudal lands: they destroyed bushes, occupied contested lands, and killed the *galantuomini* who opposed them or had opposed them in the past. There were acts of ferocious violence of the kind described by Giovanni Verga in his short story *Libertà*.

Like the sea in a tempest, the crowd foamed and billowed before the lodge of the *galantuomini*, before the town hall and on the church steps: a sea of white berets, and the axes and scythes sparkled in the sun. Then it rushed into an alley. "Take that, baron, you who had people flogged by your henchmen!" At the forefront was a witch with her grizzled hair standing up on her head, who was armed only with her nails. "Take that, priest from hell, you who have sucked our souls dry! Take that, rich glutton—you cannot even escape, you have grown so fat on the blood of the poor! Take that, policeman, you who have imposed justice solely on those who have nothing! Take that, game-keeper, you who have sold your flesh and your neighbor's flesh for two *tari* a day!" Blood was steaming and made people drunk. Scythes, hands, rags, stones: all were red with blood! Take that, *galantuomini*! Get the hat-wearers! Kill, kill! Get the hat-wearers!

Colonel Giuseppe Poulet, chief of the militias that rose up in Catania on 31 May, arrived in Bronte on 3 August and restored peace by listening to the complaints of the still bloodied crowd. He entrusted the task of maintaining order to the leaders of the revolt and proceeded to disarm the population. The conciliatory attitude toward those who had sub-verted bourgeois order did not please the consul. Nino Bixio left Mes-sina in command of an armed contingent on a "blasted mission (as he wrote to his wife), in which a man of my nature should not be involved." It consisted of making a terrible example. He arrived on 6 August and af-ter calling a special commission from a nearby town, proceeded with summary judgments, mass arrests and immediate executions by firing squad.

It was a sorry episode dictated by fears that the spread of peasant unrest could compromise the prosecution of the war against the Bourbons, which was the main objective because victory would have ensured national inde-pendence. Garibaldi and his men were not familiar with the problems afflicting Sicily and Southern Italy, which they thought to be similar to Northern Italy in terms of their societies, economies, and class relations. Although in Sicily as in other parts of Europe at the time, Garibaldi was perceived as the protector of the oppressed, his interest in the lower classes was in reality more emotional than political.

By August the dictator was thinking about how to cross the Strait of Messina and obtain a foothold on Southern Italy with the aim of taking the whole of the Bourbon kingdom. This eventuality was worrying for both Cavour and Napoleon. Cavour foresaw that the success of this extraordinary enterprise would have made Garibaldi "master of the situation" and would have tarnished the prestige of the king, whose crown would have shone only in as much as it reflected the light projected by "a heroic adventurer." And then if Garibaldi, victor and dictator in Naples "surrounded by irresistible popular acclaim," had decided to attack Austria to liberate Venice, Victor Emanuel would have had to join him in the war. To avoid such a humiliating scenario for the House of Savoy, the best solution was to get to Naples before Garibaldi and assume the government of Southern Italy "in the name of order and humanity, thus robbing Garibaldi of supreme control of the movement for Italian unification." The only problem was that Cavour did not have the capacity to mobilize Neapolitan moderates to overthrow Francis II in July, and he would not have it in the following weeks.

Even Napoleon was unable to keep Garibaldi in Sicily. The fall of the Bourbon kingdom would have compromised the Plombières plan to keep Italy divided under French protection. Already the events in Central Italy had created an unexpected situation in the Italian peninsula. The incorporation of Southern Italy and Sicily into the Piedmontese state would have meant that French military intervention in Italy had led to outcomes that damaged French interests and strengthened parties hostile to the French Emperor. In July Napoleon followed up a Russian initiative and proposed to Britain that it should obstruct the crossing of the straits with naval patrols, but Lord Russel rejected British involvement as by this stage he preferred the formation of a powerful Kingdom of Italy at the center of the Mediterranean.

One last possibility remained: the dictator could be persuaded to give up the plan, which would not necessarily succeed and could perhaps compromise the conquest of Sicily. He knew that only the king had the authority to make such a suggestion to Garibaldi, but Victor Emanuel, who was more confident of what the future held than his minister, did not fear that Garibaldi's success would damage the monarchy's prestige: he sent an invitation to desist while at the same time suggesting that Garibaldi should refuse this request.

The texts of the two letters, which have been published for some time, have been recently confirmed by the discovery of the draft copies, corrected by the king's hand, in the papers of the Court Archive of Turin where they were sent by Umberto II of Savoy. They were sent with Count Giulio Litta-Modignani, who caught up with the dictator in Milazzo on the morning of 27 July, when he was preparing to leave for Messina. In the "official" letter from the king, which emphasized that he had not given his approval for the expedition against Sicily, he advised him "to renounce the idea of moving across to the Neapolitan continent with your brave troops, provided that the King of Naples undertakes to abandon the island and leave the Sicilians free to deliberate and decide upon their destinies." He reserved the right to complete freedom of action in the event of Francis II rejecting this condition. This letter was accompanied by another with the following suggestion in the draft version:

> The General must reply that he is full of devotion and reverence for the King, and would like to be able to follow his advice, but his duties to Italy will not allow him to give undertakings not to assist the Neapolitans when they appeal to him to take action to free them from a government in which loyal men and good Italians can place no trust. That regretfully he must therefore retain complete freedom of action.

We do not know if the intermediary delivered the second letter or preferred to read out its content. The fact is that on the same day, the dictator confirmed his affection and reverence for the king and his desire to obey him, but informed him of the embarrassment in which he would be placed by "a passive attitude in relation to the populations of Neapolitan continent," who for some time he had had to hold back and to whom he had promised immediate support. "Italy would take me to task over my passivity," he asserted, "and I believe this would cause immense damage." On the other hand, once the mission was completed, he would place at the king's feet "the authority that circumstances have conferred upon me and I will be so fortunate as to obey you for the rest of my life." The necessity of disobeying in order not endanger "the sacred cause of Italy's independence" was perhaps expressed again on 10 August when the landing in Southern Italy was imminent.

In reality the letters served to exculpate the monarchy before the world of diplomacy. Garibaldi had a secret and direct line to the king. On 30 July he told him that he had decided to cross the straits on 15 August or even earlier, and needed ten thousand rifles with bayonets before that time. When Victor Emanuel forwarded the letter to the Minister of the Interior, Farini, he recommended that he should do everything he could to satisfy "the General's demands." Indeed, on 5 August, he sent his suggestions on the conquest of Naples to Garibaldi by means of Captain Gaspare Trecchi, who had been used in the past for delivering such messages. In it he showed a trust in the strength of the revolution that was no less firm than Garibaldi's. He left the decision on Le Marche and Umbria to Garibaldi and on whether he should disband the volunteers once he was master of Southern Italy. He strongly advised him to proclaim the union with the rest of Italy and to keep the Neapolitan army intact so that it could be merged with the Piedmontese army in view of the imminent Austrian attempt to take back Lombardy. He also advised him to let Francis II flee unharmed. Evidently Turin believed that the march on Naples would be a picnic and the Neapolitans were anxiously waiting for the chance to pass under the flag of Savoy.

19. Master of a Kingdom

"ONCE WE REACHED the strait, we needed to cross it. . . . We needed to cross it, in spite of the immense vigilance of the Bourbons and those who acted for them!" There are just three kilometers between the two shores—between Faro and Calabria. Garibaldi observed and remained silent. As always he gave no inkling of his plans. "Every day, and often twice a day, he traveled the road between Messina and Faro," and climbed its tower "to investigate the opposite shore with his telescope," wrote Alberto Mario. At the same time he was building up men, arms, ships and boats. The Bourbon army, which was eighty-thousand strong, was more or less intact, as it had brought back its defeated troops from Sicily. It had stationed sixteen thousand men in Calabria along the rugged coastline between Monteleone (now Vibo Valentia) and Reggio, where mountains descend straight into the sea and there are few landing places, which in any case were fortified and well-guarded. All movement was controlled by the fleet, which had complete command of the seas.

On 8 August Garibaldi made his first attempt. On a clear, star-filled night with no wind, he sent two hundred and fifty crack troops under the orders of the Calabrian officer Benedetto Musolino on some seventy boats, which formed an "invisible bridge" in that it was difficult for the Bourbon patrols to detect them. They were supposed to set up a bridgehead by taking Fort Altafiumara by surprise with the complicity of part of the garrison. Three steamships were ready to transport two thousand men immediately. The raid did not succeed and the fort put up resistance. Garibaldi's men withdrew into the mountains and, with the assistance of local liberals and reinforced by rebel bands, they escaped the troops of General Giuseppe Ruiz who were hunting them. However, crossing the strait from Faro was proving to be a difficult operation. A few days later, an attempt to reinforce the fleet with the capture of the *Monarca*, a Bourbon warship anchored in the port of Castellammare di Stabia near Naples, ended in failure. The *Tüköry*, which audaciously crossed the Tyrrhenian Sea on the night of 13 August, carried out a surprise attack counting on the complicity of some of the Bourbon crew, but they fought back and repelled the attack. The *Tüköry* had difficulty in returning safely to Sicily.

Garibaldi still believed it possible to organize a diversion in the Papal States and the mainland of Southern Italy. Six thousand well-armed volunteers had been gathered in Genoa by Bertani who was inspired by Mazzini and his dreams of opening a third front in Central Italy and challenging Cavour and Garibaldi with a policy not dependent on Napoleon. It was Bertani's intention to land in Lazio to the north of Civitavecchia. Another three thousand men ready to cross the border into the Papal States were already in Tuscany and Romagna. The preparations, which as always were carried out in the light of day, alarmed Cavour, who feared that Napoleon would take military action in Italy to protect the pope, and that this danger would strengthen Francis II's position. Cavour felt the time had come when Garibaldi's activities should not be supported militarily. On 7 August he prohibited resignations from the army to join the volunteers, something that had been tolerated up until then. On the thirteenth he prohibited the recruitment of volunteers.

Moreover Farini, the Minister of the Interior, who could not stop Bertani from leaving, imposed the condition that Bertani attack the Papal dominions not from the enlarged Kingdom of Sardinia but from Sicily, which was governed by the dictator. It was agreed that the seven steamships would stop in Golfo Aranci in Sardinia. On 12 August Bertani arrived in Faro to see Garibaldi and he put forward his proposal to invade the Papal States. Meanwhile, operations across the Strait of Messina were at a standstill. Bertani succeeded in persuading Garibaldi to accompany him to Sardinia aboard the *Washington*. The latter discovered that the situation there had changed. By order of the government in Turin, which feared becoming involved in another revolutionary initiative, a warship forced the *Franklin* and *Turin*, the first two steamships to arrive, to continue on their journey to Sicily with two thousand men. Four thousand remained, but there was now the danger of weakening the strike and creating too many objectives. The insurrection in Central Italy could only be triggered with the forces gathered in Tuscany and Romagna. "Very often, more can be achieved with two thousand men than with ten thousand," Garibaldi wrote in a letter to Luigi Pianciani, who had been appointed leader of the expedition. Garibaldi ordered the volunteers in Golfo Aranci to go to Sicily, and he rested for one day at his home in nearby Caprera.

When he returned to Sicily, he put into action a plan that he had devised in the preceding days. On 18 August he showed up in Faro, as was normal. He then returned to Messina and unexpectedly continued on to Giardini, near Taormina, some fifty kilometers to the south, where the strait widened and the enemy was not patrolling. There Bixio awaited Garibaldi with two steamships from Sardinia—*Turin* and *Franklin*—which had evaded the enemy's attention by passing along Sicily's southern coast instead of the Strait of Messina. The volunteers were already on board, but since the *Franklin* was taking on water the engineer refused to take the ship out to sea although the leak was a small one. Garibaldi, an experienced seaman, used cow dung collected from the field to seal the hole. He then took personal command, and that evening the ships weighed anchor. By dawn they were in Calabria, at Mèlito Porto Salvo, thirty kilometers south of Reggio. An over-eager Bixio ran the larger *Turin* with its deeper draught aground, but because the sea was calm and the beach close, it was easy to put the launches into the water and land the volunteers. However, they lost six hours in their vain attempt to refloat the steamship. In the meantime the volunteers had dispersed into the town in search of food.

They gathered all the foodstuffs on sale: pasta, wine, bread, meat, chicken and snow by paying up immediately and perhaps generously.

They went in search of three cows to butcher. Many peasants harvested fruit to sell to the soldiers. Carts were sent to collect snow in the valleys of Aspromonte. They summoned bakers and millers to order 3,500 sticks of bread for the following day, and gathered up all the available carts they could get their hands on, with horses, mules, donkeys and drawing equipment to transport victuals and other things on the following day to accompany the troops.

The royal judge Marco Centola, the author of this memoir, was received by the dictator on board the *Franklin*. He sat on a sofa and was entertained by Garibaldi for two hours until the attempts to refloat the *Turin* were abandoned.

He spoke at length in a very slow and often detailed manner of his heroic deeds in Sicily, and conditions in that part of Italy. He showed himself to be absolutely certain and intense about everything. He asserted that he had more than sufficient means to occupy the Kingdom of Naples which he had left behind in Sicily and spoke of his imminent arrival in Naples as though completely confident about a journey that would be carried out without difficulties or obstacles.

The telegraph brought the Bourbons news of the landing. In the afternoon two warships arrived on the scene, opened fire on Garibaldi's men, and looted and burnt the *Turin*. They killed and wounded many volunteers who were sound asleep on the shore, some did not even wake up when struck by their officers' sabers. The sleeping soldiers had arrived directly from Genoa after three days without sleep; they had not slept during the previous night as lack of space had forced them to stand. The *Franklin*, however, managed to return to Sicily safely.

At dusk (Garibaldi preferred to move by night) about 3,600 volunteers set off, leaving about a hundred men in Mèlito with the task of following with food the next day. General Giambattista Vial, commander in chief for Calabria, who had foreseen a landing across the strait from Messina, had set up his headquarters in Monteleone on the road to Naples, and had left the area south of Reggio undefended. Garibaldi's force, which linked up with the unit that had landed on 8 August and was now under Missori's command, marched without difficulty as far as Reggio, the capital of

Calabria Ultra Prima and defended by a thousand soldiers. The city was attacked during the night and taken at dawn after a fierce battle in which Bixio was wounded. The castle, in which the garrison had barricaded itself, surrendered in the evening.

When he heard from Faro the sound of battle around Reggio, Cosenz who was in Faro sent off a flotilla of boats with over a thousand volunteers, who landed between the forts of Scilla and Bagnara. Caught between the troops garrisoned in the two fortresses, this force went inland over the mountainsides of Aspromonte, where it was attacked by Ruiz's battalions on their way back from their hunt for Missori. It managed to break loose after a fierce encounter in which Paul De La Flotte died.

The Bourbons had concentrated nearly four thousand men under the orders of Generals Fileno Briganti and Nicola Melendez around Villa San Giovanni on the Calabrian side of the Strait of Messina, along which Garibaldi would have to travel to open the road to the north and where Medici could land his forces. Vial reached them by sea but did not bring any reinforcements. He conferred with them and withdrew to Pizzo. Ruiz, although close to Villa San Giovanni, withdrew to Bagnara. In vain, the government in Naples ordered both Ruiz and Vial to attack. Briganti and Melendez, surrounded by a combined maneuver by Garibaldi and Cosenz, surrendered on 23 August. Garibaldi boldly strode among the enemy soldiers, reminded them that they were all Italians, called on them to join him, and let them go free as long as they returned to their homes. Few responded to his appeal. However, the Bourbon army, which until that moment had been disciplined and combative, started to disintegrate and felt humiliated by the hesitancy of its commanders. Soldiers set off for their homes in small groups and lived by their own wits. General Briganti, who had removed his uniform to save himself, was accused of treason and killed.

The forts of Altafiumara, Torre Cavallo, and Scilla surrendered to Garibaldi's forces. The Bourbon fleet, which was now threatened from land by their artillery, abandoned the Strait of Messina. The Medici division was now free to cross. By mid-August there was a rising in Potenza, and when the Bourbon garrisons were withdrawn, Foggia and Bari also rebelled. In Calabria the local authorities had been replaced by provisional governments appointed by the dictator during his rapid march. The Bourbon generals were now operating in a country that had become hostile.

General Giuseppe Ghio, who replaced Vial, withdrew toward Soveria Mannelli. On 30 August, his troops, which Garibaldi had managed to encircle, dispersed without fighting and without a formal surrender. In less than two weeks, Garibaldi's forces had taken control of fortresses, guns, rifles, military supplies, and depots containing foodstuffs and clothing. They were beginning to be well supplied with horses and mules. They let the enemy go free because they had no means of holding prisoners.

Meanwhile, the Bourbon army was collapsing. The road to the capital seemed open to the victor, but it was still long and full of obstacles. They had covered only two hundred kilometers of the over five hundred kilometer distance from Reggio to Naples. The terrain increased the difficulties of the march, and the volunteers were exhausted and could not be subjected to further exertions. Garibaldi was conscious of this. He informed Sirtori that the stretch between Cosenza and Tarsia was very hard going, and that water could be found in just one place along the way.

On 1 September Garibaldi instructed Sirtori to take care of his soldiers, stating that "The army must march on Naples in regular stages, and care must be taken to feed the men, not to overtire them, and to ensure that they clean themselves properly and where possible repair their clothing and particularly their shoes. The corps should be strengthened with more volunteers and suitable depots should left along the way." But other more impelling considerations of a political nature meant that Garibaldi had to reach the capital quickly. The crisis facing the monarchy was creating chaos in the country. In Soveria, Garibaldi received a message from Dumas, who had reached Naples on his yacht. The French novelist had contacted Liborio Romano, a longstanding liberal and Minister of the Interior in Francis II's constitutional cabinet. He was ready to defect to the dictator, but there were fears of a reactionary coup d'état with the ensuing danger of a civil war that would reduce the city to pile of rubble or an attempt by the moderates at Cavour's instigation to take power and proclaim the annexation, which would have made it impossible for the democrats to continue the victorious march as far as Rome. Garibaldi decided to take his own units forward with a few trusted men.

In Cosenza, where he was greeted triumphantly, he met up with Bertani, who informed him that the 1,500 men of the expedition from Golfo Aranci had landed in Paola, near Cosenza. Garibaldi ordered that they should move on by sea to Sapri. By landing in Campania, they would become the advance guard of the attacking army. He went to Maratea on the Gulf of Policastro with Bertani and Cosenz on the first horses they could find and then took a vessel to Sapri. He marched inland leading at the head of his volunteers. In Padula he obtained the surrender of three thousand Bourbon soldiers who were withdrawing to Naples under the command of General Giuseppe Caldarelli, and was joined by two thousand volunteers from Basilicata.

The Neapolitan army was still a force to be reckoned with and could count on fifty thousand men under arms. It was capable of barring the way to the invader on the Plain of Salerno. However, on 5 September Francis II decided to abandon the capital and concentrate his remaining loyal troops between Capua and Gaeta in the northern part of the kingdom, basing himself in Volturno and Garigliano. He devoted the following day to his final acts of government, and had a proclamation displayed publicly in which he announced his intention of protecting the capital "against destruction and war, to save its inhabitants and their properties, places of worship, monuments, public buildings, art collections, and everything that constitutes the heritage of its civilization and greatness, and which are superior to the passions of any one period because they belong to future generations." He also sent foreign courts a protest against the "reckless enterprise" that all Europe had witnessed "with indifference." He left for Gaeta at six in the evening with the queen and a few loyal followers on a small warship, the *Messaggero*. The only ship in the fleet to follow him was the *Partenope*.

On 6 September, Garibaldi and a few of his men reached Salerno, about seventy kilometers from the capital. The government, which stayed on in Naples, decided to hasten arrival because it feared disorder now that it lacked its normal authority. Prince D'Alessandria, the mayor of Naples, and General De Sauget, the commander of the National Guard, were given the task of bearing the city's official invitation, and in the early hours of the seventh, they were received by dictator, who had already announced his willingness to cooperate by telegraph. Even though there were still six thousand loyal Bourbon soldiers in the fortresses and barracks of Naples (they would shortly move to Capua) and many thought it prudent to wait at least another day, Garibaldi decided to leave immediately, partly because he did not want Cavour's men to take advantage of the power vacuum. The railway line from Naples ran south along the Tyrrhenian coast. A ten-kilometer stretch as far as Portici had been built in 1839 and was the first railway in Italy and once the boast of the kingdom, but then works had proceeded very slowly and it still had not reached Salerno.

Garibaldi reached the end of the line, between Cava dei Tirreni and Vietri on the coast near Amalfi, in a carriage with Bertani, Cosenz, Mario, Missori, and Father Pantaleo (dressed with tricolor sash, pistol, and saber) at eleven o'clock in the morning. He acknowledged the delirious crowd and took his place on the special train which advanced slowly between the two wings of the multitude people who thronged both sides of the railway line. In Nocera the stationmaster switched a train carrying Bavarian mercenaries onto a dead-end track. At Portici an official went to meet the train and begged Garibaldi to halt, because he believed the guns in the forts were trained on the station. Garibaldi paid no heed to this warning, and at half past one the train entered Naples station.

"A son of the people, accompanied by a few friends" entered the proud capital of a kingdom. He did not show any emotion. He absented himself for a physiological need, and reappeared with his usual calm expression. Liborio Romano, the minister of the fugitive king, read out a speech in which he greeted the dictator. An enormous crowd had been waiting in the station for hours. The press had been free since the granting of the Constitution on 25 June. Liberal newspapers hostile to the government began to be published and they reported on the progress of the invaders and the defeats suffered by the Royal Army. One newspaper was even called *Il Garibaldi*. The people realized the depth of the crisis facing the House of Bourbon, and awaited the victor.

The National Guard was incapable of maintaining order, and in the confusion, Garibaldi could not reach the horse on which he was to make his martial entrance. Instead he got into a carriage. A Calabrian patriot called Demetrio Salazaro climbed up beside him and waved a flag that carried the symbols of both Naples (an unbridled horse) and Venice (the Lion of St. Mark). The carriage proceeded slowly along Via Marina, surrounded by a frenzied crowd which attempted to repeat the action of detaching the horses and carrying him in triumph. Seaman on foreign ships lying at anchor climbed the rigging and cheered him. As he passed in front of the forts of Del Carmine and Maschio Angioino, which were still garrisoned by Bourbon troops, their sentries presented arms. After an hour, he reached the square in which the Royal Palace stands, and entered the palace with the guestrooms on its right. Largo di Palazzo (which was shortly to be renamed Piazza del Plebiscito) was packed. In response to the applause, he came to the central balcony and in his Ligurian accent, thanked them "in the name of all Italians and all humanity" for what they were achieving: tyranny had come to an end, an era of freedom had commenced, and Italy was on its way to unification. To symbolize this unity, he raised his hand with index finger extended. In the days that followed, this gesture came to be widely used in Naples.

Without losing more time, Garibaldi returned to the carriage and left for the cathedral to the acclamation of the crowd along Via Toledo in the very center of the city. In Palermo the bishop had shared the rebels' hatred of the monarchy, but in Naples, Cardinal Sisto Riario Sforza, a keen supporter of the Bourbons, was not to be found in his place of worship. In Southern Italy, the majority of high-ranking clergy put up furtive resistance to their new rulers. In the cathedral Fra Pantaleo led the singing of the *Te Deum* to give thanks. The dictator received "the benediction of the Holy Sacrament while absorbed in the deepest meditation" and visited the Chapel of San Gennaro, where his miraculous blood is kept. He then returned to Via Toledo, and took up residence in Palazzo d'Angri, which belonged to Princess Doria d'Angri, who was from Nice and had put it at his disposal. The tiring day was not over. The crowd called for him repeatedly and he had to appear at the window several times. A cart in the shape of a ship was brought into the square in front of the building, while a musical band played the Garibaldi Anthem. The cart was made up in the manner used for the Piedigrotta festival and pulled by sixteen oxen with very elaborate harnesses. Finally an officer made it known with gestures that the dictator was asleep and the remaining groups of people dispersed.

The conqueror of a kingdom was at the height of his popularity and power. He knew how to make himself loved. He paid homage to the Madonna, who was worshiped in the Church of Piedigrotta, just as the Bourbons did, while thousands of worshippers rushed there from the nearby towns and villages. He replied "with words of devotion for the Christian religion and its great and sublime truths". On 10 September, he ordered that the feast of the Naples' patron saint, San Gennaro, should be celebrated "in accordance with the religious customs of this great city."

Palazzo d'Angri, which became the headquarters of the dictatorship, was constantly crowded with soldiers, civilians, and people from all classes. Garibaldi chose for himself a small room that was modestly furnished with a small iron bed, and there he received anyone who wanted to speak to him between ten and eleven in the morning. He was approached by Neapolitan and foreign women of high-ranking families and he was visited by the French writer Louise Colet, who talked to him of Venice, which she had visited a few days earlier. The dictator confirmed that he intended to liberate that city along with Rome. Esperance von Schwartz returned to his side. According to *MacMillan's Magazine*, a group of female admirers from England all kissed him and cut a lock of his hair as a keepsake, and then Türr carried out the task of tidying his flowing mane with a comb. A rumor spread that Garibaldi's officers provided him with an unwanted bodyguard to ensure that his susceptibility to the fair sex did not take too much of his energies away from his governmental duties.

Reports from Naples dominated newspapers around much of the planet. Magazines published illustrations of the countryside of Southern Italy as well as the streets and monuments of its capital. *Il Mondo Illustrato* showed Garibaldi in Via Marina standing on a carriage, and the *Illustrated London News* printed a drawing from life of a devout Garibaldi wearing his poncho in the Church of Piedigrotta and surrounded by his officers. Garibaldi was the subject of lithographs and prints in color showing him in the crowds, in a carriage, and on horseback in Via Marina, in Via Toledo, in front of Castelnuovo, or close to Palazzo d'Angri. In London nearly half a million copies of his portrait were sold. Like Napoleon, Cavour, Victor Emanuel, Pius IX, and Francis II, he was the subject of cartoons in humorous magazines. Throughout the military expeditions, the English satirical paper *Punch* sympathized with Garibaldi and aimed its barbs at Francis II and his allies in the clergy. They even believed that Garibaldi would get rid of San Gennaro, but this would not have been his intention as he was always respectful of popular beliefs, however superstitious. He showed his gratitude to Anglicans by giving them permission to build a church in Naples and donating a plot to build it on.

The dictator had the destiny of a kingdom in his hands. While public opinion around the world was electrified by the succession of incredible enterprises that had brought a modern and efficient army to its knees, the governments of the great powers were wondering how Garibaldi was going to use his extraordinary power. Italian democrats, who for the first time were in possession of a political and military force that they believed was close to achieving their program, looked to Garibaldi for the next move. But what was the program they hoped Garibaldi would implement: Mazzini's unitary republican one or Cattaneo's federalist republican one? Both Mazzini and Cattaneo rushed to Naples, where Crispi, Bertani, Aurelio Saffi, and Giuseppe Ferrari all had their own ideas on what should be done. Even without proclaiming the republic, they could have convened a constituent assembly to give the new state a more liberal constitution than the one granted by King Charles Albert in 1848. The popular revolution for the liberation of Rome and Venice still had to be prosecuted.

Garibaldi listened to everyone, including Mazzini, without being influenced on the fundamental aims: his apparent willingness to accept all manner of advice arose from his uncertainty over the appropriate means to obtain the desired results at a time of real difficulties. He was following the convictions that he had developed for some time and expressed by the slogan "Italy and Victor Emanuel." The king was the non-negotiable factor toward which he directed all his actions. He followed royal directives in his own manner when they left room for interpretation, but when they were precise, he obeyed without argument. This was what he had always done with his political masters, and was doing with complete loyalty in the case of Victor Emanuel.

In Naples as in Sicily, Garibaldi was pressing ahead with the unification around the House of Savoy without any hesitation, but he held onto the direction of the state when it came to continuing the march of freedom as far as Rome, which is what he believed the King really wanted in his heart of hearts. In his proclamation to all Neapolitans on 7 September, he asserted that providence "gave our country Victor Emanuel, who from this moment we can call the true father of all Italians" and a model sovereign. On the same day, he ordered the integration of the entire fleet of the Bourbon kingdom into the Piedmontese fleet, which he placed under the command of Admiral Persano, along with its dockyards and stores. On 9 September, he decreed that public deeds should be made out in the name of "His Majesty Victor Emanuel King of Italy," and on 14 September, he brought Charles Albert's Constitution of 1848 into force in Southern Italy.

However, Garibaldi did not want to relinquish power until he had achieved unification of the nation. He even refused to authorize the, annexation of Sicily. When Depretis pressed him to do so on 4 September while he marched on Naples, he replied that he would only do it when he reached Rome. "You understand that annexation means detaching a country from its revolutionary solidarity with the others. The revolution is our salvation, and annexation its negation: as a patriot which would you choose?" he asked on 9 September. The disputes between moderates and democrats were continuing in Palermo, and Garibaldi was forced to return there for a flying visit on the seventeenth. He accepted Depretis' resignation, and replaced him with the Tuscan Antonio Mordini. Garibaldi then launched a fierce attack on the exponents of annexation, "Rome is where we will proclaim the Kingdom of Italy. Only there will we ratify the magnificent union between free men and sons who are still slaves in this land."

Certain that he had the king on his side, he wrote to him on 11 September to ask him to send Giorgio Pallavicino as pro-dictator, "until Your Majesty will be so kind as to come to Rome, where we will proclaim you King of Italy, and I shall lay my dictatorship at your feet." On the twelfth he asked him to remove "Cavour, Farini, etc." from the government, because he believed them to be "incorrigible men who do us immense damage." On the fifteenth, he wrote in a letter to Enrico Brusco, which was published by the newspapers, that he could not make peace "with men who had injured that nation's self-respect and sold off an Italian province."

Victor Emanuel confirmed his confidence in Cavour and the policies he was pursuing, which were those of acting in agreement with Napoleon. At the end of August, the Piedmontese government obtained authorization from Napoleon III to invade Le Marche and Umbria in order to take the regular army into Southern Italy and stop Garibaldi without compromising Rome. The Papal States would lose more territory, but at least the pope's temporal power would be safe and guaranteed by France. They had to act quickly. A pretext was invented to justify the war, and Piedmontese troops crossed the border. On 18 September at Castelfidardo, they defeated the meager papal army, two thirds of which was made up of volunteers from Catholic countries who had rushed to defend the pope at the beginning of 1860. On 21 September, Garibaldi complied, "I believed that I would finish my mission in Rome, but Your Majesty commands me to finish it here and I will halt to obey you."

On 22 September, Garibaldi tried once again to persuade the king to dismiss Cavour by sending Pallavicino to see him. In Northern Italy, his demand to direct Italian politics in his own manner and to sacrifice Cavour alarmed public opinion. It made no sense to replace the great statesman when his audacious invasion of Le Marche and Umbria had nearly completed the unification of Italy without clashing with France. The dictator's popularity began to wane over the summer.

Things were not going any better in Naples. In Sicily Garibaldi had appointed Crispi, a Sicilian, as his secretary and had entrusted him with the civil administration. In Naples, however, he appointed as his secretary, Bertani, a Lombard who from 1848 had lived in exile in Genoa and had no knowledge of the problems of Southern Italy. Bertani believed that he was implementing a democratic program when in fact he was simply introducing a series of moralistic measures such as the abolition of the national lottery. There was a bitter dispute between the secretariat, which wanted to widen the revolution, and the government which was made up of moderates, whose leading figure was Liborio Romano and who wanted to restore order in the country as soon as possible under the protection of the House of Savoy. On 30 September Bertani returned to Turin to defend Garibaldi's policies in parliament, which had been convened by Cavour to resolve this dispute between Italians. On 3 October Pallavicino was appointed pro-dictator, and this strengthened the party in Southern Italy that wanted annexation.

Cavour and Garibaldi were disputing the timing of annexation without giving a thought to the fact that Francis II was still in control of part of his kingdom. The Neapolitan army had remained intact in spite of setbacks in Sicily and Calabria, which were more the result of the ineptitude of its generals and than any defect of the troops who had fought with courage at Calatafimi and Milazzo. The care that Ferdinand II had lavished on the armed forces had borne fruit. Few officers and soldiers had defected to

Garibaldi, and the majority of the army, around fifty thousand well-armed men, gathered in accordance with their king's orders in the provinces of Terra di Lavoro, Molise, and Abruzzo. In these regions, Francis II had the support of a loyal population.

Garibaldi set up his headquarters in Caserta, opposite his enemy's most advanced base, the fortified city of Capua. To protect the road to Naples, he positioned his troops along a very extended front running from Santa Maria Capua Vetere to Maddaloni. The center of the front was protected at the rear by mountains, and Garibaldi was able to move his men around by maneuvering at the rear. He knew he was in a weak position, however, and waited for his adversary to move. On 19 September, when he left Naples to rush to Palermo, Türr decided to take the initiative. He sent a column to attack Capua in the hope of repeating the miracle that had occurred at the attack on Reggio, and three hundred men to occupy Caiazzo, a hilltop town north of the River Volturno, which dominated one of the places where the river could be passed. The Bourbons came out of Capua in force and drove off their enemy decisively. Garibaldi returned to the front in the afternoon of the nineteenth. He did not consider it sensible to withdraw the garrison from Caiazzo, and so he reinforced it with another 600 men. But that was still not enough. On 21 September, seven thousand Bourbon troops left Capua, attacked the town, and took it. The volunteers lost 250 men—dead, wounded, or taken prisoner. The others withdrew across the Volturno in flood. The Bourbons had tasted their first victories and boasted of them, as they now felt that the war had changed direction and it was now time to prepare a counterattack.

General Giosuè Ritucci had been made commander in chief, and the king called on him to go on the offensive. The general hesitated, as Landi, Lanza, Clary, Vial, Briganti, Melendez, Caldarelli, and Ghio had done before him. Even though he had markedly superior forces now emboldened by success, he preferred to wait for Garibaldi to attack. Francis II insisted, and at the end of September Ritucci decided to engage in battle. He wanted to concentrate his forces against Santa Maria to break through Garibaldi's line on his left flank, cut off his lines of communication, and open up the road to the capital. However the king imposed another plan, which involved frontal attack supported on the flanks, given that they were the superior force.

Garibaldi knew he was in a position of inferiority. In the northern provinces of the kingdom that bordered with the Papal States, the House of Bourbon had the support of the population. Whereas in Sicily, bands had joined the Expedition of the Thousand and small detachments under Türr and Bixio were able to keep control of territory stretching as far as Catania and Messina, the peasant bands in Terra di Lavoro, Abruzzo, and Molise gathered to defend their Bourbon king, and were armed and integrated into the army. Legitimist uprisings occurred in various places: rebels massacred liberals at Ariano in Irpinia in mid-September and peasants gathered en masse in Molise and occupied Isernia in mid-October. A unit of volunteers commanded by Francesco Nullo, which came to assist liberals, was crushed.

The arrival of fresh volunteers was slowing down in spite of Garibaldi's proclamations ("Hasten to the general review of the army that shall become the Armed Nation to make Italy one and free," he appealed from Naples on 19 September). The dictator used the forces he had—less than thirty thousand men—as best he could. Fortunately for him, Ritucci postponed the date of the attack, which had been set for 28 September, because he first wanted to eliminate the groups of volunteers in Alto Volturno, against whom he sent Von Mechel who had now been promoted to general. Garibaldi used this brief respite to position his guns. He put Bixio, Milbitz, Sacchi, and Medici, whose valor he could count on, in command of the various corps positioned along the front. He waited and was obliged to forego the two basic principles of his military tactics—surprise and initiative.

During the night of 1 October, the Bourbon regiments left Capua and attacked at dawn. In all Ritucci threw into the battle about thirty thousand of his available fifty thousand troops, and attacked both frontally and on the flank. Garibaldi, as always, left his headquarters in Caserta, and moved into the midst of the battle at Santa Maria. Seeing that the defense was holding there, he took a carriage with Canzio and Missori toward Sant'Angelo on the slopes of Mount Tifata, from where he would be able to view the whole battlefield. On the country roads the carriage was intercepted by a squad of Neapolitan soldiers who killed the coachman and a horse. Garibaldi leapt to the ground with his sword drawn, but a platoon of volunteers arrived and chased off the attackers. He proceeded on foot, and reached a high position. He saw that the Bourbons had reached the slopes of Mount Tifata. He gathered his men, stirred them to action, and led them on a

bayonet attack. Three hours later, he felt that the situation was under control and returned to Santa Maria, where he studied the situation in light of
news brought to him by dispatch riders. On his right flank at Maddaloni
and the Ponti della Valle, the attack led by Von Mechel from Alto Volturno
had been aborted. The Swiss general had encountered the resistance of
Bixio, and without contacting Ritucci, he made his own decision to fall
back to his original positions. General Giuseppe Ruiz, whom he had sent
off with a detachment toward Caserta Vecchia, reached a position on high
ground and halted without requesting further orders from Von Mechel.
The incredible disorganization of the commanders had failed to exploit a
deadly breakthrough toward Garibaldi's headquarters.

Garibaldi took a courageous decision: he removed the garrison from
Caserta and recalled three thousand men held in reserve, who at three in
the afternoon came by rail to where the fighting was fiercest. He sent one
and a half thousand troops toward Sant'Angelo where they attacked the
Bourbons from the rear and gained the upper hand. He sent the remaining one and a half thousand between the front and Capua, where they
threatened to cut off communications with the fortress. Not knowing
how to challenge his enemy's maneuver, Ritucci withdrew his troops to
Capua after ten grueling hours of battle. Garibaldi would comment,

> They gave battle along parallel lines and clashed with positions and
> forces that had prepared to receive them. If, on the other hand, they
> had preferred to attack in a more circuitous manner, as was in
> their power because they had the initiative of attack supported by
> Capua's strong position across the Volturno and the bridges over it,
> to create skirmishes by night around five of the above-mentioned
> points (Maddaloni, Castel Morrone, Sant'Angelo, Santa Maria, San
> Tammaro, and San Leucio), and during the night to bring forty thou-
> sand men down our left flank at San Tammaro, then I have no doubt
> that they could have reached Naples with very few losses.

There is hardly any need to comment on what the political situation
would have become in such an eventuality.

But as things went the way they did, it was all over for Francis II. During
the battle on 1 October which was to take its name from the River Volturno
even though the fighting did not occur along its banks, Garibaldi did not

destroy the Bourbon army, which yet again retained nearly all its troops. Garibaldi suffered greater losses (nearly 1,900 killed, wounded, or taken prisoner, as against 1,300 for the enemy), but he had successfully countered the attack on which the Bourbon monarchy had rested all its hopes. On 2 October the consequence of the battle were all in Garibaldi's favor.

"Back in Sant'Angelo on the evening of 1 October, and tired and hungry for not having taken anything throughout the day," Garibaldi found shelter at the house of the parish priest. "I had a lavish dinner followed by coffee and then I lay down for a sound sleep I do not remember where," he recorded in his *Memoirs*. However he was not to be left in peace that night either. He was informed that Ruiz's men were encamped in Caserta Vecchia, and he had to gather his available forces. The following morning two thousand Bourbon soldiers, unaware of what had occurred the previous day, went down to the plain with the intention of looting the royal palace. Garibaldi's volunteers surrounded imprudent attackers and captured them, which meant they now had more prisoners. This was the last of a series of acts whose outcome had been considerably influenced by the lack of coordination between Ritucci and his generals, and the chronic indecision of the Bourbon commanders when it came to both strategy and tactics.

In the first and last pitched battle of the war in which thousands of men were deployed on both sides, Garibaldi displayed much better control of the situation than his adversary. He was not a military theoretician and his writings do not examine the arguments on the conduct of the war that were debated at the time, but he had a clear perception of the ways in which available forces could be deployed and of the objectives he could set himself. He adeptly maneuvered his units at Volturno, he fought in the front line during the difficult moments, as he did at Calatafimi and Milazzo, and at the same time he kept a general overview of the situation throughout its various phases and the fragmentation of the engagements. He was therefore capable of using his reserve forces intelligently and at the right moment. He proved that he was not only a skilled guerrilla leader, but also a great general.

On the day of his victory, Garibaldi's long-held dream faded. He was forced to accept that Francis II's army was large, well-armed, disciplined, backed by the fortresses in Capua and Gaeta, and supported by the population. It was therefore too strong for his volunteers. The dictator remained on the defensive. He renounced the liberation of Rome, which was clearly impossible and he prepared for the handover to Victor Emanuel.

The expeditionary force under Fanti's command defeated the papal army at Castelfidardo on 18 September and took control of the fortified city of Ancona on the twenty-ninth, where the king took supreme command and received a deputation of Southern Italians who invited him to enter the kingdom. He then crossed the border into Abruzzo. When informing the king of his victory at Volturno, Garibaldi requested that he cross the border and send troops to Naples whose position was weak. In fact some units of light infantrymen, who were being used as marines on warships riding at anchor off Naples, took part in the last phases of the hostilities.

The days of the dictatorship were coming to an end. The only doubts concerned the manner of the transfer of power and the possibility of winning political concessions from the House of Savoy in exchange for the Kingdom of the Two Sicilies. The absolute arbiter of this process was Garibaldi. A struggle was being fought around him between moderates who supported unconditional annexation by plebiscite, and democrats who proposed the election of an assembly to establish the conditions for unification with Piedmont. On 5 October Mordini, the pro-dictator in Sicily, independently decreed elections on the island. In Naples opinions were divided. The pro-dictator Pallavicino insisted on a plebiscite and on 8 October decreed that this should take place on the twenty-first for the sole purpose of accepting or rejecting annexation—"for yes or for no." The democrats, from Mazzini to Cattaneo and Crispi, applied pressure to have it combined with elections for an assembly. Garibaldi had to either ratify or reject the decree. He seemed to support first one side and then the other, as he found it difficult to put aside his hopes to liberate Rome, which required him to hold onto power a little longer. He had repeated his strongly held views on Victor Emanuel many times, and his appeal to greet the Piedmontese as brothers (published in the *Giornale Officiale di Napoli* of 29 September) left no room for doubt. Moreover the Chamber of Deputies in Turin, which met at the beginning of October, endorsed Cavour's policy of annexation.

The conflicting positions were debated vigorously at a meeting held in Caserta on 11 October in Garibaldi's presence. The question remained unresolved. The next day in Naples, a large popular demonstration gathered in support of the "yes" campaign. Pallavicino resigned and the dictator left his military headquarters to attend a cabinet meeting in the capital. He declared himself unhappy with the government's conduct, and it resigned. During the ensuing political crisis, the moderates organized demonstrations against Mazzini, who was accused of fomenting disunity. On 13 October Garibaldi, who was indignant that "people had been shouting death to this person and death to that person, and to my friends," delivered a public address and later that afternoon he convened a meeting with the leading moderates and democrats. He had received a letter from the king who congratulated him on the victory at Volturno. There was no plausible reason for postponing the handover of the kingdom to the House of Savoy. At the end of a lively discussion, Garibaldi approved the decision not to set up an assembly.

The plebiscite was held on 21 October. In Southern Italy, 1,302,064 votes were cast in favor of unification with the rest of Italy and 10,312 against; in Sicily 432,053 in favor and 667 against. The previous day Cialdini had defeated the Bourbon general Scotti Douglas at Macerone and opened up the way to Volturno. On the twenty-fifth Garibaldi crossed the river with his general staff and a few thousand volunteers over a pontoon bridge put up by British volunteers. At dawn the following day, they stopped near Teano at the Taverna Catena crossroads close to a cottage and a dozen poplar trees. A long column of royal troops was moving down the road and in the bleakness of the autumn landscape, the regimental bands attempted to add a brighter note with their martial music. Generale Della Rocca halted to speak with the dictator. Alberto Mario later recalled,

Suddenly a burst on the drums stopped the music and the royal march could be heard. "The King!" said Della Rocca. "The King! The King!" a hundred voices repeated. The King was riding a dapple-grey Arab and wearing the uniform of a general and a beret. He was followed by a train of generals, chamberlains and servants . . . . Garibaldi had tied a silk scarf under his cap to protect his ears and temples from the early-morning damp. On the King's arrival, Garibaldi lifted his hat to reveal the scarf. The King held out his hand and said, "Oh, greetings my dear Garibaldi: how are you?" And Garibaldi replied, "Well, Majesty, and you?" The King rejoined, "Very well!" Garibaldi then raised his voice and looking around like one who speaks to a crowd, he shouted, "Here is the King of Italy." All those around shouted back, "Long live the King!"

Victor Emanuel drew apart to speak with Garibaldi, and then he rode on with Garibaldi on the left. Garibaldi's officers in their red shirts followed twenty passes behind in a disorderly manner, as did the officers of the regular army in their smart uniforms. They separated when they were near Teano. The king continued along the road to the town where cooks had gone ahead of him to prepare the dinner, and Garibaldi took a side road. He stopped at a farmhouse and dined "seated on an old bench two feet from his horse's tail, an upright barrel in front of him on which his lunch was set out. A bottle of water, a slice of cheese, and a loaf. What is more, the water was contaminated." The following day, he replied sadly to Jessie White Mario when she asked him for instructions on the wounded, "Signora, they have put us at the rear!" The king had instructed him that military operations would now be carried out by the regular army and any voluntary corps still being used would take their orders from Della Rocca.

During the final days, the man who had conquered a kingdom had to swallow one bitter pill after another. "They wanted to enjoy the fruits of conquest, but drive away the conquerors," was his judgment. In reality Cavour was in a hurry to prove to diplomatic circles that the revolutionary adventure in Italy was over. There was an urgent need to reestablish social and political order in Naples, guarantee it with a universally recognized government, bring to an end the anomalous situation of Garibaldi's dictatorship, and cease all threats against Rome. In this sense, the intransigence the king and his entourage showed Garibaldi and his men in the Kingdom of Naples had its indisputable reasons. What was not acceptable, however, was the ostentation of this intransigence, the absence of any acknowledgment of the Thousand and their leader through all the actions in the monarchy's name, the shabby bureaucratic manner in which the red shirts were treated, or Cavour's insensitivity in sending Fanti and Farini at the king's side, given that Garibaldi considered them his personal enemies. Farini boasted that he had never shaken the dictator's hand.

Thus Garibaldi was alone in displaying his gratitude to the volunteers. On 31 October, he handed over the flags donated by the women of Naples to the Hungarian formations in the square next to Naples' royal palace, and on 4 November presented the medal awarded by the City of Palermo to the Thousand of Marsala (426 of them were present). On 6 November before the royal palace in Caserta, he reviewed the formations that had fought and won the war. The king had promised to be present at this solemn act, but did not turn up. Commander Forbes argued that he was engaged in an amorous encounter in Capua (which had fallen on 2 November), but it is more likely that he was persuaded by his advisers from sanctioning the actions of a revolution.

Garibaldi did not respond to these discourtesies in kind. On 7 November, he was at Victor Emanuel's side when he made his official entrance into Naples, and accompanied him on the customary itinerary from the Royal Palace to the cathedral. The next day he presented the new king with the results of the plebiscite in the throne room of the Royal Palace, and out of courtesy he participated in the subsequent reception. His authority had ceased, but he asked to remain in Southern Italy for a year as the king's representative. However, this request was rejected for the sound political reasons already mentioned. He asked that his army not be disbanded, and this request was also rejected for less plausible reasons. He was offered titles and sinecures, which as usual he rejected—the Collar of the Annunciation (the highest honor in the kingdom, which was conferred on Pallavicino), a noble title, promotion to general, a castle, a ship, a farm for Menotti, a dowry for Teresita, and the appointment of Ricciotti as the king's aide-de-camp.

He left a disappointed man at dawn on 9 November. "Well, Persano," he confided to the admiral, "men are treated like oranges: once all the juice has been squeezed out of them, the skin is thrown away." He went to the *Hannibal* to take his leave of Admiral Mundy, and he boarded the American steamer *Washington*. He was accompanied by Menotti, Giovanni Basso, Giovanni Froscianti, Luigi Gusmaroli, Luigi Coltelletti, and Pietro Stagnetti. Of all the riches of the Kingdom of the Two Sicilies, he took with him a few hundred lira (put aside by Basso without his knowledge), a few packets of coffee and sugar, a sack of pulses, a sack of seed, and a bale of dried cod.

All the Italian and foreign magazines printed full-page illustrations of the meeting at Teano with the two horsemen in the foreground, and the passage of the carriage through the crowd and the triumphal arches at the entrance to Naples with the two protagonists, the one who was about to leave the scene and the one who was taking his place. They were also the subject of colored lithographs that were widely sold. *Punch* described the meeting as one between "two kings."

There was less coverage for Garibaldi's departure. The *Illustrated London News* patriotically devoted a full-page illustration to the meeting with Admiral Mundy, who had ably expressed Britain's goodwill toward him. The popular press showed him on a boat taking him to the steamer while waving to the crowd that cheered him from other boats and from the jetty. A veil was drawn over the dramatic deeds accomplished by the Thousand. For *Punch*, while Victor Emanuel rode toward his throne, Garibaldi, "alone, took possession of a higher throne and a more noble crown".

20. From the Solitude of Caprera to the Drama of Aspromonte

ALTHOUGH HE HAD left the political and military scene, Garibaldi was not forgotten. His image appeared on illustrated calendars. Between the end of 1860 and 1861 his enterprises were recorded in collections of articles written by journalists as the events occurred (for example Dumas' *Les garibaldiens* and Louise Colet's *Naples sous Garibaldi*), the first memoirs by minor protagonists in the legendary expedition (Maxime Du Camp's observations and recollections, and Ulric de Fonvielle's memoirs, both men having taken part in Garibaldi's enterprise), and essays by political commentators on the reasons for Garibaldi's success.

Charles De Mazade, the authoritative commentator of *Revue des Deux Mondes*, acknowledged in February 1861 that only Garibaldi could have undertaken such a military expedition, because only he "could have brought along a sufficient number of volunteers inspired by his fervor and driven by his spirit," and "only he could have launched this challenge to the ungainly European diplomatic world, and attempt this diversion without bringing down an immediate tempest of repression on itself." He also showed that this challenge was assisted by mistakes made by the Bourbons. These were only some of the writings available to the public in Europe and the Americas.

Garibaldi also attracted attention because of his extraordinary personality. When word spread that he had returned to Caprera without any remuneration, Kossuth confided to a friend that such a decision was without precedent in the history of mankind, and would even obscure the example of Cincinnatus himself. Cincinnatus and Washington inspired a lithograph in which the ancient Roman was shown pointing out the supreme goal of united Italy to Garibaldi who had so clearly emulated him, and the founder of American independence was shown shaking Garibaldi's hand while offering him a rifle.

During Garibaldi's absence, Deideri acting on his own initiative built a new home partly with his own money and partly with money collected from friends. *Il Movimento*, a democratic newspaper based in Genoa, asserted in October 1860 that a considerable sum had been secretly contributed by Victor Emanuel: a curious piece of news that was neither confirmed nor denied. For a few days, Garibaldi continued to sleep in the old house, and then moved to the new one. This was built on a small plateau. It was painted white and the entrance was through a hall. On the first floor on the left, there was a bedroom for Teresita and Mrs. Deideri, and on the right Garibaldi's own bedroom, which also served as a sitting room and reception room. At the back, separated by a short corridor, there was a small bedroom, kitchen, dining room, larder, and study, which was used as a bedroom and gunroom. Stairs led to the *terrazza*. However, the house was too small, given that Menotti, Gusmaroli, and Basso lived there nearly all the time. When many people were staying, the guests slept in a tent. In February 1861 Garibaldi commenced more building work: he had a wooden house brought from the continent and erected a windmill which was sent as a gift from France.

Many gifts of all kinds arrived in Caprera. During 1861, for example, he received an assortment of English sauces sent by the Duke of Sutherland, a gold pen, seeds, vines and chestnut trees for planting, fruit, merino rams, salmon roes, a shirt (sown by Bellazzi's aunt), the works of Foscolo and issues of a magazine called *Storici italiani*, a box of cigars, carpets and curtains for his bedroom, a woolen jacket, a pair of boots and two hats from a working man's association in Milan, a pair of riding boots from Parisian shoemakers, a suitcase, a trumpet, and weapons. Authors sent books on the Expedition of the Thousand and poetry (Esperance composed a sonnet on Garibaldi). There was no shortage of prints depicting events in the war and portraits of Garibaldi's troops.

The spartan furnishing of the old house (there was only one chair and it didn't have a back) had been replaced with more comfortable ones. The crew of the *Washington* donated wooden chairs with the ship's name engraved on them. Garibaldi's room was also used as a study. He had an iron bed, a chest of drawers with mirror, a writing desk, two bookshelves stuffed with books and newspapers, and a fireplace that was constantly lit (the room was damp). On the walls he had a plait of Anita's hair in an ebony frame, a portrait of little Rosita who died in Montevideo, some photographs, a saber, and a riding whip. There was a basin and a water jug. His clothes, which he washed himself, hung from a cord that crossed the room. He was meticulous about cleaning his person and his clothes.

A guest, Candido Augusto Vecchi, left a record of daily life at Garibaldi's home. He arrived in the late morning and joined the family for lunch at midday. His presence was celebrated with "a plate of traditional *maccheroni*," followed by fish (caught by Garibaldi himself), roast wild boar and partridges (hunted by Menotti in nearby Sardinia or on the island, where woodcocks and hares could also be found), and dried fruit of Calabria and wine from Capri, which were a gift from admirers (Felix Mornand would find himself drinking wine from Asti). After coffee, everyone returned to work. Vecchi went with Garibaldi, who was building a dry-stone wall. In the afternoon more guests arrived by steamer; they were Bixio and a doctor and philosopher called Timoteo Riboli, who wanted to study Garibaldi's cranium in accordance with the theories of phrenology in the hope of uncovering the reasons for his exceptional qualities. Luckily, he found the illustrious object of his studies willing to participate.

At six they had supper. Garibaldi, who would drink water at lunch, drank fresh milk in the evening. The fellow diners were served salad and meat with milk, tea, and coffee. If in a good mood, the general would provide a lively account of events in his adventurous life. Teresita would often play the piano and sing arias from operas while her father joined in. Guests would often also join the singing, which would end with patriotic anthems.

After supper Garibaldi would withdraw to his room and read for a bit in his bed. By ten he would be asleep, and at three he would be awake. He would wake Vecchi, and they would take coffee and smoke a cigar together. Vecchi, a writer and journalist, helped Garibaldi with his correspondence, which came from all over the world. Many women, particularly Englishwomen, would ask him for a lock of his hair. Generally the correspondents wanted a signed portrait. It was tiresome to have to reply. "I am lazy about writing," he confessed to Livio Zambeccari. Usually this correspondence was dealt with by Giovanni Basso, a devoted secretary who had been with him since 1849, but entire letters with only his signature were written by another hand.

In the morning he started to get on with the daily chores. He carefully recorded the changes in the weather, work in the fields and in the house, purchases and expenditure, and events of note. Work on the farm was demanding and did not provide the satisfaction he had hoped. The soil was stony and large rocks had to be broken up before they could be removed. Guests often got involved in this thankless task, and Vecchi was no exception. Guests kept the stones of Caprera, along with its corals and twigs, as souvenirs and sent them to anyone who wanted a token of Garibaldi's life. Running free amongst the scanty vegetation were the horses, Marsala, Borbone (a black horse Menotti took off a lancer at Reggio), Said (a gift from the Viceroy of Egypt), and the donkeys (which Garibaldi laughingly named after people he disliked). There were also three hunting dogs, sheep, and poultry. On the whole, local resources were very limited. He had to import a bit of everything: hay, citrus fruit, seed, and building materials. On the other hand, the air was pure and the island's few inhabitants, as Garibaldi asserted in his novel *Clelia*, "live not splendidly but in an abundant comfort with the produce of fishing and hunting, a little bit of farming, and to a great extent the generosity of friends who send necessities from the continent."

Garibaldi's frugal life was shared by a restricted number of people with whom he was familiar for many years. Vizetelly, the illustrator for the *Illustrated London News*, recorded six sketches from life in January 1861: Garibaldi fishing at night from a canoe fitted out for the purpose with a harpoon and lamp to attract the fish; Garibaldi resting in the vegetable garden; the farm; the facade of the house (with Garibaldi and his favorite dog, Teresita skipping a rope turned by Stagnetti and Mrs Susini, and the donkey Pius IX); a group of loyal friends with Menotti; Gusmaroli asleep in the study furnished with a bed, weapons and other furniture.

It would be a mistake to believe that Garibaldi forgot the world as he lived his solitary life in Caprera. He read Italian and foreign newspapers carefully, and regularly received the *Times* and *Le Siècle*. He was in correspondence with exponents of democracy in much of Europe, and many came to meet him. He followed the hopes and plans for Poland and Hungary just as much as he followed those of Rome and Venice. His "political intuition," which surprised biographers, was the product of patient and careful attention to events. Two objectives guided the network of relationships he built up in Caprera: a proper settlement for his volunteers and the completion of Italian unification by means of a revolutionary initiative. He spoke of these things with those who had fought beside him, when they came to see him. Many of the roads of Italian democracy led to Caprera.

On 13 January 1861, Türr came to Caprera and brought Garibaldi a precious seven-pointed star decorated with diamonds, which had been bought for him by survivors of the Expedition of the Thousand. *L'Illustration* described it and provided a drawing of it. Garibaldi was tormented by the way the volunteers had been treated. He had been speaking on their behalf to Victor Emanuel since October. He had wanted them to be integrated into the regular army, but it was feared that these slapdash soldiers would damage discipline and professionalism. Immediately after his departure from Naples, the government organized them in a separate corps, favored its disbandment by offering a gratuity to those who discharged themselves, and subjecting those who wished to remain to a humiliating investigation.

The problem was a political one. The establishment did not want to leave an armed corps at the disposal of Garibaldi who in the spring of 1861 decided to recommence the revolutionary initiative. From Caprera, he reasserted his loyalty to the king: "the one indispensable [element] in the program" was to have Victor Emanuel "at the head of five hundred thousand soldiers" by the following March. The committees set up to assist the Thousand by Federico Bellazzi were transformed into Action Committees for Rome and Venice, with the task of preparing forces for action. The ideas were not very clear. "As far as plans are concerned, I don't have any," he wrote to Mazzini in February in reply to his demands. "I am restricting myself to bringing the wherewithal together and keeping alive the hope of an insurrection soon. I would suggest that you do the same, and avoid deciding on one place or another for the attack. When that place is determined, we will both inform each other." They acted without agreeing their intentions with the other democratic exponents, who in January 1861 took part in the elections for the first parliament of the Kingdom of Italy. Garibaldi was elected deputy even though he did not present himself as a candidate.

The fact was that the legend surrounding his name after the Expedition of the Thousand had become not *a* but *the* reference point for Italian democracy. This movement had never had an acknowledged leader that united all its currents. This role could not have been assumed by the unitary republican Mazzini, who was hatching his usual plots in exile in London, nor by the federalist republican Cattaneo, an isolated and scholarly man who refused to enter parliament because he would not swear allegiance to the monarchy. Only Garibaldi, who acted as a politician in Palermo and Naples (albeit with some opposition), had the prestige to unite the democratic currents in a single project, and had a national and international stature which was no less than that of Cavour.

Even those who challenged him attempted to exploit him. When Mazzini resumed his activities in October 1860, he identified two programs in Italy: Cavour's and Garibaldi's. The latter, in his opinion, consisted of the liberation of Rome and Venice by volunteers in opposition to Napoleon, and Garibaldi's return to Southern Italy. There his popularity was still enormous. Costantino Nigra, whom Cavour sent to Naples in the winter of 1861, wrote to Turin, "The gigantic figure of Garibaldi, who puts on airs of grandeur at the rock sticking out of the sea called Caprera, is throwing his vast shadow as far as here." "The day that you lack that man's name," Cattaneo pointed out in March 1862 to Bertani, who sought to gather the party around his own program, "you will come to nothing. Garibaldi . . . has always enjoyed the trust of multitude and the goodwill of the world."

Garibaldi was not going to be led by anyone. He deliberately vacillated between legality and revolution. In March Victor Emanuel II was formally proclaimed King of Italy, "by the grace of God and the will of the nation," and the parliament started to make its mark on the new state. They debated the structure of the army. Garibaldi submitted a plan to establish a rapid-response National Guard made up of citizens between eighteen and thirty-five years of age, in order to achieve a nation under arms ready to fight for complete unification. He went to the capital to promote his plan. Before leaving Caprera for Turin on 29 March, he received a delegation of workers' societies. While speaking with them, he attacked the prime minister and the men "without heart or patriotism" who surround the king and had divided the army from the volunteers, the two forces which should have been moving in unison to liberate Venice and Rome.

In Turin, he was unable to leave his hotel for five days because of rheumatic pains. Fortunately for Italy, he had not suffered from them during the military campaign of 1860, possibly because of the hot climate of Sicily and Southern Italy, but the humidity of Piedmont caused a relapse. Meanwhile on 10 April Bettino Ricasoli, as a conciliatory gesture, presented a question on the disbandment of the Southern Army, and the speaker Urbano Rattazzi visited the illustrious invalid and obtained a letter in which Garibaldi declared that he had not intended to offend the king and the parliament. It was hoped that the lion had been tamed.

On 18 April Garibaldi entered the chamber of parliament. The public galleries had been full since the morning and diplomats were present. The session started at half past one, and at two o'clock noisy applause announced Garibaldi's approach. He entered by a small door on the highest steps of the floor of the house. "He appeared," wrote Count Henry d'Ideville, a French diplomat who disliked him, "dressed in his traditional costume: the immortal red shirt, covered by a kind of grey cloak in the shape of a chasuble or a South American poncho, which gave him the air of a prophet or rather an ageing actor." He was greeted by an unceasing public ovation. Many of those present were seeing him in person for the first time.

He took the ritual oath. Ricasoli presented his question and deplored the dualism that had been created between the army and the volunteers. Fanti, the minister of war, presented the government's case in a detailed argument. Then, in a moment of profound silence, Garibaldi rose to speak. The man who had given away a kingdom spoke to the representatives of a state whose foundation he had contributed to. Everyone was aware of the historic nature of that moment. Garibaldi, "with eyes equipped with a large pair of spectacles," started to read from his notes in a disorderly manner. Then he started to gesticulate with his arms and allowed his resentment to take over. He denied that he was responsible for the dualism. "Every time that dualism could have damaged the great cause of my country, I have acquiesced and I will always acquiesce," he asserted forcefully and then added that he would not shake hands with those who had made him a foreigner in his own land. He accused the government of wanting a "fratricidal war."

On hearing these words, Cavour jumped to his feet and demanded a retraction. The chamber erupted into pandemonium. The public, which was mainly made up of Garibaldi's supporters, applauded, while the deputies of the moderate governing party crowded round the speaker and demanded that the session be ended. Rattazzi would only grant a suspension of a quarter of an hour, and when the session was resumed, he asked Garibaldi to continue and moderate his language. Garibaldi criticized the government's conduct, attributed the serious problem of brigandage in Southern Italy to the disbandment of the Southern Army, and concluded by requesting that it be re-established "as the commencement of the indispensable armament [and] as an act of justice and security."

Bixio, who had also been elected deputy, softened the meaning of his general's words and appealed for concord and reconciliation. Cavour accepted this appeal, although he repeated the political and military reasons for not forming a corps of volunteers. Garibaldi did not accept the offer. As a token of the reconciliation, he demanded the immediate reorganization of the Southern Army under his command and the arming of the nation, but the prime minister had no intention of granting this request. The debate went on for two days and concluded with the approval of an order paper, proposed by Ricasoli, that committed the government to finding positions for part of Garibaldi's officers and increasing the size of the armed forces. Garibaldi, who returned to his hotel escorted by the red shirts, softened his position and in a letter to Rattazzi expressed his "devotion and friendship" for Victor Emanuel and his respect for the parliament. He did not return to the chamber and did not use his vote.

The eventful day of 18 April had an unpleasant outcome. "You are no longer the man I thought you were," Cialdini wrote to him in an open letter published in the press, "you are no longer the Garibaldi I loved. . . . You dare to put yourself on a par with the king, and speak to him with the affected familiarity of a comrade. You think yourself not to be bound by custom and appear in the chamber in a bizarre costume." He accused him of having ordered his men to open fire on the Piedmontese in 1860, and asserted the Royal Army save the volunteers from defeat at Capua and Gaeta. Garibaldi did not stoop to justify his behavior, threw back at the Piedmontese the accusation of wanting to fight a revolution, and as far as their assistance was concerned, he reminded them that "we were at the Volturno River at the close of the greatest victory." He was ready to give satisfaction for his words.

Mutual friends attempted to mediate. The European press provided considerable coverage of the debate of 18 April. The *Illustrated London News* showed Garibaldi during parliamentary proceedings in a noble oratorical pose with a composed and inspired expression. Given that the eyes of the world were on them, it would have been scandalous to expose him to mortal danger. The duel was averted and the two generals reconciled at Pallavicino's home. The king had Garibaldi and Cavour meet in his presence. They spoke to each other coldly and did not shake hands, but they kept a channel of communication open. Cavour asked Garibaldi, when he returned to Caprera, for information on some officers to be given positions in the army. In his reply, Garibaldi went into great detail on the nation under arms and the dictatorship to be assumed by the king, which he believed was "indispensable in great emergencies." The dialogue from afar did not continue because Cavour died on 6 June following a brief illness.

Caprera was once again the center of political plots. Garibaldi's prestige was still enormous in the world. In January 1861 writing in the *North American Review*, the journalist Henry Theodore Tuckerman wrote an article on his ventures and his time in New York. In his thanks, Vecchi brought up the possibility of Garibaldi's participation in the American Civil War which pitted the abolitionist North against the slave-owning South. In America this seemed a genuine possibility, as on 2 May the *New York Daily Tribune* published his letter appealing for the split-up of the state to be avoided. On 8 June the United States consul in Antwerp wrote to Caprera with his government's authority to offer Garibaldi a command in the Federal armies. "There are thousands and tens of thousands of American citizens who would glory in being put under the orders of Italy's Washington," he asserted emphatically. Garibaldi promptly replied that the were two obstacles: the first was that Victor Emanuel needed him in Italy, and the second was that President Lincoln had not openly proposed the abolition of slavery, but had only restricted himself to prohibiting its extension to states where it was not yet practiced.

The negotiations went ahead. The news came out in August when the *New York Daily Tribune* asserted that Garibaldi had accepted the appointment as general. In reality the American ambassador in Brussels, Henry Shelton Sanford, had been instructed to meet him. He stopped in Turin to find out the intentions of the Italian government, and from there he wrote to Garibaldi, who replied that he would accept the American offer if the Italian king did not require his services.

He had in fact just contacted Victor Emanuel: "The President of the United States has offered me the command of that army, and I find myself obliged to accept this mission for a country of which I am not a citizen. Notwithstanding, I thought it my duty before taking my final decision to inform Your Majesty and find out if you believe that I might have the honor of serving you." The king replied,

> Dear General, as far as taking the command offered you by the government of the United States, I believe that you must follow the dictates of your conscience toward suffering Humanity. Dear General, whatever your decision, I am quite sure that you will never forget your Italian fatherland, just as I will never forget your friendship.

The two skillfully composed letters made known what no one wanted to say openly. The king had no intention of initiating campaigns against Rome and Venice in the short term. On 6 September, Sanford knew of the king's permission and left for Caprera, accompanied by Colonel Trecchi who had brought the reply. Garibaldi laid down his conditions: his appointment as commander in chief of the American army and the abolition of slavery. These were two things Sanford could not concede: although well-disposed, the Americans could never have accepted the appointment of a foreigner to such a high position, and the question of slavery would take time to resolve. He offered the position of major general with the promise of an independent command worthy of his fame, and he pleaded with Garibaldi to support the struggle for democracy and liberty being waged by the North. Garibaldi held firm to his position on the abolition of slavery which would have given the Civil War a universal and humanitarian significance. It should be remembered that when Garibaldi was in Brazil he freed all slaves who fell into his hands and had praised the Tsar for freeing the serfs. The American invitation was withdrawn. We can only imagine what Garibaldi's skills might have brought to the vast American plains.

In Italy, the democrats were disturbed by the idea that their most famous exponent might have left for distant shores, and feared that his departure could ruin the initiatives they were working on. Mazzini aimed to organize the Left and bring Garibaldi over to his positions. For this purpose he founded a series of associations, the Unionist Societies, which worked alongside the clearly pro-Garibaldi Action Committees for Rome and Venice, and extended his influence over the workers' friendly societies to create the basis for a popular mobilization.

The workers' friendly societies developed in liberal Piedmont, and held seven congresses between 1853 and 1859, in which they discussed how to improve working conditions without touching on arguments of a political nature. At the Eighth Congress held in Milan in 1860, they dealt with arguments that had previously been avoided, and among other things, they requested a reform of the electoral law, which because of its property qualification restricted the vote to the bourgeoisie. The formation of the Kingdom of Italy meant that the workers' movement extended its activities to all the new provinces, and these developments resulted in conflict between moderates who wanted to restrict the association to matters of mutual assistance, and the followers of Mazzini who wanted to push for political demands. At the Florence Congress of September 1861, Mazzini's followers managed to get part of the movement to follow its leadership by giving it a patriotic flavor.

By the end of the year, it appeared that the Action Party (*Partito d'Azione*) had acquired the ability to influence national politics. The branches of the Action Committees and Unionist Societies discussed the country's hopes, formulated programs, and signed appeals on behalf of the workers. However the democratic movement was divided over whether to accept the monarchy's leadership or increase popular involvement. To increase its unity, an assembly of all the associations was held in Genoa in December. Mazzini's followers gained control of the committee and elected to draw up a common statute to be approved by the next assembly. Garibaldi had to ratify these decisions, which shifted the balance of power between the different currents. He was still in Caprera, a menace to governments and an inspiration to democrats in much of Europe. According to the more persistent rumors, he was about to lead an expedition in the Balkans, a veritable tinderbox: the Turkish Empire still ruled some regions whose populations were Christian, such as Montenegro, and Austria and Russia both wanted to expand into that part of the world and encouraged independence movements. Greece was suffering from an internal crisis, which would be resolved in 1863 when George I of the Danish House of Glucksburg ascended to the throne. There was good reason to hope that a revolutionary movement would be triggered and that it could spread to Hungary and Poland. A similar blow to the heart of the Austrian Empire would have weakened its hold over its Italian possessions as well.

Garibaldi was not averse to a solution for Venice that might trigger uprisings among other oppressed nationalities. In July he asked Türr to find him "an individual suited to an important mission in Dalmatia, Montenegro, and Serbia." He did not lack suggestions about what he should do. The German democrat Ferdinand Lassalle went to Caprera in November 1861 and put forward a revolutionary scenario for Europe that would start in Italy and immediately involve Hungary. Once the Hapsburg Empire was in crisis, the revolution would break out in Berlin, Prussia would become a republic, and Germany would acquire national unity and a more influential position than Austria. Like him, Hungarian and Polish exiles were coming up with rather fantastic plans that involved landings in Dalmatia or Montenegro under Garibaldi's leadership. Everyone believed that the Expedition of the Thousand would be easy to repeat.

For the moment, however, Garibaldi was interested in the opportunities provided by the Italian situation. He did not go to Genoa, and instead delegated Avezzana to represent him. While Avezzana reassured him that the new leaders would remain faithful to his program, Bellazzi put him on his guard against Mazzini's ambitions. In the face of these conflicting pressures, he took a provisional decision. On 10 January 1862 he declared that he would not accept the presidency of the new organization, but would review his position after approval of the statute and the election of leaders. To overcome Garibaldi's diffidence, a commission led by Crispi went to Caprera in mid-February and obtained a promise that he would take part in the assembly that would take the final decisions.

The activities of the democratic associations got caught up in the king's policies and those of the prime minister. On his death, Cavour was replaced by Bettino Ricasoli, one of the protagonists of the liberal revolution in Tuscany. The government faced various pressing problems, such as the legal and administrative structure of the unitary state and the formation of a single market to develop the economy, but one of the most difficult problems was brigandage in Southern Italy, which Ricasoli believed was being instigated by Francis II who had been granted refuge in Rome by Pius IX. For this reason Ricasoli considered a resolution of the Roman question to be a priority, possibly coming to an agreement with the pope. Freedom of assembly was guaranteed by the Constitution, and he allowed the associations to propagate their revolutionary plans, but did not consider it the right time for any initiative over Venice, which was very much associated with Garibaldi. He therefore sent Senator Giacomo Plezza to Caprera at almost the same time as Crispi's visit, and Plezza argued that Venice would have to be a long-term project. It was also the government's intention to set up a National Shooting Society to train young men in the use of arms. The presidency of the new organization went to the crown prince, the future Umberto I, the vice-presidency for volunteers to Garibaldi, and the vice-presidency for the army to Cialdini. Garibaldi accepted the position and left for Genoa.

On 9 March, Garibaldi chaired the proceedings of the assembly of democratic associations and workers' societies, in which deputies from the opposition also took part. This assembly brought together all the democratic currents to present the public with the policies they were proposing for Italian problems. This intention sent shock waves amongst the moderates who condemned what they saw as an attempt to create a rival parliament. In reality, the debate aimed at drawing up a program with which all the various groups could identify. In his opening address, Garibaldi, who was elected president, appealed for unity and evoked the memory of the *fasces* carried by the lictors in ancient Rome. Differences were put aside, and the followers of Garibaldi and Mazzini came together in the Italian Emancipation Association [Associazione Emancipatrice Italiana], which above all proposed that Rome should be the capital and "armed citizens should be rallied to promote and ensure the country's unity and liberty."

Before 9 March and after the conclusion of the assembly, Garibaldi met the king and the new prime minister on several occasions in Turin. At the end of February, Ricasoli had resigned and Victor Emanuel had asked Rattazzi to lead the government. Rattazzi was trusted by the king but was not approved of by those who had supported Cavour. Lacking a ready-made parliamentary majority, Rattazzi formed one with the Piedmontese Right, which was willing to follow the king's instructions, and the part of the Left that was linked to Garibaldi. He had to make concessions: to the Left he offered the integration of the remaining officers from the Southern Army into the regular army and the replacement of some prefects with men sympathetic to democracy in Southern Italy and Sicily. For Garibaldi he was thinking of assisting in the plan to send an expedition to the Balkans. For this purpose he promised to provide one million lira in government funds and organize two battalions of volunteers in Genoa on the pretext of using them for the fight against brigandage. He did not, however, accept the proposal from some left-wing deputies to send Garibaldi to Southern Italy.

This created a mismatch between the government, which only proposed to reward the Left for its support by improving the efficiency of its administration and strengthening it in Southern Italy, and the democrats who wanted to use the Emancipation Association to initiate national armament and the liberation of Rome and Venice. Their propaganda alarmed the moderates who persuaded Rattazzi to present a bill restricting the freedom of association, which was of course strongly opposed by the democrats. The key to the ambiguous relations between Rattazzi, the Left, and the Emancipation Association was Garibaldi, who was incapable of keeping control of such a complex political game. Garibaldi did not fully understand that after the elections of 1861 the democrats had become a force within the chamber and a constitutional party, and hence many of them were no longer willing to engage in actions that were outside the law. The men who considered him the leader of their party expected him to provide leadership that took into account the exigencies of Italy's international position, and one that set clear objectives.

This was not in Garibaldi's nature as he was accustomed to keeping his plans secret and ignoring the prohibitions imposed by governments. Moreover, a climate of expectancy and enthusiasm was building up around him, much as it had done in the early months of 1860. At the home of Senator Plezza in Turin, men in authority, politicians, and working people came to see him one after the other. At the end of March, he traveled to Lombardy for the inauguration the Shooting Societies. He started in Milan, where they celebrated the anniversary of the Five Days, which was the start of the National War of 1848. He was greeted as the triumphant hero by crowds so vast that the carriage took an hour to go from the station to the hotel. He gave patriotic speeches in the cathedral square and to democratic associations and trade unions. He praised Manzoni. For his part, the great writer said that he felt small in the presence of the leader of the Expedition of the Thousand, which had freed so much of Italy, "and in the best of ways, by offering it to Victor Emanuel." Manzoni also announced that he would preserve the bunch of violets Garibaldi gave him "in memory of one of the most wonderful days of my life."

Monza, Como, Lodi, Parma, Cremona, Pavia, Crema, and Brescia were not going to be outdone in the enthusiasm with which they greeted Garibaldi, as Guerzoni reported,

> The mayors come out to meet him, the municipal councils put him up in hotels at their expense, the prefects invite him, the clergy treat him with respect and the army cheers him. Everywhere he goes, an immense crowd of people waited for him undaunted by rain or heat of the sun. They climb on roofs and trees to see him, they crowd around him delirious with devotion and they constantly shout "Rome" and "Venice" at him. And the General invariably replies, "Yes, Rome and Venice are ours, and if we are strong, we shall have them."

With the oratorical style he had so often used in 1848, Garibaldi established a dialogue with the crowds, inspired them with rhetorical questions, and provoked fervent patriotic replies. In Casalmaggiore he invited young men to take up "the carbine" and in Parma he responded to the shout of "Long live Mazzini!" by shouting "Long live Victor Emanuel!" At the end of his tour he stopped at Trescore Balneario near Bergamo in Gabriele Camozzi's villa, on the pretext of treating his rheumatism. The spa town was in a strategic position on the border with Trentino. The hot-headed speeches and activities of the Action Party's agitators, who bought arms, ordered uniforms, and collected money, made it clear that a raid was being prepared. Diplomats became alarmed and Austria protested, but the Italian government remained silent partly because the king and the prime minister were on a fact-finding mission in Naples concerning the problems of Southern Italy. On 5 May, the second anniversary of his departure from Quarto, the leaders of the Emancipation Association visited Garibaldi. Antonio Mosto, Alberto Mario, and Agostino Bertani declared that they were against a strike in Venetia. Crispi, who was absent, pointed out on 11 May that any initiative that was not supported by a "general, lightning, and immediate" insurrection would have created the conditions for an Austrian counterattack, which could have dismembered a still militarily weak Kingdom of Italy. Almost certainly in the hope of dissuading Garibaldi, General Saint-Front went to visit him on the king's instructions (although we have no record of what transpired between them).

Garibaldi held firm, and on 14 May about a hundred volunteers under Nullo's orders gathered at Sarnico on Lake Iseo. The following morning half of them started to march toward the Austrian border, but the authorities there were aware of the danger and alerted the army. Nullo and his men were captured at Palazzolo by Italian soldiers as were the others who were still in Sarnico. They were locked up in the prisons of Bergamo and Brescia. In the tense atmosphere created over the preceding weeks, this firm government action was not well received. A demonstration in Bergamo ended peacefully, but in Brescia the troops opened fire on the demonstrators when they feared they would attack the prison. There were three dead and four wounded. Garibaldi took responsibility for Nullo's actions, and publicly condemned the soldiers who had opened fire on an unarmed crowd.

In Europe passions ran high, and in Italy people were very divided. The moderates were incensed and demanded respect for the law. In military circles, the accusation that the soldiers were nothing more than "thugs dressed up as soldiers" caused resentment: Garibaldi softened his stance, but confirmed that "the duty of Italian soldiers is to fight the enemies of the fatherland and the king, and not to kill and wound unarmed citizens." On 3 June the incident was discussed in the chamber. Garibaldi did not appear, which showed little respect for parliament but removed the risk of his being carried away by his natural impetuosity. In a letter read by the speaker, he asserted that the young men who had been arrested "had no other mission than military training." Rattazzi, who returned from Naples, declared he knew nothing of these plans, but Crispi responded that the government knew about the movements of the volunteers, who were actually going to leave for Greece to support the revolt against the unpopular King Otto I of Wittelsbach (Victor Emanuel hoped to put his own son Amedeo d'Aosta on the throne), and revealed that he had provided funds amounting to one million lira. Bertani put the spotlight on Garibaldi, who with his "powerful prophetic skills" had embodied the "democratic monarchy," and whose triumphal tour of Lombardy suggested an "agreement between conspiracy and diplomacy." To clarify whether such an agreement had existed, the leaders of the Emancipation Association met Garibaldi at the Cairoli family home in Belgirate on 15 June. Garibaldi openly said that he wanted to retain his freedom of action "for his own conspiratorial ends and action with the government" (these words were minuted by Aurelio Saffi). Once the tactical difference had been established, Garibaldi did all he could to explain his intentions.

In Belgirate he went to meet Senator Plezza, who was still advising him to postpone any decision and offered to assist the expedition to the Balkans. Garibaldi did not give anything away. We only know that he returned to Caprera for a few days, and on 27 June boarded the steamship *Tortoli* of the Rubattino Line to travel to Palermo. He said he was going to fulfill a promise to visit the city and was accompanied by some loyal followers: Menotti, Basso, Guerzoni, Missori, Nullo, and Bruzzesi. They did not have a precise plan and in all probability they were thinking of an expedition to Greece. However the greeting he received in Palermo was even more enthusiastic than the one received in Lombardy, and this led him to revive his hopes of 1860.

Many of the expectations held by the Sicilian population concerned their economic and social conditions, which had not noticeably improved since the fall of the Bourbons: Garibaldi believed that the demonstrations showed a willingness to complete national unification. He encountered frenzied crowds that chanted the slogan "Rome and Venice." Garibaldi shouted the names of the two cities, and his listeners called them back with wild enthusiasm. The prefect of Palermo was the same Giorgio Pallavicino who had been pro-dictator in Naples. Neither Pallavicino nor the other government authorities dared to distance themselves from Garibaldi's fiery invective against Napoleon III, who had shed the blood of his Parisian brothers and now, "on the pretext of providing physical protection for the pope", occupied Rome and made himself the "leader of brigands and assassins."

In this same mood Garibaldi visited the places associated with his extraordinary exploits of two years earlier—Alcamo, Partinico, Calatafimi, and the field of Renna. Lastly, he entered Marsala to an indescribable triumph under a shower of flowers. A solemn religious ceremony was held in the cathedral, in which the clergy took part: a Franciscan friar, Giuseppe Martingiglio, preached with such patriotic fervor that Garibaldi embraced him and called him the "true priest of the Gospel." Then speaking from the window of Count Mario Grignani's home, where he was staying, he recalled the incredible successes of the Expedition of the Thousand and asserted that it was no longer possible to suffer the shame of foreigners on Italian soil.

The crowd responded to his concluding remark, "Yes, Rome is ours," by shouting, "Rome or death." Garibaldi took up this slogan, repeated it, and solemnly swore it the following day, Sunday, 20 July, during the mass officiated by Father Pantaleo. Another expedition to liberate Italian lands began in Marsala: only this time the destination was not Naples but Rome. Garibaldi met up with three thousand volunteers in the Ficuzza Wood near Palermo. "Hard work, discomfort, and danger: these are my usual promises," he recalled on 1 August without giving a thought to the fact that the volunteers he found in Ficuzza Wood greeted him the shout of "Bread! Bread!"

The ambiguity concerning the authoritative support that Garibaldi believed he enjoyed was quickly dispelled. Rattazzi dismissed Pallavicino, who was guilty of not having prevented the insults directed at Napoleon, and on 3 August Victor Emanuel issued a proclamation to all Italians in which he distanced himself from "inexpert and deluded young men who, forgetful of their duties and the gratitude we owe our best allies," turned the name of Rome into a symbol of war. Without mentioning Garibaldi's name, the king asked Italians to be wary of "culpable impatience and reckless rabble-rousing," and he reminded everyone that any appeal not made by himself was "an appeal to rebellion and civil war." To avert this eventuality the government decreed a state of siege and justified this serious move by arguing that Garibaldi had lent "his skill and his fame to the service of European demagogy."

The inappropriateness of the action should have been clear to anyone. Compared with 1860, too many of the factors that had made possible the miracle of the Thousand were now missing. The volunteers were not the pick of middle-class youth ready to sacrifice themselves for a great ideal. Garibaldi was not flanked by the officers who had implemented his plans in the past—men such as Bixio, Medici, Cosenz, and Sirtori, who were now generals in the Royal Army. Outside Sicily the expedition did not enjoy the support of public opinion: on 16 August the quarterly satirical magazine published in Turin, *Il Fischietto*, depicted Garibaldi at the head of a group of hooligans armed with torches, and it begged him not to burn down the house that he himself had built. Lastly, he no longer had the covert support of a sovereign state.

"Read it, put your hand on your heart, think of Italy, and think of everything that we have so miraculously achieved. Do not obstinately pursue your current course, which will inevitably lead to civil war," Medici warned him when he sent him the royal proclamation. Garibaldi was not a man to reconsider a decision once he had taken it. Besides, Rome had been his dream since 1849. In his favor was his conviction that the king secretly supported his cause. The civil and military authorities allowed three columns to run about the island in search of volunteers and later converge on an agreed rendezvous in Catania. They made no attempt to stop the procession, which by that time had become accustomed to the popular clamor in every town through which it traveled. Many, including Plezza, attempted to persuade Garibaldi to desist. Vice-Admiral Giovan Battista Albini, commander of the squadron charged with impeding their passage up the strait, sent a letter to inform him that he had a ship ready to remove him from Sicily with a group of officers. This invitation to abandon the enterprise was cunningly exploited by Garibaldi in order to pursue it, because he showed the letter to Major Gallois, commander of the garrison of Paternò, to persuade him to allow them to pass.

The democrats and the Left expressed their disagreement with Garibaldi in a letter signed by Crispi among others. Crispi would not go to Sicily, and his position was supported by a commission made up of Mordini, Fabrizi, Calvino, and Cadolini, who did go to see Garibaldi. The meeting was a failure, and Garibaldi was unshakable. The Left's ambassadors, in turn, were not won over by his charm and returned to the continent, where by an irony of fate the first three were arrested by La Marmora in Naples for sedition.

The uncertainty of the authorities contrasted with the people's enthusiasm. On the evening of 19 August at Misterbianco, the citizens of Catania came out to meet Garibaldi and their enthusiasm under the light of the torches was indescribable. The crowds detached the horses from the carriage and carried it over the ten kilometers to the city. The former dictator devoted three days to organizing volunteers. On 24 August he issued a proclamation to his fellow countrymen accusing the prime minister of provoking a civil war and deceiving the king. In Catania he found "men, money, victuals, and clothing for my naked people." He took possession of two ships, the *Dispaccio* belonging to the company Florio and the *Generale Abbatucci* belonging to a French company. The two ships were loaded so full that Garibaldi feared they might not be seaworthy, and they left at ten in the evening and coasted along the port's rocky shores to avoid the surveillance of Albini's two frigates. Their landfall in Calabria was at Mèlito, as in 1860.

This was the last piece of luck in a march that had crossed Sicily without problems and with the incredible acquiescence of the authorities charged with stopping them. Europe was holding its breath while the power of France was challenged. The army's reluctance to confront Garibaldi and his men made people think there were secret agreements between Victor Emanuel and Napoleon to strip the pope of his last few fragments of temporal power. The Italian government under pressure from Emperor Napoleon finally took decisive action. On 12 August it had turned over the political direction of Sicily to General Efisio Cugia with negligible results and on the fifteenth it granted the same powers to Alfonso La Marmora in Southern Italy, which was declared subject to a state of siege five days later. On the twenty-first Cugia was replaced by Cialdini, fresh from the triumph of taking Gaeta and ready to engage with Garibaldi without being troubled by reverence for his adversary. Cialdini, who was no longer on the island, left Genoa for Naples on 26 August, where he met La Marmora and took command of the area in which Garibaldi was active. There were many army units in Calabria and Basilicata that were fighting brigands. Cialdini easily put together seven battalions under the orders of Colonel Emilio Pallavicini di Priola and sent them toward Aspromonte, where Garibaldi had taken his men.

In Mèlito, as in 1860, Garibaldi took his two thousand men along the coast road toward Reggio. Before he had been looking for Bourbon troops in order to attack them, but this time he wanted to avoid Italian troops with whom he could not fight. Fire from a warship forced Garibaldi to leave the coast, and having been obliged to avoid a well-garrisoned Reggio, he headed inland to the slopes of Aspromonte. The volunteers, misdirected by a guide, circled for two days on a disastrous march. Peasants and shepherds avoided them because they did not want to compromise themselves. "People have eaten very little and some nothing at all," Garibaldi wrote in pencil in his *Fragments*. "A serious lack of footwear caused us to slow down the march." A potato field fed the first arrivals. At first they ate them raw, but later began to cook them. "For my part, I ate those potatoes deliciously roasted." Later the mountain people brought them bread, fruit, and cheese. That night was cold and it rained.

On the morning of 29 August Garibaldi's troops sighted Pallavicini's units. Garibaldi took the volunteers into a suitable defense position on the edge of the imposing pine forest that covered the upper part of Aspromonte. The royal troops were numerous: some three and half thousand men led by the light infantry that attacked running and shooting at the same time. Garibaldi ordered his men not to open fire. If he had wanted, he could have used his favorable position to drive off the attackers who had taken no precautions. The silence on Garibaldi's side was broken however by the odd rifle-shot from those who could not overcome the tenseness of the moment. While Garibaldi was standing to repeat more forcefully the order not to open fire, he was shot by two bullets, one in the thigh that produced a lot of blood but did not hurt, and the other deep into the articulation of his right ankle. He could not stay on his feet. The officers close by carried him under some trees at the edge of the wood and removed his boot and sock. They placed Menotti, who was wounded in the left calf and was also unable to stand, beside Garibaldi. At the shout "Garibaldi is wounded!" the troops laid down their weapons. The combat had lasted quarter of an hour and caused seven dead and fourteen wounded among the royal troops and five dead and twenty wounded among Garibaldi's men.

Garibaldi was quite calm and lit a cigar while the expedition's three doctors busied themselves around him. They were unwilling to make an incision to remove the bullet. Garibaldi was in a great deal of pain but remained calm and asked repeatedly if amputation was necessary, stating that he was ready for it. An armed officer on horse presented himself, kept his hat on, and requested surrender in a boorish manner. Garibaldi ordered his troops to disarm the officer. At his request, Pallavicini came in person. He approached holding his hat in his hand, knelt before him, spoke in a low and respectful voice, and expressed his regret.

The wounded Garibaldi had to be moved to the coast, where he was to be put on a ship at Scilla. He was placed on a stretcher made of branches and covered with coats. Around seven o'clock on the evening of 29 August, they started the descent by torchlight along difficult pathways that caused jolts and unsteadiness, which in turn inflicted agony on the patient. Eight officers carried the stretcher and a ninth continuously sprayed fresh water on the inflamed foot. At midnight they stopped at a shepherd's hut, and Garibaldi was gently placed on straw and given soup made from goat's meat. At dawn the march continued. The sun was scorching and an umbrella made from laurel branches was improvised. The prisoner had asked to leave Calabria on a British ship, but this was not permitted. They did not even want to treat him in a nearby hospital in either Reggio or Messina. At Scilla he was lifted from a launch onto the steam-frigate the *Duca di Genoa* by a hoist, "like oxen," he said smiling. This was not the first time. They allowed him to be accompanied by Menotti, the three doctors, and about ten officers. Cialdini watched the loading operations impassively from the deck of the *Stella d'Italia*. He and many other officers in the regular army thought it appropriate to teach the rebel a lesson.

21. Triumph in London

G ARIBALDI'S CAMPAIGN HAD caused bewilderment and anger in Italy and Europe because of the fear of military intervention by foreign armies in the peninsula and the consequent destruction of the kingdom that had only just been formed. The dramatic conclusion, Garibaldi's detention, his wounds, and the danger of permanent injury provoked a wave of dismay and sympathy for his plight. The indignation was expressed by popular demonstrations, collections in favor of Garibaldi and his men, and the dispatch of letters, sweets, cigars, and medicines. In Leipzig they made a golden crown of laurels for the hero of liberty and paid for it through public subscription. A Swiss poet wrote an epic poem on his life. Illustrations of a wounded Garibaldi (not always realistic as no journalists were present at the fighting) appeared in the major magazines, and there was widespread distribution of lithographs, often in color, which depicted the surrender with the red shirts and officers among the trees and surrounding their general, and subsequent moments in the prisoner's odyssey.

Rumors began to spread about the manner in which the wounded prisoner was being treated. The *Duca di Genoa* took him to Varignano near

La Spezia. There, a group of buildings, which included an ancient quarantine station and penitentiary, held two hundred and fifty prisoners condemned to forced labor. When he came off the ship after waiting a day at sea in a very uncomfortable bed, Garibaldi was lodged in a wing of the building in the commandant's quarters: a bedroom for him and five rooms for his sons and officers. Menotti and Ricciotti rushed over from Caprera; Teresita with her husband Stefano Canzio and their two-month-old child, the Deideris husband and wife, Colonel Candido Augusto Vecchi (who worked as his secretary), Julie Schwabe Salis (a German woman married to an Englishman), and Esperance von Schwartz all stayed at Varignano. Some of his most loyal followers, including Guerzoni, had been arrested at Aspromonte and were being detained elsewhere.

The rooms were large, but on the prisoner's arrival on 2 September, there was very little furniture (only Garibaldi had a bed and the others slept on the floor on mattresses) and very little for the treatment of his wounds. Adelaide Cairoli, Laura Mantegazza, and Jessie White Mario, who were among the first to rush to his bedside, had to make bandages from a bed sheet. Friends soon provided decent furniture, linen, and the necessary for his treatment. Lord Palmerston sent a special bed and paid the duty in advance to speed up its delivery. Garibaldi's admirers paid for famous surgeons to visit him: the Englishman Partridge, the Frenchman Auguste Nélaton, and the Russian Nikolaj Pirogov. Among the Italian doctors Enrico Albanese, Giuseppe Basile, and Pietro Ripari were at his bedside in the first few days, and later he was treated by the Milanese Bertani, the Neapolitan Ferdinando Palasciano, the Milanese Giambattista Prandina, and the Florentine Ferdinando Zanetti. The medical examination and treatments continued for a long time and the patient suffered greatly. It was not easy to locate the position of the bullet in the wound because of the swelling caused by arthritis. It was finally identified by Nélaton at the end of October, when Garibaldi was taken to La Spezia, and Zanetti extracted it on 23 November in Pisa.

It was not easy for the Rattazzi government to deal with the crisis precipitated by Garibaldi's campaign, which came to its unhappy end on the slopes of Aspromonte. For different reasons moderates and democrats heaped criticisms on the government for having allowed the volunteers to get as far as Calabria and having spilt the blood of their brothers. The brutal military intervention was accompanied by a fit of authoritarianism. At Fantina in Sicily, six soldiers who abandoned their units to follow Garibaldi were shot as deserters following a summary judicial process, and as has already been mentioned, La Marmora arrested Mordini and his two deputy friends in Naples without observing their parliamentary immunity. Nationwide, the government dissolved the Emancipation Association and all the democratic associations, which was a serious blow to the organization that in 1861–62 had supported the Left.

Above all they had to decide what to do with the two thousand volunteers arrested in Calabria and held prisoner in Northern Italy at Vinadio, Bard, Fenestrelle, Exilles, Alessandria, and Genoa, and what to do with Garibaldi himself. Some believed that they needed to try the prisoners and sentence them, but others more sensibly advised closing this difficult episode in Italian history without treating Garibaldi cruelly, especially when his situation was already pitiful and the international press was following events with great interest. Leaving aside the daily newspapers full of reports on the prisoner's situation, *L'Illustration, Le Monde Illustré*, and the *Illustrated London News* published illustrations of the harbor and fortress at Varignano and the landing of the wounded Garibaldi (partially sitting up on his stretcher carried by his officers and surrounded by a small crowd). When he was freed from prison, *Punch* depicted him gravely handing over his saber to shameful and contrite Italy, and allegorical lithographs printed in France showed him on a cross at Calvary. People's fondness for him showed no sign of abating. Even his prestige as a general was unaffected by defeat: on 1 September Theodore Canisius, the United States consul in Vienna, did not know the gravity of the wounds Garibaldi had suffered and renewed his invitation to Garibaldi to come and fight for the liberty and unity of the great American republic—an invitation that Garibaldi politely turned down.

Napoleon, sensitive to the moods of public opinion, advised against making a martyr of the rebel. Victor Emanuel used the occasion of the marriage of his daughter Maria Pia to the King of Portugal to grant an amnesty on 5 October to the authors and accomplices "of the events and attempts at rebellion that took place last August." Garibaldi, whom the doctors would not allow to be moved, remained in Varignano for another two weeks. He had his bed moved to the window where he could see the sea, wrote his *Memoirs* and the *Autobiographical Poem*, and read Tacitus. On 22 October he was taken to the Hotel Milan in La Spezia where he was visited by Nélaton, and then to Bocche d'Arno where he was taken up the River Arno to Pisa. There he stayed at the Albergo delle Tre Donzelle and his operation was performed on 23 November. On 20 December he was taken on his bed-stretcher to Livorno, where he boarded *Sardinia*, the post-office steamer headed for Caprera.

He needed time for his convalescence. The wound was not healing well and the stages of recovery were prolonged. On 16 January 1863 he began to get out of bed and hold himself up on crutches. "I walk on crutches and soon hope to be able to put weight on my foot," he wrote to Pallavicino on 2 February. On 11 July he mounted a horse for the first time, and on the 13th he wrote to Cucchi that the wound had healed and he hoped "to send the crutches to the devil in a few months." On 21 August he sat at the table with his family to celebrate his renewed mobility. In November he was able to write to Doctor Basile that the wounded foot had recovered its former strength. This was only partly true. Jessie White Mario would report,

> The bullet in Aspromonte changed the essence of his life. By taking away all his vigor and his presence of action on the battlefield, it stopped him even in little everyday matters from putting into practice his favorite proverb: "Those who are willing, go, and those are not, send." The wound and the resulting suffering weakened his health and prevented him from constant exercise in the fresh air, by which he was in the habit of challenging his most persistent enemy, the one that laid traps for him every day [arthritis]. At the age of fifty-six it was very hard for him to have to hold out his arm so that someone could support him—hard to be taken where *he did not want to go*. There was no choice but to bow his head and accept his destiny.

"Until '66 I led an inactive and useless life," he commented bitterly in his *Memoirs* in which he leapt from Aspromonte to the Third War of Italian Independence. This judgment concerned action, which for him was the essence of life. *La guerra es la verdadera vida del hombre* was not simply a saying he liked to repeat; it was the ideal that inspired his existence, but one that was becoming increasingly difficult to put into practice.

His physical disability, which had prevented him from accepting the invitation to take part in the American Civil War, also kept him absent from another battle for freedom closer to home. On 22 January 1863, the Poles rose up against the Russians, and Italian democrats hoped that a general revolt of oppressed peoples had started. Garibaldi immediately declared his support for the insurgents: "Do not abandon Poland," he pleaded in his appeal "To the People of Europe" of 15 February. At his behest Benedetto Cairoli and Antonio Mordini engaged in negotiations with Polish and Hungarian patriots in February and March with a view to helping Poland by setting off a revolutionary movement stretching from Galicia to Hungary and the parts of the Balkans controlled by Austria. The plan was not pursued, but in the spring another opportunity presented itself: an expedition to Constantinople with the intention of provoking a revolution in Romania and then attacking Russia from the south. Guerzoni and Bruzzesi were sent to Constantinople and Bucharest to study the chances of success for so adventurous a plan, and they advised against its implementation. A few solitary volunteers left Italy to assist the Polish; Francesco Nullo was among them and died in combat.

Rattazzi, who was under attack in parliament from both the Right and the Left, resigned in November 1862, and in December Farini formed a government that maintained the ban on associations. In 1863, the revolutionary current of the Left restricted itself to forming committees to collect funds and organize demonstrations in support of Poland as a means of rekindling popular agitation. This was not very much. An attempt to reorganize Garibaldi's red shirts on the pretext of fighting brigandage failed because the idea was rejected by the government. The problem of public order in Southern Italy was extremely serious, and the government introduced exceptional measures to deal with it. In August 1863, Pica's Law implemented a kind of state of siege in the south, and suspended most of the constitutional guarantees. The Left was against a law that gave extensive powers to the military. In December 1863 complaints about illegal and arbitrary acts in Sicily provoked a bitter debate in the chamber. Many representatives of the Left spoke against the government, which still managed to win a confidence vote. Bertani then proposed that opposition deputies should resign en masse, which would cause the chamber to be dissolved and the new elections called.

Not everyone agreed with a strategy that took the political struggle outside parliament and appealed directly to the country, as this had proved ineffective in 1862. There was fierce debate between those supporting mass resignations and those against. A great deal of pressure was brought to bear on Benedetto Cairoli, who was looked upon with warmth and respect because of his integrity, goodness of heart, and love for his country. Cairoli wished to consult with Garibaldi, whom he, like many others, considered the leader of Italy's "activist democracy."

Garibaldi decided quite suddenly, and without consulting his friends, to hand in his resignation. On 21 December, he notified the speaker from Caprera. The reasons, which he explained in his declaration "to the Electors of Naples," included parliament's shortsightedness in giving away Nice and the "abusive treatment of Sicily, which I would be proud to call my second adoptive land." His decision, which precipitated the resignations of Cairoli and others, was dictated by a lack of trust in the institutions and their aims. On 23 December, the Central Unionist Committee [Comitato Unitario Centrale] was set up in Caprera. It was made up of Garibaldi's and Mazzini's followers for the immediate purpose "of initiating, fomenting, and assisting a popular uprising against Austria in the provinces of Venetia and Trentino in the spring of 1864."

On 3 January 1864, news of the formation of the new organization was announced in a circular to which a proclamation by Garibaldi was attached. In it he invited patriots "to collect the financial means and prepare people's minds for the union of sacrifice and duty." The initiative, which the government opposed, did not produce the desired results. Failure was also the outcome of Cairoli's and Mordini's negotiations on Garibaldi's behalf with the Hungarian general Gyorgy Klapka and representatives of the Italian government over the organization of a great revolution of the peoples oppressed by Austria. The road to action, the only one in which he was interested, had been blocked off for the moment.

The long year spent in the solitude of Caprera did not completely isolate Garibaldi from the world. Looking through his correspondence, we find that he was in contact with individuals in England, France, Germany,

Hungary, Russia, Poland, and Switzerland, as well as trade unions and rifle clubs. Friends, former comrades-in-arms, Italians, and foreigners came to visit him. The fascination he exerted as a freedom-fighter remained intact; indeed his image had now been improved by a halo of martyrdom. In Britain admiration for Garibaldi had never ceased since 1845. His hostility toward Austria, Napoleonic France, and the Papacy only increased British sympathy for him. On 5 October 1862 a crowd of one hundred thousand people demonstrated their support for Garibaldi in Hyde Park in London. The Englishwoman Clara Emma Collins owned part of the island of Caprera, and following some initial disputes they had become friends. During his long convalescence she became close to him. Colonel John Chambers and his wife Emma stayed on the island and encouraged him to visit England again. He received incessant invitations from political clubs, trade unions, members of parliament, lords, and members of all classes. In March 1864 he decided to accept these offers. It is not known what persuaded him, although he said that he wanted to repay the support he had had over many years but particularly in 1860. This is quite plausible. However the British government attempted to postpone the trip. It feared that he would do something rash, and suspected he wanted to talk about the conflict over the duchies of Schleswig, Holstein, and Lauenburg, which Prussia and Austria were threatening to take from Denmark. There were also fears that he might become a rallying point for the many exiles in London from all over Europe and the cause of a major disturbance, and that he might meet up with Mazzini who had been accused (incorrectly as it happened) of being involved in a plan to assassinate Napoleon. But expectations had risen so high that the government had to put on a brave face and organize a quasi-official reception.

Garibaldi left Caprera in the second half of March, accompanied by his sons Menotti and Ricciotti, Guerzoni (now his secretary), Basso, and Doctor Basile. A British ship took him to Malta, and from there he took passage on another British ship, the *Ripon*, which arrived in Southampton on 3 April. It was a cold and wet Sunday. At one o'clock, the port's gun battery announced that his steamship had been sighted and at four in the afternoon the ship berthed. In spite of the inclement weather, an enormous crowd gathered with people arriving from all parts of the kingdom. Politicians, journalists, delegates from political organizations and trade unions, and representatives from Italian, Polish, and Hungarian committees were all awaiting his arrival and rushed to meet the ship. It was the beginning of a hectic and unprecedented succession of enthusiastic welcomes.

Garibaldi was not keen on ceremonies and feared that they could be exploited for purposes with which he did not agree. As soon as he arrived, he let it be known in a statement that he did not want "to receive political demonstrations." "I particularly implore you not to create opportunities for disturbances," he added in the postscript. All the same, he did adopt political attitudes, but not in the interests of others. Mazzini proposed that he should go to the north of England before London in the hope of publicizing his own plans and collecting money. Garibaldi was not persuaded.

The beginning of his stay was restful. For a week he was the guest of the member of parliament Charles Seely at Brook House on the Isle of Wight. Garibaldi received Herzen there, and sent for Mazzini (who sent some friends to check the lie of the land): the two then met for the first time since their disagreements in Naples in 1860. He visited the poet laureate Alfred Tennyson, who had written poems in praise of Garibaldi, and planted a tree in the garden (something he would do at other homes). A famous woman photographer knelt before him and asked his permission to photograph him. He attended receptions, including one hosted by the mayor of Southampton, and he received a similar welcome at Portsmouth when he visited the port.

On 11 April he left for London on at train flying the Italian tricolor. Over the last few kilometers the train proceeded through a dense crowd. On his arrival, he listened to welcoming speeches from the mayor and representatives of associations. The police had predicted a crowd of one hundred thousand to greet Garibaldi; in fact there was half a million, many more than had greeted Kossuth in 1851 when he had escaped from an Austrian prison, and no less than had greeted Princess Alexandra of Denmark, who had come to marry the Prince of Wales. The interminable procession of deputations that came to honor him took six hours to cover the five kilometers between the station and the Duke of Sutherland's home, where he was staying. The pressure of the crowd was such that the carriage fell to pieces on its arrival at the duke's home.

In the capital the official phase started. The Duchess of Sutherland (who was fascinated by him and would continue to write to him in an affectionate vein for many years) gave a dinner in his honor, at which the Prime Minister Lord Palmerston and his government were present. This set the tone for the rest of his tour. The most formal moment came when he was awarded freedom of the city on 20 April. At the city hall, the lord mayor wearing a wig presented him with the certificate in a solid gold casket, and compared him to Cincinnatus and Leonidas. Garibaldi thanked him in English, and recalled the many occasions on which he had benefited from the help and kindness of the British government and people. The crowd around the building was so packed that Menotti was unable to attend the ceremony.

Everyday Garibaldi attended suppers, banquets, visits, and receptions. He met nobles, politicians, and diplomats. He had conversations of a political nature with Palmerston and the home secretary, Lord Russel. He met Gladstone during a supper with Antonio Panizzi. He was introduced to Florence Nightingale and the Archbishop of Canterbury. Lord Shaftesbury brought a deputation from the evangelical church. The theaters staged *Norma* and the dance *Masaniello*. In the enormous hall of Sydenham's Crystal Palace, he was applauded by thousands of people many of whom had traveled long distances. An Italian delegation presented him with a flag on which the words "Rome" and "Venice" appeared, as well as a sword of honor for him and Menotti. Deputations of Polish, Hungarian, and German exiles came to pay their respects. He visited industrial and military sites.

He occasionally managed to escape the authorities' suffocating embrace and the unending series of ceremonies that had been programmed. On Sunday 17 April he dined at the home of the Russian exile Herzen, who had a vivid recollection of him from 1854. When he saw him that first time dressed in "heavy light-colored greatcoat, a brightly colored scarf around his neck, and a beret on his head," he had the impression of a true man of the sea and not the glorious military leader of the Roman volunteers, whose statuettes in a fantastic costume were sold around the world. When he then entered into a simple and friendly conversation, he felt "the presence of a force." At the end of the meeting, Garibaldi seemed to him to be "like a classical hero, a character from the *Aeneid*, . . . around whom a legend would have formed, if he had lived in another era." Ten years later, it seemed that there now was a legend. Mazzini, Mordini, Guerzoni,

Aurelio Saffi, and the Russian Ogareff all paid homage to Garibaldi.
Mazzini toasted "to the liberty of peoples, to the union of peoples, to the
man who in our times is the living embodiment of these great ideas, to
Giuseppe Garibaldi!"

"Today I want to carry out a duty," Garibaldi replied, "that should have
been carried out some time ago. Here amongst us is a man who provided
great services to my native country and to liberty in general." He recalled
that in his youth this man had been his guide. "He alone was awake, while
everyone around him was alseep. He became my friend, and shall always
remain my friend. The sacred flame of love for country and liberty has
never wavered in him. This man is Giuseppe Mazzini: I toast to him, to
my friend and mentor!" Those who witnessed this were moved. For the
first and last time, the two great Italians managed to put aside the arguments that divided them and acknowledged each other's enormous commitment to liberty for which they were both fighting. They toasted Poland
and a democratic Russia. Garibaldi expressed his gratitude to Britain, "the
country of independence and liberty," which offered refuge and kindness
to the persecuted.

The more conservative part of the British ruling class did not share the
enthusiasm some aristocrats and working people held for this visitor to
their shores. "Honest, selfless, and courageous, Garibaldi is certainly
those things, but he is a revolutionary leader!" Queen Victoria commented in her diary, and she refused to receive him. The government was
worried. Garibaldi's visit was having the political repercussions they had
feared, and there was no way of knowing how things would develop.
Garibaldi had met two French exiles, the radical Alexandre Ledru-Rollin
and the socialist Louis Blanc. It was rumored that London had become
a meeting place for revolutionaries from all over the world. The government in Turin was alarmed by Garibaldi's repeated meetings with
Mazzini, and let its concerns be known. It was decided that the awkward
guest needed to be sent away. On 17 April he underwent a medical in-
spection by Doctor William Fergusson, the queen's physician, who diag-
nosed exhaustion which could endanger his health. He was advised
against his tour of the country as planned by Mazzini to collect funds to
be used for revolutionary plans in Italy. Although Doctor Albanese gave
him an absolute guarantee that he was in good physical health, Garibaldi

decided to return to Italy. Although he was not ill, he was tired of a life that did not suit his habits, and he suspected that people were intriguing behind the scenes in a manner he did not approve of.

During the last few days of his stay in London he was unable to avoid further social obligations. He attended a lavish reception on 19 April, the next day he received the freedom of the city at the previously mentioned ceremony, and on the twenty-first he accompanied Panizzi to the tomb of Ugo Foscolo in Chiswick. He was later officially received at the House of Commons, and met Lady Ouseley, his friend from the Montevideo days, at another reception. On 22 April he had lunch with the American consul, and met the Prince of Wales and future King Edward VII, who was keen to speak with this exceptional man. Immediately after this, he left the capital with the Duke and Duchess of Sutherland for a rapid tour of country houses and provincial towns: during a brief stopover at Eton he was mobbed by the schoolboys. On 28 April he left with the Duke and Duchess on their yacht *Ondine*. Perhaps intending to keep him from politics, the duke suggested a cruise in the Mediterranean for a couple of months. But Garibaldi was not persuaded, and on 9 May he was back in Caprera.

The extraordinary receptions organized for Garibaldi were reported in the national and international press. They were of course immortalized in pictures produced in the *Illustrated London News*. These included the crowd scenes, such as the ship's arrival in Southampton with the quays packed with flag-waving admirers, the carriage procession through packed squares with people who had climbed up buildings and statues, the formal receptions in municipal buildings with mayors in traditional ceremonial clothes and a orderly and attentive public, and the meetings in theaters (at the Crystal Palace the platform was decorated with the words "United Italy"). The paper also honored the country's famous guest with scenes from his life, such as the house in Nice where he was born.

In little more than three weeks, the legend of Garibaldi as the champion of the peoples' liberty had received its final seal of approval. It was the conclusion of a series of exceptional enterprises that for twenty years had been turning his name into something of international significance, and kept him in the collective imagination because of the simplicity he displayed in every moment of his life. "He is of humble origins," Lord George Granville said of him. "On many occasions he has shown great courage and great moral strength. He is a valiant warrior. He has simple ways. He is naive, but in his case naivety can be considered a lack of diplomatic cunning": in other words, he was and wanted to remain a common man.

"The only great popular character of our century to have developed after 1848" (as Herzen described him) continued to live up to the selflessness for which he become so famous. His aristocratic admirers organized a collection to lift him out of his poverty. Although he was always ready to accept even very considerable sums for his military enterprises, Garibaldi refused this personal gift, and on 6 May he notified the donors that their money would be returned. However he accepted a sailing ship bought with funds collected by Colonel Chambers at the end of 1864, and the half of the Island of Caprera owned by Collins, which was purchased from a collection organized by Salis Schwabe in 1865.

22. Bezzecca, Mentana, and Dijon

For Italian democrats Garibaldi's trip to England was about the interests of various groups. Mazzini (as we have seen) had been thinking of gathering funds for his military action in Venetia, Bertani was proposing an agreement between exponents of European democracy and Britain for a war against Austria in the spring of 1865, and Mordini, who believed Garibaldi was the only person with the authority to bring together the different factions of the Italian democracy, caught up with him in London on 16 April to propose a plan for a legal party to build on the support given to the plebiscites.

Just as he rejected the idea of simply being a fundraiser, Garibaldi rejected the idea of becoming leader of a parliamentary party: "I do not belong to a party but to Italy," he wrote to Pallavicino in May 1863. The man of action did not feel he could transform himself into a politician, but he still believed that a revolutionary initiative was indispensable. He took his leave of England by proclaiming a long manifesto, in which he asserted that there would never be stability in Italy while the country was still under the yoke of two oppressive powers. In May, he instructed Mordini and

Cairoli to negotiate an agreement with Hungarian patriots and the Italian government, while working on a Mazzini-Garibaldi program for the Venetian uprising. He failed both to link up Italian goals with a great European movement and to trigger actions in Italy.

But Garibaldi did not abandon hope, and concluded secret negotiations with Victor Emanuel on an expedition to the Balkans. On 17 June he left Caprera for Ischia supposedly to treat his arthritis. While he was on the island, the usual demonstrations of enthusiasm occurred, and visitors and delegations rushed over from Naples. Garibaldi summoned some of his most loyal supporters: Cairoli, Bruzzesi, and Missori. Everyone, including Mazzini, Klapka, Mordini, and Prime Minister Minghetti, opposed the planned insurrection in Galicia, which they considered too risky and would take democracy's most authoritative exponent from Italy. On 10 July, *Il Diritto*, the official publication of the parliamentary Left, published an unsigned declaration in which it advised against revolutionary and military actions outside Italy when the political situation in the country was so serious. The king gave up on the plan once he realized the general hostility to it and the excessive publicity it had received. Garibaldi left Ischia and discharged the men he had convened.

It had become clear to everyone that Garibaldi was and felt himself to be a man of action and nothing else. From mid-1864 he lived in Caprera and continued to maintain his contacts with the world. The legend surrounding his name was as potent as ever. A leaflet printed in Naples in 1865 and entitled *Garibaldi's Doctrine: The Catechism for Young Italians Aged 15 to 25 Years* [*Dottrina garibaldina. Catechismo da farsi ai giovani italiani dai 15 ai 25 anni*], was a grotesque imitation of religious catechisms and employed their technique of brief questions and answers. It asserted that Garibaldi contained "three truly distinct persons," and these were "the Father of the country, the Son of the people, and the Spirit of liberty." While the lower classes increasingly exalted his person in an exaggerated manner, the Left was distancing itself from him as it became more involved in parliamentary business. Important events were occurring in Italian political life. By an agreement of September 1864, France undertook to withdraw its garrison from Rome within two years in exchange for Italian guarantees to secure the papal borders against any aggression. The capital was moved from Turin to Florence and according to Napoleon's interpretation of the agreement, this demonstrated that territorial claims on Rome had been renounced, but the Italians were more inclined to see it as a transitional move. In any case, the Rome question appeared to have been removed from the agenda.

However, tension between Austria and Prussia, who disagreed over how to divide up the booty from their joint victory over Denmark on the question of the disputed duchies, opened the way for a solution to the Venetian question. At the beginning of 1866, the Prussian government decided to go to war to remove Austria from the presidency of the Germanic Confederation and to initiate the process of German unification under its leadership. For this reason it sought an alliance with Italy, and a treaty was signed on 8 April. The hostilities commenced in mid-June. Italy entered the war a few days later.

Back in September 1864, the announcement of the transfer of the capital had triggered protests in Turin, and the violence with which the army suppressed these demonstrations had shocked the king. Minghetti (who had replaced Farini because of the latter's health problems) was forced to resign and General La Marmora became the next Prime Minister, but in May 1866 when war became imminent, he resigned in order to become the chief of staff. Bettino Ricasoli, who was charged with forming the next government (he took office on 20 June), wanted a government of national unity with the support of the Left.

In this cooperative atmosphere between political forces, the government decreed on 6 May the formation of five regiments of volunteers under Garibaldi's command. They were expecting fifteen thousand men, but thirty thousand turned up. With only two training depots allocated in Como and Bari, they had to open others in Varese, Bergamo, Gallarate, and Barletta, and the number of regiments was increased to ten. The Corps of Volunteers consisted of two battalions of light infantry, two squadrons of scouts on horseback, four batteries of artillery, and a company of sappers, which came to an overall force of 38,000 men, 200 horses, and 24 cannon. The red shirt was adopted as their uniform, and this was the first time that it was worn by formations of the regular army.

Garibaldi did not preside over the organization of the volunteers; he was asked instead to remain on Caprera, for fear of one of his acts of recklessness. He left the island on 10 June just before operations were to begin. He happily believed that one of his dreams had come true, but the situation on the ground turned out to be a disappointment. The enlargement of the Corps of Volunteers had not been implemented competently. The weapons were second-rate and there was a shortage of uniforms. As in 1859, he was assigned a marginal theater of action, this time in Trentino. No one gave consideration to his advice on the adoption of an offensive strategy, which was permitted by the numerical superiority of the Italian army. Nor was any thought given to his plan to land experienced units in Trieste and Dalmatia to trigger a popular revolt against the Hapsburg monarchy, even though this latter plan was looked on favorably by the king.

Garibaldi made a virtue of necessity. He set up his headquarters in Salò on Lake Garda. Recalling his experiences in South America, he proposed arming a few barges with powerful cannon, towing them into the lake, creating a flotilla, and opening fire on the shore held by the Austrians, but at the beginning of operations all he could find for military purposes was a single gunboat. He was facing an enemy of seventeen thousand well-armed soldiers trained in mountain warfare under the command of General Franz Kuhn, who could also rely upon a favorable position. Only a third of the thirty thousand volunteers under Garibaldi's orders were battle-ready. On 24 June he advanced his forces and took the bridge over the Caffaro River and Mount Suello.

The war's aims suddenly became much less ambitious. The Italian army had been divided into two corps, one under La Marmora's orders on the Mincio, and the other under Cialdini's orders on the Po (Cialdini had demanded autonomy of movement). On 24 June La Marmora's divisions advanced and engaged with the Austrians. In a confused battle badly executed by the Italians, these divisions fared poorly and were forced to withdraw; Cialdini failed to come to their assistance. It was not an irretrievable defeat, but the disorientation among the leaders and the rivalry between La Marmora and Cialdini meant that for the moment, the adoption of a defensive tactic was adopted. Garibaldi was ordered to cover Brescia, which he hurried to do, and he thus abandoned the positions he had taken earlier.

The army was reorganized during the following days, and it became possible to move onto the offensive once again. The other regiments of volunteers joined Garibaldi, and with his forces now up to strength, he moved forward to reoccupy his abandoned positions. The terrain, with its

mountains, deep valleys, and obligatory routes, was not ideal for the strata-
gems, surprise attacks, and unexpected maneuvers in which he excelled.
On 3 July, he sent two regiments into an assault on the strongly defended
Mount Suello in the rain. The Austrians responded from their well-
prepared positions with withering volleys of rifle-fire. Garibaldi, who rushed
over from Rocca d'Anfo, ordered two companies to attack the enemy from
the rear, and the main body under Clemente Corte's command to launch a
frontal attack. As often happened when the volunteers clashed with well-
trained soldiers under capable leadership, "the tired soldiers who were
soaked by the rain and whose their weapons and ammunition were in a deplorable state," were repulsed with terrible losses (they didn't have cartridge
boxes and their cartridges were wet). Garibaldi, who was wounded in the
thigh, gave orders to withdraw. The next day, Garibaldi's men suffered another setback at Valcamonica.

However, the Austrians on Mount Suello were threatened with encirclement and abandoned their position. The way forward was open. Garibaldi, who had sustained a new wound to add to his long-term ailments,
could only move around in a carriage. Nevertheless he had an overview
of his theater of operations. He encountered effective resistance as he advanced through the valleys into Trentino. At Condino, the volunteers only
managed to get control after fierce fighting in which they sustained far
higher losses than those of the enemy.

The most important military encounter occurred at Bezzecca. Garibaldi had this town occupied by General Ernst Haug, a German democrat
who had been with him since 1849. Kuhn, who was cautiously withdrawing, suddenly took the initiative by a circling maneuver aimed at annihi-
lating his enemy. On the morning of 21 July, following fierce hand-to-hand
fighting, the Austrians took possession of the town, and Garibaldi, taken
by surprise, was obliged to leave his headquarters in a carriage to salvage
the situation. At Storo, he came across units that were falling back in disorder, and as he had done on other occasions, he stopped them, reordered
them and gave orders to their officers to initiate a counter-maneuver. He
had an artillery battery set up in a dominant position and halted the enemy attack. This was not enough for Garibaldi: he ordered a charge from
a carriage riddled with bullet holes, and the Austrians abandoned their
position after vicious hand-to-hand combat. It was typical of Garibaldi's

battles in which victories were achieved by a combination of a resolute desire for victory, stubbornness, and a spirit of sacrifice. Although Kuhn had not suffered a defeat, his plan had failed. The volunteers prepared to march on Trento.

But it was too late. Along other sectors of the front, the Italians had not been able to make up for their failure at Custoza, and at Lissa Admiral Persano had been defeated by the Austrian fleet. On the other hand, Prussia had been victorious at Sadowa on 3 July, and had forced Austria to surrender. A truce was also called on the Italian front and peace was in the offing. On 10 August, La Marmora gave Garibaldi the order to withdraw from Trentino. Garibaldi replied succinctly, "I will obey."

Venetia was ceded to Italy thanks to Napoleon III who had obtained this concession from Austria before the war, whatever its outcome. The liberation of Venice occurred in a humiliating manner and was not consecrated by the success of popular forces and military valor of the new Italy, as Garibaldi had always dreamt. On 1 September the Corps of Volunteers was disbanded, but they had achieved the most during the war. On the same day, *L'Illustration*, which had given much coverage to the early phases of their operations on Lake Garda, praised the bravery of Garibaldi's men who had reached the gates of Trento.

Garibaldi was an ordinary citizen once again. He stayed in Caprera for a few months, but was tormented by the thought of Rome, the last and most important prize for unification of the nation. His anticlericalism, which had begun in the stormy months of the summer of 1849, became more extreme. In the meantime the question of relations between church and state was getting caught up in domestic politics.

During the period of political harmony embracing the Left early in the war, the democrats presented a bill to abolish some religious orders and appropriate their assets, and parliament passed it into law in July 1866. When the war ended unsuccessfully for the monarchy, Ricasoli sought the support of the conservatives, and in order to favor a rapprochement with the Catholics, he proposed that part of the proceeds from the sale of these assets be restored to the church. The determined oppositions of important sections of the moderates and all of the Left put the government in a minority position. Ricasoli dissolved the chamber and called for a general election. The question of concessions to the church became the central

issue of the election campaign. Garibaldi took part, and brought his ora-
tory to bear in favor of the opposition candidates in a tour that took him to
many large and small cities, including Florence, Bologna, and Venice,
which he entered for the first time and was greeted "with splendor." The
Grand Canal, according to Herzen, "produced the effect of one single
compact bridge." Given the situation, he indulged in invective, and
preached a religion free from dogmas. Drawn along by the fanaticism of
his admirers, he baptized children with the names of fallen volunteers.
One of his posters asserted,

> In Italy we need to ensure freedom, which is threatened and endan-
> gered by clericalism and its accomplices. . . . The clergy are subjects
> and activists of a foreign power, a mixed, universal, spiritual and po-
> litical power that commands, leaves no room for debate, spreads dis-
> cord and corrupts. We must cut off the means that these stubborn
> enemies of our country and civilization use to harm us.

He promoted associations to gather funds and set up "Liberty's pence"
as against "Peter's pence," which is collected throughout the Catholic
world. He started to agitate for popular action, as he had in 1862. Ricasoli,
who was defeated in the March elections, resigned and was replaced by
Rattazzi. The situation appeared similar to that of 1862, but this time
there was no agreement between the government and Garibaldi.

He continuously referred to Rome. In December 1866, the last units of
the French army left the city. A group of conspirators in the Eternal City,
members of the Centro d'insurrezione, invited Garibaldi to lead an uprising for unification with Italy. This was what he had been waiting for. On
22 March, he resumed the title of general conferred upon him by the
Roman Republic in 1849, and set up the Centro dell'Emigrazione in
Florence to organize Roman exiles. This organization sent out detailed instructions for the enrolment of exiles, preparation of volunteers, and collection of money. Garibaldi authorized the issue of *vaglia romani* (Roman
bonds), branches were formed in many cities, and thousands of copies of
an appeal inciting insurrection were distributed in the Papal State. By the
end of April, the plan seemed well-advanced.

He moved from San Fiorano in Lombardy, where he was Pallavicino's
guest, to Signa in Tuscany in order to be close to papal territory. Before

leaving, the French organized a corps of mercenary troops to defend the Papal State. Garibaldi intended to launch several small units into border areas to disperse the enemy troops and give Rome the opportunity to rise up in a city without a garrison. Then several units would converge on the city to provide the population with the decisive assistance. The implementation of this plan required an insurrection within the city and a simultaneous arrival of volunteer units from many directions. In June, a small unit of a hundred volunteers set off from Terni: this attempt was not successful, as it was not supported by other formations and was not coordinated with preparations by the leaders in Rome. It was dispersed by the Italian army and the few volunteers who crossed the border soon returned to the Kingdom of Italy where many were arrested.

Rattazzi felt that it was not the right time to deal with the Rome question, and on 15 April declared to the chamber that he intended to respect the agreement with France. The army had orders to stop any attempted invasion, but Garibaldi did not give up hope. From Monsummano, where he had moved at the end of June for treatment of his arthritis, he encouraged his men to continue the work they had started. The main exponents of the Left attempted to dissuade him. Crispi pointed out that the country was not in favor of an uprising, and the international situation was hostile: this might produce "another Aspromonte." "General! I beg you," he wrote, "desist from this enterprise, and prevent it from happening, if you can. Stop others from doing it without you!" The democratic press did not approve of the Terni expedition or the activities of its organizers. Mazzini, on the hand, also dissociated himself because he attributed a religious significance to the liberation of Rome, which was linked to simultaneous proclamation of the republic, and therefore did not want its achievement to benefit the monarchy.

Garibaldi would not listen to anyone. In July, he took the opportunity to give speeches in Tuscany on the need to liberate Rome. He put together a new plan which took account of the need to justify his actions to Europe. He decided that the liberation would have to start in the city. After a favorable start to the insurrection, the volunteers would move to bring outside help. This was more or less what he had demanded for Sicily in 1860: a victorious movement that makes use of an external intervention. The problem was that he was again overestimating the consistency of the conspirators willing to rise up against their government; only this time his miscalculation was even greater.

He devoted July and August to organizational work. He sent Francesco Cucchi to Rome to prepare the uprising, Menotti to Southern Italy for the invasion from the south, and Giovanni Acerbi to the border between Lazio and Central Italy. He had someone consult Rattazzi, who remained hostile. Undaunted, he continued with the preparations without giving a thought to the havoc his initiative would inflict on normal life in the kingdom. In the latter half of July he stayed with family members at the villa of the Martelli brothers near Vinci. The other guests would later recall how relaxed he was. In accordance with his usual habits, he had a frugal lunch before midday and supper around six in the evening. After the meal they chatted and sang songs: Teresita was accompanied on the piano by Roberto Martelli, who happily played the "Marseillaise" and patriotic pieces. He went to bed early, and before he fell asleep he chatted to Menotti, Ricciotti, and Teresita, and read (he kept on his bedside table Julius Caesar's *Commentaries*, Pliny the Elder, and Gaetano Filangieri's *Scienza della Legislazione*). He would get up very early in the morning and in the afternoon he would walk and work with his secretary Basso, read the newspapers carefully, carry out his correspondence and receive friends, politicians, and loyal followers such as Crispi and Acerbi, whom he informed of his intentions.

On 11 August in Siena, he asserted that they would go to Rome *alla rinfrescata,* by which he meant with the cooler weather or in the coming autumn. *Alla rinfrescata* became a slogan. Public opinion started to be won over to Garibaldi's propaganda, partly because it was offended by the obtuse activities of the French. General J.E. Dumont went to inspect the Legione d'Antibo, the name given to the mercenaries recruited to defend the church's temporal dominion, who were in reality French soldiers and still part of the French army, as Dumont pointed out in his speech and as was reported in the Italian press. The incident was proof of French interference in Italian affairs. Public meetings were held in the main cities to reaffirm Italy's claim to Rome. A petition against the pope's government was signed by thousands of Romans. Eager young men rushed to the border. Garibaldi sent Ricciotti to England to obtain financial assistance, but he met with little success; it did not seem the right moment to challenge France. At the end of August he went to Orvieto, not far from the border. Rome was not ready for the insurrection. He left the preparations to Menotti, and chose 15 September as the date to start military action with an insurrection in the province of Viterbo, followed by an invasion by the volunteers. Meanwhile he went to Geneva, where the peace conference was taking place, but soon returned. Rome was still not ready and the date of the insurrection had to be postponed. On 17 September Garibaldi was in Florence, and had unsuccessful meetings with the government. Rattazzi intended to fulfill Italy's undertakings to France, but enthusiasm for the project was spreading in the country. Garibaldi consulted those who had been appointed to lead the action and most wanted to be present at the outbreak of the insurrection in Rome. Garibaldi changed his mind as the preparations were too far advanced for any further delays. He instructed the commanders of the units to meet up in Viterbo and avoid combat with Italian troops; he asked that the enterprise proceed without him if he was held up. On the twenty-third he left Florence for the border with Basso and Pietro Del Vecchio. The next morning he was arrested at Sinalunga and taken to the fortress in Alessandria on a special train. Officers and volunteers were imprisoned.

These events caused serious repercussions including violent demonstrations against Rattazzi in the capital and many cities. Twenty-five deputies protested against Garibaldi's arrest on the grounds that he had been elected in Southern Italy and was therefore protected by parliamentary immunity. Garibaldi also invoked the protection of Britain, the United States, and Argentina as their citizen. The soldiers at the garrison in Alessandria shouted, "Rome! Rome!" General Pescetto, the Minister of the Navy, went to Alessandria in the company of Crispi and Fabrizi to offer the prisoner freedom in exchange for a promise to withdraw to Caprera and not to return to the continent. Garibaldi refused to give this promise, but he was freed on the sole condition that he would go to Caprera. In reality, he was under close surveillance in Caprera, and nine warships and numerous other vessels circled the island to prevent his departure.

Garibaldi's arrest did not stop the uprising. He gave Del Vecchio, who had been arrested with him but was immediately released, a handwritten note that incited the Italians and Romans to press ahead with the insurrection. By now it was the end of September. Exponents of parliamentary left were attempting to persuade the government to resolve the complex situation by taking the initiative over Rome. Crispi asked Garibaldi to keep calm. Nicola Fabrizi and Enrico Guastalla went to Caprera to convince him, but Garibaldi refused to give in. He drew up a plan of action: three military columns were to enter Lazio, one directed to Viterbo (under Acerbi), one to Sabina (under Menotti), and one from the south toward Velletri (under Nicotera). If the papal troops left Rome, the city would either rise up or be freed by the volunteers.

To speak of columns is not entirely correct. The Italian army had orders to prevent the invasion. The volunteers could not organize on friendly soil, so they went separately to the frontier and crossed it in small groups. They were badly armed, ill-equipped for an autumn campaign, and short of money. Menotti entered papal territory on 3 October with twenty men, and Acerbi and Nicotera moved in the following days in conditions that were not much better. The volunteers gathered around their leaders and attacked. The French legionnaires did suffer some setbacks in the early engagements, but were up to the task of defending themselves without leaving Rome short of troops. Public opinion was concerned. Europe would perceive any failure as an end to Italy's drive for unification. Demonstrations in favor of government intervention were becoming increasingly common.

Rattazzi hoped to obtain Napoleon's consent, but given that there was no insurrection in Rome, he would not grant it and threatened to send an army corps to Rome if the volunteers would not desist. Rattazzi decided to stand up to France, but Victor Emanuel vetoed the idea. The government resigned and frenetic negotiations lasted until 20 October. Suggestions for an agreement were put forward but positions were hardening, and Cialdini, who was given the task of forming a new government, gave up and claimed that it was impossible to mediate between Napoleon and supporters of Italian military action in Rome. The French expeditionary corps left Toulon.

In the meantime Garibaldi had escaped from Caprera in a manner worthy of fiction. On 8 October he boarded the postal steamer, but was recaptured. He then organized his escape using a carefully studied plan. For a few days he pretended to be ill, and then his trusted follower Gusmaroli, who resembled him, appeared in front of his house wearing his clothes. The officers put their minds at rest as they peered through their telescopes from their ships. On the evening of 14 October the real Garibaldi slipped out of the house, and with two comrades reached a small cove where, under a mastic tree, they found a small sailing boat Menotti had bought in Pisa in 1862. Garibaldi was sixty years old, his body was weakened by arthritis and wounds, but his spirit was young and indomitable. He lay down in the boat that would only take one person, and maneuvered it with a single oar as he had learnt to do in America. He slipped across the surface of the water in the darkness before the moonrise. He landed on the nearby island of Giardinelli and moved with some difficulty across its rugged terrain. He waded across the strait that divided Giardinelli from the Isle of La Maddalena, and found shelter at the home of Mrs. Collins who was expecting him. On the evening of 15 October Pietro Susini arrived on horseback, and they both crossed to the other side of the island, where Basso and Captain Giuseppe Cuneo were waiting with a boat to take them to Sardinia. They rested in a shepherd's pen, and on the evening of the sixteenth they crossed the mountains of Gallura on three horses—a tiring fifteen-hour gallop. At two in the afternoon on the seventeenth Garibaldi met his son-in-law Canzio and Andrea Vigiani, who had come with a fishing smack from Livorno. On the nineteenth they came ashore at Vada, and went to Livorno on a small cart. They took a carriage to Florence and arrived there on the twentieth to be greeted by a joyous crowd. Garibaldi's incredible escape had succeded.

As Rattazzi had resigned and Cialdini had not yet taken office, no one dared stop him. Cialdini attempted to persuade him to give up the enterprise, but he was wasting his time. Garibaldi was issuing fiery proclamations and inciting Italians to the "most sacred and glorious enterprise of our Risorgimento," while also claiming that "our brothers" had put up barricades and started the revolt. He left for Terni on a special train.

Unfortunately the insurrection in Rome failed. A handful of men led by Cucchi did not succeed in taking possession of the Capitol. Giuseppe Monti and Gaetano Tognetti (who were later condemned to death) exploded a bomb in the Serristori Barracks, but it did not produce the expected slaughter of legionnaires. Police searching for arms massacred the defenders of Giulio Ajani's woolen mill in Trastevere, and the brothers Enrico and Giovanni Cairoli were intercepted at Villa Glori while they were attempting to enter Rome with a group of comrades and carrying arms for the insurrectionists. Enrico was killed and Giovanni would die later from his wounds. The people of Rome did not get involved.

Garibaldi left Terni and 23 October reached Passo Corese, where Menotti had set up his headquarters. With eight thousand volunteers under his command he attempted to take Monterotondo, a fortified hilltop town on the road to Rome. He used one of his surprise nighttime attacks as he had done so often in the past. However, the lack of expert guides meant that the volunteers arrived at daybreak and he carried out the attack at dawn on the twenty-fifth with his typical tactic of pursuing the assault in spite of losses. But the courage of the volunteers was useless against the walls and they were cut down by enemy fire. He managed to burn down one of the gates and his men burst through.

He now had control of the position, and devoted three days to reorganizing his forces. His lieutenants began moving toward Rome (Acerbi was penetrating the Viterbese area, Nicotera occupied Frosinone on 28 October and Velletri on the thirtieth, and Pianciani entered Tivoli on the twenty-ninth). Garibaldi himself was pushing his forces up the Via Salaria, the ancient road that runs into the north of Rome. On 30 October the city came into view at Monte Sacro. He was expecting an insurrection, but found Rome peaceful. The harsh repression enacted by the papal government after 1849 had weakened the unionists, and Rattazzi's disavowal of the uprising discouraged the moderates on the Roman Committee from taking part. He waited in vain throughout the day. Without a support within the city, an attack was impossible and he returned to Monterotondo.

The game was over. In the eyes of European governments, Roman apathy provided a political justification for Napoleon's military support for the pope's temporal dominion, and militarily it left Garibaldi without the support he had counted on. He was not in a position to wander aimlessly around the countryside of Lazio. The situation had suddenly swung against him. After Rattazzi's resignation and Cialdini's failure to form another government, a right-wing government was formed on 27 October by General Menabrea. Victor Emanuel proclaimed to the nation that he nothing to do with Garibaldi's activities and emphasized once again that he would fully respect the agreements signed with the French. The French expeditionary corps landed at Civitavecchia on 30 October. The Italian army, which had entered papal territory on the pretext of ensuring order, was obliged to withdraw. Napoleon III was not in the mood for compromise.

Garibaldi did not have an efficient organization. He noticed the lack of training, esprit de corps, and trust in the officers, who in any case did not have either the experience or personality of Medici, Bixio, and Cosenz. The volunteers, having endured terrible hardships, began to desert; they dropped their weapons and crossed the border into Italy. Speaking about the attack on Monterotondo, Garibaldi expressed his pity for "our poor volunteers, half-naked, starving and their few clothes soaking." They slept along the roadsides that had been turned into mud by the recent rain. Their sole comfort was their leader who stayed with them until his officers made him seek shelter from the rain in the nearby monastery of Santa Maria, where he used a confessional to rest his legs. A shortage of supplies was exacerbated by the Italian army's roadblocks. Garibaldi did not lose his habitual calm. After the victory at Monterotondo he was optimistic. Anton Giulio Barrili described him as smiling and youthful, as in 1860, and dressed in a red and blue American poncho (in Tyrol he had worn a green one). He reminded anyone who complained there was no bread that when combatants in South America were on the march they ate roast meat not only without bread but also without salt.

As in 1862, he did not realize that it was impossible to continue the action without the Italian government's support, and simply refused to give up. He always found it difficult to suspend an action once he had started it, and his stubbornness was his strength on many occasions: but at Aspromonte and Mentana it was his ruin. He decided to move his volunteers to Tivoli and into a position in which it would be possible to fight a guerrilla war in the hope of more favorable events. On 3 November he was late in leaving Monterotondo—mid-morning rather than dawn as intended—because he had lost time in distributing shoes, the affliction of these grueling marches. Before the move to Tivoli had been completed, the four and a half thousand volunteers were intercepted at Mentana by a force of twice as many papal legionnaires and French soldiers. Combat ensued. Initially Garibaldi's men and the legionnaires fought each other; the latter fought well and by two in the afternoon had gained the upper hand. Garibaldi took action: he fired on the enemy with the only two cannon in his possession, and led his volunteers from the front. He exposed himself to enemy fire and dragged them into an attack. Their relentless charge routed the enemy.

French troops then came forward in place of the legionnaires. They were armed with a new type of breech-loading and long-range rifle, the chassepot. They blasted Garibaldi's men with intense rifle-fire while still out of their adversary's range. The volunteers scattered and fled. Garibaldi would still not give in. He managed to gather a couple of hundred men and shouting, "Come and die with me" he led another charge. The enemy stopped for a moment. Canzio took his horse by the reins and blocked the way. Garibaldi finally admitted defeat. "Pale, hoarse, somber, and twenty years older," he ordered his troops to retreat. They were not pursued.

His campaign had lasted less than two weeks. Part of the volunteers withdrew to Monterotondo, then to Passo Corese, and finally back into Italy. The one and a half thousand men barricaded in Mentana surrendered to the French the following day. Amongst its various prints, *L'Illustration* produced a wonderful panoramic scene of the Battle of Mentana and a group of red shirts being held as prisoners at Castel Sant'Angelo. This marked the end of the heroic period of the Risorgimento, in which bayonet charges brought victories to the volunteers over regular troops. These images also symbolized the end of Italy's sense of gratitude to France. Rome had again been defended by a French garrison, and Mentana had cancelled out Magenta.

After disbanding the Corps of Volunteers, Garibaldi took the train for Florence. He was arrested in Figline and imprisoned in Varignano on 5 November. The French intervention, the massacre of Garibaldi's men at Mentana, and Garibaldi's imprisonment made a great impression abroad, and in Italy there were demonstrations against Menabrea. On 25 November he was released from prison and returned to Caprera. He had lost the authority he once had, and his military defeat had tarnished the myth. Because his lack of political judgment had been so clearly demonstrated by his pursuance of an impossible enterprise, the parliamentary left no longer counted on him to lead the fight for democracy within the country's institutions.

He had never been attracted by debating in the chamber, and in August 1868 he resigned as deputy. He continued, however, to get involved in Italian affairs by issuing inflammatory proclamations and adopting clear positions. He continued his invective against the Catholic Church and in 1869 he became a member of the Anti-Council held in Naples in opposition to the First Vatican Council. He spoke for democrats persecuted by the government (even his son-in-law Canzio was accused of republican conspiracy and arrested in the summer of 1869, and Ricciotti took part in an uprising in Calabria inspired by Mazzini's ideas in 1870), and deplored the repression of a popular uprising against the grist tax and scandals of which the Left complained in the chamber. He followed the struggle for freedom around Europe with detachment and without any intention of getting involved: there was a revolt in Crete against the Turks and there were internal conflicts in Spain where the republic never put down roots and they were preparing for a return of the monarchy. Physically he seemed to be crushed. The Polish novelist Józef Ignacy Kraszewski, who visited Garibaldi on Caprera in December 1869, reported,

> The old man's health is already broken and the doctors cannot assure him of a long stay among the living. He has been in bed for more than a month, his hands are stiff from the paralysis, his face as pale as tracing paper, and his legs swollen. . . . Sadly he can only see a desert around him. The hovel in which he has made his home is damp and food—my God—cabbage and beans. He is served by two old witches, and his old friend Basso acts as his secretary and farm administrator, but the farm is in a state of decay. His children are scattered around Italy and there are very few people who are willing to risk the long and tiring journey from Genoa to see him during a period in which the sea is convulsed by tempests. . . . Correspondence is the sick man's only amusement as he lies on his wide peasant's bed.

A war in the heart of Europe engaged his interest and restored his lost vigor. In July 1870, Napoleon III was skillfully provoked by Bismarck into declaring war on Prussia. Once the war seemed likely, Napoleon attempted to enlist the help of Austria, which imposed Italy's participation in the alliance as a condition. Victor Emanuel would have been quite ready to rush chivalrously to the side of his great friend from 1859, but Giovanni Lanza's government requested that the French garrison first be withdrawn from Rome, something that Napoleon was not willing to concede.

French aggression united the whole of Germany around Prussia. The Napoleonic army immediately proved to be inferior to its enemy. On 2 September Napoleon was defeated at Sedan in a pitched battle and taken prisoner. On 4 September the republic was proclaimed in Paris. The war was continuing against the enemy who was overrunning French soil, because Bismarck was demanding very oppressive conditions.

The troops that were garrisoning Rome were recalled, and the Italian government, with the encouragement of the Left, declared that the undertakings made in 1864 were invalid. Victor Emanuel sent Count Gustavo Ponza di San Martino to Rome to persuade Pius IX to accept the occupation while assuring him of the Holy See's spiritual independence. The pope intended to show the world that he would only yield to violence, and on his refusal the Italian army entered Lazio and on 20 September entered Rome through a breech at Porta Pia. The House of Savoy thus completed the unification of the Italian peninsula. The men who had fought hardest for the liberation of Rome were absent when it was proclaimed the capital of Italy. In August Mazzini, who had been arrested in Palermo where he had gone in the hope of finding people ready for revolution, was now imprisoned in Gaeta, while Garibaldi was trapped on Caprera under surveillance by the Italian navy.

The war in France had become the war of the French people against the unjust demands of an arrogant victor. Democrats around the world sympathized with the plight of the new French Republic. Garibaldi was among the first to offer his services. "What remains of me is at your service. Give me instructions," he telegraphed the French government. He did not receive a reply. Conservatives and Catholics were strong in the republic and they saw Garibaldi as a rabble-rouser. Nor could they forget that he had fought against them in 1849 and 1867. "I have received no reply from the French government," he confessed to Canzio on 13 September. "They do not want me in France," he stated a few days later. The hesitations were overcome by pressures from popular committees formed to defend the country, and the actions of an adventurous doctor who had fought under Garibaldi in 1860, Joseph-Philippe Bordone. He left on the vessel *Ville de Paris* and stopped in Corsica. He took a boat to deceive the naval surveillance, and on 4 October reached Caprera. On the seventh Garibaldi landed at Marseille to an enthusiastic greeting. Thousands of people crowded the port and the streets were covered with flags.

The following day, Garibaldi took the train to Tours, as this was now the provisional capital and Paris was under siege. Here he was to be disappointed. Léon Gambetta, the driving force behind the resistance, had crossed enemy lines in a balloon to get there and asked him to take command of a few hundred volunteers at Chambéry in Savoy. Garibaldi was on the point of returning home as he understood that they wanted "to make use of my name and nothing else." Gambetta, who was aware of the negative effects in Europe of humiliating such a famous military leader, changed his mind and offered Garibaldi the command "of all the French corps of the Vosges from Strasbourg to Paris and a brigade of guards." This meant mobilizing forces made up of snipers, French patriots who volunteered, foreign volunteers, and soldiers drafted by the general conscription order issued after the defeat at Sedan. It also involved liaising with the regular army.

Garibaldi accepted and set up his headquarters at Dôle. The fascination of this victor of so many battles was still powerful. Apart from the French, exiles from many countries and a few hundred Italians rallied to his stand. The latter crossed the border in spite of the hostility of the Italian government, which wanted to remain neutral, and the reservations of those who sympathized with their allies from 1866. Garibaldi did not overplay his hand. "I will make no appeals," he wrote to Riccardo Sineo, "I don't want to take the responsibility for calling up Italians; it might cause misunderstandings I wish to avoid."

For the first time since his days in South America he could not rely on a strong nucleus of Italians. He wrote in an optimistic tone to Jessie White Mario, who had gone to organize field hospitals,

> It seems a repetition of the spirited days of 1860: only this time the styles of the soldiers' uniforms are more picturesque and the dialects even more varied. Snipers, of whom each company has a strangely motley crew: Italians, Spaniards, Poles, Egyptians and Greeks, who provide a range of peasant military costumes; the mobile [units], some in uniform, some in *sabot*, some in *blouse*, just as they came from the fields and smithies.

The variety of uniforms went with the unusual names of the units: the Caprera Explorers, the Nantes Bears, Snipers of Death, the Franco-Spanish Company, and the Marseille Battalion of Equality.

The downside of this colorful crowd (or "multi-dressed" soldiery to use Garibaldi's term for the Thousand) was that it was short of weapons, clothing, and provisions, and its training had been perfunctory. These problems were all the more serious because of the extremely severe winter in which temperatures fell to eighteen degrees below zero centigrade. Garibaldi who had aged considerably, suffered a great deal with his arthritis. He slept on a camp bed that he had brought from Caprera (possibly the one given to him by Lord Palmerston in 1862). In the morning he subjected himself to baths in icy water followed by a warm environment to make him sweat, and found relief in massages with camphorated alcohol. He had difficulty in walking, and had to have others lift him into the carriage in which he moved around. Only on a few occasions did he manage to mount a horse, but he was constantly in the front line and gave an example by exposing himself to enemy fire in critical moments, as in the past. This was how he held together such a heterogeneous army, which kept growing: 4,500 men in October; 10,000 at the end of November; 18,000 by mid-December; and 19,500 in January 1871.

With these troops he stood up to forty thousand well-armed, well-equipped, superbly trained Prussian soldiers who were very competently commanded by General August von Werder. He defended south of the line between the Rhine and Paris along which the invaders had drawn up their army. Werder threatened the Rhone valley held by the republicans. Garibaldi transferred his headquarters to Autun and took up a defensive position. In mid-November he entrusted Ricciotti with a surprise attack, which he carried out flawlessly in accordance with his father's instructions. The young commander (now 23 years old) marched eight hundred men for five days, and on the night of 19 October he stormed the Prussian positions at Châtillon-sur-Saône. He caught them unprepared, inflicted terrible losses, and withdrew with 167 prisoners (13 were officers), 70 horses, 6 loaded wagons, and the post cart.

The main city in his theater of operations was Dijon, which fell into German hands on 31 October. Garibaldi planned a surprise attack to be launched simultaneously with the French general Camille Crémer. The maneuver failed and he withdrew toward Lantenay, where on the twenty-sixth he was attacked. He managed to repulse them and felt it now possible to carry out a night attack on Dijon. He gave orders from a gig. When the Prussian outposts came into view, the volunteers charged the enemy and sang as they went. The element of surprise was lost and the defenders responded with deadly fire. His officers pointed out that it would be "useless to persist with the attack given the enemy's terrifying resistance. . . . I reluctantly accepted my loyal followers' assertions, and immediately thought of the unfavorable and repugnant circumstances of a retreat." Under the darkness of night, the withdrawal was carried out without difficulties.

The Prussians, emboldened by their success, launched a counterattack. On 1 December, Garibaldi who was on a reconnaissance trip in his carriage noticed, almost by chance, the Prussian column advancing on Autun. "Crushed more by shame and vexation than by fear," he sent off dispatch riders to warn Menotti, Bordone, and the other officers. Resistance was quickly organized and the enemy repulsed.

The greater part of December was spent in organizing new corps, "constantly awaiting coats, indispensable because of the severity of that season, and other items of clothing and rifles to replace our old weapons." The temperature became incredibly low and the snow packed into ice. The French armies moved in accordance with plans that treated Garibaldi as an insignificant pawn. The Prussians, who were threatened by the maneuvers of General Creuzat and General Charles Bourbaki, abandoned Dijon, which was then occupied by Garibaldi's army. On 21 January, the city was again attacked by the Prussians who returned to recapture it with an army under the command of General Edwin Manteuffel. "The attack was formidable: that day I saw the best enemy soldiers I ever came up against." The fighting lasted for three days with determination on both sides. In the end Garibaldi's men prevailed. Ricciotti took the flag of the 61st Pomeranian Regiment, the only Prussian flag taken throughout the war.

The war was coming to an end. On 29 January a three-week armistice was signed. The front on the Vosges was excluded without the French negotiators noticing. Perhaps the Prussians wanted to annihilate the volunteers and capture their elusive leader. Garibaldi found himself exposed to massively superior forces, which on 31 January started their attack. There was no time to lose. On that same night he organized the volunteers into three columns, and moved them in an orderly manner to the zone protected by the armistice, while the staff officers traveled by train. He had escaped the enemy trap. The peace treaty was signed shortly afterward and the Army of the Vosges was intact with its men and equipment.

A year later, Bakunin could rightly assert, "No one admires the popular hero Garibaldi more sincerely and more profoundly than I do. His campaign in France, indeed his entire behavior in France was truly magnificent for its nobility, its forbearance, its simplicity, its perseverance and its heroism. Never had he appeared so great."

23. Pacifism, Socialism, and Democracy

THE CAMPAIGN IN the Vosges was Garibaldi's last military undertaking. It cost him dearly because his robust health had been prematurely broken by illness and wounds, but he approached it with conscious determination. In 1837 he had started his life of military sacrifice by fighting in South America for the independence of the Republic of Rio Grande from the Empire of Brazil; it was perhaps a sign of his destiny that, after more than thirty years of battles on land and sea, he concluded it fighting for republican France oppressed by German imperialism.

His retirement from the battlefield did not mean an end to his presence in Italian and European affairs. Garibaldi was not simply a lucky guerrilla fighter who caught the imagination with incredible deeds: from 1860 he had become the symbol of the independence of nations and the liberty of peoples—of all nations and all peoples. "It was the thought of a soldier who had fought for human liberty that inflamed the hearts of most people," observed Sir John Morley on the enthusiastic manner in which he was greeted on several occasions in London in 1864.

As a champion of humanitarian ideals that went beyond national differences, his beliefs had political consequences that colored judgments on his character and divided people between enthusiastic admirers and implacable detractors. In Argentina his adversaries attempted to muddy his name with lies and accusations of looting and violence; in Europe the sensation caused by his activities destabilized long-established settlements between political forces, and above all his incessant struggle against the pope's temporal dominion, which went beyond simple anticlericalism, alarmed conservatives and provoked hatred amongst Catholics.

A startling example is the way he was viewed in France in 1870–71, which reflected the political and social disputes that were tearing the country apart. On 7 September, Garibaldi appealed to Italians from the pages of *Il Movimento* of Genoa to support the French republic which, "having learnt wisdom from the lessons of the past, will always be one of the main columns of humanity's regeneration." Louis Blanc, who was favorable to accepting his assistance, observed that he "would not come as an Italian, but as a soldier of revolutionary cosmopolitanism." This was precisely the reason why the moderate Gambetta hesitated to invite him and give him a command. Blanc's assessment was shared by democrats, republicans, and all those who saw Garibaldi as the expression of solidarity among peoples, which made up for the humiliating defeat and turned the birth of the republic into something of supranational importance.

"He has finally arrived: the commander, the most romantic hero of our century, the most famous man on the planet, the leader most certain of continuing to live in the hearts of future generations, a man whose legend— while he lives—already has the solidity of those of Wallace and William Tell," wrote Philip Gilbert Hamerton, an Englishman living in France who shared the sentiments of the French population. This interpretation explains the enthusiasm he still evoked, because as the socialist Morel asserted, "Garibaldi does not belong to Italy, but to the entire world."

In contrast, the Archbishop of Tours commented wearily on 15 October when he heard of Garibaldi's imminent arrival, "I thought that Divine Providence had already inflicted enough misery on our country; I was wrong." Unfortunately Garibaldi would provide good reason for his diffidence, because his blind anticlericalism drove him to allow a search of the bishop's palace in Autun, the closure of the Jesuit College in Dôle, and the arrest of some priests suspected of inciting the peasantry. Officers in the regular army would not cooperate with him (and he in turn condemned Colonel Chenet to death, although the French did not carry out the sentence), officials ignored him, and self-appointed moral guardians feared that his presence would attract adventurers and revolutionaries from all over the world.

The nature of this love-hate relationship became even clearer immediately after the war. The constitution of Republican France was entrusted to a Constituent Assembly. Without putting himself forward as a candidate, Garibaldi was elected in five departments of the metropolitan territory: Paris, Lower Rhine, Savoy, Dijon, and Nice. He was tired and did not want to subject himself to this further task. In the end he decided to go to Bordeaux, the provisional capital and home of the assembly, "with the sole intention of bringing my vote for the unhappy republic." The people showed him kindness and gratitude, but the majority of the assembly was made up of conservatives and clericalists who were hostile to him. He was increasingly slandered: it was said that his army had evaded combat, and that it had only distinguished itself for its looting and brutal arrogance. He was hurt by this ingratitude, and wanted to defend his record and the men who fought with him. This was another reason for wanting to speak from an authoritative forum before taking his leave of France.

He acted in a manner that demonstrated his loyalty and attention to legal process, but also his failure to understand what was appropriate. On 12 February 1871 he sent a letter to the speaker's office renouncing "the appointment I have been honored to receive," and on the thirteenth he attended the assembly. As usual, he was wearing his red shirt, poncho, and round hat. The democratic deputies (who were a minority) and the public who crowded the galleries applauded him. The majority of deputies countered with insults and wanted him to remove his hat, to which Garibaldi replied that priests were allowed keep their skullcaps. The speaker read his letter of resignation and then denied him his right to speak as he was no longer part of the assembly. Garibaldi insisted. The speaker suspended the sitting, and in the ensuing chaotic scene his supporters and detractors shouted at each other.

Another chaotic scene in which he was denigrated occurred the following month. Garibaldi was elected again in Algeria in a by-election to replace Gambetta, who had opted for another constituency. The majority proposed that the election be deemed invalid because he was not a French citizen. Victor Hugo replied that no king and no nation had come to France's aid: "just one man was the exception: Garibaldi!" That man was a power, the only one who was not defeated. He could not be considered a foreigner. Subjected to invective and denials, Hugo resigned in protest. In the meantime, a parliamentary commission examined the campaign in the Vosges, and minimized the victory at Dijon, claiming that it had been achieved by the overwhelming numerical superiority of the troops. It also accused the Italian general of having abandoned Bourbaki's army without cover, and forcing it to seek refuge in Switzerland on 1 February, where it was disarmed. These were assertions in bad faith solely for the purpose of diminishing the material and moral support the French received. Yet the loss of the regimental flag to Ricciotti was to remain ingrained in the German memory, and on 4 June 1882, when Garibaldi died, the incident was recalled in *Neue Freie Presse* and became the inspiration for a poem taught in the schools.

Garibaldi was far away. He left Bordeaux on 13 February, and the National Guard presented arms to him and a cheering crowd accompanied him to his hotel. Another crowd and more cheering awaited him in Marseille, where he stayed the following day. In his hotel, he calmly continued his work on his novel, *I Mille di Marsala*. He boarded a ship for Caprera, and would never return to France.

The French conservatives' hatred of him did not abate with the passing years. In 1882, when his death was announced in Paris, there was a lively dispute in the chamber between right-wing and left-wing deputies. The latter demanded a suspension in sign of mourning (this was approved). The deputy for Baudry d'Asson shouted, "In 1849 and 1867 Garibaldi fought against the French army," and *Le Pays* wrote, "the famous bandit has finally surrendered his soul to the devil."

Clericalists depicted Garibaldi as a terrifying warmonger and destroyer of established order. Nothing could be farther from the truth. With an apparent lack of consistency, he was actually a man of peace and a man of order. After 1860 and the campaign that turned him into an international hero, Garibaldi often spoke in favor of peace and cooperation between peoples, which would open the way for improving the material and moral condition of the poorer classes.

On 15 October 1860, after the Battle of Volturno, he sent a *Memorandum to the European Powers* in which he argued that if Europe were a single state, no one would ever consider disturbing it on its home territory.

> And in such a situation, there would be no more armies and no more fleets, and the immense riches snatched almost always from the needs and poverty of peoples to be squandered in the services of slaughter, would be redirected to the advantage of the people in a colossal development of industry, the improvement of roads, the construction of bridges, the digging of canals, the foundation of public buildings and the building of schools, which would remove from poverty and ignorance the many poor people who in all the countries of the world, whatever their degree of civilization, are condemned to brutishness and prostitution of the soul and the flesh by the calculating egoism and bad administration of the powerful and privileged classes.

In 1862 after the Battle of Aspromonte, he appealed to Britain from Varignano, where he was imprisoned, to join France in founding the United States of Europe and to put an end to wars of conquest. Moreover, he also believed that a world congress should judge disputes between nations, that standing armies should be eliminated, and that in place of bombs and armored plating there should be "spades and harvesting machines."

In the years that followed, he was always ready to encourage any initiative that aspired to peace. In the spring of 1867 Europe shuddered at Prussia's military power in the war against Austria, and anti-war sentiments quickly spread. Workers in Paris and Berlin voted resolutions against the war. Garibaldi wanted to associate himself with this sentiment. "The time has come for nations to understand each other without recourse to massacres," he stated in May. "From this time on the iron used for the terrible machinery of destruction must be used for machines and utensils that help people in need of bread."

Feverish preparations were under way for an extraordinary event, an international congress for peace and freedom to be held in Geneva on

9 September 1867. Naturally they thought of Garibaldi. In July the organizers decided to make him the honorary chairman. "This name alone is the clearest of programs. It means heroism, humanity, patriotism, fraternity of peoples, peace and liberty," went the explanation of this decision. Garibaldi wavered. He was busy with the expedition against Rome and decided to restrict his involvement to membership. On 31 July he notified them that he could not take part. In August the preparations for Rome had run into difficulties, and at the same time expectations were improving for the congress. The newspapers became interested and announced the presence of leading exponents of democracy and European culture from Fyodor Dostoyevsky to Alexander Herzen. Geneva seemed the ideal forum for announcing a crusade against the papacy and ensuring the support of the liberal world for the struggle against that institution which Garibaldi considered the greatest ally of all despots. In his opinion, the purpose of the congress was not to exalt an abstract concept of peace, but to do everything possible to establish a lasting peace by removing the causes that prevented it, even if it meant going to war to achieve this. Garibaldi made no secret of his intentions toward Rome. Everyone understood that he was going to Geneva to protest in full view of Europe against the papal misgovernment and its French protectors.

Aspromonte was distant. The pomp of his triumph in London and his victory at Bezzecca were in the recent past. The legend of Garibaldi was still very much alive. On Sunday, 8 September, his entrance into Geneva was another triumph. He was escorted by the banners of the various associations, surrounded by thousands of cheering people, and greeted by a welcoming committee. The president, James Fazy, greeted him as "the most courageous and selfless man of his century, . . . the man who personifies the democratic and philosophical aspirations of the new generation." Garibaldi spoke to the crowd from his hotel balcony: he thanked them for the asylum they gave him in 1848, extolled Switzerland's democratic tradition, and launched an attack on the pope. He received delegations from democratic and socialist associations, and was described as "dressed in his red shirt and blue trousers, legs slightly bowed from horse-riding, a blond beard with a touch of grey and receding hair at the temples."

He was accompanied by his secretary, Basso. The congress was attended by other Italians who were close to him, such as Benedetto Cairoli,

Pietro Del Vecchio, Alberto Mario, his wife Jessie (who was there as a journalist and correspondent for British newspapers), Father Pantaleo, Giovanni Acerbi, and Giuseppe Missori. Among the more famous foreigners there were Edgard Quinet, the French exile and critic of Napoleon III, and the Russian anarchist Mikhail Bakunin. Many would only declare their support from afar. Mazzini did not go, as he was skeptical about the appropriateness of such a meeting at a time when many peoples were suffering under their oppressor's heel.

The proceedings started in the afternoon of 9 September. Garibaldi was the object of even more demonstrations of support. The cheering crowd pressed around him, and attempted to touch him and shake his hand. One of the first to speak, he repeated his declaration of esteem for Switzerland, which he considered the home of the principles he had avowed throughout his life, and asserted that it was a citizen's duty to fight despotism, the scourge of humanity. He then listed and explained some articles that he wanted to add to the League's program:

1. All nations are sisters; 2. War between them is impossible; 3. Any disputes arising between nations should be judged by a congress; 4. The members of the congress shall be nominated by the democratic societies of peoples; 5. Each people shall have a right to vote in the congress irrespective of its population; 6. The papacy shall be declared to have ceased, because it is the most harmful of the sects; 7. The religion of God shall be adopted by the congress and each of its members shall be obliged to proselytize it; 8. The priesthood of revelations and ignorance shall be replaced with the priesthood of science and intelligence; 9. The religion of God shall be propagated through instruction, education, and virtue; 10. The republic is the only form of government worthy of a free people; 11. Only democracy can remedy the scourge of war; 12. Only a slave has the right to wage war against the tyrant.

"It is the only case in which war is permitted," he added and when he noted the assembly's uncertainty on this point, he stressed, "no one can separate the religious question from the political one." In another three points that only appear in the written text submitted to the president's office, Garibaldi prophetically called for the establishment of a Central

Committee in Geneva and a Congress of Nations that would prepare an end to despotism and the construction of a system of justice.

His speech was interrupted by applause and dissent, but the support was more for the man than the ideas. Quinet saluted him as a "man of truth," for the German Amandus Goegg his features "recall those of Christ," and Bakunin embraced him to much applause. He had achieved his purpose: he had called everyone's attention to the Rome question. More delegations came to pay homage, and he repeated the need to fight religious tyranny. He left Geneva on 11 September before the congress had concluded its business, while Genevan Catholics protested outside his hotel. On his way in a carriage to the railway station there were more cheering crowds. He was pleased with the outcome. On 16 September he wrote to a newspaper in Bologna,

> the representatives of the honest part of the peoples have shaken hands and laid the foundation of the cult of justice and truth that one day will prevail on earth, when the nations will understand that their money must be invested in useful works and not in purchasing shells, bombs, mercenaries, and spies.

He set off for the campaign in the countryside around Rome and the sad outcome at Mentana awaited him. He would not take part in the future congresses of the League held in other Swiss cities, but he would send his support and encouragement.

The atrocities of the Franco-Prussian War brought to the fore the question of the peaceful resolution of disputes between states. Garibaldi wrote to the German emperor William I, exhorting him to found an Areopagus made up of representatives of all the nations. In December 1872 he invited Bismarck to take the initiative in a system of international arbitration, with headquarters in Geneva, that would rule on every dispute between states. In 1873 he was ready to support a British initiative. Henry Richard, secretary of the Peace Society, presented the House of Commons with a petition signed by two hundred thousand British workers for the establishment of an International High Court. Garibaldi decided to ask Italian societies to join this initiative by sending appeals to the British parliament. On 13 January, he asked Francesco Domenico Guerrazzi through Pallavicino to write an appeal, but the Tuscan patriot failed to deliver. On

8 July, Richard's proposal was passed in the House of Commons, and Giuseppe Mazzoni, the Grand Master of the Freemasons, proposed sending a letter of congratulations to the British member of Parliament. Garibaldi signed it in September, and was followed by democrats and moderates from Cairoli and Mario to Ricasoli and Tommaseo.

Garibaldi expected governments to initiate the era of peace and concord between peoples, and he repeatedly appealed to them to act. He perhaps had expectations of legally constituted associations, as in the case of the Geneva congress, but he was not looking for a revolution to provide it. On various occasions, I have drawn attention to his respect for authority and established order, and how this affected his behavior. In South America, as in Italy and France, he worked under the orders of a government he considered legitimate either to defend or to achieve national independence or unification. The possibility of taking up arms for a social struggle in a bloody clash between the rich and the poor never entered his mind.

His solidarity with the oppressed was projected into a future in which republican constitutions, the dominance of men who are appointed by the people and concerned about the common good, and the end of warfare would have made it possible to distribute wealth equitably and prevent exploitation by the arrogant and powerful. However, Garibaldi had seen for himself that a republican government does not in itself guarantee freedom and democracy: Argentina under the tyrant Rosas was proof enough. In his opinion, a republic was "a system of honest people, a normal system desired by the majority, and consequently not imposed by violence or deception." Thus if the British, as he asserted in the preface to his *Memoirs*, "are happy with the government of Queen Victoria, . . . then their government must be considered republican."

This method of arguing based on gross simplifications irritated Mazzini, who stuck to the religious vision of *his* republic, and provoked a sarcastic response from Marx, who refused to meet Garibaldi in London. Indeed, the distinction between good and evil that arose from these simplifications caused Garibaldi to come out with contradictory statements. One example was his attitude to the Paris Commune, which was part of the political crisis that followed the fall of the Napoleonic empire.

In the capital under Prussian siege and abandoned by the government for security reasons, the acceptance of the harsh conditions for peace imposed by Bismarck was greeted with indignation. The National Guard opposed the entrance of enemy troops and surrender of the city's cannon. The people also showed their opposition in demonstrations. The decision of the assembly in Bordeaux to impose the immediate payment of rents and expired bills of exchange only increased the discontent, as did the government's decision to move with the assembly to Versailles, rather than the capital.

On 18 March 1871 an uprising led by republicans, radicals, and socialists brought popular representatives to power. "The proletarians of Paris," wrote the Central Committee of the National Guard at the beginning of the insurrection, "in the midst of defeats and betrayals by the ruling classes have understood that the time has come in which they must save the situation by taking control of the management of public affairs." The free Commune was declared the foundation of the French state that was rising up in place of the empire; this was not an administrative devolution but rather a confederation of free associations tending toward the dissolution of the centralized state. The Parisian example was followed in Lyons on 22 March; Marseille, Toulouse, Saint-Étienne, and Narbonne on the twenty-third, and Le Creusot on the twenty-fourth. On the twenty-eighth the administration of the Commune in Paris was elected by universal suffrage; during the few weeks of its existence it was mainly occupied with defense and had little time for determining precisely its political aims. But its principles were clear: "This is the end of the old governmental and clerical world," it declared on 19 April, "of militarism, mandarinism, exploitation, speculation, and privilege to which the proletariat owes its enslavement, and the fatherland its tragedies and disasters." The implementation of socialist ideas appeared to be materializing and this terrified the bourgeoisie.

The government, led by Adolphe Thiers, launched an intense propaganda campaign and accused the rebels of wanting destroy national unity and subvert social order. To quell the revolt it put together an army of 130,000 men from soldiers taken prisoner by the Germans and released for this express purpose. Paris was under siege. It fell in May after fierce combat during which public buildings and entire areas of the city were burned down. The rebels shot their hostages, including the Archbishop of

Paris, and the attackers killed twenty thousand defenders. It was both a civil and an ideological war. According to Marx's analysis, the Commune was the first experiment in working-class government.

In Italy, as in other European countries, the repercussions of the Parisian events were far-reaching. The moderate press, under the influence of the propaganda coming from the Thiers government, painted a black picture of the Communards' violence and attacked their subversive aims. In the democratic camp, judgment was not unanimous: the social nature of the Commune revealed the crisis in the ideals of the Risorgimento. For decades Italian conspiracies, insurrections, and actions taken by volunteers had been inspired by the goal of national unification, which had treated class inequalities and discontent amongst the peasantry as secondary problems. With the liberation of Rome, unification was complete. The debate now shifted to the tasks that faced republicans, radicals, and socialists.

In the Kingdom of Italy, the leadership of the moderates had never been free from excessive authoritarianism and scandals. In 1864 a commission of inquiry had discovered acts of corruption in the concession of the southern railways to Pietro Bastogi; in 1868 the introduction of the grist tax had provoked popular uprisings which were suppressed by the army; in 1869 a parliamentary commission had investigated the accusation of corruption in a joint-venture agreement for the tobacco industry and the granting of monopolies to private citizens or companies. On this last occasion, a physical attack on one of the accusers, the left-wing deputy Cristiano Lobbia, caused demonstrations and riots, which were renewed when the government persecuted Lobbia and had him found guilty of simulation. "Times worthy of the Borgias," Garibaldi commented in Caprera. The liberation of Rome and the revolt of the Commune suddenly focused attention on relations between state and society, and between the ruling classes and the subordinate classes. The young middle-class men who, full of enthusiasm, had formed the core of conspiracies and voluntary actions, awaited a word of clarification from Mazzini and Garibaldi, the historic leaders of the extra-parliamentary movements that had inspired the people's struggle up until Porta Pia was breached and the pope lost the last of his territories.

Mazzini, loyal to the theories he had been professing for forty years, was against the principles argued by the Commune and its sympathy for socialism. During 1871 he bitterly attacked the idea of a federation of communes (a negation of the unitary state that was supposed to instill moral drives in all citizens of the republic as he envisioned it), the cancellation of national identities (the engine behind the law of progress), the abolition of private property, the class struggle (in the name of solidarity), materialism, and the rejection of God (on whom duty is founded). His objective remained the republic, because it would mark the beginning of the transformation of political life. Hence he continued to form secret societies in united Italy, such as Falange Sacra (founded after Aspromonte) and Alleanza Repubblicana Universale (founded in 1866), and organized an entirely anachronistic and therefore unsuccessful republican uprising as late as the spring of 1870. In August he went to Sicily in the hope of starting a revolution against the monarchy, and was arrested in Palermo. In September he learnt of the liberation of Rome while a prisoner in the fortress of Gaeta, and when he left prison his convictions remained unchanged. He could not understand the meaning of the innovations brought about by national unification and the spread of the socialist movement around Europe.

Garibaldi found himself in a very different position. Lacking all doctrinal schemas, he expressed sympathy for all uprisings for national independence and international peace movements. Blanc had defined him as the "soldier of revolutionary cosmopolitanism" with good reason. The Communards offered him the command of the defense of Paris, as he was a combatant for liberty and had rushed to the defense of France. He did not accept and proposed the appointment of a Frenchman—Hugo, Blanc, or Quinet. His experience in Montevideo had taught him how difficult it was for a foreigner to be in supreme command. He told Ricciotti, who had remained in France to deal with the demobilization of the Army of the Vosges, to join with the Communards if war was to break out against the Germans (in which case he too would have joined them), "but if it remains a question between the French, don't get involved." According to his own rules, he was willing to fight in a war of independence to which he was summoned by a regular government, but he was not willing to fight in a civil war.

However his attitude to the Commune was ambivalent: he approved of it as an example of self-government, but criticized its call to class struggle.

The debate on the Commune had become a debate on the International Working Men's Association (later known as the First International), which was founded in London in 1864 and whose major doctrinal contribution came from Karl Marx. At a later stage, there had been a clash in the First International between Marx's positions, which aimed at organizing the class struggle for the conquest of power by the working class, and Bakunin's, which advocated an anarchist view of social revolution based on spontaneous movements from below and peasants' insurrections.

Garibaldi highlighted the aspects of the Commune and the First International that he considered positive and those he did not support. "The thing that is driving the Parisians to war," he wrote on 2 May 1871 just before the city fell, "is a sentiment of justice and human dignity . . . not communism, as the scurrilous detractors of the proletariat wish to define it, as communism consists of making the poor rich and the rich poor."

He explained his overall judgment on the First International to the Englishman Arthur Arnold in September 1871. He put aside "certain unacceptable maxims, such as 'property is theft, inheritance another theft'," because they did not merit debate. On the other hand, he found the First International's program to have its more acceptable side when it came to its basic principles.

1. Its name, which does not make any distinction between the African and the American, the European and the Asian, and therefore proclaims the fraternity of all men whatever nation they belong to; 2. The International does not want priests, and consequently does not want lies; 3. It does not want standing armies to perpetuate war, but a citizens' militia to maintain order at home; 4. It wants the administrative government of the Commune. And this is one of the greatest glories of Paris, as this means that the capital of France, which naturally has most to gain from a central government, spontaneously renounces its metropolitan domination that has lasted through all the centuries.

In conclusion, he exhorted "all governments, without distinction," to attempt to achieve all that is good in this society, "for example, the abolition of war, standing armies, priests, and privileges," and he reminded them of his appeal from Caserta in October 1860. This optimistic and oversimplified position did not take into account the First International's doctrinal premises which aimed at the struggle against all bourgeois governments for the purpose of social revolution. Garibaldi's misunderstanding and particular interpretation of the association's name triggered a dispute with the followers of Mazzini, and this unhappily descended into personal attacks.

Mazzini had always been hostile to Garibaldi's support for the House of Savoy, which handed over the voluntary units to the monarchy and in 1860 had put the seal of that dynasty on national unification. From 1848 Mazzini had attempted unsuccessfully to exploit Garibaldi's popularity for his own plans, but he had never ceased to express his contempt for Garibaldi's political intelligence. In 1864, he asked John Morley in England if he had ever observed the physiognomy of a lion, and added, "Don't you think it very stupid? Well, Garibaldi's is similar." Garibaldi in turn accused Mazzini and his followers of having continuously put obstacles in his way, in Lombardy in 1848, in Rome in 1849, and so on right up to Mentana, when after the victory at Monterotondo they supposedly incited three thousand young men to desert, thus causing the defeat against the French. In 1871, Mazzini, conscious of Garibaldi's bitterness against him, asserted that Garibaldi would not have supported the International if he had written in its favor.

In reality, the differing assessments of the International by the two leaders of Italian democracy did not result from rivalries and personal frictions; it was the natural consequence of each one's ideological and political development. The Saint-Simonian and humanitarian basis of Garibaldi's social thought is clearly revealed by his fierce debate with Giuseppe Petroni and Pallavicino. Petroni, editor of the pro-Mazzini newspaper *La Roma del Popolo*, challenged the definition of the International given to Arnold. "If you take away the rejection of nationality, property and family from the International, what remains of it that is peculiar to itself?" went his argument, and convinced that "bad faith could never find its place in Garibaldi's mind," he could only suppose that it was an excess of indulgence to some parasite that stood in his shadow.

Garibaldi replied with a very long letter in which he touched on more or less all subjects, ranging from the reasons for his defense of Gasparoni, which was based on the "romantic concept" of the honest brigand like Robin Hood, to the occasion on which he offered his services to the pope in 1847. He gave his own account of his relations with Mazzini, "who does not forgive anyone who challenges his infallibility." "I do not have to prove to my deserters in '60, at Talamone and at Mantua that I am a true republican," he said of himself. "And as a republican by conscience, I have done what little I can in my actions, but refrained from provoking discord amongst democratic ranks, as your sect does today." He constantly defended the Commune, and compared its excesses with those of its adversaries, and he repeated his interpretation of the International, which some attack "almost without knowing it."

> Is it not the product of the abnormal state in which society finds itself in the world? And when certain doctrines can be cleaned away, ones that were perhaps introduced by the malevolence of its enemies, it will not be the beginning but could certainly be the continuation of the emancipation of human law. Shouldn't a society (I mean a human society) in which the majority struggle for subsistence and the minority want to take the larger part of the product of the former through deceptions and violence but without hard work, arouse discontent and thoughts of revenge amongst those who suffer?

Garibaldi expressed his hope that the International would not let itself be led into "exaggerated positions and ultimately the ridiculous," and would carefully examine the men it put its trust in.

> Let the International be content with that to which it is entitled without touching the property and inheritance of others. And let it say loudly to the arrogant of this earth, "I come to sit at the banquet to which I am just as entitled as you. I do not touch your properties, so much richer than mine, but do not touch this little I have and earn by the sweat of my brow, by persisting in the odious methods you have always used, such as grist tax, salt tax and the many other injustices that you heap on my misery."

"But do you know the association you defend any better than Petroni,?" Pallavicino asked him. "Very noble, no doubt, this language that you attirubte to the International . . . but you are above all *a man of the heart*: might you not, by any chance, be deceiving yourself and creating an International in your own image and similitude?" he asked and reminded

Garibaldi of the horrors committed by the Commune. He had the impression that "the International, *as yet not purified of particular doctrines*, is a serious danger to existing society." He was worried that Garibaldi was putting himself in a vulnerable position during this debate: "Do you not see that this imprudent act is diminishing your prestige? I who love you and hold you in esteem beyond all expression cannot follow you down the dangerous path on which you have set out."

Garibaldi countered his friend's persuasive arguments with an act of faith:

> I belonged to the International when I served the Republic of Rio Grande and of Montevideo, long before this society was founded in Europe; I have made a public act of belonging to the same during the recent war in France. . . . I cannot tolerate the International's fanciful claims to determine the nature of man, just as I cannot tolerate those of the monarchy. Just as I would send to prison everyone who spends their life studying how to extort the basic necessities from the hungry in order to let bishops live off the fat of the land, so I would also send the leaders of the society in question, when they persist in such commandments as "War on capital," "Property is theft," "Inheritance is another theft," and so on. I have nothing to do with the International, and of course they know I do not approve of all their program, which is reason enough for their leaders to exclude me. But if the International, as I understand it, is a continuation of the moral and material improvement of the industrious and honest working class, . . . then I am with the International.

It was with this in mind that he coined a slogan that would prove a great success. He wrote to Celso Ceretti in September 1872, "The International is the bright hope of the future [*sole dell'avvenire*]." But the expression "as I understand it" and his awareness of being disliked by its leaders show the limitations on his support, based on the association's name, which reminded Garibaldi of the humanitarian ideals in which he had always believed.

Garibaldi's openness to socialism was in reality nothing more than an understanding of the urgency of the social question. Although he did not

approve of the anti-bourgeois and anti-national nature of the new movement, Garibaldi channeled youth's social protest and disappointment with
the parliamentary left into the activities of the democratic activists within
the boundaries of political struggle in the unitary state. Monarchist Italy
demonstrated its stability by remaining intact throughout the disappointment of 1866 and the Mentana crisis. It was strengthened once Rome
became its capital. The republic was a purely hypothetical alternative,
dreamt of by a tiny minority. Garibaldi also spoke of it in moralistic terms,
but when it came down to it, he would not encourage subversive acts.

His participation in the war in France in the context of a clash between
two great powers did not have the resonance of his other enterprises, but it
did help maintain his prestige. In Europe he continued a busy correspondence with the main exponents of radicalism. A personal involvement in
the Balkans which were in a continuous state of agitation, Spain which was
troubled by conflict between monarchists and republicans, or other parts of
Europe where independence revolts were raging, had become impossible
because of his age and poor health. "I am convinced that I have been involved in too many things in my life, and therefore everything I have undertaken has remained unfinished," he confided in Pallavicino on 31
December 1867. In 1871 when his military career finally came to an end,
reflection on any future role led him to concentrate on Italian politics.

In place of socialism Mazzini put forward his long-held ideas on solidarity. In January 1871 he confirmed the importance of association "as the
only normal means of collective and individual progress at the same
time," in which authority and liberty cease to be in conflict. In November
he organized a congress of workers' societies in Rome, which signaled the
resumption of his project to use the workers' movement as the popular
base for his republican party. It approved a Fraternity Pact, undertook the
publication of a weekly called *L'Emancipazione*, which was the official
publication of the societies affiliated to the pact, and promoted the establishment of Regional Republican Associations. The fervent activity did not
last long. Mazzini's death on 10 March 1872 created a crisis that the devotion of his disciples failed to overcome.

For Garibaldi the democratic project had to be entirely rewritten, and
had to start with resolving the fragmentation of the forces of the Left
both inside and outside parliament. His proposal to overcome the triple

despotism "of monarchies, priests and privilege" was "unification in a single society of all the existing societies that tend toward the moral and material improvement of the Italian family." He asserted in a manifesto dated
18 January 1872 that the freemasons, trade unions, and democratic associations all had to be forced into a single organization. He entrusted the task
of unification to the freemasons. He wrote on 15 April 1872 that it had to
"identify with the present times and therefore force all the associations
that promote good in Italy into a single organization."

His relations with the freemasons had been constant. A member with
little commitment in Brazil and Montevideo, Garibaldi again received the
first three degrees in Palermo in 1860. In recently united Italy the freemasons established themselves in the main cities of Turin, Palermo, and Naples, and the lodges came under the influence of either the moderates or
the democrats. After 1862 the democrats were in the majority. Garibaldi,
who received testimonials and tokens of appreciation from many lodges,
was raised to the position of Grand Master for life by the Supreme Council of Sicily in March. Between the end of 1863 and the summer of 1864
his name was exploited to overcome divisions. In May 1864, he was elected
Grand Master at an assembly held in Florence without the participation of
the Palermo masons. He accepted and appointed Mordini to represent
him in the hope of uniting the two factions, both of which treated him as
their leader. He resigned when he discovered that it was impossible to bro-
ker an agreement, but he stayed close to the freemasons. He continued to
hold his position in Palermo until 1868, and in 1865 the other Grand
Lodge hailed him "the leading Italian mason and Honorary Grand Master for life" (an honor that was confirmed two years later). In 1867 he
argued that "unity amongst masons will drag Italy political unity behind
it" and he expressed his hope that the masons create "the Roman group-
ing that we have not yet managed to create in politics in spite of many
great efforts."

In 1872 he returned to this idea and used the freemasons to bring the
democratic forces together. For the moment, he observed, republicans
could not hope to establish a republic—they would have to discuss the
question of an achievable program. Garibaldi was a charismatic presence:
over three hundred associations, clubs, and trade unions appointed him
their honorary president. The congress he was promoting was held in

Rome in November. Unable to attend, he pointed to the implementation of universal suffrage as the most important objective of the time, because it was a fundamental condition for the establishment of a true democracy, and to a series of other measure such as the struggle against the church and the decentralization of administrative powers.

The Rome Pact, a compromise between Garibaldi's supporters and Mazzini's disciples, was not effectively implemented. Garibaldi realized that it was difficult to take direct action in the country outside legal channels. In 1873 he advised Felice Cavallotti to use "the parliamentary arena, where I think it possible to move forward our sacred cause." In November 1874 he was elected deputy in Rome in two constituencies. He decided to take part in parliamentary proceedings. In January 1875 he left Caprera with his family—the woman he had been living with for two years and their two small children—and Menotti, who had gone out to fetch him. He went to Civitavecchia by sea, and then to the capital by train, where he was greeted by an enormous demonstration of support. He had aged a great deal, and being semi-paralyzed he had to be carried bodily from the train to the carriage that would take him to his hotel. In spite of this, he visited the places associated with the city's defense in 1849, and met veterans, trade-union delegations, and politicians. In the chamber his voice was firm as he was sworn in. On 30 January Giacomo Medici and Giuseppe Dezza, now generals in the Royal Army, accompanied him to meet Victor Emanuel, whom he had not seen since 1866. The king stood throughout the encounter with his head uncovered, while Garibaldi remained seated and wore his usual hat. The two were alone in each other's company for some twenty minutes.

Garibaldi moved from Caprera to push for an enormous project involving the control and canalization of the Tiber. Rome was subject to ruinous floods (the one in December 1870 provided the pretext for Victor Emanuel to make an informal visit to the city which was not yet the capital). Control of the river's course would have produced the twin result of eliminating the danger of flooding and opening a navigable channel for trade. An early project, which involved the total redirection of the flow of water and the construction of a road on the old riverbed, was shelved because of the enormous cost. Garibaldi, with the assistance of the gifted engineer Alfredo Baccarini, proposed another less onerous project to embank the urban course of the Tiber and construct a drainage canal in Aniene, with a view to creating a port basin between San Paolo and Fiumicino and reclaiming part of the land around Rome. These grandiose plans, possibly inspired by the Saint-Simonian concept of economic development or possibly by less noble business aims, did not find financial backing. Garibaldi remained in the capital for a few months and unsuccessfully pleaded with the parliament and asked for the support of the moderate government led by Minghetti. They did not go beyond promises and later less ambitious works were carried out to bring the Tiber under control.

Garibaldi went to Rome for the last time in 1879. Many things had changed. The Left came to power in March 1876 and Victor Emanuel died in January 1878 to be succeeded by his son, Umberto I. The hopes placed in the government of the Left were disappointed. An Extreme Left was established in the chamber on progressive lines that were anti-government and secretly anti-monarchy, and it had links with political currents outside parliament. Republicans in the tradition of Mazzini declared at a congress in April 1878 that they intended to achieve "the sovereign right of Italy in the formation of a Constituent Assembly and a National Pact." There was increasing demand for an agreement between all the democratic forces in order to be more effective in parliament and the country. They needed to identify the areas of agreement. Bertani, Saffi, and many others were sounding out the terrain. The republican deputy Giovanni Bovio took the initiative and wrote a circular on 1 April 1879 to convene a conference in Bologna.

Garibaldi took over his plan. He returned to Rome and wrote to Bovio himself on 12 April: he agreed that there was a clear duty to bring together all the forces engaged in legal agitation, announced his wish to reach an agreement with all the principal exponents of democracy, and declared that universal suffrage was "the main and fundamental reform." He used his prestige to force everyone to speak to his own program. With the assistance of Alberto Mario, who shared his ideas, he convened a conference in the capital, and invited ninety-two politicians and intellectuals in the democratic camp in a signed letter. Sixty-two of them came to the meeting on 21 April. The proceedings were opened by Garibaldi, who was seated between General Avezzana and Mario on one side and Bovio and Campanella on the other. He asserted that he had convened them "to organize the meager forces of republican and parliamentary democracy in Italy around a common undertaking and a common purpose." He listed a series of demands which he considered to be shared by all democrats. He proposed that the common undertaking should be "agitation in the press and through public meetings in favor of universal suffrage and the abolition of the political oath of allegiance, in the belief that the country can achieve stability and unity around a national agreement."

It was a skillful speech written by Mario along the conciliatory lines suggested by Garibaldi who wanted to avoid a complete rupture with the monarchy: in the background there were far-reaching reforms to keep the extremists happy, in the short-term there was the objective of universal suffrage and the abolition of the oath of loyalty by deputies in order to make it possible for republicans to enter parliament and to form a progressive majority.

In the debate that followed, Garibaldi's gradualism was attacked by those who supported the Mazzini line. They argued with Campanella's support that the national agreement should be "dictated by the Constituent Assembly," while Garibaldi, who was present throughout the debate, firmly defended the prepared text. Antonio Fratti, a Mazzini supporter, acknowledged that "the poor old man" behaved well: "he was steadfast against Campanella, but he was calm, smiling and dignified." At the end of the debate, his agenda was approved by a large majority.

During the proceedings, which lasted from one-thirty to four o'clock, Garibaldi suffered greatly from the heat and the lack of food. His health had deteriorated. On arrival in Rome, he was taken off the train on a stretcher. His arthritis tormented him. He could not take part in the second session held the following day, but the strategic direction he imposed remained unchanged. In a manifesto published on 26 April, he informed Italians of the foundation of the League of Democracy created out of an agreement between various factions "with the adoption of the same method of propaganda and the same means of agitation, which shall be open, sincere and within the law." The league's declared aimed would be to campaign for the "effective implementation of national sovereignty, for a less harsh existence for those disinherited by fortune, and for social justice and inviolable freedom."

The event was widely commented upon in the press. Unsurprisingly it provoked concerns amongst the moderates, who feared the transition from peaceful means to revolutionary ones, concerns that were shared by Depretis' government and even the Extreme Left in parliament. In the opposing camp, the Mazzini faction attacked the initiative for not being radical enough. Sara Nathan argued,

> Garibaldi has always been disastrous for Mazzini's work. Every inch of territory gained in the field of Mazzini's ideas has been challenged more relentlessly by him than by those openly hostile to Mazzini. But Mazzini will be as immortal as the ideas he put forward, while Garibaldi will pass along with era of opportunism.

In the meantime the organizational wheels began to turn. They set up a committee of forty-four members and an executive commission of sixteen, whose leading members were Mario, Bertani, Bovio, Campanella, Canzio, Cavallotti, and Saffi. In January 1880 they launched a newspaper, *La Lega della Democrazia*. Garibaldi followed these developments from afar. He spent the summer at Castelli Romani, Albano, and Civitavecchia. He encouraged the league to promote activities by writing letters to the newspapers. He put pressure on deputies of the Left who looked up to him, to make them demand urgent reforms from the government. He wrote personally to Depretis, and in July while he was in Albano he received Benedetto Cairoli, who had become prime minister. But when he lost hope of an annulment of his marriage to Raimondi (he had hoped the new government would have provided this), he left for Caprera on 1 September.

But he did not abandon the battle. In the spring of 1880, once the campaign had built up steam, he was again exercising a leading role. He did away with some of his conciliatory tone. When he was re-elected in the First Constituency of Rome in May 1880, he thanked his electors and then went on to make some harsh criticisms of the country's institutions and the monarchy. In his opinion, the monarchy during the Risorgimento had acted as a center "around which those who wanted a strong and respected nation could rally," including republicans, but afterwards the monarchy had failed to work for the greater good and had "trampled on the people's rights and reduced them to poverty." The remedies he advised were savings on salaries and pensions, an armed nation, suppression of fiscal contributions to the clergy, smelting of church bells to make coins, and reform of electoral system. On 30 May he appealed to the league's commission to work harder. He sent a leaflet to Italian democrats in which he unleashed a polemic against the followers of Mazzini and called for "a persistent campaign by means of public meetings in favor of universal suffrage, considered the great opportunity of this period."

A large number of public meetings were held around the country. The citizens excluded from the vote, the *non-electors*, spoke up at a large demonstration held in Rome on 13 June 1880. Garibaldi increased the enthusiasm. On the twenty-third he told Mario that "the campaign must be peaceful and legal, but also continuous and resolute," and in August he issued another proclamation to Italians announcing a public gathering in Rome that "must take on the semblance of a national plebiscite in terms of both its number and its solemnity." Preparations started for the Roman assembly to be held at the beginning of the following year. But there were doubts about whether Garibaldi would be present, because since the autumn of 1879 the aggravation of his crippling arthritis had forced him into a wheelchair, made him increasingly dependent on his family, and turned public appearances into a sufferance. Then an unexpected event made him leave Caprera. In September 1880 Stefano Canzio was imprisoned in Genoa and found guilty of rebellion against the forces of public order during a republican demonstration. Incensed by what he considered a personal affront, he resigned as a deputy and sent his electors a letter to using strong words against the Cairoli-Depretis government and expressing the hope that universal suffrage would renew the representation of the country. He then went to visit his son-in-law in the company of family members and loyal supporters. On his arrival in Genoa on 8 October he was greeted by massive demonstrations of support. He also went to San Damiano d'Asti, where his wife Francesca Armosino had been born. At the beginning of November he moved to Milan to attend the inauguration of a monument in memory of the dead at Mentana. On 8 November he left for Alassio, where he spent the winter.

The leading advocates of democracy dutifully went to pay their respects. Alberto Mario asked him to preside over the public meeting in Rome that was set for 10 February 1881. Garibaldi hesitated because he no longer felt he had the energy to fight off the inevitable attacks from the Mazzini faction against whom he was conducting an ill-timed polemic, and he was held back by some members of his family who did not think it prudent to make an enemy of the government. Mario's insistence proved unsuccessful. Cavallotti, who went to Alassio on 6 February, only obtained a letter, the last important text sent to the league and one of the last documents demonstrating his political commitment. Cavallotti read it to the crowd:

> My fellow citizens know who I am. A mixture of good and bad like so many others, but accustomed to speaking the truth at any cost and practicing it: therefore a republican, an enemy of despotism and fraud, which lord over this world in spite of the widely heard boasts of liberty and civilization. The reason for this meeting of representatives of all Italian democrats is the achievement of universal suffrage, the indisputable right of free peoples, or in other words the ability to send one's true representatives to the government of the nation and not men of privilege. What is more, those who find themselves at the helm of the state must realize that the democratic campaign will not only continue but will become more demanding if its just aspirations are not immediately implemented.

The public meeting that was the climax of the campaign voted a resolution in which it "invited the people to regain universal suffrage as one of the constituent rights of the sovereignty from which the law of the new Italian life arose." Bovio concluded with a speech to the people of Rome to give the vote the value of a plebiscite. In the weeks that followed, plebiscites spread to the whole of Italy. The reform movement achieved some success, but not universal suffrage. A considerable extension in voting rights, which until then had been restricted to the most affluent classes, was approved by parliament in 1882. In the elections that October the number of electors increased from 620,000 to over 2,000,000.

Garibaldi died before he could witness this victory. During his final years his prestige made him the leader of Italian democrats and he had the ability to direct his meager forces toward *possible* goals in the constructive manner that had always typified his activities. At the age of seventy-three he performed his last service to the consolidation of unified Italy to which he had devoted so much of his life.

24. The Final Years: Family, Literary Activities, and Financial Concerns

GARIBALDI SPENT MOST of the final decade of his life in Caprera. They were melancholy years. His health was deteriorating. His wound from Aspromonte made it difficult for him to get the physical exercise with which he fought off arthritis, and prevented him from riding and rambling around the island among the fields and animals. On the other hand, he had remarried; he had small children and a family around him, so he did not miss Menotti, Ricciotti, and Teresita during their frequent absences.

The turning-point in his private life occurred in 1865 when Francesca Armosino came to the island to assist Teresita, who like Anita's other children, had had a difficult childhood in Montevideo and Nice, had been deprived of her mother at an early age and then entrusted to the affections of the Deideris. Her transfer to the restricted community of Caprera had suffocated her adolescence. There were many visitors—comrades-in-arms, fellow conspirators, and the inquisitive. There was talk of political and military projects, and of battles fought or to be fought. Even the few women who came to the island were infatuated with her father. Inadvertently being Garibaldi's daughter became over time a heavy burden. She had few adult figures on whom she could rely (Mrs. Deideri and Mrs. Susini being two of them) and she completely lacked company of her own age and a social life.

Some personal observations by Candido Augusto Vecchi give us an idea of her dissatisfaction. When the king sent her the gift of a diamond necklace, it was received and put aside without enthusiasm: there was no way in which she could have shown it off. Her desires lay in different directions. At the end of carnival in February 1861, Teresita had just had her sixteenth birthday, and knew that on the nearby Island of Maddalena they were having fun with a masked ball. She envied her brother Menotti, who was in Milan and undoubtedly dancing. She could not hide her sadness. Her father noticed this and dressed elegantly to dance a waltz with her while Eliodoro Specchi, a tenor in his youth and later one of Garibaldi's officers, played the piano.

According to Vecchi the episode demonstrates Garibaldi's solicitude for his daughter, while for us it demonstrates how the adolescent girl experienced her condition as repression. Her marriage to Canzio did not transport her to a different world. Her husband was a fervent republican ready to follow his father-in-law on all his enterprises and distinguished himself for extremism. He lived in Genoa, but sent his wife to Caprera whenever he went away. Moreover, he loaded her with children: she had nine by the age of twenty-seven. Still disappointed in her hopes of a more varied life and physically exhausted by pregnancies, Teresita started to show signs of restiveness and derangement. She was suffering a breakdown. In April 1865 Garibaldi sent for the robust young Francesca Armosino from San Damiano d'Asti to help her, and did so reluctantly because he had always believed that hiring a companion was exploitation of the poor.

The gilded isolation of Caprera was also creating problems for Garibaldi, the greatest of which was the absence of women. As an experienced seaman he probably took advantage of easy opportunities that presented themselves when he went to Maddalena or Sardinia on hunting trips or to make purchases. The presence of a young and unpretentious woman was a temptation to which he willingly succumbed. He was not in the habit of taking precautions and on 16 February 1867 a daughter was born. He called her Clelia, a Roman name he had given to the female protagonist of a novel he was writing. He saw her for the first time in November, when he returned to the island after Mentana. Another child, Rosa, was born on 10 July 1869, and repeating the misfortune of her namesake many years before, she died on 1 January 1871 while her father was in France. On 23 April 1873 the sixty-three-year-old general became a father again, this time a son they named Manlio. The little children who grew up around him gave him the joys he had forgotten or rather never experienced in his wandering youth. As his arthritis and his immobility worsened, Francesca became increasingly indispensable. "Since we have known each other," she would say many years later, "no one else has touched my husband. I was the only one who lifted him, changed him, put him in the bath, put him to bed and pushed him in his wheelchair."

She was devoted to him and showed a sensitivity that was not expected of an unpolished woman. Garibaldi did not plan a nice room for himself with a view of the sea, and his longing for the sea increased as his mobility diminished. On 4 July 1880 Francesca, who had only just got married, thought up a splendid birthday present for her husband: she had another room built on the front of the house without his noticing (it was the last of many modifications to the building over different periods), and furnished it with new furniture she had brought from Livorno (a metal bed with mosquito net, chandelier, chairs, and an armchair). She decorated it with flowers and tricolor flags. Then she took him backwards on his wheelchair into the sunlit room while the band from Maddalena played his anthem in his honor. Garibaldi, overcome by emotion, cried uncontrollably, kissed her, and asked his children to thank their mother.

The other side of the coin was that this illiterate woman from a poor family pestered the father of her children to marry her and make her and her children's position respectable. The group of friends associated with Garibaldi in Caprera, which felt entitled to protect his image with the agreement of Anita's children, attempted to drive her away as had occurred with Battistina Raveo. But Battistina had met him in an unfavorable moment when he became infatuated with the daughter of Marquis Raimondi. Francesca did not have rivals amongst the upper-classes. The rumors about her doubtful morality, which may have been true or may have been purposefully exaggerated, made little impression. This time, the woman was calling the tune. She gradually brought her relations over to the island and kept away his old friends. She greeted visitors with an ill grace and they began to come less frequently, partly because Garibaldi's political and military role was becoming less important. Anita's children rarely came.

By 1870 Francesca was already indispensable to Garibaldi. When he left for France in October, he wrote,

> As I have to leave my home for an unknown period of time, I leave my woman, Francesca Armosino, in charge of it. She is the owner in my absence, and shall take care of everything inside and outside my house and all my property on Caprera. Any of my children who come here shall be treated as family. If Menotti comes here, he shall be considered to be myself, i.e. the owner. But no one shall have the right to send away my woman Francesca and my family from the house without my orders.

He left her with instructions for the work to be carried out on the farm in the autumn and he remained continuously in contact throughout his stay in France. On 7 October, he wrote "on arrival in Marseille" to inform her that he felt better, "even though I have started to miss your kind assistance." He sent her frequent letters with news and instructions on working and managing the farm. He claimed that he was happy to hear that her father and brother had joined her in Caprera. Francesca had succeeded in becoming someone he could rely on.

The ultimate success came in January 1880, with the annulment of his marriage to Raimondi. On the twenty-sixth the marriage took place between Giuseppe Garibaldi, farmer, and Francesca Armosino, housewife in Caprera. There were not many guests: Menotti with his wife, Teresita with her husband (Ricciotti was far away in Australia), a few of the bride's relations, the odd friend, and representatives of the local authorities. They ate their usual frugal dinner. Then music was played: Teresita sang, as did Garibaldi, just like the good times. The downside to this happy occasion was that the bridegroom had had to humiliate himself to obtain the annulment. "I would be willing to become a protestant, even Turk," he wrote to Crispi in June 1874, "if by this I could manage to give my name to my children, Manlio and Clelia!" He therefore went to great lengths and appealed to Victor Emanuel, Umberto I, politicians, and lawyers. He even thought of sending a petition to the pope.

Another negative aspect of Francesca's influence was the torment she inflicted on him by massively increasing his financial worries to the point of causing him to tarnish his magnificent and well-merited image of a self-less man. For reasons that are now clear, Francesca realized how precarious her position was. She wanted economic security, something that could not be provided by the meager proceeds from the farm on Caprera. Garibaldi was unable to work: he had to walk on crutches from 1873, and he was obliged to use a wheelchair from 1880. He had neither salary nor pension. He had always expected a Spartan lifestyle of himself, Anita and their children: Francesca did not want luxury for herself and her children, but she did want the security of owning her own home and some form of income to provide for them after her husband's death which could not be far off.

Garibaldi returned to writing to supplement his income. He published historical novels. The first, *Clelia*, came out in English with the inexact subtitle, *The Monks' Government*, which was then repeated in the first Italian edition of 1870, but later modified to the more sensible *Il governo dei preti [The Government of Priests]*. It is set in 1849 and Mentana. The protagonist Clelia, who has a sentimental attachment to the patriot Attilio, is the object of the insane passions of Cardinal Procopio, who attempts to seduce her. The two lovers experience complicated adventures which take them as far as Venice and ultimately to the expedition into the Roman countryside where Attilio dies. *Cantoni il volontario* was also published in 1870 in Milan, and is set in the Roman Republic of 1849: the Jesuit Gaudenzio attempts to come between Cantoni and his virtuous Ida; the two manage to get married, and die eighteen years later at Mentana. *I Mille* was published in 1874. Against the background of the famous Expedition of the Thousand, it narrates the story of a young woman, Marzia, who joins the expedition dressed as a man; in Palermo she is kidnapped by Monsignor Corvo and taken to Rome, where he rapes her without knowing that she is his illegitimate daughter; he has her shut up in a convent, from which she escapes to rejoin the Expedition of the Thousand. The novel obviously concludes with the punishment of the evildoer who goes mad, unlike the other damned souls, his predecessors Procopio e Gaudenzio, who pay for their crimes with their lives. In a fourth novel, *Manlio*, which for some time remained unpublished, the author looks into the future: the protagonist leaves for South America in 1874 where he stays for five years and experiences extraordinary adventures further complicated by passionate love affairs; he returns to Italy at the age of thirty and is imprisoned on trumped-up charges; in the final part, he escapes from prison, attacks the Austrian navy, and gives Italy dominance of the Adriatic.

Garibaldi was driven to writing by a moral imperative and a practical aim. He explained this in his preface to *Clelia*: "1. To remind Italy of all those brave men who laid down their lives on the battlefield for her . . . 2. To dwell with Italian youth on their exploits and the sacred duty to finish the job while pointing out the foul deeds and treachery of governments and priests. 3. Lastly to live off my own earnings". Having decided to write, he adopted the historical novel as his genre: he believed that he was an accurate commentator as far as the historical side was concerned. As far as the "novelistic side" was concerned, he would not have vexed the public "during the century in which Manzoni, Guerrazzi, Victor Hugo, and other such authors have written novels," if it were not for the historical side in which he was competent, and the need to reveal "the vices and iniquities of the clergy."

These brief summaries of the plots and his declaration demonstrate how he drew heavily on his political and military experiences in Italy, and gave vent to his feelings and resentments during the years that followed Mentana. The novels were, as he asserted in the preface to *I Mille*, "the product of someone who feels the misery and shame of his own country." Hence the novels—although failures artistically because of the excessive depiction of characters as wholly good or wholly bad, and the overly emphatic narration—"have importance as historical and autobiographical documents," as Sacerdote explains.

In these novels, not only does Garibaldi narrate his major exploits in Rome, Sicily, and Naples, but he also heaps in his own feelings and thoughts, and directs his ideas toward the most pressing political, religious, and social problems. At every turn, we see the author's figure loom up to admonish, preach, theorize, praise, and curse. But then the novelist turns into partisan and the story becomes a polemic, and while such digressions help us to understand better Garibaldi's thought, they certainly do not enhance the artistic value of the work.

For this reason, Garibaldi is most effective as a narrator in his *Memoirs*, which he revised and completed in 1871–72. This brought the account of his life up to the Vosges campaign. The fact that he ended the work with his last military enterprise shows that he perceived war as giving meaning to "his tempestuous life, made up of good and bad as I believe is the case for the majority of people." In the final version, he drops the novelistic and exaggerated episodes that embellish the works of Dumas and Esperance von Schwartz, omits any reference to meeting the Saint-Simonians or his sympathy for Mazzini's ideas, fails to examine the political causes of events, and is not interested in the continuity of the narration. Instead he depicts men, landscapes, and moments that he considered striking and of interest to the reader. We should not forget that he initially started work on the first draft in the autumn of 1849 with the intention of awakening the curiosity of an apolitical public. This was partly why he wrote about his personal military experiences in great depth and conjured up the most exciting situations with an extraordinary memory for details, which have generally proved to be correct in the light of recent historical research.

Where the final version really differs from the *Memoirs* of 1859 is in the much more polemical tone against the church, priests, Mazzini, his followers, the monarchy, and the succession of different governments in Italy. In spite of this, the work retained all the freshness of its impressions and lively narration, and this is why I have frequently quoted from it. In the climate of the 1870s, it would have found favor with the public, but the negotiations that Dr. Albanese entered into with Palermo Council came to nothing. Garibaldi preferred to consign it to posterity: he gave the manuscript to Menotti, and instructed him to make it public after his death. It was in fact published in 1888, and went through nine editions in that same year, with reviews and recognition in Italy and abroad. Much later, in 1912, another rather singular form of memoir was published. The *Poema autobiografico*, which he started on in 1862 during his long period of unavoidable inactivity due to his wound at Aspromonte, was the product of his love for poetry rather than a genuine poetic bent.

The novels did not produce the hoped for financial returns, although they were published in various editions, particularly in 1870 when his international fame reached new heights. During that year *Clelia* was published in Paris, London, New York, Boston, St. Petersburg, Novi Sad,

Stockholm, Pest, and Vienna. In Montevideo, it was published in the literary supplement to *La Tribuna*. There were further translations in Prague in 1871, Lisbon in 1874, and Moscow in 1876. Garibaldi received thirty thousand lira from the proceeds. *Cantoni il volontario* was printed in Geneva and Vienna in 1870, and republished in Italy in an illustrated edition in 1873. We know, however, that Garibaldi received barely 1,500 lira for the first edition in 1870 and 1,000 in 1874, and we think that he earned little or nothing from the majority of the translations.

Meanwhile his popularity was fading. It was difficult to find a publisher willing to guarantee thirty thousand lira for *I Mille* as the author requested. The work was not helped by the ambiguity of its title. Garibaldi put his hopes on the English market, but the translation did not find promoters: his admirers wanted an historical narration of the expedition (the *Memoirs* only went up to 1859 at the time), and they did not like the blood-curdling plot. The freemasons came to his rescue to ensure sales. In 1874, as was the custom of the time, Timoteo Riboli distributed 12,640 order cards to Garibaldi's friends and admirers—4,322 were signed and produced revenues of 21,610 lira, of which 11,360 lira went to the author after deducting costs. A subscription for the French translation was launched by the leading Masonic official Charles Silvain, secretary of the International Peace League, and achieved 2,199 subscriptions.

The fact is that by 1874, the time of the book's publication, people were becoming increasingly aware of the Garibaldi's misfortunes and precarious financial condition. In 1869 he sold the yacht donated by British admirers, the *Princess Olga*, to the state for 80,000 lira, but the proceeds were stolen by the intermediary. Menotti became involved in some industrial enterprises that failed (he had no experience in this field and was the victim of dishonest advisors) and to avoid his bankruptcy his father mortgaged Caprera to the Banco di Napoli. Canzio, who was equally maladroit in business, went bankrupt.

Garibaldi appeared a poor old man fallen victim to the culpable improvidence of his family members. There was a wave of indignation and it seemed only right to give assistance to someone who had sacrificed himself for his country. Plans were made for collections, but Garibaldi let it be known that he did not want this, partly because, as he wrote to Timoteo Riboli on 4 November, he had received an unsolicited the gift of a bill of exchange for five thousand lira in gold against the Rothschild bank from Mr. John Anderson of New York. He did not feel poor. He was accustomed to "adapting to his condition," and he had always done this "since the time in which my wealth consisted of a shirt under my horse's saddle in America and up to the one in which I found myself the dictator of the Two Sicilies in Caserta."

Firm plans for a more secure future were taking shape. The municipal councils of Reggio Calabria, Salerno, and Velletri sent sums of money, and Palermo Council voted a life annuity of three thousand lira per annum (which the one-time dictator accepted). Pasquale Stanislao Mancini presented a bill to grant a pension to the man who had contributed so much to the Risorgimento and provided the lofty example "of a life of self-abnegation and freely-accepted poverty after having had the treasuries of kingdoms at his disposal." In May 1875 the two chambers decreed that Garibaldi receive in the form of a "national gift" a five-per-cent annuity bond of 50,000 lira and a pension for life of another 50,000 lira. Fearing a maneuver by the moderates to lessen his opposition, Garibaldi did not accept because it involved, in his own words, "a government culpable for the people's miseries and of whom I do not wish to be an accomplice." However, he accepted the offer in 1876 when the Left took power and Depretis, who had been his Sicilian pro-dictator in 1860, became prime minister.

This was a lapse for the man who in 1845 had refused a gift from Rivera. Jessie White Mario found him to have "aged twenty years he was so broken-hearted." Supporters of the church did not lose the opportunity to make biting comments, and for Federico Campanella, the heir to Mazzini's intransigence, "the ruination is now complete. It is terrible to say that in the hands of those scoundrels the exceptional man, the modern Cincinnatus and magnificent mendicant has ceased to exist, and in his place there is nothing more than the monarchy's pensioner." Garibaldi replied brusquely, "I was never a member of the chattering republicans, but I always fought for republics in my deeds and therefore there has been no defection," and he shared the sum gifted to him among his children and sent an allowance to the widows of his two officers, Perla and Lobbia.

He was saddened by political disappointments and family tragedies. In 1871 he wept for the loss of his little Rosa, and in 1875 Anita, his daughter by Battista Raveo, died, which caused him much suffering because he felt he had been an inattentive father and had not given her the affection she needed.

In politics he suffered barbs from followers of Mazzini. In his novel *I Mille*, he renewed his accusation that Mazzini and his supporters had impeded his campaign in 1860. Maurizio Quadrio, loyal to his mentor's doctrine, confuted this point by point in a series of fourteen articles in *L'Unità Italiana e Il Dovere*, until this Genoese publication closed in November 1874. The published and unpublished articles were then published in a posthumous collection by Sara Nathan in 1879. The Left's rise to power did not bring about those measures he had so often supported in relation to budget savings, the nation under arms, and improvements to workers' conditions. Neither Depretis nor Benedetto Cairoli, who replaced him in 1878 with a more progressive program, acted with the incisiveness and rapidity that the former dictator would have wanted from a government. However, he still remained at the breach.

"I can hardly read and still less write," he wrote to Mario Aldisio Sammito in August of 1877. "And I speak really very little and to the desert." This was not strictly true as is demonstrated by the success of the League of Democracy. It was not even true that he spoke very little. He often adopted a public position on national and international events: he supported the cause of the Christian populations of Bulgaria and Macedonia who had rebelled against the Turks; he expressed his hope that Austria, having strengthened its position in the Balkans, would let "our brothers in Trento and Trieste" return to Italy; he protested against the French expansion into Tunisia; and was pained by the anti-Italian demonstrations in Paris and Marseille, which threatened to mar an old friendship between the nations. He also continued to voice his unflagging hostility to the church (the slogan "Get the priest to dig the soil" came up in 1880), disassociated himself from the plans to colonize distant lands, and insisted on the importance of reclaiming and cultivating Italian land.

In 1882 he was invited to the celebration of the sixth centenary of the Sicilian Vespers, the ancient demands for Sicily's independence from Angevin rule. He wanted to see once again the island he had not visited since 1862. His health was poor and he suffered from bronchitis. His family tried to dissuade him, but he was adamant. The government put a patrol vessel, the *Esploratore*, at his disposal. He left Caprera on 18 January in bad weather with the intention of first stopping at Naples, which he had not revisited since 1860. On the twenty-first an ailing Garibaldi was brought ashore on a hospital bed and taken directly to Villa Maraval, property of a Colonel MacLean. The villa, overlooking the Posillipo Sea, was built like a castle with small towers and battlements, as well as a large terrace. It had been rented by the Calabrian deputy Achille Fazzari, who had been close to Garibaldi since the Expedition of the Thousand: he was responsible for sending Francesca Armosino to Caprera and was a witness at their wedding. Garibaldi stayed there with his wife and two children, his trusted friend Froscianti, Clelia's governess, two maids, and two men-servants, and Menotti came down from Rome. For many weeks the former dictator convalesced and was visited by some of Naples' most distinguished doctors. He was trapped in his bedroom and could not receive guests. The mild climate was good for his health, which improved. Francesca with Clelia (a beautiful young girl of fifteen) and Manlio (now nine years) went to the theater, watched carnival floats file by, and took a trip into the surrounding countryside.

Garibaldi recovered. He read the newspapers for three hours every day, received the Minister of Justice Giuseppe Zanardelli (in Naples on official business), and on 19 March, his saint's day, the "survivors of the nation's battles" serenaded him from the sea on a steamer and several boats. Anthems and songs continued for a long time and finally the object of these festivities stepped out onto the terrace and into the lamplight. *L'Illustrazione Italiana* devoted its entire cover to the event: Edoardo Matania depicted Garibaldi who "thanks the veterans and the people" in an illustration imbued with the magic of the Posillipo Sea.

His much-improved health made it possible to continue his journey to Palermo. He left Naples on 24 March by train: he wanted to see Southern Italy, barely glimpsed in 1860. It was raining and he crossed the city in a closed carriage to the station at Portici: the population of the ancient capital of the Bourbon Kingdom was unable to see him. A special train took him down the recently opened railway line, along the more circuitous route, stopping at Salerno, Eboli, Potenza, Catanzaro, Reggio Calabria, and Copanello where he stayed for twenty-four hours at Fazzari's home. Needless to say, the usual rapturous crowds turned out at every station: reports spoke of a storm of cheering in Salerno, and one hundred thousand people in the square at Reggio. He crossed the strait and slept in Messina, before continuing by rail for Catania and then to Palermo. The train passed between cheering crowds on either side of the rails, and on 28 March he reached Palermo. He was exhausted. The crowd packed the streets and watched him pass in his carriage in religious silence. Many were weeping.

He was unable to take part in the ceremonies, but received representatives of the authorities and admirers at the villa of the Marquises of Favare, with whom he was staying. He continued to exhort Italians to action. The people of Palermo had shown that "while Italy was and is obedient to its faith in the brotherhood of nations, she also holds her head high and although she does not threaten others, she is not afraid of aggression from the arrogant and powerful." He left for Caprera on 17 April. His journey through the kingdom he had liberated so magnificently was his last triumphal procession amongst the people and marked the end of his public life.

25. Epilogue

ON 2 JUNE 1882, there was increasing concern at Caprera. Garibaldi had returned from Sicily with his health deteriorating, but they did not yet fear the worst. In Palermo he had talked about poetry with Senator Francesco Paolo Perez and recited from memory passages by his precious Foscolo and from Voltaire's *Zaïre*. His mind was lucid. Doctor Albanese left and on 29 May Garibaldi asked Gaetano Cacciatore, the director of the Palermo observatory for the position of a comet and day on which it was largest. Then his condition suddenly deteriorated. The invalid was running a fever, and wanted to stay in the open and drink cold drinks. His bronchitis worsened, his catarrh made it difficult for him to breath, and an inflammation of the throat hampered his speech. Then he was struck down by pharyngeal paralysis: for three days he could not swallow even a drop of water and had to be fed artificially.

He was treated by Alessandro Cappelletti, the doctor from the warship *Cariddi* lying at anchor off Maddalena. Menotti was at home and the first to realize that his father's condition was deteriorating. They telegraphed

Ricciotti, Teresita, and Albanese, whom Garibaldi trusted as a doctor; they would arrive too late. The invalid was peaceful. On the morning of 2 June he absolutely insisted on taking a warm bath against the advice of his doctor and family. They gave him vapors to inhale to free his air passages. After eleven in the morning his life started slipping away. He had difficulty in uttering a few words with long intervals between them. He saw two blackcaps at the window, and thought of his two dead daughters. He did not want them to be chased away. He asked to see Manlio, who was in bed with a fever. He died at twenty-two minutes past six in the evening. News of his death was telegraphed around the world and appeared in the newspapers the following morning.

The grief was immense and immediate. In Rome the Chamber of Deputies remembered him with great feeling. "Neither the passing years nor the occurrence of other events can erase our eternal gratitude," announced the speaker Domenico Farini. Bovio quickly followed up,

> The man cannot be separated from the myth. Future generations will see him alive in their midst, whenever they stand up for a human ideal. They will see him, and they will not know what to call him, nor in what language to speak of him. Was he the man of Montevideo, Rome, Dijon, or Marsala? Make way for him: his path goes beyond nations and beyond generations.

The chamber decreed mourning for two months, the suspension of sittings until 12 June, the granting of a national pension to his widow and children, a state-funded funeral, and a monument in Rome. "My father taught me as a small child to honor the General's virtue as a citizen and a soldier," Umberto I telegraphed the family.

In many cities shops were closed, shows postponed, and citizens displayed black drapes at their windows. Municipal councils named streets, monuments, and honors after him. Demonstrations of mourning were arranged for Sunday, 4 June and celebrations to commemorate the Constitution were postponed. In some cities, famous orators gave speeches in the theaters, and these were then reported in the newspapers. In Bologna Giosuè Carducci imagined how the legend of Garibaldi would be remembered in the centuries to come: "He was born from an ancient god of the fatherland, who made love to a fairy of the north." The daily newspapers published dispatches, reports from correspondents, biographical information, and combatants' memories.

Messages of condolence arrived from every part of the world, including India. "Garibaldi belonged to Italy and equally to the peoples who fought to reform their nations," telegraphed the speaker of the Romanian Chamber of Deputies. And Victor Hugo added his voice, "It is not Italy that is mourning, nor is it France; it is all humanity." Official expression of condolence came from Paris and London; enormous and solemn demonstrations were held in Montevideo to honor the great defender of Uruguayan independence, the *Héroe de ambos mundos*; municipal councils and democratic associations organized public celebrations of his life in many European and American cities.

Meanwhile decisions were being made for a funeral worthy of him. Garibaldi had long thought about death. He wanted to be cremated. On 27 September 1877 he gave written instructions to Doctor Prandina on how it was to be done. He indicated a depression in the ground where

> a two-meter pile of wood will set up using acacia, mastic, myrtle, and other aromatic woods. An iron base should be placed on the woodpile and on that the open coffin with the corpse dressed in his red shirt. A handful of ashes should be conserved in a commonplace urn, and this must be placed in the burial grounds that contain the ashes of my daughters Rosa and Anita.

The family wanted to respect his wishes which were reiterated in further instructions in July and September 1881, even though there was some uncertainty over the urn's final destination. However, they argued over the method of cremation, because the experts did not believe that a funeral pyre would work with a pile of wood, and proposed the construction of an oven (something Garibaldi had specifically rejected). The materials for this were sent from Rome to Civitavecchia and shipped from there to Caprera.

The authorities however opposed the implementation of Garibaldi's wishes, and insisted on the body being buried in accordance with tradition so that future generations could show their reverence at his place of burial. Public opinion was in fact opposed to cremation, which was prohibited by the church and practiced in Italy only by a few free-thinkers. Friends managed to put pressure on the family, which bowed to general expectations. Thoughts turned to a tomb in Rome on the Janiculum, and the funeral plans increasingly took on the appearance of an official occasion. A tricolor flew over Caprera showing the shield of the House of Savoy.

His body lay on the bed in the room where he died, and he was dressed in the clothes that he wore during his most recent visit to Milan, with his hat and his gold pince-nez resting on his chest. These were to be kept by Teresita to remember him by. There was an old copy of Foscolo's poetry on a small table beside his bed. The guard of honor was made up of seamen from the *Cariddi*. His veterans and admirers arrived in large numbers and filed past his corpse; many broke into uncontrollable tears. By 6 June it was already impossible to find lodgings for so many people. All the beds were taken, as were the mattresses, and there were arguments over the chairs. More people were expected. Caprera was surrounded by warships, freighters, and vessels of every kind. There was a shortage of foodstuffs. Plans were made for the authorities and deputations to disembark from steamers for the funeral ceremony and then leave immediately afterwards.

On 7 June an "infinitely long" train (as one journalist described it) left Rome for Civitavecchia with the official funeral guests. The king was to be represented by Prince Thomas of Savoy, Duke of Genoa, and he was accompanied by ministers, generals (including Gaetano Sacchi, who had fought at his side in Montevideo), deputies, officials, and mayors. The weather deteriorated and they were to have a bad crossing. A road was opened in Caprera for the funeral party to parade along, and poles flying pennants and banners were erected at its sides. The funeral took place at three in the afternoon on 8 June. The procession included the authorities, representatives of over 1,200 associations with a hundred flags (including that of the Expedition of the Thousand), veterans, representatives from the army and navy, and a military band. The *Washington* and the *Cariddi* fired a salute. Once the customary speeches had been made, the coffin was carried by veterans from the Expedition of the Thousand, and placed next to the tombs of his little daughters Anita and Rosa. It would be covered with a granite slab on which only the word "Garibaldi" appeared. Within the next few days the pilgrimages started.

This moving ceremony had an unexpected postscript. The sea was so rough that some deputations had been unable to land and inhabitants of the Isle of Maddalena were unable to come to the funeral. During the afternoon of 8 June a storm blew up. Ships were unable to leave and it was even difficult to travel from Caprera to Maddalena. The Garibaldi family opened the barns and all the rooms. There was a lack of food and water, and everyone had to wait for the sea to calm down. On the morning of 10 June people could finally leave.

The following Sunday the last honors were completed with an imposing ceremony in Rome, where some would have liked the body to have been brought for burial. The immense procession with flags, wreaths, and musical bands, made its way through the crowded streets of the city and accompanied a carriage carrying a colossal bust of Garibaldi, the work of the sculptor Ettore Ferrari, and images commemorating episodes from Garibaldi's life. Forty men who had fought under him marched alongside the carriage, and each held a banner with the name of one of his victories written on it. Many foreign deputations were also present. The commemoration was held in the Capitol Square, and the official speech was made by Giovanni Bovio. Finally, the bust was taken into the grand Capitoline Hall and handed over to Duke Torlonia, the Mayor of Rome. The triumph was complete.

The illustrated magazines recorded this final dazzling display of popularity. *L'Illustrazione Italiana* devoted the entire issue of 11 June to the deceased. There was an extensive and accurate biography with various chapter headings, which was possibly written by Jessie White Mario, given that there was also advertising for her *Vita di Giuseppe Garibaldi* which had been published a few days before. The most important episodes from his youth, his South American campaigns and up to the battles of the Vosges came with illustrations that were often full-page. Other illustrations showing Garibaldi on his deathbed, the commemoration in parliament, and the funeral in Caprera appeared in the issue of 18 June, whereas the great procession through Rome covered a two-page spread on 26 June. *L'Illustration* devoted the issue of 10 June to Garibaldi's life and on 24 June there was a full-page illustration of the procession in Rome as it passed through the Fori Imperiali. The *Illustrated London News* narrated the story of his exploits, showed him on his deathbed, and depicted the funeral in Caprera and the placing of the bust in Capitol.

The weighty biographies by White Mario and Guerzoni were quickly put on sale, and were accompanied by an array of slim and easily read volumes. Lithographs were popular among the working class, as were color vignettes depicting noteworthy episodes in Garibaldi's life.

The family felt they were in the full glare of publicity worldwide. Menotti, Ricciotti and Canzio received dignitaries; Menotti accompanied Prince Thomas to pay his last respects to the dead hero. Caprera was visited by two ministers, the speaker, the vice president of the Senate, an admiral, and five generals. The parliament awarded a national pension to the surviving family. They had to respond to these solemn acts of esteem with their own demonstration of selflessness. On 9 June Anita's children and Francesca Armosino, on her own behalf and on behalf of the children, decided that Caprera should never be divided up and should be held in perpetuity as "a natural and lasting monument to [Garibaldi's] greatness."

This gift to the nation was a means to avoid unpleasant disagreements. There was no love lost between Francesca and Anita's children. In his first will, Garibaldi had left Caprera, his only property, in equal parts to his wife and his children, but a few days before his death he altered the will and gave most of the island to Francesca Armosino. Indeed, she would live on the island until she died in 1923, while Clelia, her constant companion who would never marry, remained custodian of her father's house until she died just before her ninety-second birthday in 1959. Manlio, a naval officer, died young in 1900. The ownership of the island, which was declared a national monument on 4 July 1907 (on the centenary of his birth), was later transferred to the Italian military and became part of the naval base established on the Isle of Maddalena. Garibaldi's tomb is still where he was buried in 1882, and the proposed transfer to Rome never took place. However, Anita's remains were moved to the capital in 1932, the fiftieth anniversary of Garibaldi's death, and buried on the Janiculum.

The elder children's loyalty to their father's memory took a different course. It was not easy to live up to Garibaldi's moral legacy: both Menotti and Ricciotti ended up involved in shady business affairs and were criticized for their political views. However the former, who was the deputy for

Velletri for many years, followed in his father's footsteps by devoting his energies to a successful land-reclamation scheme on an enormous farm in the Roman countryside. Ricciotti would keep alive his father's ideal of voluntary military action in favor of the oppressed peoples, and in this spirit he commanded a corps of red shirts assisting the Greeks against the Turks, and fought at Domokos in 1897 and Drisko in 1912. Later, recalling Garibaldi's Vosges campaign in 1870, his sons went to fight for France against the German invasion in World War I, while Italy was still neutral: in 1914 Peppino (born in Melbourne in 1879, the first of ten children) formed a legion that fought at the Ardenne. His youngest, Bruno and Costante, died heroically in December 1914 and January 1915 respectively, and thus demonstrated their support for their grandfather's teachings by sacrificing their lives. A very popular anthem, *Torna Garibaldi*, inspired by the number of Garibaldi's descendents who were being cut down, renewed the laurels won by the Expedition of the Thousand.

Caprera remained intact with its memories and the mortal remains of the man that made it famous, and was for a long time the object of patriotic pilgrimages. As time passed and events changed Italy's political structure, Italian reverence for one of the principal founders of national unification began to fade. The centrifugal forces, which were entirely overcome by history during the period between 1859 and 1870, appear to have revived and cast doubt on the unification that was so widely supported at the time. But such doubts cannot detract from the extraordinary qualities that made Garibaldi one of the main protagonists of the events that banished foreign domination and absolutism from Italy, and opened the way for a state in which the liberty guaranteed by the Constitution made it possible for the needs of the country's various components to assert themselves.

In any case, no assessment of Garibaldi's life can be limited to his contribution to the achievement of Italian unification. He was a complex character who cannot be summed up in a formulaic manner or assigned to a particular party or state. In his youth he developed an original view of the tasks "men of feeling" should undertake, and up until an advanced age he committed himself to these. He worked in a manner that was consistent with his inner self in very different moments and environments, and he left his indelible imprint on the political and military history of American and European nations. I have attempted to give as realistic an interpretation as

possible of his adventurous life, by eliminating the exaggerations and rhetorical excesses of the early biographers while demonstrating his openness
to love, friendship and the beauty of nature and showing how public and
private events were interwoven. I have also attempted to put his life in the
context of the events affecting the countries in which he became involved.
But however accurate and convincing, the rewriting of the bare plot containing many episodes would not give the measure of the uniqueness of
this human adventure if it were not augmented with accounts and comments by contemporaries.

Garibaldi's greatness was in his legend, which was formulated after his
death by posterity: it became part of his character through the extraordinary impression that his exceptional American and European exploits produced in the world, the fascination he exercised over men, the masses,
intellectuals, and the dispossessed, the moral and emotional force triggered by his incredible selflessness, and the hopes of national independence and social improvement he inspired. "Garibaldi was quite rightly the
symbol of popular revolution, and a model of a people's military leader,"
the Polish historian Jerzy W. Boreisza has recently observed. Contemporaries understood this when they started to reflect upon his significance of
his death. Over time, historical research has uncovered biographical details, argued over his abilities as a military leader and examined his cultural
background and the politics behind his actions. This hard scholarly slog
(whose results I have always observed) has not modified the judgment on
his unique qualities and has not tarnished his transfiguration into the ideal
combatant inspired by the dream of universal brotherhood.

A rapid review of the views expressed in the international press on the
occasion of his death gives an idea of how the legend was historicized.
The Parisian newspapers made no secret of their admiration. "Garibaldi
was a citizen of the world. Like the knight errant, the medieval paladin,
he had as many homelands as there were oppressed peoples. His image
has replaced that of Napoleon in many of our peasants' hovels," and is
found "in the Bulgarian's shack just as in the Indian's tent on the pampas," wrote *La France*. He was "a great heroic figure" for *Paris*, and "a
kind of chivalric hero, inspired and naive" for *Le Temps*, while "posterity
would salute him as the precursor of all the great ideas of liberty" according to *La République Française*. "Garibaldi's loyalty and courage cannot

be challenged," wrote *Le National*. "We salute these robust virtues in the old warrior at a time when this dying century is bringing its epic stories to an end, one by one."

German and Austrian newspapers preferred to remember him with sympathy rather than as an adversary. "The most ideal figure of our time," *Wiener Allgemeine Zeitung* defined him, "a man who at his feet had everything that human fantasy can imagine—power, wealth, splendor, honors, and titles—a man who despised everything that others so eagerly sought and who devoted his life to what he considered his duty." The liberal *Neue Freie Presse* considered him "a hero and a child, full of that strong and unshakable faith that is the guarantee of victory. . . . He will live on immortal in history . . . and will be an example of noble self-abnegation and fervent patriotism." For *Neues Wiener Tagblatt*, the legend of Garibaldi will be "a blessing for Italy and all other peoples, because it is the legend of liberty." According to *Deutsche Zeitung*, "a new Homer should appear who is worthy of singing the Odyssey of this life, and such a new Odyssey would not sound less marvelous and fabulous than the old one."

This review of articles expressing grief and exalting the deceased could also include the Spanish, Portuguese, Polish, Hungarian, Romanian, Greek, and South American press. We will limit ourselves here to the North American and Japanese press. His death revived enthusiasm in the United States to the levels of 1849, 1859, and 1860: he was compared with Lincoln for the same image of a common, honest and selfless man (the *New York Times* and *Chicago Weekly Journal*), and was perceived as a "majestic reminder of the creative period of a nation's golden youth" (the *New York Daily Tribune*). In Japan the most authoritative government daily newspaper, *Tokyo Nicinici Shinbun*, told the story of his life in four installments in 1882 and perceived it as a great adventure. In 1887 Yukici Yasuoka published a detailed biography, and Garibaldi, who was compared with Tagamori Saigo, one of the protagonists of the Meiji restoration, became a popular figure.

I have left Britain to last, as it was the county where he was most loved and where yet another biography was published in 1881, this time by J. Theodore Bent. I will not quote the many admiring assessments by so many newspapers ranging from the liberal *Daily Chronicle* to the conservative *Daily Telegraph* and *Morning Post*. I will dwell on the more profound assessment provided by the *Times*, which observed both the light and shade, and asserted that Garibaldi would merit close attention even after he had lost "the shining aura with which he has been covered by popular excitement." He was not only a warrior, according to the paper. Although he was no strategist and showed little or no interest in organization, he had leadership qualities, "firm expression, rapid decision-making, and re-sourcefulness." He read a great deal, "but he lacked the basic rudiments in politics as in soldiering. He rushed to conclusions without struggling through the intermediate argumentation. Crude notions of democracy, communism, cosmopolitanism, and positivism mixed in his brain . . . draw-ing him into contradictions of which he was not aware," so that he spoke of everything "in his emphatic, incisive and peremptory tone."

However, "with a heart like Garibaldi's a man can certainly permit his brain the odd distraction. . . . Have Garibaldi's biography written by his worst enemy, and he will still seem the most sincere, the most selfless and the least ambitious of men." The journalist writing the article dwelled at length on these qualities and his ability to electrify the motley hordes of volunteers who came running to his orders.

> Among the various favorable circumstances that conspired to bring about the triumph of the Italian cause, nothing proved more provi-dential than this singular man, this *conquistatore misterioso* (as he was called) and the almost mythic prestige surrounding his military feats, which were moreover such extraordinary successes that they silenced every criticism and appeared to an astonished world in the light of supernatural events. Of the three figures who contributed to Italian unification—Victor Emanuel, Cavour, and Garibaldi—the third will appeal to the imagination as a legendary reality (similar to that of William Tell), as something fabulous and of an elusive nature.

So the *Times* wrote that in the case of Garibaldi you need to appeal to the imagination "as a legendary reality," and brought together contrasting concepts in an audacious manner. "You cannot separate him from the legend," asserted Bovio. "Future generations will see him alive in their midst, whenever they stand up for a human ideal." The truth of Garibal-di's incredible appeal is to be found in his legend, his having moved "from nationalism to humanity" (in accordance with the teachings he received from the Saint-Simonians), having appeared a sincere defender of human brotherhood, having given genuine space to cosmopolitanism, and having lifted the Expedition of the Thousand from an episode in a merely Italian struggle to a symbol of liberty for all humanity.

The Russian revolutionary Sergei Mickailovich Kravchinsky observed in 1882 that Garibaldi was himself a symbol of liberty and humanity:

> he was one of those people who never allow life to overcome them and never put restraints on a further development. They are the people who remain in the vanguard of the fighters for progress because their love for the people is not mediated through the screen of some doctrine and they therefore sense what leads most directly and rapidly to human happiness. Garibaldi was one of the major representatives of this kind of man, so rarely found amongst politicians. Right up until the last days of his life he conserved the sensitivity and freshness of his soul.

Chronology of Events

1807   Garibaldi is born on 4 July in Nice, during the brief period in which it belongs to France. In 1814 the city is returned to the Kingdom of Sardinia.

1815   The Congress of Vienna decides to divide Italy into five regional states and three small duchies.

1824–1833   Garibaldi enters the merchant service and works on the Mediterranean routes as a seaman. In 1832 he obtains a second-class master's ticket.

1833   He develops a passionate interest in the ideas of Saint-Simon and Mazzini, who founded Young Italy in 1831 for the purpose of creating a unified, independent, and republican Italy. At the end of the year he joins the Sardinian navy.

1834   He takes part in a failed uprising in Genoa, which has been organized by Mazzini. He is discovered but manages to escape. He is condemned to death by a military tribunal.

1834–1835   He seeks refuge in Marseille, where he works as a sailor under a false name. He joins Young Europe. In the summer of 1835 he leaves for Brazil.

1836   In Rio de Janeiro, he establishes an association in support of Mazzini among the Italian exiles.

1837   He becomes a privateer in the service of the Republic of Rio Grande do Sul, which is fighting for its independence from Brazil. He is attacked by the Uruguayans on the River Plate. He is wounded and seeks asylum in Argentina, where he is imprisoned for a few months in Galeguay. Once he has been freed, he spends some time in Montevideo.

1838–1841   He moves to Rio Grande, where he fights the Brazilians on land and sea. He meets Anita in Laguna in 1839, and in 1840 his son is born; named Domenico, he will always be called Menotti.

1841–1848   He returns to Montevideo. There he fights for Uruguay, which is now under attack from Argentina, which is support-ing the rebel Oribe. In 1842, he is given the task of leading a naval expedition up the Paranà River and then takes part in the defense of Montevideo, which is under siege. In 1845 he commands an expedition up the Uruguay River, and in Feb-ruary 1846 he repulses superior forces at the battle of San Antonio near Salto, which causes a considerable sensation. He then returns to defend the capital. His fame begins to spread in Europe. His children Rosita (who dies very young), Teresita, and Ricciotti are all born in Montevideo.

1848   On 15 April, he leaves Montevideo for Italy and arrives there in June. The First War of Independence has already commenced. Convinced that all Italians should be united in the fight against Austria, he offers to fight for King Charles Albert of Sardinia. Rejected by the Sardinian army, he obtains command of the army of the provisional govern-ment in Milan. He fights in Lombardy against the Austri-ans as an irregular after the Salasco Armistice. He returns to Nice, and from there he sails with a group of volunteers for Sicily to assist the rebellion against the Bourbons. In Livorno he decides to remain in Tuscany and then moves to the Papal States.

1849   He fights in the defense of the Roman Republic, which was proclaimed after Pius IX fled the capital. When the republic falls in July, he decides to take a few thousand volunteers to Venice, which is under siege from the Austrians. He is obliged to disband his troops in San Marino and attempts to reach Venice with a few comrades. He fails, and in August while he is on the run, Anita dies. In spite of great difficulties, he manages to evade the Austrian manhunt. In September, he is safe in Liguria.

1849–1853   He returns to exile. He stays in Tangiers and then moves to the United States. He works on Pacific trade routes. At the end of 1853 he leaves for England.

1854–1859   He returns to Italy. He stays in Nice. His father has died in 1841, and his mother in 1852. He purchases part of the Island of Caprera and goes to live there. From a political point of view, he puts aside his republican ideals and joins the National Society, as he believes it right that Italians assist the House of Savoy, the only constitutional monarchy in Italy, in forming a coalition against Austria.

1859   In the Second War of Independence, he is a general in the Sardinian army, in command of the Cacciatori delle Alpi. He has a daughter called Anita by Battistina Raveo. Following the Armistice of Villafranca, he takes command of the army of the League of Central Italy. He resigns when he is prevented from invading the Papal States.

1860   In January he marries the daughter of the Marquis Raimondi, from whom he separates a few days later. In April, he unsuccessfully opposes the transfer of Nice to France. On 6 May, he leaves Quarto with a thousand volunteers to assist Sicily in its revolution against the Bourbons. On 11 May he lands in Marsala; on the fourteenth he takes on the title of Dictator in Salemi; on the fifteenth he defeats the Bourbon army at Calatafimi; on the twenty-seventh he enters Palermo; on 6 June he is in control of the city; on 20 July he again defeats the Bourbons at Milazzo; on 19 August he crosses the Straits of Messina and lands in Calabria; and on 7 September he enters Naples. On 1–2 October, he halts the Bourbon counterattack at the Battle of Volturno. After the union of Southern Italy and Sicily with the Kingdom of Sardinia has been decided in a plebiscite, he meets King Victor Emanuel II at Teano on 26 October, and he hands over power to him in Naples on 7 November. On the ninth he returns to Caprera.

1861   The Kingdom of Italy is proclaimed in March. In April Garibaldi clashes with Cavour in Parliament over the treatment of his volunteers.

1862   With the intention of liberating Rome through a popular uprising, he departs from Sicily with two thousand volunteers, but on 29 August he is halted by the Italian army at Aspromonte in Calabria. He is wounded and held prisoner until October.

1864   In April, he is greeted in triumph while touring in England.

1866   In the Third War of Independence, he commands a corps of volunteers who fight in Trentino. At Bezzecca he wins the only victory during an unsuccessful campaign for the Italian army.

1867   Clelia, his daughter by Francesca Armosino, is born. He returns to his plans to liberate Rome with a military expedition. In September, he takes part in the Peace Congress in Geneva. In October, he leads the volunteers in an invasion of Lazio, but the Rome campaign ends unhappily at Mentana on 3 November.

1869   Rosita, his second child by Francesca Armosino, is born (she is to die young in January 1871).

1870   From October to January 1871 he fights in the Franco-Prussian War on the side of the republic that has just been declared in France. He embarks on his literary career, which will eventually produce three novels and the completion of his *Memoirs*.

1871   He returns to Caprera. He adopts a position in favor of the Paris Commune and socialism.

1872   On the death of Mazzini, he orders that the flag of the Thousand should fly over his coffin, even though he dissented from Mazzini's political position. In November, he attempts to unite all the democratic forces in Italy through the Pact of Rome.

1873   Manlio, his son by Francesca Armosino, is born.

1875   He stays in Rome to campaign for a project to build a canal on the Tiber to prevent flooding.

1876   He accepts the National Gift, once the Left has attained power.

1879   In April, he establishes the League for Democracy in Rome to promote a legal campaign for electoral reform.

1880   He obtains an annulment of his marriage to Raimondi and marries Francesca Armosino.

1882   He returns to Naples and Palermo. He dies in Caprera on 2 June.

Bibliography

The bibliography on Giuseppe Garibaldi is immense and was considerably expanded at the time of his centenary celebrations. The principal bibliographical work is the monumental *Giuseppe Garibaldi e la tradizione garibaldina. Una bibliografia dal 1807 al 1970* by Anthony P. Campanella (Geneva, 1971), which contains 16,141 entries. There are, however, many more titles, as some entries include several works. A short annotated bibliography covering the same period is Emilio Costa-Bianca Montale, *La Liguria*, in *Bibliografia dell'Età del Risorgimento in onore di Alberto Maria Ghisalberti*, vol. 1 (Florence, 1971). For the period after 1970, see Giuseppe Armani's preface to Giuseppe Garibaldi, *Memorie* (Milan, 1982); Stefania Magliani, "Giuseppe Garibaldi: bilancio di un centenario," *Rassegna Storica del Risorgimento* (April–June 1992); Stefania Magliani, "Nuove prospettive di studio: gli inediti di Garibaldi recuperati dalla storiografia nel decennio 1982–1992," in *Giuseppe Garibaldi. A dieci anni dal centenario della morte. Bilancio storiografico*, edited by Gaetano Massa and Romano Ugolini (Rome, 1999), which also includes Salvatore Candido's appraisal of *Il rivoluzionario Garibaldi (1831–1854)*.

Garibaldi's countless writings are a source of primary importance. The National Edition produced for the fiftieth anniversary of his death contains volumes 1–6 (Bologna, 1932–1937): *Memorie* (1–2), the novel *I Mille* (3), and *Scritti e discorsi politici e militari* (4–6). The editorial committee, which was reestablished in 1956, is currently publishing his *Epistolario*: the first ten volumes, which were edited between 1973 and 1997, include his correspondence up to the first half of 1866. For the years from 1866 to 1882, serviceable alternatives can be found in *Epistolario*, edited by Enrico Emilio Ximenes (Milan, 1885), and *Scritti politici e militari. Ricordi e pensieri inediti,* edited by Domenico Ciampoli (Rome, n.d. [1907]). His parliamentary speeches have been collected in *Garibaldi in Parlamento* (Rome, 1982), vol. 1, *Dalla Repubblica Romana a Aspromonte,* vol. 2, *Dalle dimissioni del 1864 alle commemorazioni in morte;* the essay in the appendix by Silvio Furlani, "Garibaldi candidato elettorale," examines Garibaldi's involvement in elections from 1848 to May 1880.

Of the biographies that are still of interest although not necessarily reliable, the most significant are Giuseppe Guerzoni, *Garibaldi* (Florence, 1882), and Jessie White Mario, *Vita di Giuseppe Garibaldi* (Milan, 1882), with an expanded edition in *Garibaldi e i suoi tempi* (Milan, 1884) (with illustrations by Edoardo Matania), because they were written by people who knew him and worked with him. The most successful of recent works, which have become slightly outdated by the onward progress of a scholarship, are Gustavo Sacerdote, *La vita di Giuseppe Garibaldi secondo i risultati delle più recenti indagini* (Milan, 1933), which is well documented and richly illustrated; Jasper Ridley, *Garibaldi* (New York, 1974), which covers the contemporary American and British press in detail; Mino Milani, *Giuseppe Garibaldi. Biografia critica* (Milan, 1982); Romano Ugolini, *Garibaldi. Genesi di un mito* (Rome, 1982), which covers only 1848. There is an effective summary in Giuseppe Monsagrati's entry for "Garibaldi, Giuseppe" in *Dizionario Biografico degli Italiani,* vol. 52 (Rome, 1999).

In *Garibaldi vivo* (Milan, 1982), Aldo A. Mola provides us with an annotated anthology of Garibaldi's writings, along with unpublished documents and further biographical and bibliographical notes.

The most useful of the recent works and the conference proceedings for events held in many Italian cities throughout 1982 are Angelo Tamborra, *Garibaldi e l'Europa. Impegno militare e prospettive politiche* (Rome, 1983); *Giuseppe Garibaldi e il suo mito,* Proceedings of the Fifty-first Congress of the History of the Risorgimento (Rome, 1984); *Garibaldi condottiero. Storia, teoria, prassi,* edited by Filippo Mazzonis (Milan, 1984); *Garibaldi e il socialismo,* edited by Gaetano Cingari (Rome-Bari, 1984); *Garibaldi generale della libertà,* edited by Aldo A. Mola (Rome, 1984); *Garibaldi, Mazzini e il Risorgimento nel risveglio dell'Asia e dell'Africa,* edited by Giorgio Borsa and Paolo Beonio Brocchieri (Milan, 1984).

The brief notes that follow on the individual chapters have been restricted to information on the most important contributions in recent decades and the works that have been quoted in the main text.

For Garibaldi's *Memorie* we rely on the text produced in the National Edition, vol. 2, and the letters up to 1866 in the text of the *Epistolario* published by the National Commission.

The following abbreviations will be employed:

> *Bollettino Domus* = *Bollettino della Domus mazziniana*
> *Mito* = *Giuseppe Garibaldi e il suo mito*
> *RSR* = *Rassegna Storica del Risorgimento*

In order to demonstrate Garibaldi's popularity around the world, we have systematically sorted through the French magazine *L'Illustration* and *Le Monde Illustré* and the British magazine *The Illustrated London News*.

Introduction. The term "pirate-centaur" comes from Gino Doria, "Il pirata-centauro, notizie e documenti ignoti sulla vita di Garibaldi in America," now in *Mondo vecchio e nuovo mondo* (Naples, 1966).

Chapter 1. To put the events of Garibaldi's life in their Italian historical context, see Giorgio Candeloro, *Storia dell'Italia moderna* (Milan, 1956), vols. 1–6; Alfonso Scirocco, *L'Italia del Risorgimento*, 2nd ed. (Bologna, 1993). For the economy of Liguria and Nice, see Luigi Bulferetti and Raimondo Luraghi, *Agricoltura, industria e commercio in Piemonte dal 1814 al 1848* (Turin, 1966).

For Garibaldi's family history from 1600, see Lorenzo Caratti, *La genealogia di Giuseppe Garibaldi*, RSR (October–December 1979). Chapter 1 of Pino Fortini, *Giuseppe Garibaldi marinaio mercantile. Pagine di storia marinara* (Rome, 1950), provides information on the ships on which Garibaldi sailed, the names and types of vessels, and the routes he followed. This allows us to reconstruct his seagoing career up to the time of his arrival in Rio de Janeiro.

Augusto Vittorio Vecchi, *Memorie di un luogotenente di vascello* (Rome, 1896).

Description of Garibaldi's character and physical appearance can be found in Bartolomeo Mitre, "Un episodio troyano. Recuerdos del sitio grande de Montevideo," in *Obras Completas*, vol. 12 (Buenos Aires, 1949); Louise Colet, *Naples sous Garibaldi. Souvenirs de la guerre de l'indépendance* (Paris, 1861); Giovan Battista Cuneo, *Biografia di Giuseppe Garibaldi* (Turin, 1850); G. Guerzoni, *Garibaldi* (Florence, 1882); Malvida von Meysenburg, *Ricordi di una idealista* (Rome, 1905); Alexandre Dumas, *Mémoires de Garibaldi traduits sur le manuscript original, précédé d'un discours su Garibaldi par Victor Hugo et d'une introduction par George Sand*, 3 vols. (Brussels, 1861–1862).

Chapter 2. Jessie White Mario, *Vita di Giuseppe Garibaldi* (Milan, 1882); G. Guerzoni, *Garibaldi* (Florence, 1882). On the events of 1834 and Garibaldi's support for Mazzini, a convincing account can be found in chapter 2 of R. Ugolini, *Garibaldi. Genesi di un mito* (Rome, 1982). All the quotations by Mazzini have been taken from Giuseppe Mazzini, *Scritti editi ed inediti. Edizione Nazionale* (Imola, 1906).

Chapter 3. On the history of South America: *Storia del mondo moderno*, vol. 10, *Il culmine della potenza europea (1830–1870)* (Milan, 1970).

On trade between Italy and South America, see Elio Lodolini, "Rapporti marittimi e commerciali fra Stato pontificio e America Latina nella prima metà del secolo XIX," *RSR* (October–December 1979) (it contains specific information for the Kingdom of Sardinia); Chiara Vangelista, "Traders and Workers: Sardinian Subjects in Argentina and Brasil," in *The Italian Diaspora: Migration across the Globe* (Toronto, 1992).

Careful examination of the South American context in which Garibaldi's action took place can be found in Ivan Boris, *Gli anni di Garibaldi in Sud America (1836–1848)* (Milan, 1970) (chapters 1 and 2 deal with his stay in Rio); R. Ugolini, *Garibaldi. Genesi di un mito* (Rome, 1982), chapter 3; Salvatore Candido, "L'azione mazziniana in Brasile ed il giornale *La Giovine Italia* di Rio de Janeiro (1836) attraverso documenti inediti o poco noti," *Bollettino Domus*, no. 2 (1968).

Chapter 4. S. Candido, *Giuseppe Garibaldi corsaro riograndese (1837–1838)* (Rome, 1964) (an essential work); I. Boris, *Gli anni di Garibaldi in Sud America (1836–1848)* (Milan, 1970), chapter 3 and 4; R. Ugolini, *Garibaldi. Genesi di un mito* (Rome, 1982), chapter 4.

Chapter 5. I. Boris, *Gli anni di Garibaldi in Sud America (1836–1848)* (Milan, 1970), chapters 5–14; R. Ugolini, *Garibaldi. Genesi di un mito* (Rome, 1982), chapter 4; S. Candido, *La rivoluzione riograndese nel carteggio inedito di due giornalisti mazziniani: Luigi Rossetti e G. B. Cuneo (1837–1840)* (Florence, 1973).

Chapter 6. I. Boris, *Gli anni di Garibaldi in Sud America (1836–1848)* (Milan, 1970), chapter 9; S. Candido, *La rivoluzione riograndese nel carteggio* . . . ; Gustav Hoffstetter, *Giornale delle cose di Roma nel 1849. Documenti della guerra santa d'Italia* (Capolago, 1851).

Chapter 7. I. Boris, *Gli anni di Garibaldi in Sud America (1836–1848)* (Milan, 1970), chapters 15–17; S. Candido, *Giuseppe Garibaldi nel Rio de la Plata. 1841–1848*, vol. 1, *Dal ritorno a Montevideo alla spedizione suicida nel Rio Paraná 1841–1842* (Florence, 1972); S. Candido, "La Giovine Italia a Montevideo (1836–1842). Contributo alla storia mazziniana nelle Americhe," *Bollettino Domus*, no. 1 (1975). The Argentinean and Uruguayan presses are examined in Jasper Ridley, *Garibaldi* (New York, 1974), chapter 9.

Chapter 8. I. Boris, *Gli anni di Garibaldi in Sud America (1836–1848)* (Milan, 1970), chapters 17–22; R. Ugolini, *Garibaldi. Genesi di un mito* (Rome, 1982); S. Candido, *La Giovine Italia a Montevideo* . . . .

Chapter 9. I. Boris, *Gli anni di Garibaldi in Sud America (1836–1848)* (Milan, 1970), chapters 23–26; Georges Bourgin, "Garibaldi et la France en Uruguay. 1840–1848," *RSR* (July–September 1965); S. Candido, "Giuseppe Garibaldi sulla via del ritorno in Italia (April 1848)," *RSR* (October–December 1968).

Chapter 10. Jasper Ridley, *Garibaldi* (New York, 1974), chapter 8; B. Mitre, "Un episodio troyano. Recuerdos del sitio grande de Montevideo," in *Obras Completas*, vol. 12 (Buenos Aires, 1949); H. F. Winnington-Ingram, *Hearts of Oak* (London, 1889); Ouseley's account can be found in Denis Mack Smith, *Garibaldi* (London, 1957); R. Ugolini, *Garibaldi. Genesi di un mito* (Rome, 1982), chapter 6; R. Ugolini, "L'esperienza latino-americana nella formazione politica di Garibaldi," *Nuova Antologia* (January–March 1985); S. Candido, *Giuseppe Garibaldi sulla via del ritorno.* . . .

Chapter 11. Carlo Jean, "Garibaldi e il volontariato italiano nel Risorgimento," *RSR* (October–December 1982). Still useful is Piero Pieri, *Storia militare del Risorgimento* (Turin, 1962) (1848 is covered in chapter 10).

Chapter 12. P. Pieri, *Storia militare del Risorgimento* (Turin, 1962), chapter 12; Gabriella Ciampi, *Roma: la difesa del 1849*, in *Il 1848. La rivoluzione in città*, a cura di Angelo Varni (Bologna, 2000); Giuseppe Monsagrati, "La popolazione di Roma al tempo dell'assedio," in *España y la Republica Romana de 1849*, edited by Manuel Espadas Burgos (Rome, 2000); Emilio Dandolo, *I volontari ed i bersaglieri lombardi. Annotazioni storiche* (Turin, 1849); Candido Augusto Vecchi, *La Italia. Storia di due anni 1848–1849* (Turin, 1851).

Chapter 13. P. Pieri, *Storia militare del Risorgimento* (Turin, 1962), chapter 12; Jan Philip Koelman, *Memorie romane* (Rome, 1963).

Umberto Beseghi, *Il maggiore Leggero e il «trafugamento» di Garibaldi. La verità sulla morte di Anita* (Ravenna, 1932). The report from the archbishop of Ravenna's secretary on Anita's death can be found in G. Sacerdote, *La vita di Giuseppe Garibaldi secondo i risultati delle più recenti indagini* (Milan, 1933).

Chapter 14. Corrado De Biase, *L'arresto di Garibaldi nel settembre 1849, con un'appendice di documenti* (Florence, 1941); Paolo Castagnino Saetta, "L'arrivo di Garibaldi a Chiavari," in *Garibaldi condottiero. Storia, teoria, prassi*, edited by Filippo Mazzonis (Milan, 1984); for the state subsidy, see Emilia Morelli, "Garibaldi nel processo unitario," in *Mito*.

Jasper Ridley, *Garibaldi* (New York, 1974), chapter 23, quotes the views of Dwight and Tuckerman; P. Fortini, *Giuseppe Garibaldi marinaio mercantile. Pagine di storia marinara* (Rome, 1950), chapters 2–5; Philip Kenneth Kowie, "Nuova luce su Garibaldi in Perú (1851–1853)," *RSR* (July–September 1981); Philip Kenneth Kowie, "Garibaldi in Nicaragua e nel Regno di Mosquito nell'agosto–settembre 1851," *RSR* (January–March 1984); Philip Kenneth Kowie, "Garibaldi in Oriente, aprile–settembre 1852," in *Garibaldi, Mazzini e il Risorgimento nel risveglio dell'Asia e dell'Africa* (Milan, 1984); Philip Kenneth Kowie, "Contro la tesi di «Garibaldi negriero»," *RSR* (July–September 1998).

For the move to Caprera, see G. Sacerdote, *La vita di Giuseppe Garibaldi secondo i risultati delle più recenti indagini* (Milan, 1933), which quotes a comment by Galante; Giacomo Emilio Curatulo, *Garibaldi agricoltore* (Rome, 1930), which includes notes and accounts for the years 1856–57 and the *giornale di apicultura* for 1873–74, as well as anecdotes taken from well-known works.

Chapter 15. For the formation of the Garibaldi legend, see chapter 18.

Alexander Herzen, *Garibaldi a Londra* (Milan, 1950); Alexander Herzen, *My Past and Thoughts*, translated by Constance Garnet (London, 1974).

Alfonso Scirocco, *I democratici italiani da Sapri a Porta Pia* (Naples, 1969), chapter 1; Luciano Russi, "Garibaldi, Pisacane e la repubblica romana," in *Garibaldi generale della libertà*, edited by Aldo A. Mola (Rome, 1984); Nino Bixio, *Epistolario*, edited by Emilia Morelli, vol. 1 (Rome, 1939); P. Pieri, *Storia militare del Risorgimento* (Turin, 1962), chapter 16.

Chapter 16. Gideon Scott Lang's letter to the *Times* is published in Jasper Ridley, *Garibaldi* (New York, 1974), and Roslyn Pesman Cooper, "Garibaldi e l'Australia," *RSR* (April–June 1985); Emilia Morelli, "La Sinistra rivoluzionaria da Villafranca ai plebiscite," in *Atti del XLII congresso di Storia del Risorgimento italiano* (Rome, 1966); A. Scirocco, *L'Italia del Risorgimento*, 2nd ed. (Bologna, 1993), chapter 1.

For Speranza von Schwartz, see Luisa Gasparini, *Un amore di Garibaldi* (Milan, 1932); G. Garibaldi, *Lettere a Speranza von Schwartz*, with a preface by Natalia Aspesi (Florence, 1982). On the short-lived marriage, see Mino Mulinacci, *La bella figlia del lago. Cronaca intima del matrimonio fallito di Giuseppe Garibaldi con la marchesina Raimondi* (Milan, 1978).

Chapter 17. Many aspects of the expedition are examined in *Atti del XXXIX congresso di Storia del Risorgimento italiano* (Rome, 1961); A. Scirocco, *L'Italia del Risorgimento*, 2nd ed. (Bologna, 1993), chapter 2; J. Ridley, "Le ripercussioni internazionali della spedizione di Garibaldi nel 1860," in *Garibaldi generale della libertà*, edited by Aldo A. Mola (Rome, 1984).

Giuseppe Bandi, *I Mille. Da Genova a Capua* (Florence, 1903); Marziano Brignoli, *I Mille di Garibaldi. Volti di protagonisti e comparse* (Milan, 1981); Germano Bevilacqua, *I Mille di Marsala*, vol. 1, *Vita, morte, miracoli, fasti e nefasti* (Calliano [Trento], 1982), vol. 2, *Album fotografico* (Calliano, 1985).

For the military operations, see P. Pieri, *Storia militare del Risorgimento* (Turin, 1962), chapter 18; Guido Landi, "Il generale Francesco Landi," *RSR* (April–June and July–September 1960); George Rodney Mundy, *Hannibal at Palermo and Naples, during the Italian Revolution. 1859–1851* (London, 1863).

Chapter 18. For how the expedition was perceived, see Ferdinand Boyer, "La presse progaribaldienne a Paris en 1860," in *Archivio Storico Messinese* (1859–1961);

Franco Venturi, "L'immagine di Garibaldi in Russia all'epoca della liberazione dei servi," in *Rassegna Storica Toscana* (October–December 1960); Robert J. O. Van Nuffel, "Il Belgio e la spedizione dei Mille," in *Genova e l'Impresa dei Mille* (Rome, 1961); Robert Van Nuffel, "L'opinione reazionaria belga e gli avvenimenti di Sicilia," in *La Sicilia e l'unità d'Italia* (Milan, 1962); Marina Milan, "Opinione pubblica e antigaribaldismo in Francia: la querelle sull'unità d'Italia (1860–1866)," *RSR* (April–June 1983); Karl Marx and Friedrich Engels, *Sul Risorgimento italiano* (Rome, 1959). A. Tamborra, *Garibaldi e l'Europa* (Rome, 1983), examines the effects of the expedition on European public opinion and subsequent displays of admiration in relation to the formation of his legend up to his death; *Mito* develops this argument in relation to the Garibaldi myth in Mexico, the United States of America, Spain, Britain, France, Austria, Belgium, Scandinavia, Poland, Romania, Japan, and Central and Eastern Europe; *Garibaldi e il socialismo*, edited by Gaetano Cingari (Rome-Bari, 1984), does the same for Hungary, Romania, Bosnia-Herzegovina, the Balkans, and the Danube river basin; *Garibaldi generale della libertà*, edited by Aldo A. Mola (Rome, 1984) for Hungary, Romania, Poland, Bulgaria, Spain, and France (Sergio Romano examines French hostility to Garibaldi in great detail); *Garibaldi cento anni dopo* for Switzerland and Eastern Europe. For Garibaldi's philo-Hellenism and his legend in Greece at the time of King Otto, see *Garibaldi e il filellenismo italiano nel XIX secolo* (Athens, 1985); Philippe Gut, "Garibaldi et la France, 1848–1882. Naissance d'un mythe," *RSR* (July–September 1987).

P. Pieri, *Storia militare del Risorgimento* (Turin, 1962), chapter 18; Mariano Gabriele, *Sicilia 1860, da Marsala allo stretto* (Rome, 1991); A. Scirocco, *L'Italia del Risorgimento*, 2nd ed. (Bologna, 1993), chapter 2; G. Guerzoni, *Garibaldi* (Florence, 1882); Denis Mack Smith, *Cavour and Garibaldi. 1860* (Cambridge, 1954); Giuseppe Cesare Abba, *Da Quarto al Volturno. Noterelle di uno dei Mille* (Bologna, 1891).

The texts of Victor Emanuel's two letters—one requesting him to desist from his campaign in Sicily and the other in draft form telling him exactly the opposite—whose existence has been known for some time, were recently corroborated by the discovery of the rough drafts with corrections in the king's hand, among the papers lodged in the Court Archive by Umberto II of Savoy (Turin State Archive, *Court, Bequest by Umberto II*, First Lodgment, Batch 29).

Francesco Brancato, *La dittatura garibaldina nel Mezzogiorno e in Sicilia* (Trapani, 1965), dealing only with Sicily; "Garibaldi e la Sicilia nel 1860," with reports on the political situation internationally and on the island, in *Archivio Storico Siciliano* (1983); Salvatore Francesco Romano, "I contadini nella rivoluzione del 1860," in *Momenti del Risorgimento in Sicilia* (Messina-Florence, 1952); Francesco Renda, "Garibaldi e la questione contadina in Sicilia nel 1860," in *Garibaldi e il socialismo,* edited by Gaetano Cingari (Rome-Bari, 1984).

Chapter 19. Alberto Mario, *La Camicia Rossa* (Turin, 1870); Tommaso Nardella, *Marco Centola e lo sbarco garibaldino a Melito* (Naples, 1969); P. Pieri, *Storia militare del Risorgimento* (Turin, 1962), chapter 19; D. Mack Smith, *Garibaldi* (London, 1957); A. Scirocco, *L'Italia del Risorgimento,* 2nd ed. (Bologna, 1993), chapter 2; A. Scirocco, *Il Mezzogiorno nella crisi dell'unificazione (1860–1861),* 2nd ed. (Naples, 1981). The documents locating the meeting between Garibaldi and Victor Emanuel can be found in the pamphlet *Storico incontro di Taverna Catena,* edited by the Commune of Vairano Patenora (Vairano, 1982).

A great deal was written on the conduct of the war and Garibaldi as a general at the time of the centenary. Here we recall Lucio Ceva, "Garibaldi soldato in Europa," in *Mito*; Giorgio Rochat, *Il genio militare di Garibaldi,* and the articles by Luciano Russi, Silvio Furlani, Ferruccio Botti, Lucio Ceva, and Carlo Crocella in *Garibaldi condottiero. Storia, teoria, prassi,* edited by Filippo Mazzonis (Milan, 1984); Oreste Bovio, *L'arte militare di Giuseppe Garibaldi,* the articles by Piero del Negro, Salvo Mastellone, Franco Della Peruta, and the one by Carlo Moos in *Garibaldi generale della libertà,* edited by Aldo A. Mola (Rome, 1984).

Carlo Pellion di Persano, *Campagna navale degli anni 1860 e 1861. Diario privato-politico-militare* (Turin, 1880); Charles Stuart Forbes, *The Campaign of Garibaldi in the Two Sicilies* (Edinburgh, 1861). When describing his last meeting with Garibaldi, Admiral Mundy, *Hannibal at Palermo and Naples, during the Italian Revolution. 1859–1851* (London, 1863), sketches a rapid portrait of Garibaldi's moral character and physical presence that does not disagree with others we know.

For lithographs, satirical vignettes, illustrations in magazines and books, and portraits of Garibaldi on objects, particularly after 1860, see Salvatore Abita and Maria Antonella Fusco, *Garibaldi nell'iconografia dei suoi tempi* (Milan, 1982); *Garibaldi. Arte e Storia* [catalog for the exhibition with the same name held in Rome] (Florence, 1982), the section titled "Garibaldi: Il mito e l'immagine"; photographs have been produced in Wladimiro Settimelli, *Garibaldi. Album fotografico* (Florence, 1982).

Chapter 20. Charles De Mazade, "L'Italie depuis Villafranca. Le roi François II et la révolution de Naples," *Revue des Deux Mondes,* 1 February 1861.

Elpis Melena (Speranza von Schwartz), *Excursion à l'île de Caprera* (Geneva, 1862); Candido Augusto Vecchi, *Garibaldi a Caprera* (Naples, 1862); Felix Mornand, *Garibaldi* (Venice, 1867); Timoteo Riboli, *Craniografia di Garibaldi e mio viaggio a Caprera. Sunto di un più esteso e circostanziato lavoro* (Turin, 1861); Antonio Monti, "L'agricoltore Giuseppe Garibaldi (con inediti del «Diario agricolo» di Caprera)," *Nuova Antologia,* 16 September 1934 (the notebooks of the diary start in June 1864 and end in December 1874, and contain notes on family and political matters); Vincenzo Amat Di San Filippo, "Un epistolario inedito riguardante Giuseppe Garibaldi a Caprera (dicembre 1860–marzo 1861)," *Archivio Storico Sardo* (1984). For the celebratory gifts sent to Caprera from all parts of the world after the Expedition of the Thousand, see Alberto Maria Ghisalberti, "Garibaldi in Giamaica," *RSR* (July–September 1982) (a small silver statuette of Garibaldi); Roslyn Pesman Cooper, "Garibaldi e l'Australia," *RSR* (April–June 1985) (a celebratory silver sword from Melbourne).

R. Ugolini, "L'attività politica di Garibaldi nei silenzi di Caprera," in *Miscellanea in onore di Ruggero Moscati* (Naples, 1985); A. Scirocco, *L'Italia del Risorgimento,* 2nd ed. (Bologna, 1993), chapters 5–6; Henry D'Ideville, *Il re, il conte e la Rosina* (Milan, 1967). Raimondo Luraghi, "Garibaldi e la guerra civile Americana," in *Garibaldi e il socialismo,* edited by Gaetano Cingari (Rome-Bari, 1984); Garibaldi's letter to Victor Emanuel and the king's reply are in the Turin State Archive, *Court, Bequest by Umberto II,* First Lodgment, Batch 58.

P. Pieri, *Storia militare del Risorgimento* (Turin, 1962), chapter 20; there are several contemporary accounts in the Aspromonte issue of the *Rivista Popolare* of September 1912, which was edited by Napoleone Colajanni.

Chapter 21. A. Scirocco, *L'Italia del Risorgimento,* 2nd ed. (Bologna, 1993), chapter 7; John A. Davis, "Garibaldi e il movimento radicale e operaio inglese (1848–70)," in *Garibaldi e il socialismo,* edited by Gaetano Cingari (Rome-Bari, 1984); J. Ridley, "Il mito di Garibaldi in Inghilterra e la visita del 1864," *Rassegna degli Archivi di Stato,* nos. 2–3 (1982).

For information on Julie Salis Schwabe and Englishwomen who were friends of Garibaldi's, see Giacomo Emilio Curatulo, *Garibaldi e le donne* (Rome, 1913), chapters 2, 8, 11, 12, and 13, which is also interesting for the information on a few women who were drawn to Garibaldi, including Louise Colet and Princess Elena

Ghika (better known by her pseudonym Dora d'Istria), a Romanian writer who lived for a long time in Italy and corresponded with Garibaldi about the independence of the Balkan peoples. See also the *Lettere inedite di Giuseppe Garibaldi alla marchesa Anna Pallavicino*, edited by Giovanni Praticò (Pavia, 1982).

Alexander Herzen, *Garibaldi a Londra* (Milan, 1950). Lord Granville's thoughts on why Garibaldi became "a popular idol" in England are to be found in a letter to Queen Victoria, published in Jasper Ridley, *Garibaldi* (New York, 1974).

Chapter 22. A. Scirocco, *L'Italia del Risorgimento*, 2nd ed. (Bologna, 1993), chapters 8–14; his stay in Ischia is described in Nino D'Ambra, *Giuseppe Garibaldi. Cento vite in una* (Naples, 1983); the pamphlet *Dottrina garibaldina* is examined in the article by Giuseppe Oreste in *Mito*.

P. Pieri, *Storia militare del Risorgimento* (Turin, 1962), chapters 21–22; Ambrogio Viviani, "Garibaldi a Bezzecca," in *Garibaldi generale della libertà*, edited by Aldo A. Mola (Rome, 1984).

The memoirs of the Martelli brothers were published in *Nuova Antologia* and have been republished in Giovanni Spadolini, *Il mito di Garibaldi nella «Nuova Antologia»* (Florence, 1982).

Anton Giulio Barrili, *Con Garibaldi alle porte di Roma (1867)* (Milan, 1895); Robert J. O. Van Nuffel, "I belgi e Garibaldi. Mentana," in *Studi in memoria di Nino Cortese* (Rome, 1976); Camillo Brezzi, "La «mano di Dio» a Mentana," in *Garibaldi condottiero. Storia, teoria, prassi*, edited by Filippo Mazzonis (Milan, 1984).

On the involvement of the Ricciotti and the red-shirts in the Cretan revolution of 1867, see A. Tamborra, *Garibaldi e l'Europa* (Rome, 1983).

For the state of Garibaldi's health during the Vosges campaign, see Max Gallo, *Garibaldi. La forza di un destino* (Milan, 1982) (a generally hurried and inaccurate work); Jens Petersen, "Garibaldi e la Germania. 1870–71. Mito e realtà," in *Garibaldi e il socialismo*, edited by Gaetano Cingari (Rome-Bari, 1984).

Bakunin was sent into internal exile in Siberia in 1860 and managed to escape in 1861. In January 1862 he wrote to Garibaldi and informed him that news of the Expedition of the Thousand had reached Irkourtsk, and in January 1864 he went to visit him on Caprera. But because of his theories of social revolution based on anarchism and rejection of the state, he later distanced himself from Garibaldi, whom in 1869 he considered to be "an exponent of greater Italian unity and the glory of the Italian state, and a loyal servant of the monarchy." However, this did not stop him from admiring Garibaldi as a popular hero and for his defense of the Commune in 1871: see A. Tamborra, *Garibaldi e l'Europa* (Rome, 1983); P. C. Masini, *Garibaldi e Bakunin*, in *Garibaldi cento anni dopo*.

Chapter 23. The quotations from Morley and Hamerton appear in Denis Mack Smith, *Garibaldi* (London, 1957); William Wallace (1272–1305) is the national hero in Scotland who led the resistance in the First War of Independence.

Michele Sarfatti, *La nascita del moderno pacifismo democratico ed il Congrès international de la paix di Ginevra nel 1867* (Milan, 1980); A. Tamborra, *Garibaldi e l'Europa* (Rome, 1983); Danilo Veneruso, "Garibaldi e l'Europa. Un progetto di unificazione europea," *RSR* (April–June 1982); Giuseppe Fonterossi, "Garibaldi e la lettera gratulatoria a sir Enrico Richard," *RSR* (April–June 1932); Aldo A. Mola, "L'internazionalismo massonico di Giuseppe Garibaldi," in *Garibaldi e il socialismo*, edited by Gaetano Cingari (Rome-Bari, 1984); Luigi Polo Friz, *La Massoneria italiana nel decennio postunitario. Lodovico Frapolli* (Milan, 1998).

Letterio Briguglio, *Garibaldi e il socialismo* (Milan, 1982); Franco Della Peruta, "Garibaldi tra mito e politica," *Studi Storici* (January–March 1982); Giorgio Spini, "Garibaldi e le origini del socialismo," in *Le radici del socialismo italiano*, a cura di Lucia Romaniello (Milan, 1997); Franco Molinari, "La religiosità di Garibaldi," in *Garibaldi generale della libertà*, edited by Aldo A. Mola (Rome, 1984); *Gli inconciliabili eroi. Lettere di Mazzini e Garibaldi a Petroni*, edited by Anna Maria Isastia and Giulio Petroni (Rome, 1987); Romano Ugolini, "Petroni e Garibaldi," in *Giuseppe Petroni. Dallo Stato pontificio all'Italia unita*, edited by R. Ugolini and Vincenzo Pirro (Naples, 1991).

G. Garibaldi, *Il progetto di deviazione del Tevere e di bonificazione dell'Agro romano (Scritti e discorsi del 1875–1876)*, edited by Agostino Grattarola (Rome, 1982).

A. Scirocco, "Garibaldi «politico» e la Lega delle Democrazia," *Clio* (January–March 1983).

Chapter 24. Candido Augusto Vecchi, *Garibaldi a Caprera* (Naples, 1862). Ugo Ojetti's interview with Francesca Armosino can be found in Sacerdote, *La vita di Giuseppe Garibaldi secondo i risultati delle più recenti indagini* (Milan, 1933). The letters from France appear in G. Spadolini, *Il mito di Garibaldi nella «Nuova Antologia»* (Florence, 1982). On the family conflicts and financial affairs of his final years, see Francesco Bidischini, *Garibaldi nella vita intima* (Rome, 1907), which contains a wealth of information on their financial problems and the strategies adopted to deal with them, on the National Gift, on the transfer of Caprera to the state, on Francesca Armosino, and on the financial position of family members after 1882; Curzio Cornacchi, *Le discordie di Caprera e Francesca Armosino. Rivelazioni documentate* (Florence, n.d. [1907]), which argues forcefully that Armosino was responsible for making Garibaldi aware of a worrying financial situation and for keeping away Anita's children and his old friends; information on how the Gift was shared out can be found in the *Diario*: Antonio Monti, "L'agricoltore Giuseppe Garibaldi (con inediti del «Diario agricolo» di Caprera)," *Nuova Antologia*, 16 September 1934.

Danilo L. Massagrande, "Una disavventura editoriale di Garibaldi," *Il Risorgimento*, no. 1 (1990) (it covers *Cantoni il volontario*); Milly Martinengo, "Garibaldi narratore. Vicende editoriali e stato attuale dei manoscritti," *Il Risorgimento*, no. 1 (1996).

On the 1882 trip to Sicily, see Achille Fazzari, *Garibaldi da Napoli a Palermo*, facsimile reprint (Florence, 1965); Domenico Viggiani, *I tempi di Posillipo dalle ville romane ai casini di delizia* (Naples, 1989); at the time, the newspapers followed events concerning this trip and his sojourns in Naples and Palermo on an almost daily basis.

Chapter 25. The funeral in Caprera and the commemorative events in Rome were depicted in great detail in newspaper illustrations of the time. The review of the national and international press was drawn from these and from the proceedings of the conferences referred to in chapter 18. Carducci's speech "Per la morte di Giuseppe Garibaldi" is published in *Discorsi letterari e storici* (Bologna, 1935). For the commemorations in Australia, see Roslyn Pesman Cooper, "Garibaldi e l'Australia," *RSR* (April–June 1985).

For Menotti and Ricciotti, see the biographies written by Giuseppe Monsagrati in *Dizionario Biografico degli Italiani*, vol. 52 (Rome, 1999). In the *Dizionario*, which currently has reached the letter G, one may consult the biographies of many of Garibaldi's comrades and friends: Abba, Acerbi, Anzani, Avezzana, Bertani, Bixio, Benedetto Cairoli, Canzio, Cosenz, Crispi, Cuneo, Depretis, and Fazzari.

For the involvement of Garibaldi's descendents in the freedom struggles of Europe, see the bibliography in the section "La tradizione garibaldina dopo la morte di Giuseppe Garibaldi," in Anthony P. Campanella, *Giuseppe Garibaldi e la tradizione garibaldina. Una bibliografia dal 1807 al 1970* (Geneva, 1971), and A. Tamborra, *Garibaldi e l'Europa* (Rome, 1983).

Rosario Villari, "La prefigurazione politica del giudizio storico su Garibaldi," *Studi Storici* (April–June 1982). Jerzy W. Borejsza's assessment can be found in *Mito*, and that of Kravchinsky, better known by his nom de guerre Stepnjak, in A. Tamborra, *Garibaldi e l'Europa* (Rome, 1983).

The legend of Garibaldi has been used for political reasons in successive periods both in Italy and in other parts of the world. In the case of Italy, I draw attention to the following: Pier Giorgio Franzosi, "Garibaldi tra mito e storia nell'Italia umbertina e giolittiana"; Mario Isnenghi, "Usi politici di Garibaldi dall'interventismo al fascismo"; Arrigo Boldrini, "Dal primo Risorgimento alla resistenza"; Elisabetta Lecco, "Garibaldi nella letteratura scolastica per l'infanzia durante il fascismo," all published in *Garibaldi condottiero. Storia, teoria, prassi*, edited by Filippo Mazzonis (Milan, 1984); Santi Fedele, "Tradizione garibaldina e antifascismo italiano," in *Garibaldi e il socialismo*, edited by Gaetano Cingari (Rome-Bari, 1984); Ugoberto Alfassio Grimaldi, "L'utilizzazione del mito garibaldino ad opera del fascismo," in *Garibaldi generale della libertà*, edited by Aldo A. Mola (Rome, 1984). Rossella Certini, *Il mito di Garibaldi. La formazione dell'immaginario popolare nell'Italia unita* (Milan, 2000), examines the influence Garibaldi exerted on the Italian imagination as "an exemplary hero, particularly as presented in the biographies of Cuneo, Dumas, Guerzoni, Jessie White Mario, and Achille Bizzoni."

The survival of Garibaldi's memory in other regions of the world, such as China, Japan, parts of Europe, and the Americas, is demonstrated by many of the articles in *Garibaldi generale della libertà*, edited by Aldo A. Mola (Rome, 1984), and *Garibaldi, Mazzini e il Risorgimento nel risveglio dell'Asia e dell'Africa* (Milan, 1984), as well as some recent biographies: Madan Lal, *Vir Garibaldi* (New Delhi, 1982); Fusatoshi Fujisawa, *Garibaldi. Hero in a Red Shirt: From the Legend to the Myth* (in Japanese) (Tokyo, 1987); Donn Byrne, *Garibaldi: The Man and the Myth* (Hong Kong, 1988).

Index